Mexican Cinema

Third Edition

Mexican Cinema

Reflections of a Society, 1896–2004

Third Edition

Carl J. Mora

McFarland & Company, Inc., Publishers

Jefferson, North Carolina, and London

LIBRARY OF CONGRESS CATALOGUING-IN-PUBLICATION DATA

Mora, Carl J.
Mexican cinema : reflections of a society, 1896–2004 ;
third edition / Carl J. Mora.— 3rd ed.
p.   cm.
Includes bibliographical references and index.

ISBN 0-7864-2083-9 (illustrated case binding : 50# alkaline paper) ∞

1. Motion pictures — Mexico — History.   I. Title.
PN1993.5.M4M6   2005   791.43'0972 — dc22   2005009058

British Library cataloguing data are available

On the cover: Regina Orozco and Daniel Giménez Cacho
in *Profundo Carmesí* (1996); camera art ©2005 clipart.com

Manufactured in the United States of America

McFarland & Company, Inc., Publishers
Box 611, Jefferson, North Carolina 28640
www.mcfarlandpub.com

I dedicate this book to the memory of my father,
who passed away some years before its first publication.
By leading the family for over a decade on weekly excursions
to various Spanish-language movie houses in New York City,
he sparked within me the earliest stirrings of what has
become an obsessive affection for Mexican cinema —
"el cine cristiano," as he jestingly called it.

In loving memory of
EDUARDO DOUGLAS MORA
1899–1976

Contents

Preface to the Third Edition

In 1982, I completed and sent in the manuscript for the original edition of this book. At that time, the furthest thought from my mind was that by 2005 I would be preparing a third edition (a second, revised edition was published in 1989). Much has changed in the intervening years: the original research entailed many hours at the library while this time most of the information I needed was accessible on the World Wide Web. And not to forget that the 1982 edition required a lot of old-fashioned typing on a real typewriter (remember those?), and in 2005 all the new text and revising of the old was written and easily edited on a computer.

Also in 1982, I had to make arrangements well ahead of time for movies to be projected for me at film archives or I had to catch them in movie theaters (a haphazard process). In recent years the easy availability of many old and new Mexican films on videotape and DVD has simplified things enormously for researchers, students, teachers, and just plain movie buffs — and more films are being added constantly.

This new edition was necessitated because of the great changes in Mexico's film industry from 1990 to 2004. In 1982, no Mexican films were attracting attention in the United States or any other country. In 1985, however, two films did receive some limited recognition outside of Mexico: Paul Ledúc's *Frida* and Jaime Humberto Hermosillo's *Doña Herlinda y su hijo*. But that was pretty much it for the remainder of the 1980s. Of course, many films were made for domestic consumption, but most were lowbrow sex comedies and sex and violence action movies. There were some state-funded "quality" films that did not travel far from the national territory.

In the early 1990s, however, a number of Mexican films received international recognition: Nicolás Echevarría's *Cabeza de Vaca* (1991), Alfonso Cuarón's *Solo con tu pareja* (1991), Dana Rotberg's *Angel de fuego* (1991), Guillermo del Toro's *Cronos* (1992), and María Novaro's *Danzón* (1990). These successful films culminated with Alfonso Arau's huge breakaway international hit, *Como agua para chocolate* (1992).

Later in the decade and in the first two years of the twenty-first century, several Mexican films and their directors would achieve international commercial success and critical acclaim and put Mexico on the cinematic world map. These were Alejandro González Iñárritu's *Amores perros* (2000), Alfonso Cuarón's *Y tu mamá también* (2001), and Carlos Carrera's *El crimen del padre Amaro* (2002), the last nominated for an Oscar as best foreign-language film. Guillermo del Toro became solidly established in Hollywood with big studio productions like *Mimic* (1997), *Blade II* (2002), and *Hellboy* (2004).

It was quite unprecedented in motion picture history that three films from one country (other than the United States) should in three consecutive years have enjoyed such global success. How did Mexican cinema rise from its moribund state in the late 1980s to success in the 1990s and 2000s? There is no one all-encompassing reason: just the serendipitous confluence of talented and dedicated filmmakers. There were also important changes in the Mexican cinematic infrastructure, as well as significant social and cultural transformations.

All these developments I attempt to describe in my new Chapter 7, which appropriately is the longest. The earlier chapters did not require much revision, since what is past is past. I did, however, amplify discussion of some films, e.g., *Enamorada* (1945).

Finally, it is a source of great personal satisfaction to me that this book has been almost continually in print since 1982. It has become the standard English-language survey of Mexican cinema. The first two editions were brought out by the University of California Press. After a brief hiatus, McFarland & Company is publishing this edition. They are also the publisher of one of the two important books in English on Mexican cinema that came out in the 1990s: David Wilt's *The Mexican Filmography, 1916–2001*, an exhaustive survey of Mexican movie production. The other valuable general work is Paulo Antonio Paranaguá's *Mexican Cinema* (London: British Film Institute; Mexico City: Instituto Mexicano de Cinematografía, 1995), an anthology of translations of many Mexican scholars' writings.

My profuse thanks to the many people who made possible the prior editions are contained in those volumes. There is an additional roster of friends and colleagues to thank for the present version. First of all, my gratitude to the following individuals who read the new chapter and offered valuable comments: Alejandro Pelayo, the late Edward Moseley, Dana Evans, Jon Bowman, David Wilt, Dave Herzel, and David Dent. All mistakes are of course my fault entirely (although I hope there aren't too many!).

Persons in Mexico City who generously made time in their busy schedules to talk with me are Alfonso Arau, María Novaro, Víctor Ugalde, Juan Roberto Mora Catlett, Alfredo Joskowicz, Susana López Aranda, and Moisés Jiménez. I am very grateful to Angeles Sánchez Gutiérrez and Félix Bermejo at the Cineteca Nacional for providing most of the movie stills used in Chapter 7. Rogelio Agrasánchez, Jr., kindly made available a number of stills from his extensive collection. My old friend Alejandro Pelayo, cultural attaché at the Consulate General of Mexico in Los Angeles, set aside most of a day for me and treated me to a delicious sushi lunch.

Others who helped me with the logistics of finding lodgings and getting around Mexico City are my cousin Arturo Mora Rivera, his wife, Carmela Fernández, and their son, Arturo Mora Fernández. Extravagant thanks to my daughter Valerie who typed the entire manuscript, and whose keen eye spotted a number of stylistic infelicities. And my love and gratitude to my wife Gigi, who has accompanied me on several research jaunts through the years, including this last one to Mexico City.

Carl J. Mora
Albuquerque, New Mexico
Spring 2005

1

The Silent Film Era: 1896–1929

Mexico in the 1890s was one of the *belle époque*'s success stories. Buoyed by his country's economic progress, progress at least by the standards of Positivism and the prevailing wisdom of the era's liberal tenets, the old authoritarian president, *don* Porfirio Díaz, presided over a nation whose future, like that of all Western civilization, was perceived to be bright indeed. Mexico's international credit standing was excellent; British, American, Spanish, French, and other European firms, along with a number of Mexican entrepreneurs and ranchers, built and operated the country's railroads, extracted its mineral wealth, cultivated its fields, herded its cattle, and managed its factories.

According to the preponderant belief of the times, progress was being achieved by the only effective course: to entrust the economy — and the political system — to an elite of Mexican and foreign capitalists. To this end the resources of Mexico, along with its laws and government, had in effect been put at the disposal of entrepreneurs who were willing to invest in the country's development — upon the guarantee of favored treatment and assured profits.

Since Mexico was prosperous, politically stable, and a member in good standing, at least peripherally, of progressive European civilization, it was not surprising that the projectors and films developed and produced by Louis and Auguste Lumière should appear in Mexico almost immediately after their popularization in Europe. Mexican audiences flocked to the *cinematográficos* as enthusiastically as did their European and North American counterparts. Elsewhere in Latin America, newly opened theaters in Buenos Aires,[1] Rio de Janeiro,[2] and Havana[3] were also hard put to keep up with the crowds that flocked to be enraptured by these early flickering films.

The silent film era in Mexico has not been well documented and can only be pieced together from scattered journalistic sources of the time. Emilio García Riera (1931–2002), Mexico's leading film historian, decried the lack of sources necessary to form a comprehensive picture of his country's early filmmaking, since most of the movies made between 1897 and up to the 1920s have been lost.[4] The most complete reconstruction of the silent film era has been accomplished by Luis Reyes de la Maza who, culling accounts from Mexican newspapers and popular magazines of the time, put together a tantalizing glimpse of the social milieu of those bygone times. The following account is based largely on his book.[5]

The very first "moving pictures" in Mexico were provided by Thomas A. Edison's kinetoscope in January 1895; a certain John R. Roslyn invited the press to witness the novelty prior to initiating public showings. The kinetoscope, or nickelodeon, did not prove to be very popular since it was subject to frequent breakdowns, and the viewer had to watch the brief show through an eyepiece. The effort to provide musical accompaniment by means of a pair of headphones through which the faint melodies of a scratchy recording could be heard was also unsuccessful. The pictures themselves seemed to be largely restricted to "the contortions of a clown or the somersaults of an acrobat."[6]

In August 1896, however, the newspapers announced the arrival of Louis and Auguste Lumière's famous invention, the *cinématographe*. Reportedly it was a Frenchman, Gabriel Vayre, who obtained authorization to set up the first projector in Mexico, at number 9 Plateros Street, today Madero Avenue, and called the location "Cinematógrafo Lumière."[7] The Lumière projector caused an immediate sensation in the capital, and the city's residents lined up in Mexico's first movie queues to see such one-minute films as *The Card Players*, *Arrival of a Train*, *The Magic Hat*, and other such brief performances that had premiered in Paris as recently as December 1895 and were already being shown around the world.

Luis G. Urbina attended the performances at the Cinematógrafo Lumière and wrote an article about the experience, making him, in effect, Mexico's first film critic:

> The cinema is the fashion in Mexico. Its appearance has excited the capital, if the capital is considered to be limited between Peter Gay's Bar Rhum on Plateros Street, and the Escandón Palace on San Francisco Street. The new contraption has triumphed here over the kinetoscope.... For the moment all eyes are on the cinema.
> This new contraption which tries, as do its rivals, to entertain us by reproducing life, also lacks something: it lacks color. Perhaps with time it will acquire sound.... When fantasy, that curious dreamer, recovers from its amazement it gives thanks to Science, so abused, which Spencer has characterized as Cinderella. And there are those who still maintain that science is arid![8]

By December 1896 a more varied and attractive program was being offered the enthusiastic public by Vayre. The following is a typical program as advertised in the newspapers:

> Cinematógrafo Lumière. No. 9 Plateros Street. Program for Monday, December 14, 1896. 1st. Military parade in front of the Royal Palace in Madrid. 2nd. Women of the island of Tenerife supplying coal to ships of the squadron. 3rd. Parade of the Queen's Lancers. 4th. A Spanish engineer regiment en route to Cádiz to embark for the Cuban campaign. 5th. Spanish artillery in combat. 6th. Spanish infantrymen on bivouac. 7th. View of Berlin. 8th. Two Bengal tigers in the Paris zoo.[9]

These brief views of the colonial war raging in neighboring Cuba, along with those of the Parisian tigers, bore no comparison with the newsreels that in later years were to become part and parcel of every moviegoer's experience. But such films, though intended primarily to entertain with their novelty rather than inform, pointed up the immense importance of the new medium of cinematography. Distant events in faraway countries could be captured on celluloid and reproduced on a white screen in a darkened salon.

No longer would the conflict in Cuba, or the Kaiser reviewing his troops in Berlin, or the crowded streets of New York be items solely to be read about, or frozen in photographs — such events from the world's vast panorama could now be magically brought to life anywhere. These first films, obtained from the Lumière firm, brought Europe to life before Mexican audiences, but it would not be long before these audiences would see *actualidades* of their own country. The early cinema not only enabled audiences to see real-life views of foreign countries, but it also better acquainted them with their own societies.

The origins of filmmaking in Mexico are immediately associated with the name of Salvador Toscano Barragán (1872–1947), a young engineering student who was the first Mexican to open a movie salon, make films of real-life events, and create in 1898 the first of his country's "fiction films," *Don Juan Tenorio*, a one-reeler starring the popular actor Paco Gavilanes.[10] During the Revolution, Toscano was to record extensively many of the historic events that shaped modern Mexico, footage that in 1950 would be compiled by his daughter, Carmen Toscano, into a full-length documentary, *Memorias de un mexicano* ("Memories of a Mexican").

In 1897 Toscano ordered a projector and camera, a *toma vistas* (view taker), from the Lumière brothers. Opening a salon at number 17 Jesús María Street, he began to show Lumière films with musical accompaniment provided by an Edison phonograph.[11] At around midyear, Toscano transferred his salon to a larger, more comfortable site at the corner of Plateros and Espíritu Santo (today Madero Avenue and Isabel la Católica). It is misleading to think of Vayre's Cinematógrafo Lumière and Toscano's unnamed salon as true movie houses; they were simply large rooms into which these early entrepreneurs crowded as many chairs as they could for their brief shows.

However, in March 1898 a projector of United States manufacture was set up in the Grand National Theater; this was a "veriscope," touted as being superior to the Lumière projector but in reality the same apparatus. It was simply an early instance of misleading advertising in the cinema industry, designed to fool the patent office as much as the spectators. The program was the Fitzsimmons-Corbett fight, the first American film shown in Mexico.[12]

By 1900 the cinema's popularity was solidly established and it enjoyed the loyal following of thousands. The programs still consisted of short comedy routines and acrobatics, in addition to the varied scenes of dignitaries and events in foreign countries. Thus the cinematic novelty had not yet encroached on the popularity of the traditional theater, but in the same year the latter's first real challenge arrived in the capital: the first "full-length" feature to be shown in Mexico, a French import called *The Passion of Jesus Christ*, in three reels.[13]

In 1901, Salvador Toscano returned from Paris bringing with him a load of brand-new films and the latest Lumière projector, the *biograph*. He rented the Orrin

Lobby card for _Memorias de un mexicano_.

Circus Theater and there screened his new movies, among which was probably the first bullfight ever shown on a Mexican screen, although it was either a French or Spanish _corrida_.[14]

Between 1901 and 1904, many new cinematic salons opened throughout Mexico City. The largest cigarette manufacturer of the time, El Buen Tono, opened its own salon on the top floor of the building which housed the company offices, just across the street from the site on which the Palace of Fine Arts would shortly be erected (Juárez Avenue and San Juan de Letrán). Instead of charging admission, El Buen Tono would simply accept a certain number of its empty cigarette boxes. In January 1904, it premiered the first version, probably of French origin, of _Don Quijote de la Mancha_. It was also one of the longest films seen in Mexico up to that time, being more than 450 meters in length and lasting about forty-one minutes.[15]

In 1905 another name famous in the early annals of film in Mexico made its appearance: Enrique Rosas (d. 1920) introduced the new Pathé projector, setting it up in the Orrin Circus Theater. Soon his performances gained greater popularity than Toscano's. Rosas presented such talked-about films as the farce _Un carbonero en el baño_ ("A Coal Man in the Bath") and the dramatic _Un drama en los aires_ ("A Drama in the Skies").

Like Toscano, he had his own camera and soon was able to announce the show-ing of Mexican-made films. Every week he would offer highlights of the previous Sunday's bullfights; on June 25 Rosas announced film of the funeral procession of don Manuel Azpiroz, Mexico's ambassador to Washington, who had died in that city and whose remains had recently been brought back for burial. The audiences flocked to these and other programs principally to see the familiar streets of Mexico City on the screen and to catch glimpses of recognizable faces. So successful were Rosas's pro-grams that he moved to the more comfortable Riva Palacio Theater on Ayuntamiento; here he initiated such innovations as special children's admission prices on Thurs-days and free admission for ladies on Mondays.[16]

The competition between Toscano and Rosas continued unabated through 1905, a year that saw more than two hundred short films screened in the capital's two or three salons. On October 29, Toscano showed *The Great Train Robbery* (1902); another landmark film projected in Mexico City that year was G. Méliès's *A Trip to the Moon* (1902). Toscano again showed his 1898 one-reel effort, *Don Juan Tenorio*. In addi-tion he screened his current films such as *Guanajuato Destroyed*, showing the effects of a disastrous flood on that picturesque city; *Horse Races*, showing President Porfirio Díaz at the Hipódromo de la Condesa; *Automobile Races*; *Bullfight by Fuentes*; *Jota Danced by the Beautiful Romero*; *The Villa of Guadalupe* and other such movies. Some-what out-of-date films from abroad were shown, such as *Alfonso XIII in Paris*, *Great Fire in Denver*, *The Workers' Strike in Russia*, *The Revolution in Russia*, *The Portsmouth Peace Conference*, and *The War in the Transvaal*.[17]

The year 1906 began with the premiere of the first "cops and robbers" serial — Pathé Frères's *Los rateros de París* ("Thieves of Paris"). In February a new salon, La Boite, was opened on San Juan de Letrán, using the latest 1906 Lumière-Pathé pro-jector. Faced with the increased competition of an additional moviehouse, Toscano announced his acquisition of a brand-new 80-ampere Pathé "Lantern."[18] Not to be left behind, Enrique Rosas advertised in March the following program for his Riva Palacio Theater:

> The management announces for today two shows in which will be screened the highly interesting views of the presidential visit to Yucatán.... 1st. Departure from Mexico of General Díaz. 2nd. Bay of Veracruz. 3rd. The Wharf. 4th. The gunboat Bravo. 5th. The port of Progreso. 6th. General Díaz disembarks in Progreso. 7th. The president in Mérida. 8th. Panoramic view of Mérida. 9th. General Díaz visits the Institute. 10th. Mrs. Romero Rubio de Díaz visits the Cathedral and the Bishopric. 11th. The lake of the San Cosme suburb. 12th. General Díaz leaves Mérida. 13th. The president makes his farewell to Yucatán.[19]

Although the greatest cinematic activity was to be expected in Mexico City, provincial audiences in the other states of the extensive country were also being drawn into the new medium. Jorge Stahl (1886–1979), one of the true pioneers of the Mex-ican film industry, was one of the early entrepreneur showmen. His father owned a hat factory in Guadalajara and young Jorge, at the age of fifteen, began a photogra-phy business. He sold it so as to acquire an Edison Kinetoscope at the St. Louis Expo-sition of 1904. With this machine he traveled around the country — Guanajuato, San

Luis Potosí, Chihuahua — renting theaters in these cities for one peso. Stahl recounted the following experience:

> In 1906 something curious happened to me. I opened a projection salon in Guadalajara and called it Cine Verde, with four hundred chairs and a pianola. It was a small area, but since it was the first cinema, it was the gathering place for Guadalajara society. At that time the governor was Mr. Miguel Ahumada; he sent for me a few times to tell me that that was a very dangerous locality because, in the event of a fire, a real disaster could take place. For this reason he passed various ordinances: for more doors, an evacuation route.... All of these things we carried out. Since the salon was always filled and people were always waiting for the second or third show ... he says to me one day: "Listen friend Stahl, you get that cinema out of there ... because with that nonsense you're making more money than I do as governor." He did not at all appreciate our success. And it wasn't at all difficult to fill a little locality of four hundred capacity, at twenty-five centavos per show. Everyone in Guadalajara was always there.[20]

The popularity of the cinema, and consequently the demand for films, increased markedly in 1906: whereas at the beginning of the year there had been just three movie salons in Mexico City, by the end there were sixteen.[21] Luis G. Urbina, writing in the December 9, 1906, issue of *El Mundo Ilustrado*, commented on the increased traffic and crowds in that part of the city where the movie salons were concentrated:

> They go to ... cinema because it fills and entertains them with a pacifying, child-like innocence, and later upon returning to their bare and melancholy abode, their fantasy, like an Aladdin's lamp, continues decorating with ephemeral delights the sadness of existence.[22]

It was natural that the disadvantaged sectors of society, in Mexico and elsewhere, should respond with enthusiasm to the cinema. The developmental policies of the Díaz régime transformed Mexican society by creating the industrial infrastructure that was to make possible Mexico's economic advances after the 1940s; in the process of creating an industrial proletariat, however, a great many people were uprooted from their rural homes (now increasingly being taken over by large landholders and speculators) and forced to seek livelihood in the factories of the cities, or, starting at this early date, in the southwestern United States.

Between 1810 and 1910, the population of Mexico increased 148 percent from six million to fifteen million inhabitants (less than the population of greater Mexico City in 2005) — and the greater part of this increase was registered during the Díaz dictatorship from 1876 to 1910. This largely urban demographic growth has been generally attributed to the improvement of communications, industrialization, and the era's peace and stability.[23] Mexico's internal and external migration prior to 1910, though significant in itself, was dwarfed by unprecedented population growth in the following decades, a growth greatly accelerated by the Revolution, and by developments in our own day. The increasingly greater visibility of the "underclasses" was already evident by 1906, and Urbina was moved to observe:

> The popular masses, uncouth and infantile, experience while sitting in front of the screen the enchantment of the child to whom the grandmother has recounted a fairy

tale; but I fail to understand how, night after night, a group of people who have the obligation of being civilized can idiotize themselves at the Salón Rojo, or in the Pathé, or the Monte Carlo, with the incessant reproduction of scenes in which the aberration, anachronisms, inverisimilitudes, are made *ad hoc* for a public of the lowest mental level, ignorant of the most elementary educational notions.[24]

Although the above may be interpreted as a "Positivist" view of the cinema's social effects, there is no evidence that the authorities felt that the burgeoning number of movie salons and the intermingling of classes within them posed any great threat to the existing social order. On the contrary, and no doubt contributing to Urbina's consternation, hundreds of individuals fanned out across Mexico armed with projectors rented from firms like E. Moulinié or J.D. Tippett. Just as Jorge Stahl described, they carried a few films with them and set up mobile salons in even the tiniest of villages. Nevertheless these showmen realized tidy profits. Some of them eventually became distributors, as did Stahl, who came to acquire a stock of seven thousand films.[25]

The major French and American producers also sought to sell their films to the proliferating number of exhibitors. One of the first advertisements to this effect appeared in 1906:

> Mexican National Phonograph Co. No. 77, 5 de Mayo extension. Three Edison films of the San Francisco earthquake are offered for sale.[26]

The Pathé Frères company soon opened its own offices in Mexico City for the sale of the parent firm's products: the Spanish titles of some typical films and their prices were *El cofrecito del Rajá* ("The Rajah's Small Trunk"), 660 meters, 123 pesos; *Romeo cogido en la trampa* ("Romeo Caught in the Trap"), 60 meters, 36 pesos; and *Los hermanos rivales* ("The Rival Brothers"), 145 meters, 87 pesos.[27]

However, an ambitious distributor by the name of Jorge A. Alcalde placed his orders directly to the United States and France. Strangely, the parent companies, Pathé in particular, felt no compunction about bypassing their authorized representatives in Mexico and selling films to Alcalde. When he placed an advertisement in the paper listing a large number of new acquisitions, the Pathé Frères office in turn announced that all other film vendors were its branch offices. Alcalde was so incensed by being referred to as a "branch office" that he countered with an advertisement in which he indignantly asserted his autonomy at the same time naming all the firms in the United States, France, and England with which he did business.[28]

The Mexican Pathé office countered by reducing the price of all their films to sixty centavos a meter (heretofore prices had ranged between 1.70 pesos and 75 centavos per meter). This led to an all-out price war between Pathé and Alcalde which the latter won, in a manner of speaking, by offering all his films at one centavo per meter. Pathé of course retreated and priced their films at the standard rates; in a few months the Paris office realized its unethical conduct and dealt only through its representative office in Mexico City. This curious episode, according to Reyes de la Maza, is an example "of the astute and determined businessman in the first years of the cinema in Mexico, when this was an open business and did not see itself suffocated by official agencies or powerful unions."[29]

While Mexicans from a wide social spectrum were increasingly spending more of their leisure time at the cinema, momentous events were in the offing. The country was approaching the centennial of Father Miguel Hidalgo y Costilla's 1810 uprising which eventually led to independence from Spain. The year 1910, however, was to bring much more to Mexico that just a grand nationwide celebration, but the citizenry was of course unaware of the portentous events in its future.

Meanwhile, Mexicans went to the movies. Anticipating the upcoming centennial celebrations, the country's first major film made from a script[30] was premiered at the Salón Vista Alegre; this was Felipe de Jesús Haro's production of *El grito de Dolores* ("The Cry of Dolores") (1908)[31] which attempted to recreate the events surrounding Father Hidalgo's (played by Haro) abortive 1810 uprising. This movie also set a significant precedent for many subsequent Mexican films in that it was the first to be panned by the critics, in this case the reviewer for *El Imparcial*:

> In one of the capital's salons we were surprised a few nights ago to see a movie ... which should have deserved its audience's applause. What we saw was nothing less than the conferences that the priest Hidalgo had with his allies a few hours before uttering his famous *grito*. This was followed by Hidalgo's arrival at the atrium of the temple of Dolores, the gathering of the people who, summoned by the bell, slowly began arriving until there was a very large number of insurgents ... right there he was given the standard with the Virgin of Guadalupe. The old man, in spite of his age, bounded rapidly, flag in hand, onto the saddle (which was of the type used nowadays). He rode off like lightning and the mob followed him.... After what seemed to be endless running around over a vertiginous road without any kind of rhyme or reason that the public could discern, that phalanx of patriots arrived at the town of San Miguel el Grande — of this we were assured by the more alert viewers — and as it seemed they were going to stop there for awhile, the disorder grew and about a dozen gendarmes appeared, but not just in any old way but ... with their Colt pistols. The insurgent mob, determined as it had been to crush whatever enemy stood in its path, fell in with the orders of the police of a hundred years later ... and from that point the hero took off for parts unknown, since he was not seen again until the apotheosis, in which he appeared reclining over a tricolor flag, which Iturbide had undoubtedly lent him.
>
> And so it occurred to me, as I think it would have to any person of average intelligence: why were not the gendarmes eliminated, or the conference with the Corregidora in Dolores, the contemporary saddle, the transfer of the standard at the time of the *grito*, and so many anachronisms that even children could notice? So many errors can be excused only if this is seen as the initiation of one of the most useful applications that the cinema will shortly have: to provide history lessons for schoolchildren, but in the meantime it is ludicrous to see the picture presented by Hidalgo and his army running around the mountains aimlessly on a brute horse, and obeying the orders of the police of San Miguel el Grande.[32]

It is quite possible that Haro's apparent *faux pas* in showing the revolutionary throngs meekly responding to the fictitious gendarmes' orders was not entirely an innocent blooper; given the Díaz regime's obsession with law and order it conceivably would not have looked with favor on scenes in which unruly mobs defied the established authorities, even if these happened to be Spanish colonial authorities. Whether any censorship was exercised on Haro's film, or whether he prudently wrote the scene into his script, is impossible to document.

Since Mexican cinema was to all intents and purposes nonexistent before 1910, moviegoers flocked to see principally American and French productions, but especially the latter. Toward the end of the nineteenth century the influence of France in literature, painting, and the theater had become predominant in Mexico, at least among the educated classes. This "detestable end-of-the-century taste ... takes possession of architecture and the great lesser arts such as fashion and jewelry."[33]

The theater, notwithstanding the apparent competition of the film salons, was to enjoy a revival thanks to the work of Virginia Fábregas, "the first modern actress in Mexico."[34] Born María Barragán in Yautepec, Morelos, she debuted in the 1890s with a popular Spanish actor, Leopoldo Burón. In 1904 she acquired the Renacimiento Theater and renamed it the Virginia Fábregas Theater; here she presented the latest works of the Paris stage, which were very popular with society under Díaz, as well as recent productions from Spain.[35]

Concurrent with the urbane, cosmopolitan theatrical trend personified by Virginia Fábregas, another quite different one was germinating among the lower classes. This *género chico* (short plays based on folklore, popular themes, and with certain political overtones) of popular culture was not to come into full flower until after the initiation of the Revolution when "beginning in 1911 we find the panorama of a nation which, complacent and between belly-laughs, approaches the humorous reduction of its own existence. The repertory: gendarmes with hanging mustaches, pulque parlor drunks, unrequited lovers, clownish ranchers, Spanish tavern owners, *peladitos*, Indians from Xochimilco, 'outsiders.'"[36]

The *carpa*, or tent show, was the medium in which these popular genres flourished; it was also the training ground for many of the performers who would later graduate to the *revistas*, or music halls, of the cities, and finally to films. The quintessential *peladito*—a picaresque "wise guy" from the slums of Mexico City—was Mario Moreno "Cantinflas" (1911–1993) who got his start in a carpa in Jalapa; other early Mexican comics who were the creators of a distinctly national style of humor were Roberto Soto, Leopoldo Beristain, and *don* Catarino whose costume was a forerunner of Cantinflas's.[37] The legitimate theater and the *género chico* were to have a strong effect on the later cinema, both in subject matter and acting styles.

But it would still be some time before such popular expressions of the national culture were to reach Mexican screens. Meanwhile, in 1909 the "pax Romana that the dictator Porfirio Díaz imposed on Mexico did not encourage a popular brand of laughter, even though the people did not appear to be suffering. If their ruler did not distribute bread equitably, at least he kept them entertained with the circus of his court. They enjoyed his parades and the idea that they were governed by yesterday's hero."[38] In this enterprise, the cinema was admirably suited to advance the interests of the *porfiriato*; that year a filmic record was made of the president's visit to Manzanillo in December 1908 to inaugurate the opening of the railroad between that port and Mexico City. The Ministry of Public Education hired Gustavo Silva to photograph the entire journey and the final result was announced in the following glowing terms:

THE PRESIDENT'S JOURNEY TO MANZANILLO FILMED! Last night the rushes of the motion picture taken during the presidential trip to Manzanillo ... were

shown at the hall of the Superior Council of Education. The rushes were seen by the
Minister of Public Instruction and Fine Arts, *Licenciado don* Justo Sierra; by the sub-
secretary Lic. Ezequiel A. Chávez; by Lt. Colonel Porfirio Díaz, Jr.; by Lic. *don* Pablo
Macedo and by Mr. *don* Luis G. Urbina. The film in question has a length of more
than 500 meters and reproduces the most interesting details of the trip.... It commences
with the departure of the presidential party from the Buenavista station in this city,
and the dirigible El Buen Tono, which escorted the train in which the president was
riding, could be clearly seen. The most attractive parts of the route to Colima can be
admired, and the reception for the presidential train in that city, as well as in Manzanillo and Guadalajara. The precision of all the most important details reproduced
by the film is notable: the cruise around the bay aboard the "Ramón Corral," the presentation of the "Catinat's" commander, the reception in Colima, the parade and
reception in Guadalajara, and the banquets in Manzanillo; everything can be seen with
clarity and exactness.[39]

It was reported that *don* Porfirio watched the movie a few days later and expressed
satisfaction with the new invention and the cameraman's work. Soon after, the Ministry of Public Instruction and Fine Arts released the movie to a distributor who
either sold or rented it to exhibitors around the country.[40] In October 1909 Enrique
Rosas filmed the meeting in Ciudad Juárez between Díaz and President William
Howard Taft; the documentary was announced with great fanfare and screened exclusively at the Academia Metropolitana.[41]

Clearly, Mexican filmmaking was limited in the prerevolutionary period to what
we would now call propaganda features designed to enhance the glory of the dictatorship. "Popular" culture was still excluded from the better urban stages and had not
made its appearance on film if one excludes from this category the first screening of
the bullfights in the El Toreo Plaza of Mexico City.[42] In such features, the weekly
bullfights and the eulogistic recordings of the chief executive's official peregrinations,
it can be said that a style had already been established that succeeding decades of
Mexican newsreels would faithfully follow.

Since Mexican humor was absent from the screens, as it also was from the legitimate stage, audiences laughed at French slapstick shorts, especially those featuring
the great comic Max Linder.[43] In the pre–1914 period, French film studios practically
monopolized the world market and, in the silent film era, comedy, being entirely
visual, was instantly communicable to audiences of any national or cultural background. Even in Italy, which had a well-established comic tradition in the *commedia
dell'arte*, the influence of French comedy was all-pervading in this early period.[44]

It is apparent that conventions in comedy, as in melodrama, were quite universal, at least in societies sharing Western cultural traditions. Virginia Fábregas was most
instrumental in breathing new life into the Mexican theater. But also in the prerevolutionary period, the best French, Spanish, and Italian companies regularly toured
the country, and some of the major international artists appeared there.[45] Such already
strong cultural ties were strengthened by the popularity of the cinema before the regular tours of foreign and domestic actors were interrupted by years of civil war.

The year 1909 also marked a tragic event in Mexican cinema history: the first major
fire in a crowded movie salon, at the Flores Cinema in Acapulco. When it was over,
two hundred persons had been burned or suffocated to death. The early phosphate

film was extremely flammable and the merest spark from the projector might ignite the film being run; this is what happened in the Acapulco salon. The rest of the four hundred meters of film in the projector quickly caught fire and the conflagration immediately spread to other film stock in the wooden projection shed.

The disaster in Acapulco shocked the entire country and for a few days following the tragedy, the capital's movie salons were practically empty.[46] The Salón Rojo, which came under the management of Jacobo Granat in June, boasted of its four fire exits. The suppliers of projectors took advantage of the disaster to hawk their wares: "The terrible fire in Acapulco and the enormous loss of life would not have occurred if an Edison cinematograph had been used."[47]

Nineteen hundred and ten, the centennial year, arrived and Mexico proceeded to grandly celebrate its first one hundred years of independent existence.[48] Military parades, official ceremonies, foreign delegations, balls, all testified to the prosperity and respect that Mexico enjoyed in the international community. Mexican cinematographers, especially Salvador Toscano and Enrique Rosas, dedicated themselves to capturing on celluloid the highlights of this important occasion. Many of these have been preserved in *Memorias de un mexicano*, splendorous scenes which form an ironic backdrop to the disaster that was shortly to overtake the *porfiriato*. In addition to the documentaries, the country's second commercial film was produced in honor of the centennial: *El suplicio de Cuauhtémoc* ("The Torture of Cuauhtémoc") by Unión Cinematográfica, S.A., the second, albeit short-lived, Mexican movie company (the Alva Brothers' was the first, producing *El grito de Dolores* in 1908). Although no written sources seem to be available regarding the film itself, its subject matter is significant in that it "reflected the revived interest in Mexico's Indian past, also notable in music, literature, dance, and art,"[49] prior to the Revolution.

In 1910 Francisco Madero, a wealthy Chihuahua rancher and opponent of Díaz, issued his Plan of San Luis Potosí, a manifesto that ignited the widespread resentment against the government. He set November 20 as the day on which the people should revolt against the tyrant Díaz. Even though scattered, tiny bands of revolutionaries did launch attacks against government installations on November 18–20, "the inability of the Díaz government to quell these small revolutionary brush fires revealed the hollowness behind its impressive façade."[50] The situation steadily worsened for the government and finally, on May 25, 1911, Díaz resigned: Madero's call for a revolt, "essentially a colossal bluff,"[51] had succeeded.

The year 1911 was therefore rather devoid in movie news since the public and the newspapers naturally enough had much more serious matters to contend with. But it was not long before Mexican cinematographers were to begin bringing to the public views of the fratricidal struggle that was shaking the country. In 1912 the first newsreel of which there is any record curiously seemed to be reflecting a peaceful Porfirian society:

> Salón Allende. Today we inaugurate the film series entitled *Revista Nacional,* produced by the firm Navascue's y Camus. This bimonthly newsreel will show local and national events of palpitating actuality. The first film to be exhibited today shows the following events: Exhumation of the journalist don Trinidad Sánchez Santos, Olympic games,

September 16th parade, Triumphal arches on San Francisco Avenue, Festivals of Covadonga, Disturbances in the Chamber of Deputies, Regattas in Xochimilco.[52]

European newsreels remained very popular as Mexican audiences learned, perhaps with a sense of morbid fascination, that in the Old World the primary concern seemed to be "enlisting troops."[53] Escapist films also increased in appeal, including the showing at the Salón Rojo of Sarah Bernhardt's *Camille*; other major films shown on the capital's screens in 1912 were, from Italy, *The Divine Comedy*, from France, Victor Hugo's *Les Misérables*, and in a neighborhood theater, *The Adventures of Sherlock Holmes*, which the copywriter for the advertisement, after repeatedly gallant efforts, still could not get quite right. The film's title appeared on different occasions as *Las aventuras de Charley Colms* and *Las aventuras de Shaley Colmmes*.[54]

Another odd exercise in publicity was Jacobo Granat's advertisement for films of "the centennial of Independence, in which appears the illustrious figure of General *don* Porfirio Díaz, which is enthusiastically applauded even by the ladies."[55] The Revolution, however, was not entirely ignored on the Salón Rojo's screen: *La revolución en Chihuahua* ("The Revolution in Chihuahua") aroused great interest since it showed scenes of the Madero government's military campaign against the rebel forces of Pascual Orozco in the north; musical accompaniment was provided by a military band. The Hidalgo Theater showed *La revolución en Veracruz* ("The Revolution in Veracruz") which also helped to make audiences realize "the sadness of a war between brothers and the cost in lives."[56]

The cinema was accused of fostering immorality almost from its inception and there are reports of the Federal District authorities prohibiting showings of "pornographic" films exhibiting "secrets of the *boudoir* and spasms of the bedroom." It was even said that the Pathé cinema in Irapuato, not content with projecting "immoral" films, also passed out "pornographic pamphlets."[57] In both the capital and the provinces moralists decried the fact that on Sunday afternoons children gazed at "scenes of adultery, of crude lasciviousness, of brutal revenge, of horrifying cynicism, all skillfully projected. They saw rapine, assassinations, robberies, and suicides."[58] The guardians of the public morality agonized over the temptations that middle-class Mexican youth might encounter in darkened screening halls, even if properly chaperoned:

> Vamos al cine, mamá
> Mamá ... matógrafo,
> Que eso de la "oscuridá"
> Me gusta una atrocidá[59]
>
> (Let's go to the cinema, Mama
> Mama ... matograph
> Because I like the darkness very much)

The perils were not only moral but physical as well; in 1918 a certain Dr. Chacón gave a learned discourse in the Medical Academy to ophthalmologists regarding the ill effects that the cinema could cause to eyesight.[60] Such concerns reflected an ever-growing awareness of the social impact that this new form of entertainment could have. Thus regulation came early: in 1913 the first ordinances governing the licensing and operation of movie salons in the Federal District were published. These also included safety measures designed to avoid disasters like the Acapulco fire in 1900. In addition, the regulations stipulated that all descriptive subtitles were to be written in "correct Spanish," those in any other language being prohibited unless a corresponding translation was also provided.[61]

It was during the waning days of Madero's provisional regime that the first Italian costume drama played in Mexico. *Quo Vadis*, "indubitably the first great hit of the new form of entertainment,"[62] enjoyed a worldwide success and directed Italian filmmaking toward the lavish historical spectacular. It premiered at the Arbeu Theater in July 1913 and was billed as "the biggest event in the history of Mexico!"[63] In November the Salón Rojo followed suit with the second Italian "superproduction," *Marc Antony and Cleopatra*, with music provided by an orchestra "formed by professors of the National Conservatory of Music."[64]

But the make-believe carnage of ancient Rome that Mexican moviegoers enjoyed on the screen was soon to be supplanted by agonizingly authentic bloodshed in the very heart of the capital. *Porfirista* (pro–Díaz) elements in combination with some foreign business interests had been planning to topple the well-meaning but largely ineffectual Madero almost from the time he arrived in Mexico City.

On February 9, 1913, Bernardo Reyes, a Díaz supporter still smarting over the old caudillo's overthrow, and Félix Díaz, nephew of the deposed dictator, initiated a coup attempt designed to terminate the provisional government. This led to an artillery duel in the middle of Mexico City between Díaz and General Victoriano Huerta whom Madero had ordered to put down the still-unimportant flareup. The fighting lasted from February 9 to 17 ("La Decena Trágica" or the "Tragic Ten") in which hundreds of innocent bystanders were slaughtered.

The result was that Huerta himself toppled Madero and probably arranged his assassination. Huerta's bloody assumption of power caused widespread repercussions: immediately Emiliano Zapata in Morelos and Francisco "Pancho" Villa in Chihuahua rallied to Venustiano Carranza's call for a drive to unseat the "usurper" from the presidency. In this effort, the "Constitutionalists," as the Carranza-Villa-Zapata coalition was called, had the support of the new American president, Woodrow Wilson, who could not abide Huerta. This all led to years of bloody civil war and complex political maneuverings involving principally the various Mexican factions and the United States, but also, at various times, Germany, Britain, and Japan.

Meanwhile, the so-called epic Revolution forged ahead with Zapata's movement encompassing the more radical elements and Carranza's the bourgeois, reform-minded groups. Francisco Villa's host composed of northern cowboys, railroad workers, and farmers was a populist surge lacking any well-defined political or ideological thrust.

Movies of this epochal, fratricidal struggle were in great demand, and an enterprising producer sent his cameramen to film the *zapatistas* in Morelos. The result was a three-thousand-meter documentary, *Sangre hermana* ("Blood of Brothers"), in which "the public could see with clarity the horrors of *zapatismo*." This film was premiered at the Lírico on February 14, 1914, and reportedly was very well attended. The advertising for it, as the above example illustrates, had to be couched in terms acceptable to Huerta's censors, but the film itself apparently displayed considerable sympathy for the revolutionary cause, and the capital's citizens through it could vent some of their hatred of the government.[65]

In May 1914 the Salón Rojo presented a film of the "terrifying April 10 battle at San Pedro de las Colonias":

> The formidable encounter between the federal forces commanded by the heroic generals J. Refugio Velasco, De Moure, Maas, Romero, Ruiz, Jaso López, García Hidalgo, Almazán, Alvarez, Monasterio and others, with the revolutionary forces. A realistic, effective movie, without artifice, taken on the battlefield at great personal danger by an expert cinematographist of the Pathé Frères firm of Paris. The most definitive and truthful demonstration of the cruel fratricidal struggle that has caused a sea of blood to run across the soil of the tormented Mexican nation. All of the scenes are authentic, exact, as can be confirmed by the above-cited heroic generals. The heroism of the combatants and the bitterness of the struggle will accentuate in the spirit of all Mexicans the desire for unity so as to calm the anguish of our shattered nation.[66]

Jacobo Granat's injection into his advertising of a plea for reconciliation among his countrymen seems to have gone unnoticed by the *huertistas* who, in any event, had much more serious problems on their hands than movie publicity. The basic antagonism between Wilson and Huerta had, through an involved series of events, resulted in the bombardment of Veracruz on April 21 by the United States fleet and that city's occupation by American troops.

By June, film of the event was being shown on the capital screens. The following advertisement for the Trianon Palace gives an indication of the contents of the movie along with widely shared Mexican sentiments:

> The very interesting motion picture, The North American Invasion, will be exhibited. Events in Veracruz. A film of actuality which reveals the iniquitous deed committed by the *yanqui* invader. The interesting scenes reproduced by the cinematographer already indicate the contrast between the active Veracruz of yesterday, of the free and sovereign Veracruz, with today's Veracruz, trampled upon by our eternal enemy. On the screen you will see all the port's social classes attending the funeral of the heroic captain Benjamín Gutiérrez, giving the lie with this act to that segment of the capitaline press that has placed in doubt the conduct of this noble city. Among the diverse scenes reproduced by this interesting movie, we will cite the following: Panoramic view of the Bay of Veracruz. San Juan de Ulúa. Mexican artillerymen. The North American squadron in combat formation facing the heroic port on the morning of April 21. The Ipiranga. The *Prairie* bombarding the Naval School. The streets of Veracruz after the combat. The neutral White Cross volunteers its service ... Damages caused by the bombardment ... the invaders' camp ... What the *yanquis* mean by equality. Seaplanes maneuvering.[67]

War had broken out in Europe in August 1914 and by November the first films of that conflict were shown in Mexico at the Salón Rojo, which announced that the latest views from the fighting fronts would be shown weekly. The domestic civil war continued to receive good coverage as well as sympathetic treatment for Huerta's enemies if one is to judge by some of the copy in one of Granat's advertisements for a program featuring scenes of Villa's attack on Nuevo Laredo followed by the "triumphal" entry to that border city of the "Supreme Chief of the Constitutionalist Army," Venustiano Carranza. It was described as a "national motion picture which reproduces a great historical event."[68]

Such films, which were also being shown throughout the cities and hamlets of Mexico, played an important role in familiarizing the citizenry with the leaders of the factions contending for power at that time. In fact, the cinemas of the republic became lively centers of political commentary as these well-known figures — Huerta, Carranza, Alvaro Obregón, Villa, Zapata, and many others — were jeered[69] or applauded according to the public's preferences. Sometimes the audience's reaction was a good deal more volatile as in Martín Luis Guzmán's following description of movie-going Conventionists, as the supporters of Villa and Zapata were known, in Aguascalientes in 1916 watching a newsreel:

> We, nonetheless, did not see the end of the movie because something happened unexpectedly that obliged us to flee the spot we occupied just behind the screen. Don Venustiano of course was the personage who most often appeared on the screen. His appearances, increasingly more frequent, had been becoming, as was to be expected, more and more unappreciated by the Conventionist audience. From the hissing mixed with applause on the first occasions he was seen, it progressed to frank hissing; then to hissing bordering on whistling; to open hooting, and finally to bedlam. And in that way, by stages, it finally resulted, when Carranza was seen entering Mexico City on horseback, in a hellish uproar culminating in two gunshots.
>
> Both projectiles punctured the screen in the exact spot on which was outlined the first Chief's chest, and they struck the wall, one, half a meter above Lucio Blanco: the other, closer even, between Domínguez's head and mine.[70]

The years between 1916 and 1920 were tumultuous ones for Mexico, but in spite of grave domestic and international problems the epic phase of the Revolution was winding down. Venustiano Carranza's provisional administration was able, through the military prowess of Obregón, to eliminate the threats from Villa and Zapata. War with the United States was narrowly averted and a new constitution promulgated in 1917, a document that in its labor, land tenure, and social welfare provisions was the most radical in the world at that time. It provided the political and juridical infrastructure that guides the country to this day, the "institutionalized Revolution," as Mexican politicians have been fond of saying these many years.

The Mexican film industry was born in the midst of this profound transformation of the nation's society and it was to grow with the rest of the economy, as the latter became more diversified and acquired more complex technologies through the subsequent decades. In purely economic terms, films were to become an important export and thus a source of badly needed foreign exchange; by 1961 they were in sixteenth place among Mexico's export commodities. In that year films brought in 100 million pesos in revenues from foreign markets, greater than such important export items as henequen and tomatoes.[71] The cinematic medium's great propaganda value had already been recognized by the political authorities:

The government quickly appreciated the ability of films to speak to mass audiences. The Ministry of War, as one example, expressed a lively interest in filmic interpretations of the Revolution which kept Mexico in chaos throughout much of the 1910–1920 decade, and financed such films as *Juan Soldado*, *El precio de la gloria* [*The Price of Glory*] and *Honor militar* [*Military Honor*].[72]

In spite of war and uncertainty — or perhaps because of it — the movies thrived. The great Italian spectacle film, *Cabiria*, opened to enthusiastic audiences in 1916. General Pablo González, the man who was to bring about Zapata's assassination in 1919,[73] was quoted as saying that *Cabiria* was "the most gorgeous work I have seen in my life."[74] Foreign serials were introduced, including the famous Pearl White adventures, and Charlie Chaplin made his first appearance on Mexican screens. The popularization of "police" films brought forth a denunciation of "*Sherlockholmismo cinematográfico*" by the editors of *El Tiempo*. They were concerned lest the showing of such movies, especially in lower-class theaters, serve as training if not inspiration for criminal elements, a concern that continues to our own day. The alarm that *El Tiempo* expressed over the mixture of classes in neighborhood salons — bourgeois, workers, foreigners, soldiers, ruffians, respectable women, secretaries, maids, and prostitutes — would indicate just as well the democratizing influence of the cinema, whether it itself was a factor in this process or simply reflecting the changes that were occurring in the larger society as a result of the Revolution.[75]

More important, however, was the vigor displayed by Mexican filmmakers at this time. On September 15, 1916, the first full-length film made in the country was premiered at the Hidalgo Theater. This was *1810 o los libertadores de México* ("1810 or the Liberators of Mexico"), produced in Mérida, Yucatán, by the firm Cimar. The screenplay was written by the Yucatecan poet Arturo Peón Contreras.[76]

Manuel de la Bandera, an actor and founder of the México-Lux production company, attempted to establish a school to train performers for the cinema. His first effort in September 1916 came to naught, but by 1917 Mexican filmmaking was promising enough to come to the attention of President Carranza who ordered that a cinematic school to be headed by the same Bandera be formed as part of the National School for Theatrical Music and Art.[77]

Mimí Derba (1893–1953), a popular stage actress, is an important name in the nascent film industry; with Enrique Rosas she cofounded Azteca films which produced *En defensa propia* ("In Self Defense") in 1917. The first full-length (one-hour) film to be made in the Federal District was, however, *La luz* ("The Light"), produced by Bandera's company, Mèxico-Lux. Starring Emma Padilla and Ernesto Agüeros, it was directed by Ezequiel Carrasco, a photographer at the National Observatory. It had its premiere at the Salón Rojo in June, a gala event attended by Venustiano Carranza. It was the first Mexican film to employ such cinematic techniques as closeups and tracking shots.[78] It was based on a 1915 Italian film, *Il Fuoco*, starring the *diva* Pina Menichelli,[79] but transplanted to a Mexican setting, shot on location in Chapultepec, Xochimilco, and Viveros de Coyoacán.

Azteca Films's *En defensa propia*, starring Mimí Derba, was released in July. According to *El Pueblo*, which termed it the "first artistic nationally made film" it was a great success (the same newspaper had severely criticized *La luz* which in turn had been well received by all other writers). It would be of interest to briefly outline the plot here in order to get an idea of the stories favored by the Mexican public at the inception of the national movie industry. *En defensa propia* tells of Enriqueta, recently orphaned, who is obliged to work and finds employment as a governess for the widower Julio Mancera's small daughter. In time Enriqueta and Julio fall in love and marry, but it is not long before a cousin of Julio's, Eva, arrives from Europe. The unscrupulous woman, obviously a typical vamp, sets about to break up Enriqueta and Julio's idyllic marriage. Eva is close to succeeding but she is foiled at a party that she has insisted on giving for all of Julio's friends; at an unguarded moment she is surprised in the garden by Julio, Enriqueta, and all the guests in a compromising situation with Mauricio, Julio's best friend.[80]

Except for the backgrounds, it is evident that this plot outline was not terribly unique to the Mexican ambience. The story was most probably inspired by a European model in much the same way that *La luz* was. Since Italian cinema was at its peak at this time it seems likely that *En defensa propia* was, like *La luz*, adapted from one of Italy's upper-class dramas, a form already in decline.[81] Mimí Derba's second effort for Azteca Films was *La soñadora* ("The Dreamer," 1917). Writing of this movie, an anonymous reviewer for *El Pueblo* expressed his misgivings over the already evident tendency of his country's filmmakers to portray a nonexistent, artificial Mexico. In one party scene the guests, "dressed in Louis XV style" dance a "clumsily executed" minuet which has no relation to "these violent times, of the danzón and fox-trot.... How much better it would have been if Mimí's 'national beauty' had been presented clad in the typical Mexican dress tracing out the steps of a daring and gay *jarabe*."[82]

The years between 1915 and 1923 have been termed the "Golden Age"[83] of the Mexican silent cinema, although production was extremely modest, especially if compared with the output of the major filmmaking countries, but still impressive according to Latin American standards.[84] In this period new production companies were organized in Guanajuato[85] and Mazatlán as well as in Mexico City, but unlike Brazil, in which a regional filmmaking pattern was to arise,[86] the Mexican cinema industry, like the Argentine, was soon to be centered in the capital city's environs. By 1919 Enrique Rosas had left Azteca films and with the Alva brothers formed Rosas, Alva, y Cía, which produced the most distinguished Mexican film of the silent era, *La banda del automóvil gris* ("The Gray Car Gang").

After 1917 the main studio facilities were those belonging to Azteca Films (on the corner of Balderas and Juárez) and the ones belonging to Manuel de la Bandera's company, México-Lux or Productora Quetzal.[87] Since they were located within the city they cannot have been very extensive. Jorge Stahl recalls that in Mexico City "there was no studio adequate for the achievement of a better-quality film," and opened one in the Condesa suburb, on no. 117 Montes de Oca Street. He does not mention what year he did this but refers to "more than two hundred and fifty films made in ten years," and states that *Tiburón* ("Shark"), starring Joaquín Coss, was the first one produced there.[88] It must have been around 1919, since it is in that year that the Stahl name first appears as a movie producer (Jorge's brother, Carlos, directed a good many

Scenes from *La banda del automóvil gris* (1919)

of the Stahl studio productions). The figure he quotes of 250 films would seem to indicate that Mexican film production was more significant than the extant sources show; however, Stahl says that these were all very brief, amateurish efforts, and of them no trace or memory remains.

The upswing in film production from 1917 reflects the return to Mexico of at least the beginnings of political of not economic stability. On February 5 the Constitution of Querétaro became the new law of the land, replacing the Constitution of 1857. On that day, too, the last American troops of Pershing's "punitive expedition" quietly retreated across the border. On March 11 elections were held and Venustiano Carranza emerged victorious.

Mexico managed to stay clear of the European conflict and most people in the country were undoubtedly relieved to see American troops in the trenches of France instead of galloping around the Chihuahua deserts. Tensions with the United States flared up again after the end of the World War, mostly over the touchy subject of American properties in Mexico, especially oil fields. In 1919 revolts against the Carranza administration broke out: Félix Díaz again trying his luck in Oaxaca, and Pancho Villa initiating anew his nuisance raids.

In October an anti–Carranza band captured the United States consul in Puebla, William O. Jenkins, and held him for ransom. Carranza was either unable or unwilling to obtain his release and Jenkins finally had to ransom himself. As soon as he was free, however, federal authorities arrested the American consul on the rather doubtful charge that he had arranged his own abduction. The affair caused excitable elements in both countries to talk of war for awhile. The strongly anti–Carranza Jenkins remained in Mexico and went on to become an important figure in the film industry.[89]

Carranza, by contrast, was the victim of Mexico's last successful military coup. Alvaro Obregón unseated him in May 1920 and Carranza was machine-gunned while trying to flee with a good part of the treasury. The 1920s was the period of the "Northern Dynasty," called thus because Mexico's leaders were from the northern states, principally Coahuila, Sonora, and Chihuahua (Carranza had been governor of Coahuila when the Revolution began in 1910). Howard Cline has summarized Obregón's administration in the following manner:

> His court was composed of an interlocking directorate of military men, intellectuals, labor leaders, and agrarians. From 1920 through 1933 these leaders hacked away at the roots of Mexican difficulties; slowly and painfully they wrestled with the undramatic chores of reconstruction and rehabilitation. By historical accident national leadership for the Revolution had come primarily from the North; this circumstance goes far to explain the peculiar cast, the emphasis, and the goals of their programs. The general tone of the golden twenties everywhere in the world provided the atmosphere in which they toiled.[90]

The apparent vigor of the fledgling film industry seemed to reflect the Obregón presidency's business-like approach to the rebuilding of Mexico. By the early 1920s, however, film production was falling off in spite of the construction of new facilities like Jesús Abitia's Chapultepec studios.[91] Mexican films at this time had no foreign

markets and their hold on the domestic one was precarious indeed. Silent films moreover were almost strictly visual, and the plots could easily be followed without much
recourse to the brief intertitles.

Mexican moviemakers generally attempted to copy European, especially Italian,
cinema: the stories, the acting styles, and even the institution of the diva, in the persons of Mimí Derba, Emma Padilla, and Elena Sánchez Valenzuela, were adopted by
Mexican filmmakers.

An exception was the previously mentioned *La banda del automóvil gris* (1919).
Produced and tautly directed by Enrique Rosas, it was patterned after the highly popular serials from France and the United States. The film related the exploits of an
actual criminal gang that had operated in Mexico City — a gang, it was rumored, with
political connections. The criminals utilized a gray automobile for their capers, hence
the film's title. Rosas was inspired to make the movie when he photographed the exe-
cution of the real gang. Joaquín Coss played the leading role and assisted with the
direction. The movie debuted on December 12, 1919, in twenty-eight Mexico City
theaters. Of it García Riera has remarked, "*El automóvil gris* conserves its flavor and
freshness. Efficiently realized and with a good rhythm, the film constitutes a magnificent testimony of its time, of the revolutionary epoch."[92]

From a peak production in 1919 of fourteen films, including a newsreel series
that reached seventy editions, Mexican filmmakers' output gradually declined until
in 1923 only two films were made, and in 1924 apparently none. Production increased
to about seven movies in 1925 but the popularity of Hollywood films was a challenge
that the undercapitalized and largely unoriginal national companies were unable to
overcome. The United States was producing between five hundred and seven hundred features a year by the early 1920s, a gargantuan industry that was backed by an
aggressive marketing organization throughout the world. In 1923, for instance, First
National Pictures opened its own distribution offices in Mexico City and not long
afterwards Universal, Paramount, and Fox followed suit.[93]

While Mexican filmmakers in the silent film era seemed little preoccupied with
depicting, either negatively or positively, their neighbors to the north, Mexico was
becoming an important thematic component of early American moviemakers. The
great majority of representations of Mexicans or Mexico on American screens were
distinctly negative and almost entirely within the "Western" genre. It must be remem-
bered that this was a period in which racist attitudes were freely expressed in the media,
not only in the United States but throughout most of the world. The most famous
example of this in film is probably D.W. Griffith's *Birth of a Nation* (1915) — an unde-
niably great film, it nonetheless represented blacks in a highly offensive manner, but
the portrayal was undoubtedly concurrent with the image of blacks held by the great
majority of white Americans at the time.[94]

The traditional enmity toward Mexicans in the Southwestern United States,
extant even before the two nations warred in 1848, had generated a legacy of hatred,
suspicion, and bigotry. These attitudes were exacerbated by the Mexican Revolution,
whose social effects spilled over the border into the United States. The sporadic official
hostility between Washington and Mexico throughout the 1910s to the 1930s did little
to uplift the Mexican image in American films. Although Westerns were the principal

genre to draw upon both then-current attitudes and literary stereotypes to depict Mexicans as "conniving, untrustworthy persons, who usually operate outside of the law,"[95] other films addressed themselves to contemporary issues.

For instance, in 1915 William Randolph Hearst helped to finance a fifteen-part serial entitled *Patria* starring Irene Castle. The film depicted a Japanese-Mexican invasion of the United States and clearly was designed to capitalize on the nervousness many Americans felt over revolution in Mexico, Japanese involvement south of the Rio Grande, and United States–Japanese tensions. The serial was vastly popular but so offensive to the Japanese ambassador that President Wilson asked the film company to withdraw *Patria* from public exhibition.[96]

It seems likely that such American films, for obvious reasons, were not exported to Mexico. Thus moviegoers in the Mexican capital were for the most part unfamiliar with the Hollywood Western's portrayal of the "Mexican greasers" so familiar to American Western folklore. More concern was expressed over American films made in Mexico and the image they presented of the country. The pilgrimage of American filmmakers to Mexico is as old as the cinema industry itself: in 1898 the Edison Company sent photographers south of the border to make such brief films as *Mexican Rurales Charge*, *Mexico Street Scene*, and *Train Hour in Durango, Mexico*.[97]

One of the first complaints against the "distortion" of Mexico on American screens appeared in 1920. An unidentified American offered to make films in Mexico so as to familiarize foreign audiences with the country — an offer that apparently elicited a subsidy from the Mexican government. The movie later appeared in the United States under the title, *The Real Mexico*, including scenes of "the Texcoco market with a couple dozen seminaked Indians selling firewood with an explanatory title stating 'productive transactions.'" The commentator reserves his most indignant reaction for a shot of Madero Avenue with the title, "The capital's most aristocratic avenue"; it was shown almost deserted, but at the moment the camera was filming, two or three burros loaded with coal passed by.[98]

In spite of the many troubles between Mexico and the United States, the Salón Rojo saw fit to celebrate the American independence day in 1918 with a "solemn commemoration ... program dedicated to the honorable and dignified American colony and its allies."[99] This was the introduction to a showing of the latest newsreels from the European battlefields. It seems strange that the Salón Rojo's management, whose business depended on the public's good will, would refer to the United States in a manner that must certainly have been anathema to a good number of Mexicans. Perhaps it can most readily be explained as still another manifestation of the peculiar love-hate relationship that has always existed between the two countries — that perplexing blend of mutual attraction and antipathy that many Mexicans and Americans feel toward each other.

The decade of the twenties witnessed the emergence of a fabulous movie industry in Hollywood and, as a consequence, a decline in production in Mexico. The highly professional American films offered their audiences fantasy and glamour, and this was the period of the great "stars": Rudolph Valentino, Douglas Fairbanks, Mary Pickford, Theda Bara, Charles Chaplin, and many others. The film industries of Western Europe, especially Italy and France, failed to recover their prewar vigor. Only in

Germany, traumatized by defeat and narrowly avoiding a Marxist revolution, did directors such as Fritz Lang attempt to interpret and explain the anxieties of German society, and through their efforts German expressionism made a deep impression on filmmakers throughout the world. The Bolshevik government of Russia was among the first to realize the enormous propaganda potential of the cinema and directors like Sergei Eisenstein raised "expressive realism" to an art.[100]

In view of such developments in Europe it is somewhat puzzling that the revolutionary government of Mexico did not place more emphasis on the utilization of film as an educational and propaganda tool. Under the dynamic leadership of the enigmatic José Vasconcelos, Minister of Education under Obregón from 1921 to 1924, a great cultural, educational, and artistic movement got underway.[101] Artistic and musical festivals were organized among schoolchildren in which native traditions were revived and glorified; painters like Diego Rivera, José Clemente Orozco, and David Alfaro Siqueiros resurrected and gave new significance to an ancient tradition of mural art — "the message was Marxian, the technique Mexican."[102]

Clearly Mexico in the 1920s had a monumental task of reconstruction before it, and perhaps its disorganized, suffering, and poverty-stricken society was not in a position to respond to a government educational program in which film would play a major role. The problem was basic education — the need to eliminate widespread illiteracy and to raise the self-esteem of the Mexican masses. This is what Vasconcelos's program attempted to do and evidently he did not recognize the part that films could play in the process. Even if Vasconcelos had realized the potentialities of motion pictures, it is doubtful that his Ministry of Education with its painfully inadequate budgets could have subsidized much filmmaking.[103] The troubled Mexican film industry, such as it was, remained solidly in private hands.

If Mexican films per se had not made a particularly strong impression on the world cinema, Mexican and other performers from Spanish-speaking countries were achieving international stardom. Spanish-born but Mexicanophile Antonio Moreno (1887–1967) appeared in a 1920 American production released in Mexico under the title of *Los peligros de la montaña del trueno o Aventuras de Moreno* ("The Dangers of Thunder Mountain or Adventures of Moreno"). It was made by the Vitagraph Company and was reportedly premiered in Mexico even before it was shown in the United States.[104] Moreno's Hollywood career spanned more than forty years during which he made 150 films. His initial reputation was established by the Latin lovers he portrayed opposite Greta Garbo, Pola Negri, Clara Bow, and Gloria Swanson. Ramón Novarro (1899–1968) was a transplanted Mexican who became a romantic star of the silent era in Hollywood whose most famous role was in *Ben Hur* (1925).[105]

But far and away the most successful performer, and the one who achieved true stardom, was Dolores del Río, born Dolores Asúnsolo y López Negrete in Durango in 1906. The Revolution forced Dolores's father, who was director of the Bank of Durango, to seek refuge in the United States. In the meantime, his wife and their four-year-old daughter sought a measure of peace in Mexico City. There Dolores attended an exclusive French private school and, as was proper for a well-bred young lady of the Porfirian aristocracy, she studied Spanish dancing.

In 1921, at the age of fifteen, she married Jaime Martínez del Río, a wealthy lawyer and *hacendado*, eighteen years her senior. After a two-year honeymoon in Europe, during which on one occasion she volunteered to dance for Spanish soldiers wounded in the Moroccan war and drew plaudits from Alfonso XIII, the happy couple returned to a comfortable yet uneventful life in Mexico City. Their placid existence was radically changed by a chance visit from their friend, the painter Adolfo Best Maugard, who brought some American friends with him — the film actors Claire Windsor and Bert Lytell, and the director, Edwin Carewe.

The American filmmaker was highly impressed with Dolores and asked her if she would be interested in working in a movie. The idea excited both Dolores and Jaime, both of whom longed for a change as well as a chance to get away from the insecurities of Mexico. By August 1925, they were in Hollywood and Dolores del Río's international film career, spanning almost fifty years, had started, beginning innocuously enough with a bit part in United Artists's *Joanne* (1925).

In keeping with a long-established American tradition by which any Latin American, and especially Mexican, with positive personal attributes was perceived as being "Spanish," so too did Dolores's billing tout her as a "Spanish actress." Quite possibly also, the continuing uneasy relations with Mexico might have persuaded studio publicists that it would not do for them to go out of their way to inform the moviegoing public that their newest glamorous property hailed from that troublesome neighbor full of rampaging Indian bandits and revolutionaries.

In rapid order, Dolores del Río appeared in *All the Town Is Talking* (1925) with Edward Everett Horton, and *Upstream* (1926) with Walter Pidgeon. When she appeared in Raoul Walsh's *What Price Glory?* (1926) as Charmaine, the French peasant girl pursued by Victor McLaglen and Edmund Lowe, Dolores was established as a star. She starred in *Resurrection* (1927) directed once again by Carewe, this time playing a Russian peasant. Other notable silent films that Dolores made were *Ramona* (1928) and *Evangeline* (1929); she made fifteen in all, including the films already mentioned.

Dolores del Río had not yet learned English (she was directed through interpreters), a not insurmountable problem in silent films. She made the difficult and surprising transition to sound, having learned English, and went on to an equally successful career in the "talkies."[106] She was not to make a Mexican film until 1943.[107]

While Dolores del Río was achieving international stardom and other Mexican performers, most notably Ramón Novarro, Lupita Tovar, Raquel Torres, Lupe Vélez, and Gilbert Roland, were establishing careers in Hollywood, the Mexican silent film industry languished, unable to offer even token competition to American products. Even though Mexican production could be characterized as flourishing when compared to that of Argentina and other Latin American countries,[108] this was small consolation to the country's filmmakers.

In the late 1920s however, some names appeared that were to become important in the 1930s and 1940s and to contribute to the Mexican film industry's commercial, if not artistic, success in ensuing years. Among these were the Stahl brothers, Jorge and Carlos, who produced *La linterna de Diógenes* ("The Lantern of Diogenes," 1925), and especially Miguel Contreras Torres (1899–1981), a revolutionary officer-turned-filmmaker, who made *El sueño del caporal* ("The Corporal's Dream," 1922), *De raza azteca* ("Of Aztec Race," 1922), *El hombre sin patria* ("The Man Without a

Country," 1922), *Fulguración de la raza* ("Resplendence of the Race," 1922), *Almas tropicales* ("Tropical Souls," 1923), *Atavismo* ("Atavism," 1923), and *Oro, sangre y sol* ("Gold, Blood and Sun," 1925). According to García Riera, Contreras Torres's work is "without doubt the most important of the twenties." His films were "imbued with a patriotic spirit similar to that which animates commemorative political speeches."[109]

The advent of sound was to cause profound changes in the international cinema. The popularity of Hollywood films was not to diminish by any means, but forces would be brought into play that were to revitalize or initiate the movie industries of many countries. Mexican reality would begin to find its voice, however fitfully, in the films of the 1930s.

2

The Coming of Sound:
1930–1939

From the very inception of the cinema, the synchronization of sound with the screen image had been a cherished dream. We need only recall Luis G. Urbina's musings on the subject after attending a performance at the Cinematógrafo Lumière in the late 1890s: "It ... lacks something.... Perhaps with time it will acquire sound."[1]

Experimentation with sound had started early although such attempts invariably failed. In Mexico the first public demonstration of synchronization of sound with film occurred at the Colón Theater in June 1912, an experiment mounted by one of M. León Baumont's assistants — or at least it was thus reported. The French filmmaker had preferred not to display his untried chronophone in Paris just yet and supposedly arranged to have it tested in Mexico instead. It was no more than a phonograph record synchronized with the film and it was a complete failure, not only because the supposed Gaumont assistant was not really what he pretended to be but also because he was inept at operating the equipment. He was incapable of correctly synchronizing the record with the screen images and only succeeded in eliciting some "frightful noises which had nothing in common with what was being seen on the screen." The cronófono, as it was called in Mexico, was kept in the Colón's storage room until 1927 when a second unsuccessful attempt was made to work it.[2]

The coming of sound, in Eric Rhode's telling words, was to release "energies that had long been suppressed."[3] As this chapter will describe, the energies generated by the Mexican Revolution sought expression through the new medium of sound films and resulted, toward the end of the decade, in the establishment of a sophisticated industry. The movies produced by Mexican studios in these years reflected a variety of societal, cultural, and political concerns. They also provided an outlet for the ambitions of some members of the new entrepreneurial class created by the Revolution. A number of producers were revolutionary officers or cronies of influential politicos.

Foreign influences also played a major role in the development of the Mexican film industry and the two major sources will be discussed: the artistic and intellectual ferment of interwar Europe, and the techniques and styles of Hollywood. The latter's ill-fated attempt to make "Hispanic" films for the international Spanish-speaking market was especially important, providing a training ground for directors and performers who later went to Mexico. Although Mexico was in the process of recovering from a destructive civil war and developing ways of continuing and institutionalizing its revolution, it was also caught up in the complexities of the postwar world.

The intellectual and political reactions to the revolutionary changes taking place both in the Old and New Worlds were reflected in the new art of the cinema. The "talkies" were to acquire great importance in many countries as a medium for expressing vague national anxieties. The world was in turmoil, and social and political change was occurring faster than most people could come to terms with it. The *belle époque* of prewar days had signified the end of an era of smug self-complacency in Western societies. The World War shattered the security of the middle classes and tragically demonstrated the fatal flaws in the sacred double pillars of European claims to superiority: capitalism and nationalism. Imperialism, the manifestation of this system in Asia and Africa, had also been dealt a death blow although its weakened structure was not to collapse completely until after 1945.

The "roaring twenties" exemplified the general rejection of traditional social restraints in the West. What was known in the Anglo-Saxon countries as Victorian morality had been rent asunder by the brutal stresses of total war. The rejection of prewar ethical and sexual standards resulted in a more or less "liberated" class, among the elites at least. Another kind of liberation — and much more ominous to many — was represented by the Bolshevik triumph in Russia and the founding of Comintern-affiliated Communist parties throughout the world. The middle and upper classes in capitalist countries lived in fear of what they considered a proletariat subverted by Bolshevik agents.

Perhaps the cinema could be ideally adapted to further the interaction of social change and art. Working from this premise, Lev Kuleshov, at the Moscow State School of Cinematography, came to believe that editing was the basic tool for adapting the cinema to artistic or social purposes. He worked out a theory of montage which a short time later would be taken up by Sergei Eisenstein (1898–1948), a filmmaker who was to have a profound effect on the Mexican cinema.

The struggle to understand and express the social and technological changes that were taking place assumed many forms. The Futurist movement, for example, attempted to find artistic inspiration in the industrialized urbanism of the twentieth century and its influence soon spread to film. This group of artists was the first willing to cooperate with the Bolsheviks, who accepted for a time the Futurists' views as official policy.[4]

The Futurists' restlessness and preference for the bizarre was one attempt aesthetically to come to terms with and respond to the multifaceted uncertainties of postwar life. In painting, surrealism and cubism reflected this intellectual restlessness. These forms found their way into the cinema in such films as *The Cabinet of Dr. Caligari* (1920), for which the presurrealist Alfred Kubin, "who ... made eerie phantoms invade harmless scenery and visions of torture emerge from the subconscious,"[5] designed the sets. The Futurist style was also incorporated in the work of French avant-garde filmmakers: in Louis Feuillade's *Fantômas* (1913) the main character "pierces a white wall and blood gushes out of it ... and five men in identical masks and black tights pursue each other at a ball."[6]

Louis Delluc, in his use of objects to convey his central characters' mental states, especially in the lost film *Le Silence* (1920), strongly influenced both Jean Epstein and the Spaniard Luis Buñuel (1900–1983). In fact, Delluc's techniques can be said to have reached their fullest expression in the 1960s, in Alain Resnais's *Last Year at Marienbad* (1961) and Buñuel's *Belle de jour* (1966).[7] Buñuel, along with his fellow Spaniards Pablo Picasso and Salvador Dalí, was intimately associated with prewar and postwar Parisian artistic circles. Buñuel and Dalí collaborated in the classic but bizarre surrealist experiment *Un Chien Andalou* ("The Andalusian Dog,"1928). Its imagery "includes hands and armpits covered by ants, soiled bodies, an emphasis on buttocks and the usual apparatus of sadistic practice."[8] In *L'Age d'or* ("The Golden Age," 1930) Buñuel developed further these symbols:

> Less brittle and more wide-ranging than its predecessor, *L'Age d'or* brings this anality even more into the open: lovers roll ecstatically in mud beneath the shocked gaze of some dignitaries: later the woman dreams about her lover as she sits on the lavatory. From its opening sequence — a documentary in the manner of Painlevé about the death rites of scorpions — to its concluding quotation from de Sade's *140 Days in Sodom*, in which various noblemen dressed in robes imitative of figures from the past, including Christ, totter from their debauchery into the snow, *L'Age d'or* extends caustically over many notions of civilization and style, including the manners of polite society, the corruption and suicide of a minister and even the founding of Rome.[9]

Diego Rivera, who along with David Alfaro Siqueiros and José Clemente Orozco was to found the Mexican muralist movement under the sponsorship of Vasconcelos, was also a part of this European artistic and intellectual maelstrom. He was in Europe during the war and in the immediate postwar years "joined the Cubist movement, became a friend of Picasso ('I have never believed in God,' he said, 'but in Picasso, yes.') fraternized with Apollinaire, quarreled with and made up with Modigliani.... He stayed a long time in Italy studying the frescoes of the Renaissance. He glowed with enthusiasm for the new Russia that was emerging from the revolution."[10]

Rivera participated in and absorbed the intellectual excitement of the European avant-garde and returned to his native Mexico to create a muralist genre that received inspiration from both pre–Columbian fresco painting and Old World traditional and revolutionary concepts. Simultaneously, Luis Buñuel was developing his unorthodox film techniques and antibourgeois posture in silent films — a style he was to bring to fruition in Mexico during the 1940s and 1950s.

Nationalists in Mexico and elsewhere in Latin America were concerned that the advent of sound films represented "the most powerful weapon" in the American "peaceful invasion" of their countries. If all films henceforth were to be made in the English language, they worried, the Latin American publics would "by force have to learn that tongue if they wished to be entertained and after a few years Castilian would be forgotten, passing into the category of dead languages."[11] The newspaper

El Universal launched a campaign to convince all Latin American governments to prohibit the showing of English-language films, an objective which most other Mexican newspapers and magazines enthusiastically supported. One exception was the monthly magazine *Continental* which attacked *El Universal's* position and defended the screening of movies in any language, especially English, since it would help "Mexicans learn that language which was indispensable in the business world." The magazine's spirited defense of foreign-made "talkies" (as they were also called in Mexico at this time) might very well have been based on the fact that foreign film distributors regularly bought twelve pages of advertising in *Continental*; in addition, the editors displayed rather bad timing in publishing, in the very same issue in which they stated their pro–English-language "talkies" position, a letter from Paramount Films de México, S.A. congratulating them on the editorial.[12]

Sound films were not greeted with enthusiasm elsewhere in the world either: Chaplin felt they were unsuitable to his sophisticated comedy style of mime and characterization; and the Soviet directors, Eisenstein among them, felt that sound introduced additional technical and marketing difficulties.[13] The advent of sound ended the careers of some box office idols, notably Douglas Fairbanks and Mary Pickford. Many foreign artists in Hollywood were unable to handle dialogue adequately, although, as has been seen, Dolores del Río, whose English was certainly almost nonexistent in the 1920s, did make the transition quite successfully to the talkies, as did Greta Garbo. However, other performers, such as Emil Jannings, Pola Negri, and Conrad Veidt, returned to Europe.

As pointed out in chapter 1, Mexican filmmaking was practically at a standstill by the end of the silent film era. The only moviemakers of any consequence were the ex-revolutionary fighter, Miguel Contreras Torres who cultivated a superpatriotic genre, and Jorge Stahl, who had run the gamut from pioneer cameraman *à la* Toscano to distributor and studio owner. Both Contreras Torres and Stahl were to achieve greater prominence after the production of Mexican sound films began. Other directors, producers, and performers of the early 1930s were to arrive in Mexico by way of Hollywood's Spanish-language film production.

The major American companies, in an effort to retain and widen their lucrative Latin American markets, and undoubtedly concerned about the implications of campaigns against English-language films such as the one waged by *El Universal*, imported stage actors and directors from Spain and Latin America. Initially, the films were simply Spanish-language versions of English-dialogue originals or sound remakes of silent originals. Toward the end of Spanish-language movie production, especially at Fox, some films were produced in Spanish only.[14]

By 1929 all of Hollywood's production facilities had converted to sound but American films could obviously only be marketed in English-speaking countries. Therefore the large studios began simultaneously to produce silent versions of their films for foreign consumption. This ploy was a resounding failure in countries like France, Germany, and the Soviet Union that were already making their own sound films. Movie production in Spain and Latin America, on the other hand, was incapable of supplying a market of one hundred million people who demanded films in Spanish. Movies with Spanish subtitles were unsatisfactory because of the high illiteracy rate generally throughout Latin America.[15] In addition, the Mexican government, as did others in Latin America, demanded "absolute Castilian purity in the subtitles of foreign films."[16] Hollywood thus began the production of features in Spanish, French, and German but soon found that European audiences much preferred seeing the original versions starring popular American stars.

Only film production in Spanish, however, became established in Hollywood. In spite of these "Hispanic" pictures' general unpopularity with Latin American audiences, more than 113 were made between 1930 and 1938.[17] Strangely enough, Hollywood never utilized its best-known Latin American stars, Dolores del Río and Lupe Vélez, in Spanish-language films, although Ramón Novarro did appear in a few. Marlene Dietrich and Emil Jannings also never made Hollywood films in their native tongue, while Greta Garbo and Maurice Chevalier did.[18]

There seem to have been two principal reasons for the nonacceptance by the Latin American publics of these Hollywood Spanish-language films. First, there was the jumble of accents — Spanish, Cuban, Mexican, Argentine, Chilean, and others — which imbued these movies with an air of unreality. For the first time, through the medium of sound films, the average person of one country came to realize how his language was spoken in another. Though Spanish theatrical companies had for generations been touring throughout Spanish America, the legitimate theater was usually restricted to a relatively well-educated elite who expected national and regional variances in the spoken language.

But the cinema exposed mass audiences to a sort of collective culture shock; they heard their own language emerging from the screen images' lips, but a language that sounded bizarre and alien — even if understandable. Part of the problem was the American producers' assumptions — even if they knew a little Spanish — that the so-called Castilian Spanish, the language as spoken in the central plain of Spain, was acceptable everywhere in the Western Hemisphere. The immediate result of this linguistic confusion was that Argentina declared that she would not permit the importation of the multiaccented films or those in "Castilian."[19] Spain, for its part, stated that its moviegoers "could not bear to listen to the irritating Latin American accents" and that if the "c" or "z" were not "orthographically pronounced," the American studios "need not bother" sending their films.[20] Lest it be assumed that all of this bickering over language was simply an isolated case of Hispanic xenophobia, it should be pointed out that in Britain at this time, movie audiences began to complain of pictures in "American" and that there were demands that actors should speak English "correctly."[21]

The second factor that rendered Hollywood Hispanic films unacceptable to their intended audiences was the same one that doomed the making of American pictures in French, German, or Italian: the Latin American audiences enjoyed seeing American stars and "would not easily accept their substitution by José Crespo or Luana Alcañiz."[22] On the surface, the two factors would seem to contradict each other since the linguistic dispute was ultimately an expression of a particularly strident nationalism that was emerging throughout the world in the 1930s. Yet this xenophobia was transcended by Hollywood's "dream factories" which had already established the American movie as the favorite entertainment of millions throughout the world irrespective of nationality or ideology.[23]

A rather interesting film that was made after the regular production of Hispanic films ended was Columbia's *Verbena trágica* ("Tragic Festival," 1938).[24] It starred the eminent Mexican actor, Fernando Soler, playing the role of Mateo Vargas, a Spanish immigrant in New York. As the film begins, we are shown a, or perhaps *the*, Hispanic neighborhood in Manhattan, whose multinational residents are making preparations to celebrate *El día de la raza*— Columbus Day. This small, improbable neighborhood is a paean to Pan-Americanism since the inhabitants seem to represent every Latin American country. However, the principal characters are Spaniards and as the fiesta celebrations — more reminiscent of a typical Little Italy street *festa*— proceed, we see Mateo just released from a short stint in jail for hitting a policeman. Mateo is a boxer and neighborhood hero and his return is eagerly awaited by everyone except his wife Blanca (Luana de Alcañiz). This is because she happens to be a couple of months pregnant, and since Mateo has been in prison for eight months it does not take him long to realize that something has been going on in his absence. Blanca's lover is Claudio (Juan Torena), Mateo's best friend and fiancé of Blanca's half-sister, Lola (Cecilia Callejo).

It is soon evident that the basic problem with all these emigré Spaniards (they are not refugees from the Civil War raging at that time; in fact references to Spain make the country appear completely normal) is their difficulty in adapting to life in New York. Claudio is disgusted because he cannot find a job and has no money to marry Lola; Mateo's problems, as reflected in his unexplained act of hitting a policeman, stem from his homesickness and his unhappiness with American ways — the "noise," the "bluff," the "hypocrisy." The rest of the film is a melodramatic account of Mateo's finally realizing that it is Claudio who is Blanca's lover; with the street festivities as a backdrop, Mateo pursues Claudio, catches up with him on a fire escape, and punches him, causing Claudio to fall to his death in the street below. This time Mateo's temper and his exaggerated sense of honor have brought him serious trouble.

Verbena trágica is interesting in that it seems to be a last-ditch attempt by Hollywood to find some formula that would appeal to Latin American audiences. Although it is difficult to know what kind of distribution the film had in Latin America, it probably was not extensive. By 1938–39, Mexican filmmaking was well established and expanding rapidly.[25] It was well on its way toward exploiting the Latin American markets that Hollywood had failed to reach with its Spanish-language productions. It is difficult to tell whether *Verbena trágica* was designed to utilize Columbia's remaining Spanish production facilities in an attempt to find a market among Hispanics in the United States. Employing an already-familiar actor like Fernando Soler with a back-up cast of leftovers from Hollywood's Hispanic heyday would seem to indicate some such intent.

In the late 1930s, the major Hispanic group would have been the Mexican-Americans of the Southwest. This was before the great Puerto Rican influx of the late 1940s and 1950s that was to make New York City a major foreign market for the Mexican film industry[26]; it also predated the much larger immigration, both legal and illegal (of Mexicans, Dominicans, South Americans), of recent decades. The Cuban population of Florida, centered at this time in the Tampa area, was minimal and unimportant as a motion picture market.

In any event, Fernando Soler recalls that when he went to Hollywood in 1938 to make *La verbena trágica* and *El caudal de los hijos* ("The Fortune of Children") he was "unimpressed" with either film; the experience served only to corroborate his opinion that in Mexico they "performed technical miracles."[27] Yet, whether the Columbia studio executives' intention was to appeal to Latin American audiences or United States Hispanic audiences, their choice of an aggressively Spanish group of principal characters in *Verbena trágica* seems to betray a basic misconception of their market. The imagined problems of Spanish immigrants in New York would presumably hold little interest for movie audiences in Bogotá or Lima and perhaps even less for a Mexican-American public in Los Angeles or San Antonio, even if one ignores the fact that Spanish immigration to the United States has always been statistically insignificant. It is true that throughout the film other obvious national types make brief appearances — Argentines, Mexicans, and a black man who is supposed to be either Cuban or Puerto Rican. Yet such obvious contrivances imbue the entire film with an air of unreality, and *Verbena trágica* serves as a fitting epitaph to Hollywood's ill-conceived and ill-fated attempt to make movies in Spanish for Latin America.

The sound era in Mexico began on July 6, 1929, when *The Jazz Singer* starring Al Jolson was premiered at the Olimpia Theater. It was the first film with a complete sound track although for some years incidental sound effects or background music had been included in some movies,[28] one of numerous examples being the metallic sound of gold coins being dropped on a table in the scene where Judas is being induced to betray Jesus in Cecil B. DeMille's otherwise silent *King of Kings* (1927).

It is also at this time that Luz Alba (pseudonym of the journalist Cube Bonifant) began writing her highly regarded film reviews in *El Universal Ilustrado*. Jorge Ayala Blanco considers her, along with Xavier Villaurrutia, the only writer in this period who foresaw and sensed the rudiments of a specifically cinematic culture. In her reviews Luz Alba was one of the first in Mexico to take always into account the "decisive participation" of the director.[29] Fittingly, the premiere of *The Jazz Singer* was favorably chronicled in Luz Alba's movie column.[30]

The excitement caused by the novelty of sound soon led to the various international controversies already described and Hollywood's failed venture into foreign-language motion picture production, especially in Spanish. The way was now clear for the rebirth of a Mexican film industry symbolized by the 1931 production of *Santa*, a remake of the 1918 silent film based on the Federico Gamboa novel. The Compañía Nacional Productora de Películas was formed on the initiative of a wealthy film distributor and ex-revolutionary associate of Madero, Juan de la Cruz Alarcón, the journalist Carlos Noriega Hope, and the veteran cineast Gustavo Sáenz de Sicilia. The Spaniard Antonio Moreno was brought from Hollywood to direct Mexico's first sound movie. Also from the United States came the Oaxaca-born Lupita Tovar to play the title role[31] (fresh from portraying Eva in Universal's Spanish-language production of *Dracula* [1931] directed by George Melford), Donald Reed (professional name of Ernesto Guillén), and Alex Phillips to supervise the filming.

Among other significant names associated with *Santa* were: Roberto and Joselito Rodríguez who devised an original sound system for the film; Agustín Lara, who wrote the music; and Miguel Lerdo de Tejada, musical director.[32] Shooting began on

Donald Reed and Lupita Tovar in *Santa* (1931) (Cineteca).

November 3, 1931, in the Nacional Productora studios; on March 30, 1932, *Santa* was premiered at the Palacio Theater. It cost 45,000 pesos to make and ran for eighty-one minutes.

Santa is a humble country girl who lives happily with her family in Chimalis-tac until she is seduced and abandoned by the army officer Marcelino (Donald Reed). Her brothers, learning of the dishonor she has brought on the family, cast her out. Santa makes her way to Mexico City where she finds work at a brothel run by *doña* Elvira (Mimí Derba) and where Hipólito (Carlos Orellana), a blind piano-player, is also employed. Both Hipólito and the bullfighter El Jarameño (Juan José Martínez Casado) fall in love with Santa who has by this time become quite renowned in her trade. She goes to live with El Jarameño but when he surprises her one day with Marcelino he throws her out of his house. Santa sinks to the lowest depths and devel-ops cancer; Hipólito arranges for an operation but she dies during surgery. He has her buried in Chimalistac.

García Riera says that Santa is "mysteriously lacking in the poetry that time tends to attach to even the worst of films."[33] Yet, as Salvador Elizondo comments, the film represents a "peculiar condition" that occupies a "preeminent place in the Mexican soul; the idealization, through moralizing, of the prostitute, that irresistibly attractive yet veiled being.... Terror of the mother [the opposing and equally prevailing

symbol of Mexican popular culture]
drives us with ever-increasing fury
into the arms of the prostitute."[34]

Another significant event for
the future of Mexican cinema was
the arrival in the country in late
1930 of Sergei Eisenstein, the eminent Soviet director, accompanied
by his collaborators Grigori Alexan-
drov and the cameraman Eduard
Tissé. Eisenstein had been traveling
through Western Europe and the
United States studying the latest
cinematic technology, especially
that of sound. He was under contract to Paramount to film Theodore
Dreiser's *An American Tragedy*, but
the restrictions placed upon him by

Lupita Tovar and Juan José Martínez Casado in a scene from *Santa* (Cineteca).

the studio executives prompted him to leave in disgust. Eisenstein had already agreed
to carry out a filmmaking assignment for the Japanese government when he met

Santa and her brothers, right to left, Lupita Tovar, Antonio R. Frausto, and an unidentified actor (Cineteca).

Sergei Eisenstein meets Mickey Mouse at Walt Disney Studios in Hollywood, 1930.

Upton Sinclair and Diego Rivera. The latter tempted the Russian with beguiling descriptions of the stark beauty of Mexico and Sinclair assured him of financial backing if he would undertake a film project in that country.

Eisenstein and his crew traveled throughout Mexico filming the land and the people, and most of his actors were picked from the peasants and average villagers — a technique that was to be adopted by the postwar Italian neorealists. The Russian filmmaker immersed himself in the culture and life of postrevolutionary Mexico; he sought out the country's most remote corners and assiduously studied Mexican history and customs. Eisenstein also made contact with the young artists and writers of Mexico and benefited from their advice and help. Among these were the artist and poet Isabel Villaseñor who played the role of Mariá in the second episode, "Apotheosis of the Magüey," of Eisenstein's projected epic which he was going to call *¡Que viva México!* There were also Agustín Aragón Leiva and the painter Adolfo Best Maugard, who had been instrumental in starting Dolores del Río on her Hollywood career.

Difficulties, however, soon emerged. A manager, Sinclair's relative, was imposed on Eisenstein who proceeded to hinder and delay the filming. After thirteen months of work, the Russian director left Mexico with eighty thousand meters of unedited film; at Laredo, Texas, he was obliged to wait almost two months for authorization to reenter the United States and then, because of contractual commitments, he had to go directly from there to the Soviet Union.

¡Que viva México! was never released in any form approved by Eisenstein. Sinclair sold Sol Lesser (producer of the Tarzan pictures) the authorization to use whatever stock he needed for his feature, *Thunder Over Mexico*. Somewhat later, Marie Seton, Eisenstein's biographer, utilized some of this film for her picture, *Time in the Sun*. All this resulted in a good deal of controversy in the United States, but the most tragic aspect of the affair was that Eisenstein himself was never given the opportunity to fashion the film on Mexico that he had originally envisioned.[35] In 1979, the two surviving members of Eisenstein's crew, Sergei Bondarchuk and Grigori Aleksandrov (the cameraman Eduard Tissé died in 1961), released *¡Que Viva Mexico!— Da zdravstvuyet Meksika!* Using Eisenstein's notes and sketches, they edited a film they believed came very close to Eisenstein's projected motion picture.

Still, Eisenstein's unrealized film was to have an important influence, even if indirect, on subsequent Mexican filmmakers who were to develop a "national" style of cinema, especially Emilio "El Indio" Fernández.[36] García Riera comments that Eisenstein's work in Mexico

> Permitted various Mexican cineasts more or less solidarized with populist currents to create a style which would be characterized by meticulous camerawork [concentrating on clouds and magüey plants] and would gratuitously pay tribute to a hieratism by which they pretended to attain a national essence.[37]

Although 1932, the year in which *Santa* was released, saw only six films produced, it was significant in that it witnessed the debut of two directors who would soon make valuable contributions to their country's cinema. These were Fernando de Fuentes (1894–1958)[38] who made *El anónimo* ("The Anonymous One") and Arcady Boytler (1893–1965), a pre–Bolshevik Russian filmmaker who had studied under

Stanislavsky and, in Mexico, met Eisenstein.[39] He directed *Mano a mano* ("Hand to Hand"), the first *charro* sound film. Boytler's cameraman was Alex Phillips (1900–1977), a Canadian who had met Mary Pickford in Europe while he was serving in his Canadian unit in World War I; she later helped him get a start in Hollywood from where he went to Mexico to photograph *Santa*. Phillips made Mexico his home and was to become one of the industry's leading cameramen.[40]

In 1933 Mexican film production was at the forefront of Spanish-language moviemaking with twenty-one feature films, among them these important works: Fernando de Fuentes's *El compadre Mendoza* ("Godfather Mendoza") and *El prisionero trece* ("Prisoner Number Thirteen") and Arcady Boytler's *La mujer del puerto* ("The Woman of the Port"). The industrial infrastructure behind this spurt in production consisted of two studios: those of Nacional Productora with three sound stages, and Jorge Stahl's México-Films studios with three sound stages. By the end of the year, the Industrial Cinematográfica, S.A. studios were also in operation. The average cost of making a film at this time was between twenty thousand and thirty thousand pesos (between $5,700 and $8,500 in 1933 dollars); the director usually earned fifteen hundred pesos ($425) and the "star" between five hundred and a thousand (between $140 and $285). The total number of personnel in the industry came to somewhere between two hundred and three hundred, none as yet unionized.[41]

Domingo Soler and Andrea Palma in Arcady Boytler's *La mujer del puerto* (1933) (Cineteca).

Arcady Boytler's *La mujer del puerto* was described by Luz Alba as "the first national movie which truly deserves the qualification of excellent." An uneven film, it did not elicit unqualified praise from all critics when it first appeared. Yet, later students of the film have continued to find merit in it: according to Carlos Monsiváis, "Boytler realizes the first singular Mexican film, absolutely personal ... [it] possesses atmosphere and personages, it is endowed with a certain unusual intensity." Tomás Pérez Turrent, a Mexican critic and filmmaker, says of it: "Much has been said of the influence of German expressionism on Boytler. In effect, it exists, but it is not the only influence; present also are Jacques Feyder ... Lacombe ... except that Boytler surpasses them all." And Georges Sadoul thought it had a "captivating and sensitive atmosphere."[42]

The story of *La mujer del puerto*, based on a short story by Guy de Maupassant, is a sordid one of betrayal, prostitution, and incest. In Veracruz, Rosario (Andrea Palma) cares for her gravely ill father. She learns that her fiancé is having an affair with another woman; when her father confronts the fiancé with this charge, the latter hurls the old man down a flight of stairs, killing him. Rosario buries her father while the joyous sounds of the carnival reverberate in the background. Time passes and she has become a prostitute. Alberto (Domingo Soler), a sailor on a Honduran freighter, visits the cabaret in which she works. Rosario takes Alberto to her room where they have sex. Afterwards, as they talk, they realize that they are brother and sister, having lost contact long before (although this is never fully explained). Rosario, horror-stricken, hurls herself from the sea-wall and drowns in spite of Alberto's efforts to stop her.[43]

Another significant film is Fernando de Fuentes's *El compadre Mendoza*, adapted by De Fuentes from an idea by Mauricio Magdaleno and Juan Bustillo Oro. During the Revolution, the landowner Mendoza (Alfredo del Diestro) works out a modus vivendi with both the *zapatistas* and the *huertistas*. When troops of one or the other band ride up to his hacienda, he displays pictures of either Huerta or Zapata, as appropriate, and throws a party for his guests. On one of his trips Mendoza marries Dolores (Carmen Guerrero). While he is away, the *zapatistas* surprise a band of federal troops partying in Mendoza's house; on his return they detain and are going to shoot him but General Felipe Nieto (Antonio R. Frausto) spares Mendoza's life. In gratitude, he asks Nieto to be his son's godfather and makes him his *compadre*. Nieto, on his frequent visits to the hacienda, falls in love with Dolores and grows very fond of her son. Meanwhile, after the revolutionaries capture a wheat-laden train that Mendoza was sending to the capital, he finds himself in severe economic difficulties. He is forced to accept a deal from the huertistas to betray Nieto. While his *compadre* is being assassinated, Mendoza hurries from the hacienda with his wife and child.[44]

El compadre Mendoza is a film of rare sensitivity, insight, and dramatic power. It continued to draw praise from Mexican critics like García Riera, Ayala Blanco, and Tomás Pérez Turrent, who tend to be hypercritical of their country's cinema. Georges Sadoul, who was largely responsible for the rediscovery of De Fuentes by young Mexican critics, says of the film in his *Dictionnaire des Films* that *El compadre Mendoza* "is one of the great accomplishments of the Mexican cinema during the rich 1932–1952 period. The satire is carried along with enthusiasm, good humor, a vivid sense of

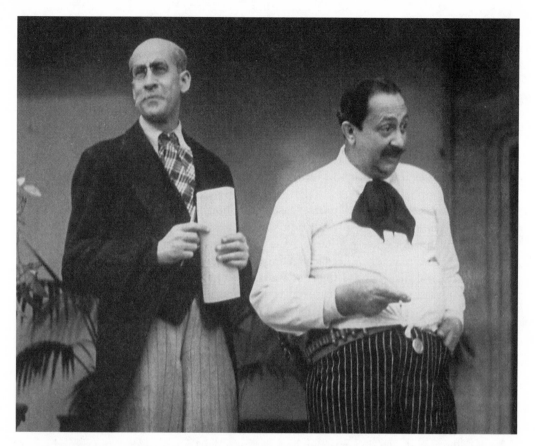

Fernando de Fuentes's *El compadre Mendoza* (1934) with Luis G. Barreiro (left) and Alfredo del Diestro (Cineteca).

observation, and the memories of the Mexican Revolution (still quite recent) contribute to make of the 'compadre' a true social type."[45]

El compadre Mendoza is an important film that escaped international notice when it was released in 1933. The reason for this is clear enough: Mexico, with the rest of Latin America, was outside the mainstream of Western culture — and somewhat so it remains today. Western intellectuals, and by "Western" here is meant the United States, Britain, France, Italy, and Germany, had tended to dismiss, if not disparage, the culture of Latin America by characterizing it as simply an "extension" of Spain and Portugal. For many years Latin American literature was unknown to Western audiences, until critics and publishers in first Europe and then the United States "discovered" Jorge Luis Borges, Pablo Neruda, Gabriela Mistral, and later Gabriel García Márquez, Carlos Fuentes, and Manuel Puig, among others. It must be said, however, that French and Italian intellectuals tended more than the "Anglo-Saxons" to follow and appreciate the literature of Latin America.

To a lesser extent the same is true of Latin American films. The French especially have generally been more aware of them perhaps as a result of the Cannes Film Festival. Since World War II, Mexicans and other Latin Americans have always participated at Cannes, and at Venice as well. This being the case, a good many French film critics and scholars tended to be more aware of Latin American cinema than their American or British counterparts. Mexico's past isolation from world film audiences explains why *El compadre Mendoza* originally passed unnoticed by international critics and film scholars and why in later years both the film and its director began to receive the credit due them.

Like the contemporaneous literary movement referred to as the "Novel of the Mexican Revolution," the significance of *El compadre Mendoza* lies in its expression of a feeling of disillusionment at the corrupted ideals of the Revolution. The *hacendado* Mendoza, in his cynical manipulation of both sides, represents the newly emerging postrevolutionary bourgeoisie that replaced the Porfirian aristocracy but which in its principles differed little from the deposed elite.

The following year, 1934, marked the inauguration of President Lázaro Cárdenas who was to usher in the most radical political climate that Mexico had experienced since the epic phase of the Revolution. During his six-year administration, the distribution of land was dramatically stepped up and Communist influence in labor and education circles was to reach its peak. However, the dramatic highlight of the Cárdenas years was the expropriation of the American and British oil fields in 1938, which many Mexicans came to look upon as the "economic emancipation" of their country.

As if auguring *cardenismo*, there was in 1934 briefly a cinema of "*contenido social,*" as García Riera terms it, expressed through two films, *Redes* ("Nets") and *Janitzio*. *Redes* was produced by the Ministry of Education (Secretaría de Educación Pública), the first time since before 1920 that the government had financed a full-length feature film. The project had its origins in 1932 when the New York photographer, Paul Strand, arrived in Mexico with the intention of putting together a book of photographs on the country. In this he was supported by the distinguished conductor and composer, Carlos Chávez, and a prominent Marxist, Narciso Bassols, who was then Minister of Education. The three concocted an idea to make government-financed films "with the people and for the people." The critic and art historian, Agustín Velázquez, joined the group and they soon had a script for a full-length film and a director in the person of a young Austrian, Fred Zinnemann.

The story of *Redes* concerns a young fisherman, Miro (Silvio Hernández), who organizes his fellow workers against the monopolist (David Valle González) who buys their catch at very low prices. The monopolist bribes a local politician to seed discord among the fishermen who then quarrel among themselves; when the police are called in to quell the disturbance, the politician takes advantage of the confusion to shoot Miro. His death, however, serves to unite the fishermen and they carry Miro's corpse to the city in a demonstration of labor solidarity.

Redes expressed for the first time the elements considered by the country's intellectuals as "ideal for a good national cinema":

> A combative social content, good photography that reveals the beauty of native faces and the on-location filming, an accomplishment and montage inspired by Eisenstein's example. With all this, a linkage was attempted with the themes and forms of the

most advanced currents of plasticity, music, and the other Mexican arts which came together in a necessity to revindicate and uplift the Indian in the picture of national culture.[46]

Continuing in this short-lived vein of "social content" cinema was *Janitzio* directed by Carlos Navarro and written by Luis Márquez who based the story on an Indian legend from the Pátzcuaro area. The plot was based on a true incident that transpired on the island of Janitzio: an Indian girl had become the mistress of an outsider — a Spaniard who lived in Pátzcuaro and who was already resented by the Indians because he bought their fish catch at a low price and sold it at a large profit. The girl, on her return to Janitzio, was stoned by the islanders and banished from the community. The cast included Emilio "El Indio" Fernández (1904–1986) who was to enjoy a long career as performer and director. He later wrote and directed two films based on *Janitzio*: the famous *María Candelaria* (1943) and *Maclovia* (1948).

According to Ayala Blanco, the "fundamental influences" on Navarro and cameraman Jack Draper were the photography of *Thunder Over Mexico* (Eisenstein's cannibalized footage from his projected *¡Que viva México!*), Robert Flaherty's *Moana* (1928), and F.W. Murnau's *Tabu* (1929–1931). Of *Janitzio* he says: "By means of elaborate images and a very slow interior rhythm, we come into contact with the primitive paradise of the Rousseauan savage who lives in harmony with nature, but an imperfect paradise since tabus exist and the white man mars it."[47] In the screenplay for *Janitzio*, the story of the Indian girl who was disgraced for loving a white man is essentially retained. Her lover is not a Spanish buyer but an engineer (Gilberto González) who arranges to imprison the fisherman Zirahuén (Emilio Fernández) so he may seduce his fiancée Eréndira (María Teresa Orozco). Ayala Blanco considers the film's principal attributes to be the images of the "fishermen's butterfly-like nets

floating over the lake and the innocence of the native characters."[48]

Redes and *Janitzio* can be considered as superior films that served to initiate an "Eisenstinian" current of "Indianist" films that were to be a distinguishing feature of the Mexican cinema for the next twenty years. Romanticized, and often melodramatic, such films, along with those dealing with the theme of the Revolution as in De Fuentes's *El compadre Mendoza*, were to constitute a "national" style of cinema and stand in counterpoint to

Emilio "El Indio" Fernández in Carlos Navarro's *Janitzio* (1934) (Cineteca).

the horde of melodramas based mostly on French and Spanish theater pieces that Mexican filmmakers were to churn out in the following decades. An example of this attachment to nineteenth-century European models, so typical of the Porfirian middle class and emulated by the postrevolutionary elite, was *Bohemios* ("Bohemians," 1934). Instead of drawing on the vigorous contemporary artistic and literary life of Mexico, the film based itself upon the outmoded theme of the penniless artist enamored of a sickly girl.[49]

The first year of the Cárdenas presidency was marked by increased labor-management frictions culminating in a great number of government-backed strikes. This was reflected in the growing film industry by the creation of the UTECM (Unión de Trabajadores de Estudios Cinematográficos de México), with Enrique Solís being named as General Secretary. The UTECM was affiliated with the Communist-run labor union, the CTM (Confederación de Trabajadores Mexicanos), founded in 1936 by Vicente Lombardo Toledano.[50]

The government of Lázaro Cárdenas, buoyed by the commercial and artistic success of *Janitzio, Redes,* and *El compadre Mendoza,* took the first steps signaling active official participation in the movie industry and, as some feared, its possible nationalization. Certainly there was sufficient precedence for such a step, at least in the minds of the independent producers. In Germany from the time of World War I, the government had exercised control over filmmaking by buying out the largest private producers and acquiring ownership over all studio facilities; now, under Adolf Hitler, German filmmakers were totally at the disposal of the State. In Italy also the Fascist regime of Benito Mussolini had stepped in to build Cinecittá, the great studio complex outside of Rome and thereby to take a commanding role in film production. In the Soviet Union the process had been completed even earlier. Another leading film producer, Japan, was experiencing a similar evolution under the increasing political power of the militarists.[51]

The Mexican government largely subsidized the construction of the new CLASA (Cinematográfica Latino Americana, S.A.) studios which were equipped with the latest equipment and were as up to date as any Hollywood or European facility. For the first time in Mexico, a movie studio was supplied with Mitchell cameras, re-recording (or synchronization) equipment, a "gamma" processing laboratory, and "back-projection" equipment, among other of the latest advances. The first film to be made at these studios was Fernando de Fuentes's *Vámonos con Pancho Villa* ("Let's Ride with Pancho Villa," 1935); the government was generous with assistance to the similarly named production company, CLASA Films. It made available a complete military train, a regiment of regular army troops, ordnance, artillery, uniforms, horses, and assorted military equipment. When CLASA, after the film was completed, declared bankruptcy (the movie had cost one million pesos), the government subsidized it for the same amount thus saving the company.

However, in spite of these developments which seemed to presage a state cinema industry, filming was to remain a private enterprise preserve in which investors placed their money in order to realize a profit in the shortest time possible. Without a rational system of financing and credit, lacking an effective distribution system and with no foreign markets to speak of, Mexican production went from crisis to crisis.

In 1935 twenty-two films were produced, one fewer than the year before. By contrast, Spain had almost doubled its production over the previous year's to forty-four thus placing her first among Spanish-speaking countries. Argentina slowly expanded its film industry by releasing thirteen full-length features. In the same year, Hollywood produced eight Hispanic movies, the most important of which were Paramount's *El día que me quieras* ("The Day That You Love Me") and *Tango Bar* with Carlos Gardel, the Argentine singing idol who was to perish that same year in a tragic plane crash in Medellín, Colombia while on a tour of Latin America.[52]

The second of Fernando de Fuentes's great "trilogy"[53] of films, *Vámonos con Pancho Villa*, was completed in 1935, although because of CLASA's financial difficulties its premiere was delayed until 1936, after De Fuentes' third and most popular picture, *Allá en el Rancho Grande* ("Out at Big Ranch"), had been released. In *Vámonos con Pancho Villa*, De Fuentes views the Revolution as a cataclysmic event that sweeps away its uncomprehending participants; he portrays the disillusionment that arises from the dichotomy "between the Revolution understood as an ideal and the Revolution itself, chaotic, contradictory, and relentless."[54]

Fernando de Fuentes's *Vámonos con Pancho Villa* (1935). (Clockwise) Rafael F. Muñoz (lying down), Antonio R. Frausto, Carlos López Chaflán, Ramón Vallarino, and Manuel Tamés (Cineteca).

The year is 1914. Miguel Angel (Ramón Vallarino), a deserter from the federal army, rejoins his friends Tiburcio (Antonio R. Frausto), Melitón (Manuel Tamés), Martín (Rafael F. Muñoz), and the Perea brothers, Máximo (Raúl de Anda) and Rodrigo (Carlos López "Chaflán"), a group of adventuresome ranchers who dub themselves the "lions of San Pablo." They decide to join the forces of Pancho Villa (Domingo Soler) whom they find distributing corn to the troops from a train. The film consists of a series of episodes in which either one of the *leones* or another individual is killed. Miguel Angel and Tiburcio, the only survivors of the group, are en route to Zacatecas on a *villista* train when Miguel Angel contracts smallpox. Tiburcio is forced to kill him and cremate the body. In the face of Villa's fear of the epidemic, Tiburcio leaves the train and returns, disillusioned, to his village.

Vámonos con Pancho Villa is a remarkable film which looks back on the still-recent events that constituted a traumatic part of the lives of most Mexicans of the time, and coldly demythologizes them, revealing the Revolution for what it was in a multitude of major and minor details. That this could have come about in a time of renewed radical activity, and that the government, while heavily supporting the film, made no attempt to influence the theme, speaks highly of the open political climate of the time.[55] *Vámonos con Pancho Villa* was the last Mexican motion picture to deal honestly with the country's recent past. What seemed to be the auspicious beginnings of a serious national cinema, however, were soon to be overwhelmed by a commercialist trend given impetus by events in the world beyond Mexico's borders.[56] Ironically, it was Fernando de Fuentes himself who was to powerfully influence this development of the cinema with his next film.

Allá en el Rancho Grande (1936) "opened to Mexico all of the markets of Latin America and changed the course of the industry."[57] It demonstrated to Mexican filmmakers that the Latin American publics expected of them "Mexican" movies — that is, "films that would be vehicles for the unique 'national color' of Mexico."[58] They were not interested in Mexican movies that were simply duplication of Hollywood Hispanic films. The majority of the country's production had been "family melodramas" such as the Spaniard Juan Orol's *Madre querida* ("Dearest Mother," 1935), a tear-jerking, shamelessly sentimental paean to motherhood which was rushed through production so as to be premiered on Mother's Day. It was a great hit at the box office in Mexico and its success inspired other producers to emulate it — a phenomenon of the mass entertainment business with which we are quite familiar in the United States. Outside of the country, however, such films were not popular enough to establish a firm foothold for the Mexican cinema.

The success of the *comedia ranchera* was not simply a case of adapting the internationally popular Hollywood Western to a Mexican setting. The American cowboy picture was a popularization of the Turner thesis of the expansion and conquest of the frontier: the rugged individualist confronting a hostile and primitive environment and overcoming it through sheer will power, thus ensuring the extension of democratic institutions. In innumerable Westerns the theme is repeated again and again wherein the hero, on behalf of the "little people," confronts the local tyrant (usually the owner of a big cattle spread who is headquartered in the local saloon)

Fernando de Fuentes's *Allá en el Rancho Grande* (1936) with (left to right), Lorenzo Barcelata, Esther Fernández, and Tito Guízar (Azteca Films).

who aspires to reduce the entire region and its people to the status of a fiefdom. This is contrary of course to the American democratic ideal and the petty bourgeoisie (small farmer, sheepman, shopkeeper, newspaper publisher, town officials, the pretty school marm), inspired by the hero's example of personal courage and moral integrity, rather than being "led," are galvanized into corrective action.

There is no comparable universe in the Mexican experience; a similar myth of the frontier did not develop in the popular consciousness. The *charro* might ride a horse like his American counterpart and be dressed in what appears to resemble the cowboy's dress but there the similarity ends. The Yankee cowboy costume is that of a working man — plain, homespun with no fancy frills (with the possible exception of the costumes that Gene Autry and, particularly, Roy Rogers wore).

The *charro* is magnificently attired in an embroidered riding suit that bespeaks a hoary tradition of rural aristocracy. His environment is not a wild frontier area but a minutely ordered feudal society in which the *hacendado* presides with paternalistic yet firm authority over his socioeconomic inferiors — the hacienda's employees, tenants, and, of course, women. The *charro* glories in his masculinity and he exercises it not so much to right a wrong but rather to enhance his male self-esteem and social prerogatives. It is the idealization of an attitude firmly rooted not only in the Porfirian past but in Mexico's colonial tradition and can be said to reflect a powerful conservative tendency in the society. In other words, the *charro* or *ranchero* was generally not trying to initiate social change but rather to maintain the status quo. He came to represent the traditional and Catholic values in defiance of the leftist, modernizing tendencies emanating from the cities.[59]

Allá en el Rancho Grande brought to life just such a traditional society but tellingly placed it in contemporary Mexico at a time when the Cárdenas government was making it very clear that its objective was to extirpate all traces of prerevolutionary institutions and create a "classless" society. Fernando de Fuentes rejected such "socialistic" pretensions by exalting the traditional *patrón-peón* and male-female relationships, and by so doing he struck a responsive chord in the Mexican middle class which was fearful of the "spread" of communism under the leftist Cárdenas. The Mexican film industry in fact reflected the conservative forces that were gaining in power and influence and which were to displace the left-wing reformists in 1940 with the inauguration of President Manuel Avila Camacho (1940–1946).

De Fuentes, who had himself given strong impetus to the development of a politcal "message" cinema with *El compadre Mendoza* and *Vámonos con Pancho Villa*, reversed the trend (and in the process rejected his own incisive probings into the Mexican condition as epitomized in these two films) and put Mexican cinema on a solidly commercial, *petite bourgeois* track. In *El compadre Mendoza*, De Fuentes was first critical of the apolitical, opportunistic class that went along with the Revolution as long as its interests were not threatened, yet readily turned against it to maintain its economic position. In *Vámonos con Pancho Villa* he then examined the Revolution and saw it as a cataclysm which sucked in helpless individuals and destroyed them, and which in the end did not really improve conditions. Finally, in *Allá en el Rancho Grande*, he rejected the uncertainties and perils of revolutionary change and opted for an idealized prerevolutionary social order in which individuals of different classes each knew their place and were the happier for it.[60]

On a less socially symbolic level, *Allá en el Rancho Grande* was the prototype for the most enduring genre of the Mexican cinema — the musical *comedia ranchera*. It established its star, Tito Guízar (1908–1999),[61] as a favorite of millions throughout the hemisphere; he eventually became quite well known in the United States and for a number or years was to be the "typical" Latin American in a number of American films.[62] *Allá en el Rancho Grande* made music de rigueur for all subsequent ranch comedies and it helped to establish the *mariachis*, those stringed instrument and vocal groups originally from the state of Jalisco, as what in effect have become the national musical ensemble.[63] In fact the latter is a good example of what Carlos Monsiváis describes as the development by the Mexican establishment of an "official" yet spurious folklore which has been useful not only in attracting tourism but, much more importantly, in blurring regional differences so as to create a more integrated society.[64]

The resounding success of *Allá en el Rancho Grande* inspired the "entire Mexican cinema to move to that very productive Rancho which had also given it its first figure of international prestige, Tito Guízar."[65] Of the thirty-eight films made in 1937, more than half were based on folkloric or nationalistic themes. The civil war

Tito Guízar in the cantina scene from *Allá en el Rancho Grande* (Azteca Films).

in Spain reduced that country's production to only ten motion pictures while
Argentina's output rose to twenty-eight.[66]

Some details of interest in an otherwise undistinguished roster of films that year
were: the first Mexican color film was made, Roberto A. Morales's production of
Novillero ("Novice Bullfighter") directed by Boris Maicon and photographed by Ross
Fisher (the color process used was "cine-color")[67]; the debut of Alejandro Galindo
(1906–1999), who was to become one of the most important and prolific of his country's filmmakers, directing *Almas rebeldes* ("Rebel Souls") which was produced by
Raúl de Anda[68]; the inauspicious debut of Jorge Negrete (1911–1953), the future box-
office idol and singing charro par excellence, in *La madrina del diablo* ("The Devil's
Godmother")[69]; and the first Mexican film directed by a woman (there were to be
precious few), *La mujer de nadie* ("Nobody's Woman") directed by Adela Sequeyro.[70]
This year also saw the film debut of Mario Moreno "Cantinflas" in a minor supporting
role in Miguel Contreras Torres's *No te engañes corazón* ("Don't Deceive Yourself, My
Heart").[71] Fernando de Fuentes enticed Lupe Vélez from Hollywood to appear in *La
Zandunga*, a folkloric comedy set in the Isthmus of Tehuantepec. In spite of her participation, the film was a commercial and artistic failure.[72] The reluctance of the
other Mexican Hollywood star, Dolores del Río, to appear in one of her own country's films did not endear her to many of her countrymen; she justified her absence

from Mexican screens by arguing that the national industry was not as yet "of sufficient solidity."[73]

Dolores del Río was certainly accurate in her assessment of Mexico's film industry, especially since she was viewing it from the standpoint of the huge American industry — huge not only physically but in capitalization, investment, distribution, and profits. Put in the simplest terms, the moguls of Hollywood were not only hard-nosed businessmen but also dedicated filmmakers; they plowed their profits back into the movie business. In Mexico, on the other hand, producers were often businessmen out to make a quick profit who had little interest in building a solidly based production company.[74]

Thus directors were hampered in their efforts to make quality films by a strong commercialist imperative: the producers were reluctant to invest large sums of money in an industry in which they had little faith, and when they did they expected monetary returns as quickly as possible.[75] Thus shooting schedules were impossibly short — two to three weeks on the average — and budgets as restricted as could be gotten away with. The possibilities of a state-sponsored cinema were demonstrated by the success of De Fuentes's *Vámonos con Pancho Villa* which had enjoyed the Cárdenas government's generous support and was produced in the modern and largely officially financed CLASA studios.

Yet the specter of "socialism" thoroughly frightened both bourgeois investors and filmmakers even though the administration's measures stopped far short of nationalization. The most radical actions taken by the government were in its encouragement of unionization in the film industry as well as in other Mexican industries. Another measure taken by Cárdenas was the requirement that all theaters show a minimum number of Mexican films, a reflection of the difficulty of competing with Hollywood and its well-organized distribution systems. Another unsettling development was the entrance of American capital into Mexican filmmaking as exemplified by RKO's direct participation in the production of national films.

When compared with the problems that, say, French and Italian cinema had experienced after World War I, the organization, or rather lack of it, that characterized the Mexican industry was far from unique.[76] Most film production was carried out by small companies, some of which were formed solely for the purpose of making one film and then dissolved; studios, like those of CLASA and Estudios Azteca, were privately owned and the facilities rented to filmmakers.

The movie industry was indeed on a shaky footing in spite of the 1936 success of *Allá en el Rancho Grande*; the popularity of that film demonstrated the potential, and the need for, international markets. Unfortunately, in 1937 the commercialism and lack of creativity of most producers led them to try to capitalize on De Fuentes's triumph by churning out more than twenty "*Rancho Grandes*," that is, musical melodramas based on folkloric or nationalistic themes. During 1939 only thirty-seven films were made, twenty less than the previous year, even though the membership of UTECM had grown steadily every year since its founding until it numbered 410.[77] Another indication of the "crisis" was that Argentina's production surpassed Mexico's for the first time with fifty films in 1939, making it the largest producer in the world of Spanish-language movies.

The last years of the decade of the 1930s were tumultuous and significant ones for Mexico. Lazaro Cárdenas had injected a new vitality into the Revolution, an energy that was to be quickly dissipated after 1940. Mexico had defied the great capitalist powers — the United States and Great Britain — by expropriating their oil properties in 1938 after a prolonged and bitter labor dispute. In addition, the Cárdenas government had extended open and full support (as far as Mexico's limited means allowed it) to the beleaguered Spanish Republic. After Franco's victory in 1939, Mexico opened its doors to thousands of Spanish refugees. This sudden inflow of immigrants constituted in its majority an elite of Spanish society — writers, artists, intellectuals, and political activists. Among this number were many filmmakers and performers whose names in a few years were to become standards of the Mexican movie industry[78]: Angel Garasa,[79] José Baviera, Emilio Tuero, Emilia Guiú,[80] and Luis Alcoriza.[81]

Yet these dramatic events were not reflected at all in the Mexican cinema of the period — it was the beginning of the "detachment from reality" that was to characterize the greater part of the filmmaking of the 1940–1965 era.[82] For instance, Alejandro Galindo's *Refugiados en Madrid* ("Refugees in Madrid," 1938), although set in the Spain of the civil war and concerning a group of presumably anti–Franco Spaniards taking refuge in a Latin American embassy in Madrid, managed to avoid all reference to the contending factions and convert the subject into a stock melodrama.[83] *El indio* ("The Indian"), made that same year, was based on the prize-winning novel of the same name by Gregorio López y Fuentes. Obviously a cinematic effort to parallel the "Indianist" literary genre, it instead presented an idealized and exotic view of the Mexican Indian.[84] Alejandro Galindo, although blatantly inspired by the Hollywood gangster film, made a technically competent movie, *Mientras México duerme* ("While Mexico Sleeps," 1938), which established him as one of the more talented Mexican directors working at the time. It starred Arturo de Córdova and was photographed by Gabriel Figueroa.[85]

As if to symbolize the declining days of the Cárdenas regime and the desire of the country's bourgeoisie for "normalcy," Juan Bustillo Oro's 1939 production of *En tiempos de don Porfirio* ("In Times of Don Porfirio") was that year's most successful film at the box-office. The nostalgia it evoked of a simpler and more peaceful epoch could also be interpreted as a rejection by the middle class of the more socialistic aspects of the Revolution. The appearance in the film of such popular actors as Fernando Soler, the Spanish immigrant Emilio Tuero, and the fine comic actor Joaquín Pardavé were also potent factors in the movie's success.[86] Another historical note of importance is the formation of Posa Films which featured the popular *carpa* (tent show) comic, Cantinflas, in two short features, *Siempre listo en las tinieblas* ("Always Ready in the Shadows") and *Jengibre contra dinamita* ("Ginger versus Dynamite").[87]

Just as 1939 signified the end of the civil war in Spain, this fateful year was to see the long-awaited and feared outbreak of war in Europe. The effects of the world conflict on Mexico — not only on its film industry but in almost all aspects of the economy — were to be fortuitous indeed. The ambitious rising entrepreneurial class, anxiously awaiting the welcome end of Lazaro Cárdenas's presidential term, looked forward to a regime that would place its greatest priority on the expansion of the

Mexican economy rather than on unsettling and even dangerous notions of "social justice" and "class struggle." It was the attitudes of this *nouveau riche* petty bourgeoisie, ambitious yet unsure of itself and identifying somewhat with Porfirismo, that were to set the tone for Mexican movie production of the following decades. With the official denouement of *cardenismo*, the danger (if ever it existed) of a nationalized film industry was safely past; the cinema was firmly in private hands and was to remain so during the boom years of the 1940s and 1950s, and well into the crisis-ridden 1960s.

Bolstering the Mexican middle class's identification with international democracy (and the business opportunities inherent in such an alignment), Franklin Delano Roosevelt's "Good Neighbor" policy sought to emphasize to Latin America that the nations of the area were full and equal partners in the struggle against fascism. An important part of this campaign was the effort to "improve" the Latin image in Hollywood films.

To the United States's favorite Latin American, Tito Guízar,[88] was now added Arturo de Córdova (1908–1973) who appeared in an English-language film, *Miracle on Main Street* as well as in the Hispanic feature, *El caudal de los hijos.* Even Miguel Contreras Torres wrote, produced, and directed an English-language feature, *The Mad Empress*, for Vitagraph.[89]

However, the principal example of Hollywood's response to Washington's new Latin American policy was Warner Brothers' major production of *Juárez* with Paul Muni in the title role. Bette Davis played Carlotta, Briane Aherne was Maximilian, and John Garfield — of all people — portrayed the young Porfirio Díaz. Perhaps one of the most incongruous scenes in all film history (and there are many) is the sight of Díaz (Garfield) kneeling at Juárez's feet (Muni) and asking the deliberately Lincolnesque president to explain democracy to him. The movie never went on to reassure its viewers as to how well Juárez's definition of this elusive political art had been absorbed by his eager protegé. *Juárez* nonetheless was given first-class treatment in Mexico, being premiered at the Palace of Fine Arts by decree of Lázaro Cárdenas himself.[90]

Such an auspicious event was a fitting demonstration of the increased respect in which the Latin American "partners" were to be held, even though some cynics might have pointed out that the formerly scoffed-at nations south of the Rio Grande were practically the only friends the United States had left in the world who were not directly threatened by Axis military might. Whatever Hollywood did or did not do to bolster the Good Neighbor policy, events beyond its control were to facilitate the growth of a major and competing movie industry right on its doorstep.

3

War and Growth of a
Major Film Industry:
1940–1946

Replying to a reporter's query on his attitude toward the Catholic Church, the new president of Mexico, Miguel Avila Camacho, answered, "*Soy creyente*" ("I am a believer").[1] In the context of Mexican politics since the Revolution, which had been stoutly anticlerical, this was tantamount to an American chief executive refusing to attend the church of his choice on Sunday. Although the Mexican left was disconcerted, it was exactly the message that the country's fretful middle classes had been hoping for. As if to symbolize the transition from Cárdenas's activist administration to a more conservative regime, the last film produced in 1940 bore the title, *Creo en Dios* ("I Believe in God")—coincidentally it was also the last motion picture made under the Cárdenas presidency.[2]

During the administration of Avila Camacho (1940–1946), the Mexican film industry was put on a commercial footing through state support to private producers. In one sense this official interest in the cinema was a very real indication of the importance in which it was held; but the other side of the coin demonstrated a voracious acquisitiveness typical of all areas of Mexican economic life in which fortunes were waiting to be made by those individuals aggressive (and unscrupulous) enough to take advantage of the opportunities presented by World War II.

The war raging in Europe and Asia proved a windfall for Latin America whose raw materials were in great demand by the Allies. The curtailment of imported manufactured goods from the United States and Europe also was a significant impetus to industrialization in the major countries of the area like Argentina, Brazil, and Mexico. The Mexican and Argentine film industries reflected this industrializing process as they stepped in to supply national and foreign Spanish-speaking markets with a commodity formerly supplied by Hollywood and, to a lesser extent, European producers. Portuguese-speaking Brazil, being practically a continent unto itself, did not require foreign markets for its films. The war did create a demand within Brazil for national films and the 1940s saw its studios produce up to one hundred movies a year.[3]

Argentina in the late 1930s and early 1940s was Mexico's strongest competitor and its production was still ahead of the latter's in 1941—forty-seven films[4] to thirty-seven for Mexico.[5] One of the more significant commercial and artistic successes of the Argentine cinema at this time was Lucas Demare's *La guerra gaucha* ("The Gaucho War"), which dealt with the struggle for independence against Spain. The film "employed the sun as a major symbol, implicitly linking it to the Inca past as well as to the new Argentine nationality."[6] The popularity of this movie clearly indicated, as *Allá en el Rancho Grande* had a few years before, that Latin American audiences responded to and enjoyed seeing Latin American themes on the screen, even if the settings were not in their own particular countries.

The Mexican cinema of 1941 sought to tap this current of Pan-Americanism with *Simón Bolívar*, produced, written, and directed by Miguel Contreras Torres. However, that year's most popular and profitable film was Julio Bracho's initial directorial effort, *¡Ay, qué tiempos, señor don Simón!* ("Oh, What Times, Mr. Don Simón!")—an appealing and lively musical exercise in Porfirian nostalgia starring Joaquín Pardavé, Arturo de Córdova, and Mapy Cortés. It took in just over 137,000 pesos at the box-office in its first three weeks of exhibition, a record for the time.[7] The film's success also indicated that Mexican middle-class audiences were still much more attracted to the *belle époque* than to Pan-Americanism.

In 1940, Mario Moreno "Cantinflas" had scored an international success with *Ahí está el detalle* ("There is the Detail"), his first full-length feature. The former *carpa* comic transcended the conventional theatrical humor of Juan Bustillo Oro's direction "with the effect of a bomb."[8] His irreverent, street-wise language was the perfect counterpoint to Joaquín Pardavé's polished but superficial phrases—in other words, the *pelado* (lit. "hairless"—a penniless nobody) meets the hypocritical creole and shows him up. The film's high point, which created a following for Cantinflas throughout the Spanish-speaking world, was the final courtroom scene in which he delightfully flouts social and legalistic conventions and succeeds in so confusing the arrogant judge and attorneys that they end up talking in *cantinflismos*.[9]

Cantinflas's second full-length feature in 1941 was *Ni sangre ni arena* ("Neither Blood nor Sand"), a parody of Vicente Blasco Ibáñez's bullfight novel *Sangre y arena*, which had recently been filmed in Hollywood (*Blood and Sand*, 1941) starring Tyrone Power, Rita Hayworth, and Linda Darnell. Hoping to capitalize on the American motion picture's popularity, Posa Films, hereafter to be Cantinflas's exclusive producer, signed Alejandro Galindo to direct the popular comic. The association was reportedly not a happy one and the two were never to work together again; however, Galindo's assistant, Miguel M. Delgado, hit it off much better with Cantinflas and became his favorite director.[10] *Ni sangre ni arena* was vastly popular and took in 54,000 pesos in four days at the Alameda Theater, another box-office record.[11] This success was followed in short order by *El gendarme desconocido* ("The Unknown Policeman"), with Mapy Cortés and Gloria Marín, considered by many to be among Cantinflas's best movies. Commenting on the reasons for Cantinflas's popularity and of this film in particular, García Riera writes:

> No other Spanish-speaking actor has enjoyed Cantinflas's popularity, and this can perhaps be readily explained by the fact that, apart from a great personal charm, this actor

Mario Moreno "Cantinflas" (right) with Joaquín Pardavé in *Ahí está el detalle* (1940) (Azteca Films).

does not employ any dramatic artifice. In other words, Cantinflas is the first real and living personage in a cinema characterized by its attachment to cheap histrionics. Such an accomplishment favors the unsophisticated spectator's identification with the character, something which has rarely occurred in any other case.

The ridiculization [in *El gendarme desconocido*] of the police, generally detested by the public, is established from the first moment in which *Cantinflas* appears in his uniform. Seeing "one of their own" converted into a guardian of law and order gives the spectator a sensation of freedom. The public solidarizes itself with *Cantinflas* for the very reason that the character's ridiculousness and his encyclopedic ignorance place him at a disadvantage in relation to any spectator. Thus, the weapons employed by *Cantinflas* [the weapons of a picaresque character] to flout authority are within reach of the most humble and ignorant of men.[12]

A classic of the "family drama" genre was *Cuando los hijos se van* ("When the Children Leave") directed by Juan Bustillo Oro, now more in his element. It starred Fernando Soler, Joaquín Pardavé, and — Latin America's favorite self-sacrificing mother figure — Sara García. This film attests perhaps to the Mexican public's capacity for self-punishment since for four weeks it kept drawing crowds eager to sit through its 139 minutes of unrelenting melodrama and nostalgia. Directed in a strictly theatrical style by Bustillo Oro with a seemingly immobile camera, the film tells in excruciating detail the story of a staunchly *petite bourgeois* Córdoba family.

The complicated plot essentially concerns the father Pepe Rosales's (Fernando Soler) misjudging of his "good" son Raimundo (Emilio Tuero). The young man is falsely incriminated by the ne'er-do-well son José (Carlos López Moctezuma), whom the father considers a model of filial responsibility. The mother, Lupe (Sara García), with her unerring maternal instinct, never doubts for a moment the innocence of the disgraced Raimundo who later proves his devotion by returning from Mexico City, where he has

Cantinflas in *El extra* (1962) (Azteca Films).

triumphed as a singer, to save his parents from bankruptcy brought about by José's dishonesty. Raimundo is shot to death by the usurer Patricio Gómez (Miguel Inclán, at his most deliciously villainous), but before dying Raimundo manages to destroy

El gendarme desconocido (1941) with (left to right) Carlos López Moctezuma, Mapy Cortés, and Cantinflas (Cineteca).

the falsified note that Patricio held on the Rosales house. With the entire family gathered at Christmas eve dinner, José confesses his guilt and is dutifully forgiven by Pepe who finally recognizes the moral superiority of the departed Raimundo, whose empty chair forms part of the family gathering.[13]

In Bustillo Oro's universe, the family, "autonomous, victorious, omnivorous,"[14] stands coldly aloof from the world around it. The Rosales household seems to be suspended in time with its walls effectively keeping out the disturbing society outside. Disaster invariably comes to any of its members who seek to break their bonds with the sacrosanct family, and it is only when they have rejected the world outside and all personal ambition that they find security, a security disconcertingly based on their individual failure and dependent on a stultifying submersion within the family. Such a regressive idealization of the traditional values was an effective way, if only for 139 minutes, of shutting out not only the changes that Mexico was undergoing but the unsettling Axis victories and the radically altered world order that they portended.

Another type of retreat from reality, yet a considerably more entertaining one, was represented by the box-office success of Joselito Rodríguez's *¡Ay Jalisco no te rajes!* ("Oh Jalisco, Don't Back Down!"), which was Jorge Negrete's first great triumph and definitely established him as the quintessential Mexican singing charro.[15] In Alejandro Galindo's words, Negrete was the most faithful representative of the Mexican ideal: "dark-complexioned, tall, proud, romantic, pistol-packing, and who sings his sorrows as readily as his joys."[16] Finally, 1941 saw also the directorial debut of Emilio "El Indio" Fernández who had been involved in films for some years in Hollywood and Mexico — he was the male dancer in the *jarabe tapatío* sequence in the cockfighting arena in *Allá en el Rancho Grande*. His *La isla de la pasión* ("The Island of Passion") concerned a group of Mexican soldiers stranded on Clipperton Island off the coast of Central America.[17]

Thus Mexican film production in 1941, as exemplified by *Simón Bolívar, Ni sangre ni arena, El gendarme desconocido, ¡Ay, qué tiempos señor don Simón!, Cuando los hijos se van,* and *¡Ay Jalisco no te rajes!,* demonstrated several of the basic formulas that were to find favor with Latin American audiences. First was the historical/patriotic epic, by no means new to Mexican filmmaking. However, such productions, because of the necessarily limited budgets and consequently short shooting schedules, suffered in comparison with Hollywood films on which millions of dollars were spent.[18] Of course, it should be kept in mind that Hollywood rarely filmed Latin American themes and when it did, the results were as often as not offensive to the sensitivities of the country concerned.[19]

The second formula, and commercially a resoundingly more successful one, was the Cantinflas movies. It was enough simply to have the enormously popular comic on the screen for the film to make money. This success, unsurprisingly, tended to fossilize Cantinflas's performances and, according to some observers, he continued making essentially the same film for the next three decades.[20]

The melodrama based on attachment to traditional values — "God, Nation, and Home"[21] — was already an important component of the Mexican cinema as exemplified by *Cuando los hijos se van*. In the next decade there were to be variations on this theme; for example, the sacrosanct family is threatened by carnal or material temptation from the outside world, whether it be a cabaret girl as in Alberto Gout's *Sensualidad* ("Sensuality," 1950) or a vacuum-cleaner salesman as in Alejandro Galindo's *Una familia de tantas* ("An Ordinary Family." 1948).[22]

The continued utilization of a limited number of themes within a handful of well-defined genres would quickly have bored audiences were it not for a corresponding "star system" as the key element in marketing the product. Thus certain performers specialized in defined roles and the films being discussed here provide outstanding examples of actors already established in their particular genres.

Among the "star" fixtures of the cinema was "the mother of Mexico," Sara García (1895–1980). Born in Oriz-aba, Veracruz of immigrant Spanish

Sara García (Cineteca).

parents, she began her distinguished acting career in in the theater, principally doing Spanish plays. Her first movie role was in the silent feature *En defensa propia* ("In Self Defense," 1917), and her first sound film was *El pulpo humano* ("The Human Octopus," 1933), but the role that made her a star was *No basta ser madre* ("It's Not Enough to be a Mother," 1937). Of *Cuando los hijos se van* she said:

> It is an immortal motion picture, no matter what is said against it. The cinema might end, but *Cuando los hijos se van* will go on, because in every home the children eventually leave: or they become monks or nuns, or they elope, or they go to work in a foreign country, or they marry, or whatever. In effect, life itself is contained in the title.... The public goes to see it, they feel it, they cry.... Because of all this ... it is a classic film.[23]

The other enduring cinematic formula, the *comedia ranchera*, was represented by *¡Ay, Jalisco no te rajes!* The predictable succession of love affairs, personal misunderstandings, conflicts, and spurious folklore — all liberally garnished with *ranchera* music — could not have retained the public's interest without the appearance of a "superstar" such as Jorge Negrete. Soon Pedro Infante (1917–1957) was also to achieve star status in this genre, although his signal triumph was in *Nosotros los pobres* ("We the Poor," 1947), a melodrama of the urban poor that was to be one of the greatest box-office hits in the history of Mexican cinema.

The debut of Emilio "El Indio" Fernández was, in hindsight, perhaps the most significant event of this year. A man of complex personality, withdrawn, and occasionally violent, Fernández was to be the founder of a "Mexican school" that achieved international recognition in the late 1940s and 1950s. His work, at its best, was

Sara García in scenes from different films: (top left) *No basta ser madre* (1937), with Maria Fernández Ibáñez, (top right) *El capitán aventurero* (1938), and *Papacito lindo* (1939) (Cineteca).

intensely nationalistic and overly sympathetic to the Indian whose culture has been under relentless attack from the mestizo and creole sectors of Mexican society.

Fernández, in close collaboration with the renowned cameraman Gabriel Figueroa (1907–1997), was to glorify Mexico's landscapes, dramatic, cloud-laced skies, and, more importantly, its stoic, beautiful Indian faces. And of the latter, he utilized two of the most magnificent: Dolores del Río and Pedro Armendáriz. It has often been said of Fernández (and, of course, Figueroa) that he is the principal Mexican

Emilio Fernández and Dolores del Río in *Flor silvestre* (1943) (Azteca Films).

exponent of the "Eisenstinian" style as embodied in the never-completed *¡Que viva México!* Whatever inspiration Fernández received from Eisenstein was apparently far from direct, and the photographic techniques were most probably passed on to "El Indio" (as to many others) through Fred Zinnemann's *Redes*.[24] Whatever the processes through which Fernández developed his style, his name was to become synonymous with "quality" Mexican cinema, especially in Europe, and he would be the only Mexican director whose work was to become somewhat known in the United States, principally through *The Pearl* (1945) and *The Torch* (1947), both starring Pedro Armendáriz.[25]

In order to begin organizing the film industry on a more rational financial basis, the Banco Cinematográfico was founded on April 14, 1942, "on the initiative of the Banco Nacional de México and with the moral support of President Avila Camacho."[26] The Banco began as a private institution although the government's interest in this new credit agency was no secret; Avila Camacho "did not think it opportune to give the Banco an official subsidy because it was his wish that private enterprise develop by its own efforts."[27] Nonetheless, the Banco Cinematográfico was backed by official agencies like the Banco Nacional de México and the Nacional Financiera which held 10 percent of its stock.[28] The board of directors was made up of six bankers and industrialists and two filmmakers, Mauricio de la Serna and Jesús Grovas.[29]

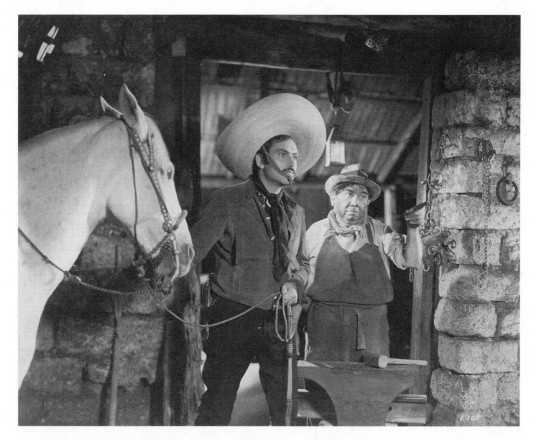

Emilio Fernández's *Flor silvestre* with Pedro Armendáriz (left) and Hernán Vera (Cineteca).

The creation of the Banco Cinematográfico was a solid indication of the importance in which the national film industry was held in high official circles. In an effort to centralize the sporadic activities of small, undercapitalized producers, the Banco in its first year extended credits of 5 million pesos to nine production companies (out of a total of about thirty): Grovas, S.A., Films Mundiales, América Films, Ixtla Films, CLASA, Juan Bustillo Oro, Cinematografía Miguel Zacarías, Vicente S. Piques, and Producciones Fernando de Fuentes.[30] Of these, the largest firms were Grovas, which produced eight films in 1942, and Films Mundiales with six motion pictures.[31]

Partly as a result of the creation of a centralized credit institution for production and distribution, the following year, 1943, saw the Mexican cinema show promise of fulfilling its potential and becoming a true industry. Seventy films were produced in "the great year,"[32] while Argentina's output declined sharply to thirty-six and Spanish studios made only fifty-three.

A number of factors contributed to this impressive performance. First, because of a common language and similar cultural background, Mexican movies undoubtedly appealed to the tastes of the mass Latin American audience[33]; second, and closely connected with the first factor, Hollywood production, at this time entirely given over to supporting the war effort, held little appeal for Latin Americans. In addition, the pro–Axis inclinations of various Argentine governments during the war years motivated the United States to apply certain sanctions against that country, and among these was the cutting off of raw film to Argentine producers. Fortunately for Mexican producers, their government's declaration of war on Germany, Japan, and Italy and its subsequent support of the Allied cause led to reciprocal actions on Washington's part. Most important for Mexico's film production was the allocation by the United States of raw film and cinematic equipment to bolster its movie industry. Now that Hollywood had to resign itself to the temporary loss of its Latin American market, it was quite willing to support the Mexican film industry.[34]

A number of creditable films were produced in 1943. Emilio Fernández achieved his greatest artistic triumphs with *Flor silvestre* ("Wild Flower") and, especially, *María Candelaria*. Julio Bracho's *Distinto amanecer* ("A Different Sunrise") suggested the possibility of a sophisticated, urban-oriented cinema in the *film noir* vein. There was also Fernando de Fuentes's *Doña Bárbara*, based on the novel by the Venezuelan Rómulo Gallegos and starring María Félix, an actress of great beauty who was to be one of the leading box-office attractions of the Mexican cinema. The influence of Orson Welles was evident in Alejandro Galido's *Tribunal de justicia* ("Tribunal of Justice")

Fernando de Fuentes's *Doña Bárbara* (1943) with María Félix (left) and María Elena Marqués (Cineteca).

María Félix in *Doña Bárbara* (Azteca Films).

and Norman Foster's *La fuga* ("The Escape"). The latter also made the best version of *Santa* to date.[35] Miguel Contreras Torres directed the interesting *La vida inútil de Pito Pérez* ("The Useless Life of Pito Pérez") based on the novel by José Rubén Romero, and Bustillo Oro made *México de mis recuerdos* ("Mexico of my Memories"), perhaps his best film.[36]

The chaos of war had its disrupting effect on such matters as copyright conventions, and Mexican producers took advantage of the situation to adapt for the screen the works of more than twenty foreign authors. This tendency was denounced by some as a perpetuation of a "Porfirian inferiority complex" in which "culture, good taste, and intelligence were [considered to be] European specialties which America* should import without taking the trouble to comprehend."[37] Whatever the merits of this argument, the inevitable reaction was a nationalist cinema which the Banco Cinematográfico encouraged by granting more generous credits to those producers making such films. Agustín J. Fink, president of Films Mundiales, backed Fernández and Bracho in their efforts to reflect the contemporary Mexican reality on the screen.[38]

Flor silvestre and *María Candelaria* were Fernández's two great triumphs of 1943. The latter won international renown for its creators when it was entered in the first

By way of explanation, "America" as used in Mexico and the rest of Latin America encompasses the entire Western Hemisphere, including the United States and Canada.

postwar international film festivals at Cannes (1946) and Locarno (1947). The film won several important prizes at both festivals and helped to establish a European market for the Mexican cinema. Fernández's choice of Dolores del Río to star in both films was also an effective way of assuring that international film circles would focus some attention on his work.

María Candelaria was loosely based on *Janitzio* (1934). The setting is shifted from the island of Janitzio to Xochimilco. As the film begins, a group of journalists are interviewing a world-famous artist (Alberto Galán). A young woman reporter asks him about a painting of a nude Indian girl he had done years before and which he never revealed. The painter replies that it was the cause of a tragedy and proceeds to tell its story.

It is Xochimilco in 1909. María Candelaria (Dolores del Río) earns her living by gathering flowers and selling them at the market. She is in love with Lorenzo (Pedro Armendáriz) and they plan to marry. However, the villagers resent María because her mother was a prostitute and at one point Lorenzo has to intercede when the Indians threateningly block María's way. She owes a small sum of money to *don* Damián (Miguel Inclán), a villainous mestizo who owns Xochimilco's only general store and ruthlessly exploits the Indians. *Don* Damián demands that María pay the money she owes him or he will take her little pig with which she hopes to sell and raise money so she and Lorenzo can get married.

Lorenzo and María are at the market. The artist is painting in the street when he notices María. Struck by her beauty, he buys all her flowers and asks her to pose for him but Lorenzo won't allow it. Undaunted, the artist sends an Indian to follow María and find out where she lives. Meanwhile, *don* Damián is determined to take María's pig, having been frustrated once in the attempt at the blessing of the animals ceremony at the village church. He paddles up to María's shack and just misses getting a shot at Lorenzo before he disappears into a cornfield. In a rage, he then shoots the little pig. Shortly after, María falls ill with malaria; Lorenzo, in desperation, brings the dead pig to *don* Damián and asks him for quinine tablets (since he is the only one in the village authorized by the government to distribute them). *Don* Damián refuses to hand over the tablets and holds Lorenzo at bay with a rifle. After Lorenzo leaves, Damián decides to close the store and get away for a few days because he fears "these Indians' treachery."

The artist, however, had learned of María's illness and sends a doctor to tend her, although too late to prevent Lorenzo from breaking into *don* Damián's store where he takes not only the malaria tablets but also a dress. A few days later, *don* Damián has Lorenzo arrested in the middle of the wedding ceremony in which María is wearing the stolen dress. Lorenzo is sentenced to one year in prison. María seeks help from the artist and the priest (Rafael Icardo), but they can do nothing to help Lorenzo. The artist tells the priest that he considers María to be the "essence of Mexican beauty"; the priest then assures María that there is nothing wrong in her posing for the artist. However, she refuses to pose in the nude, leaving the painting unfinished. The artist completes it by using another model.

The villagers, however, are scandalized when they learn of the painting, thinking that María posed in the nude for it. Egged on by *don* Damián, a mob gathers

Pedro Armendáriz and Dolores del Río in *Flor Silvestre* (Azteca Films).

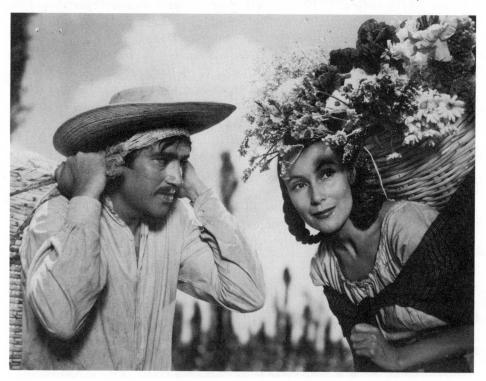

Dolores del Río and Pedro Armendáriz in *María Candelaria* (1943) (Azteca Films).

and goes in search of María. Terrified, she flees back to the village with the mob in pursuit; she attempts to reach the jail and Lorenzo but is cornered by the villagers and stoned to death. Lorenzo hears the commotion and breaks down the cell door but too late to save María. In the film's final scene, he has placed María's body in a dugout canoe and surrounded it with flowers as he sadly takes her to be buried.

In spite of the criticism leveled at *María Candelaria*, it remains a classic of the Mexican cinema and the work that created an international following for "El Indio." The film has been faulted for presenting a "tourist's" Mexico, an image of stoic, attractive Indians patiently paddling their flower-laden dugouts along the scenic canals of Xochimilco, and for creating a stereotype of them that subsequent cineasts would perpetuate.[39] Yet the film retains a simplicity and lyrical beauty that can still be appreciated over sixty years later. Moreover, false idealization or not, Fernández presented a positive view of Indians — a group that more often than not had been the butt of music-hall jokes. Not everyone was happy with *María Candelaria* for this reason. As Fernández himself commented:

> We filmed *María Candelaria* in Xochimilco, with many problems caused by the weather and many personal differences. A few good people couldn't go along with the film. It seemed to them — imagine! — exotic and also depressing. They were scandalized and ousted me from the production company ... because I had made "such shit about Indians." I had to resolve to starve to death.[40]

The film was boycotted by Emilio Azcárraga who refused to run it in his Alameda Theater. Agustín J. Fink then stepped in and rented the Palacio Theater where it was premiered to a full house, which included the Soviet ambassador, Constantin Oumansky, who was enthusiastic about the film.[41]

Julio Bracho's *Distinto amanecer* was another of 1943's distinguished films. Set in a realistic yet threatening urban setting, *film noir* style,[42] it tells the story of an idealistic labor leader, Octavio (Pedro Armendáriz), fleeing the gunmen of a corrupt state governor because he has evidence that the functionary suppressed a strike at the bidding of foreign interests. The incriminating documents are in a box at the post office which Octavio is trying to reach. He is being tailed by one of the governor's men; to elude him Octavio slips into a theater where a lively musical number from *¡Ay, qué tiempos señor don Simón!* is in progress on the screen. Octavio sits next to Julieta (Andrea Palma). When she starts to light a cigarette he blows out her match and tells her to obey the no-smoking sign. Julieta answers that she obeys cigarette advertisements instead and gets up to go to the ladies' room. Octavio follows her right in after he notices the governor's man in the theater. Once inside the ladies' room, Julieta and Octavio discover they know each other; they had been politically active university students years before. She tells him that she married the third member of the group, Ignacio (Alberto Galán), now an unemployed diplomat. Julieta lets Octavio out a side door from the ladies' room and she takes him home to a run-down building to meet Ignacio.

Thus a sequence of events is set in motion in which the personal relationships between Julieta, Octavio, and Ignacio are subsumed by their social obligations. Julieta and Octavio have always loved each other and his reappearance is a troubling

Pedro Armendáriz and Dolores del Rio in *María Candelaria* (Cineteca).

experience for her. Their emotional problems are intertwined with the danger that now faces all three, and Julieta and Ignacio decide to help Octavio obtain the evidence that will expose the corrupt governor.

The entire action of *Distinto amanecer* transpires in the course of one night. During that time Julieta is forced to kill the governor's henchman, and she and Octavio have to get rid of the body. In the meantime, Ignacio obtains the critical document from the post office box. He is aware of Julieta's love for Octavio and is prepared to step out of the way so they can be together. At the last moment, in the railroad station, she changes her mind and stays with Ignacio. Octavio leaves on the train for the south with the valuable evidence safely in his possession.

Distinto amanecer was a laudable attempt to interpret the tensions of contemporary Mexican society. Of the three once-idealistic university companions, only Octavio has continued the struggle as an activist labor leader. Julieta and especially Ignacio are disillusioned by the increasing materialism of Mexican life—he comments bitterly about "a country in which politics drags everything with it, and a time in which a chauffeur earns more than a teacher." Yet Octavio is still fighting the good fight, and he enthusiastically tells Julieta that the scandal will cause high government officials to fall and that his group will then demand radical changes. The film was

Andrea Palma in Julio Brancho's *Distinto amanecer* (1943) (Cineteca).

criticized in some quarters for Julieta's "melodramatic" decision to stay with Ignacio,[43] but Salvador Elizondo said of *Distinto amanecer* that it

> well deserves the place of honor that New York's Museum of Modern Art has conferred upon it. It was the first Mexican motion picture to focus upon life as a phenomenon in which two forces come together: love and solidarity. Unfortunately, timidity, or perhaps caution, prevented the very interesting problems set forth there of being resolved with frankness. To *Distinto amanecer* belongs the honor of being one of the very few Mexican movies that does not moralize. It would have been enough for the characters to succumb to the amorous passion set forth from the beginning for this to undoubtedly have been one of the more formidable films made in this country.[44]

The three existing studios — CLASA, Azteca, and México-Films (Stahl) — were hard put at this time to keep up with the increased production. Many producers had to wait weeks before sound stages were available.[45] An American industrialist, Harry Wright, began construction of extensive new studio facilities on a 92,000-square-meter area between the Azteca and CLASA studios in the Churubusco suburb.[46]

All this activity attracted the attention of N. Peter Rathvon and Phil Reisman, president and vice-president respectively of RKO Radio Pictures which had been

Pedro Armendáriz and Alberto Galán in *Distinto amanecer* (Cineteca).

involved in movie production in Mexico since the late 1930s. Reisman was also a member of Nelson D. Rockefeller's Office for Coordination of Inter-American Affairs, the agency through which the Mexican film industry was receiving so much valuable assistance.

Rathvon and Reisman arrived in Mexico City in September 1943 with the intention of investing heavily in the increasingly lucrative Mexican movie business. They offered to distribute worldwide the entire production of CLASA Films and Films Mundiales; they tried to buy 51 percent of Posa Films's shares and proposed that Cantinflas, their exclusive artist, make several films in Hollywood. The RKO executives also tried to share equally with Harry Wright a controlling interest in the company that was building the new Churubusco studios. Even though most of these grandiose projects failed to materialize,[47] they caused concern among many Mexican film executives who feared the "Americanization" of the industry. Already there was consternation at Wright's construction of new studios since it was feared that production capabilities were not yet broad enough to justify the extensive new facilities.[48]

Still, in 1944 the industry produced an unprecedented seventy-five films, and witnessed the debut of fourteen new directors, the most significant being Roberto Gavaldón with his splendid motion picture, *La barraca* ("The Cottage"). Just as this increased output signified that filmmaking in Mexico was now indeed on an industrial footing, the outbreak of serious intra-union disputes could be taken as another indication of the industry's growing pains. Other observers looked upon this unionization as an attempt by the film industry's skilled workers to protect their own jobs by systematically excluding new blood. In spite of the industry's impressive growth, everyone concerned fully realized that such expansion had its limits — each had to retain his slice of a limited pie. This "closed door" policy was evident in the formation in 1944 of a Director's Guild of which Alejandro Galindo was named secretary-general; whereas in 1944 fourteen new directors made their appearance, only one director was admitted into the organization in each of the following two years.[49]

By 1944 all film workers — from performers, directors, cameramen, and technicians right down to ticket-sellers and popcorn salespeople in movie theaters — were represented by the Sindicato de Trabajadores de la Industria Cinematográfica (STIC), founded in 1919 as the Unión de Empleados Confederados del Cinematógrafo.[50] The actors were grouped in Section 2 of STIC, along with technicians and lesser-skilled studio employees — in effect putting internationally known performers at the same level as a carpenter. Objecting to this categorization, the actors, led by Jorge Negrete and Mario Moreno, led a movement to form their own section. STIC's chief, Enrique Solís, opposed such an action, citing what some newspapermen characterized as "socialist" reasons; however, "the times had changed: Avila Camacho and not Cárdenas was president ... and Fidel Velázquez had substituted Lombardo Toledano at the head of the CTM."[51] The National Committee of the CTM supported the actors' secession and authorized their formation of a section 7. The workers then went on strike halting filming during all of April.[52]

In 1943 the STIC had seven thousand members organized in forty-seven sections with three thousand workers in the Federal District.[53] But dissatisfaction with Solís's stand on separate sections for actors, cameramen, and directors had already led to a dispute between him, his secretary-general Salvador Carrillo and Gabriel Figueroa, the head of section 2, Técnicos y Manuales (cameramen and technicians' section).[54] The motive for this splitting off of the artists and skilled workers — the actors, cameramen, and directors — from STIC was that the industry's growth was greater in distribution and exhibition than in production. Thus, these members of the union felt threatened; "they felt that the industrial union did not take into account their needs and, if matters continued thus, that soon they would have neither voice nor vote in union matters."[55]

After many bitter recriminations and some threat of violence, the Sindicato de Trabajadores de la Producción Cinematográfica (STPC), incorporating the seceding sections from the STIC, was officially recognized by the CTM on March 14, 1945, as the official bargaining agent for its members, an action bitterly protested by the STIC.[56] A projected strike against the studios by STIC personnel was to be met by armed actors led by Mario Moreno, Jorge Negrete, and Arturo de Córdova. Their militancy had its effect and the STIC called off the work stoppage.

Finally, on September 3, 1945, Avila Camacho issued an executive order delimiting the areas of responsibility of the two contending unions: STIC over the distribution, exhibition, and production of newsreels and short films, and STPC over the production of feature-length films. In effect two competing unions were now in existence, each with a full complement of performers, directors, and technicians. The STPC, of course, had the "name" personnel authorized to make profitable full-length features. STIC-affiliated directors, that is, those who made short features, were barred from the STPC's Directors' Guild because they lacked "experience" in directing full-length movies.

However, it was obvious that the only way to obtain this experience was in the STPC. It was simply a way for the established directors to keep out new blood and assure themselves work. The creation of the STPC and the division of responsibilities between it and the parent STIC resulted in much bitterness and incessant conflict. In the 1960s and 1970s, rising production costs led many producers to work illegally with the STIC to produce full-length features thus reversing the situation for the STPC-affiliated Chrurubusco-Azteca studios who now saw their own production drastically curtailed and many of their workers unemployed.

The presidential support for the STPC was dramatically symbolized by the appearance of Mario Moreno, Jorge Negrete, María Félix, and other film luminaries on the presidential balcony alongside Avila Camacho on the occasion of a parade organized by the STPC to show its gratitude to the president. In the face of such massive official opposition, the STIC had no other choice but to accept the situation.[57]

Luana Alcañiz and José Baviera in Roberto Gavaldón's *La barraca* (1944) (Cineteca).

In spite of the complicated union problems, production continued. One film, *La barraca*, stood out in 1944, outshining by far the other mostly mediocre seventy-four motion pictures. Among the latter, to be sure, were a number of interesting productions. Fernández directed *Las abandonadas* ("The Abandoned Ones") and *Bugambilia*, both starring Dolores del Río and Pedro Armendáriz. Norman Foster made a creditable bullfight movie, *La hora de la verdad* ("The Hour of Truth") with Ricardo Montalbán; and María Félix continued establishing herself as the "*devoradora de hombres*" ("devourer of men") in such films as *Amok* and *La monja alférez* ("The Ensign Nun").

Roberto Gavaldón's *La barraca*, based on the novel by Vicente Blasco Ibáñez, was a paean to a lost Spain, that is, to the pre–Franco era. With the screenplay written by Blasco Ibáñez's daughter, Libertad, and the participation of more than sixteen Spaniards in the production, the film was "much more Spanish than anything else."[58]

Set in Valencia in the 1880's, *La barraca* faithfully reproduced the Valencian countryside and folkways. The story of Batiste and his ill-fated struggle against intolerance and superstition can be seen as an allegory of the dark night which Spain had been enduring since 1939, at least in the view of Spanish republican exiles and their many sympathizers in Mexico and throughout Latin America. But now with the end of the war clearly approaching, hopes were being raised that Franco's fascist regime would soon go the way of those of Hitler and Mussolini. Thus, *La barraca*, recreating in loving detail the rural Valencian society of a bygone era, paid tribute also to the enduring values of the "eternal" Spain.[59]

Barret (Pascual Guillot), a bankrupt farmer, has been driven off his land. He gets drunk and kills the usurer responsible for his ruin. Barret dies in prison, his wife expires in the hospital, and his four daughters become prostitutes. His friends and neighbors, led by Pimentó (José Baviera) and his wife Pepeta (Luana Alcañiz), vow that no one will ever work the lands that once belonged to *tío* Barret.

Ten years later, however, Batiste (Domingo Soler), his wife Teresa (Anita Blanch), and their five children move into the abandoned farmhouse as tenants. Even though they work hard to improve the property, they have to cope with the hostility of their neighbors. This culminates in a fight between Batiste's sons and a group of boys during which Pascualet, the youngest, is thrown into a stagnant pond. He becomes seriously ill.

In the meantime, Pimentón accuses Batiste of irrigating out of turn. Batiste has to appear before the Tribunal of the Waters, an ancient body dating back to pre–Visigothic times. He cannot prove that Pimentón is lying, and is found guilty and fined five pesetas. Soon after, Pascualet dies almost at the instant that Batiste's horse is killed. Grief-stricken and furious, Batiste challenges Pimentón to face him man to man, but Pimentón cowers in his darkened house.

After the tragedy of Pascualet's death, the villagers make amends and welcome Batiste and his family into the community. Things seem to improve for awhile until Pimentón is chastised by the landowner for always being late with his rent; she taunts him by saying "*Muchos recuerdos a Batiste*" as he is ordered from her house. At the cantina, a drunken Pimentón complains that the landlord "is not afraid of us anymore" because Batiste defied the community and got away with it. Batiste arrives at this point; he is attacked by Pimentón but breaks a chair over his assailant's head. The old hostility reemerges and Batiste and his family find themselves once again isolated. While hunting in the swamp, Batiste is shot and wounded. He pursues his attacker and kills him. It is Pimentón. Batiste and his family are burned out of their house. Resigned to defeat, they sadly pack up their meager belongings and leave, joined by Tonet (Manolo Fábregas) who has fallen in love with Batiste's daughter Roseta (Amparo Morillo).

La barraca is a story of irrational intolerance and the inability of a good man to cope with it. An allegory, certainly, of the Spanish Republic, but an allegory submerged in nostalgia and folklore. Gavaldón went to great pains to reproduce as realistically as possible a nineteenth-century Valencian *huerta*; an elaborate outdoor set was constructed that portrayed a Spanish farming community down to the smallest detail. The same care was lavished on the actor's dress, the dialogue, and the customs of Valencia, the Tribunal of the Waters scene being an especially noteworthy instance. Aside from its many artistic and technical merits, the significance of *La barraca*, according to Ayala Blanco, is:

> The phenomenon of Spanish emigration following the republican collapse and the numerous Hispanic population that refuses to assimilate form perhaps the principal motor nerve of the film. A work of collective inspiration, *La barraca* departs from [and directs itself to] a specific audience of refugees and residents, a restricted audience but one which counts for much and predominates in the Mexican cultural order.[60]

As Avila Camacho's presidential term was drawing to a close, so too was the war. For Mexico the bloody struggles on far-flung battlefields had meant prosperity for many areas of economic activity besides the film industry. The conflict had also attracted a host of foreigners to Mexico's peaceful and profitable shores, King Carol of Rumania among them. Mexico City was now more cosmopolitan and sophisticated than it had been in the halcyon days of the Porfiriato. The nouveau riche, both Mexican and foreign, required smart activities on which to spend ostentatiously — night clubs, restaurants, horse racing, and other patrician pastimes.[61]

While the wealthy were converting the capital into a mild Latin American version of prewar Paris, the Bracero Program sent thousands of humbler Mexicans to toil in the fields of the Southwestern United States, an arrangement that enabled additional millions of dollars to flow into Mexico in the form of remittances from its temporarily expatriated farmworkers. And since the war had closed off overseas travel, American tourists discovered Mexico and found to their delight that it was no longer populated by bandelier-clad revolutionary *bandidos* (or Marxist presidents that expropriated American properties). Quite the contrary, Americans could run down to Mexico and be free of ration books and other wartime exigencies.

A marked change had taken place in relations between Mexico and the United States in just a few short years. Mexico's adoption of a more conservative stance and its support of the Allied cause (war had been declared against the Axis powers on May 30, 1942) certainly softened some previously strong anti–Mexican attitudes in the United States.

It is fascinating to reflect also on the role that Hollywood might have had in this process of implementing the Good Neighbor policy at the urging of the Roosevelt administration. For instance, Nelson D. Rockefeller's Office for Coordination of Inter-American Affairs asked Walt Disney to make a goodwill tour of Latin America, an area where he enjoyed great popularity.[62]

The result was two films, *Saludos Amigos* (1943) and *The Three Caballeros* (1945). In *Saludos Amigos*, Donald Duck met the parrot José Carioca, the feathery incarnation of Brazil, an important South American ally. It was a musical romp combining animation and live action that had the effect of showing to American audiences that South America was a magic land full of color, vivacity, and appealing people, not to mention cute animals. Then the United States's other important Latin American ally, Mexico, received its turn in *The Three Caballeros* in the person of Panchito, a sombrero-wearing, charro-clad, pistol-packing rooster. True, a bit of the old stereotype remained in Panchito but he was a thoroughly likable, fun-loving albeit assertive type who showed *"el pato Pascual"* and José Carioca the wondrous beauties of Mexico: piñata parties, the *jarocho* dances of Veracruz, a charro-clad girl dancing with enormous animated cacti to the tune of "Jesusita en Chihuahua," posadas, and other celebrations of Mexican folklore.

Mexico had never been given such a benign and positive image by Hollywood, and *The Three Caballeros* undoubtedly aided tourism to that country if not necessarily contributing to greater international understanding. At least the theme of Pan-Americanism was sounded in the film's title song (set to the music of the popular *ranchera* "Ay Jalisco no te rajes"):

> Oh, we're three caballeros
> Three gay caballeros
> They say we are birds of a feather...

Thus in the persons of Donald, José, and Panchito, the United States, Brazil, and Mexico were three pals, none more equal than the others. Latin American audiences were enchanted with both *Saludos Amigos* and *The Three Caballeros* since never before had a *yanqui* filmmaker presented their countries in such a favorable and appealing way. Disney's attention to accuracy was also a major factor in his films' popularity in Latin America; the music, dances, and costumes were authentic and properly placed. No *chinas poblanas* dancing flamenco or gauchos doing rhumbas, as most Hollywood films had for years freely lumped together without regard for what musical style or mode of dress was typical of a particular country.[63]

As to the war itself, very little of it was reflected in Mexican films. A projected movie on the sinking of the *Potrero del Llano*, a Mexican freighter torpedoed by a German submarine off the Florida coast on May 14, 1942, and which was the *casus belli* for Mexico's declaration of war, was never realized.[64] A number of low-budget, uninspired efforts usually dealt with very *macho* charros besting Axis saboteurs and spies who were in Mexico obviously up to no good, as in Emilio Fernández's quite amusing *Soy puro mexicano* ("I'm Pure Mexican," 1942).[65] One film, *Tres hermanos* ("Three Brothers," 1943), told of three brothers in the American army. But then the Mexican film industry's specialty was not combat films, a topic that in any event reflected very little of the Mexican experience.[66] If anyone in Mexico or the rest of Latin America wanted to see war movies, Hollywood was supplying plenty of those. Mexican films appealed generally to lower-class audiences who were by and large uninvolved in the global struggle.

The war years were a crucial period for the Mexican movie industry. Vital foreign markets were carved out by producers and distributors quick to take advantage of the effect of the war on Hollywood and other foreign producers. Genres — the *comedia ranchera*, the urban melodrama, the musical comedy — were refined and linked to a star system for maximum exploitation. This formula proved a great success with most Latin American audiences, who were generally uninterested in the war propaganda movies emanating from Hollywood and Great Britain.

Quality cinema was also created, that is, films that attempted to portray the realities of Mexican society. Thus Fernández made his compatriots deal with the problems of Indians in *María Candelaria*, and with the meaning of the Revolution in *Flor silvestre*. Julio Bracho with *Distinto amanecer* explored the relevance of old values in the face of a changing, ever more materialistic social and political order. Gavaldón's *La barraca*, although dealing allegorically with the anguish of Spain, dramatized universal problems applicable to Mexico as well as to any other society.

4

"Golden Age," Crisis, and Retrenchment: 1947–1959

With the war over, Mexico entered a "boom" period of unprecedented economic expansion and prosperity under the administration of Miguel Alemán (1946–1952). These years also constitute the film industry's "Golden Age," at least in production and profits. Yet even though filmmaking in this era was at its peak and a number of significant films were made, the outlines of a crisis were there for all to see. The main problem was the very success the industry had been enjoying—producers became wedded to audience-tested genre pictures not only because such movies were popular with the public but also because the Banco Cinematográfico would only back projects with the greatest possibility of commercial success.

The unionization of the industry's workers also contributed to the general artistic stagnation. This was perhaps most serious in the Directors' Guild, which zealously limited the number of new directors so as to protect the livelihoods of the older members. Another flaw inherent in such a closed system was that many of the directors prized by producers were those who could crank out formula movies as quickly and cheaply as possible.

The major factor sustaining such a movie industry was the "star system." Mexican producers and directors were indeed fortunate in that during the 1940s and 1950s a fortuitous confluence of talented, charismatic, and attractive performers appeared who could assure commercial success for even the worst of films. The problem with this was that a motion picture became a vehicle for the star and consequently the director and the script became of secondary concern. This was the situation faced by Luis Buñuel when he arrived in Mexico in 1946 to work for Oscar Dancigers.

Buñuel, the renowned creator of *Un Chien Andalou*, *L'Age d'or*, and *Las Hurdes—Tierra sin pan* ("Las Hurdes—Land Without Bread"), had been in the United States since 1938 working at various times for the Museum of Modern Art in New York, for Hollywood's Hispanic productions, and in the making of military training films.[1] His first film in Mexico was *En el viejo Tampico* ("In Old Tampico"), later renamed *Gran Casino*, and it starred Jorge Negrete and the great Argentine star, Libertad Lamarque (1908–2000). Negrete, afraid that his career was in the doldrums, was determined to upstage Lamarque who was equally determined to be successful in her first Mexican film and establish herself as the star she had been in Argentina.[2] The result, according to Buñuel, was a "tourney to see who could sing more tangos, Lamarque or Negrete."[3] In spite of the two stars' participation, *Gran Casino* was a commercial failure and it would be two years before Buñuel was to make another film.

Under Alemán, steps were taken to assure the government a major role in the film industry, a policy in keeping with the increasing public sector participation in the Mexican economy. The pattern had been well established under Avila Camacho:

> Assessing the development of state capitalism during the regime of General Manuel Avila Camacho, we can conclude that if it indeed received a strong impetus with the creation of a series of state-controlled organs and firms and by the widening of governmental faculties and actions in the economy, it also lost much of the nationalist and popular content exhibited during the government of General Cárdenas.[4]

In the film industry, this tendency meant increasing official protectionism in order to safeguard an important national "cultural" activity. Thus on February 12,

Libertad Lamarque and Lola Beltrán in *Canción del Alma* (1963) (Cineteca).

1946, a law (retroactive to the previous five years) was enacted exempting the movie industry from income taxes. The drafting of a cinematic law was also initiated under Avila Camacho, although the legislation would not be passed until 1949.[5]

The activities of William O. Jenkins, the former United States vice-consul in Puebla who was the central figure in a much-publicized political kidnapping in 1919, serve to illustrate the byzantine workings of the film business in Mexico at this time. Jenkins had settled in Puebla and

Libertad Lamarque in *Canción del alma.*

proceeded to make a fortune in the distribution of alcoholic beverages, medicines, and drugs. His partner, Gabriel Alarcón, built the Reforma Theater in Puebla with financial assistance from the state governor, Maximino Avila Camacho (the president's brother), who also had extensive business dealings with Jenkins. Alarcón and Jenkins then took over ownership of the movie houses in Puebla owned by the Spaniard Jesús Cienfuegos. Alarcón and Jenkins then formed a partnership with the Espinosa Iglesias brothers, the only remaining independent theater operators in the city.

From these modest beginnings, the consortium extended its control to all movie houses in the State of Puebla, forcing out the small, independent operators. Eventually, Jenkins, who functioned as a silent partner, and Manuel Espinosa Iglesias extended their monopoly over a large part of the country: Guadalajara and parts of Jalisco, and the states of Michoacán, Guanajuato, Aguascalientes, Querétaro, Zacatecas, and Durango. Jenkins was also the principal stockholder in the original Banco Cinematográfico which happened to sell its controlling interest in a number of Mexico City theaters to Espinosa Iglesias who formed his exhibition chain, Operadora de Teatros, S.A. Espinosa Iglesias forced Emilio Azcárraga to sell his Alameda Theater and string of movie houses; he accomplished this by informing both Mexican producers and American distributors like 20th Century Fox, Paramount, and Universal that "if you rent films to the Alameda Theater and its circuit, I will not exhibit any motion picture of yours in our movie houses of Mexico, Puebla, Veracruz, Torreón, and other cities I am beginning to control."[6] And what Espinosa did not take over, Alarcón, Jenkins's other partner, absorbed into his empire.

Jenkins's financial interests were not limited solely to movie house chains and the Banco Cinematográfico; he was also an important figure in the Nacional Financiera, an official credit agency, where he was in a position to influence contracts and investments "in almost fabulous amounts."[7] Jenkins was also an associate of Rómulo O'Farrill in the building of the Packard automobile assembly plant in Puebla and later joined with him in establishing the largest television station in Mexico, now in partnership with Emilio Azcárraga, the displaced owner of Operadora de Teatros and founder of XEW, Mexico's leading radio station.[8]

The multifaceted operations of Jenkins had to depend on the friendship and protection of powerful politicians. His personal and business relationships with President Avila Camacho's brother, who also happened to be governor of Puebla, make this evident enough. Jenkins's almost total control, through his cohorts, over the country's exhibition houses caused public alarm and resentment during the Alemán presidency. Led by the flamboyant ex-revolutionary officer and producer/director, Miguel Contreras Torres, a group of independent producers protested against the Jenkins monopoly.

To counter Jenkins and assist the film industry in the face of foreign competition, President Alemán created the National Cinematic Committee (Comisión Nacional de Cinematografía). The Banco Cinematográfico, heretofore a private firm, was reorganized as the Banco Nacional Cinematográfico with a capitalization of 10 million pesos provided by the federal government on the one hand and the Banco de México, Nacional Financiera, and the Banco Nacional de México on the other.[9] Whether this effectively checked the Jenkins consortium is questionable, given his pervasive influence in Mexican high finance.

Despite this move, in 1953 Eduardo Garduño, the Banco Cinematográfico's director, publicly attacked Jenkins, saying that "the monopoly hangs heavily over the nation and, in addition, prevents the healthy development of production."[10] A state distributor, Películas Nacionales, S.A., was founded in 1947 presumably to provide an alternative to the Jenkins group; participating in it were: Filmadora Mexicana, CLASA Films Mundiales, Producciones Rosas Priego, and the Banco with a capital of approximately 200,000 pesos.[11]

An outstanding example of official interest in filmmaking was "El Indio" Fernández's *Río Escondido* ("Hidden River," 1947). Coming on the heels of *Enamorada* ("Woman in Love," 1946), his successful adaptation of "The Taming of the Shrew" to a revolutionary setting, these two films signified a high point in Fernández's career.

Enamorada starred Pedro Armendáriz (1912–1963) as General Juan José Reyes, a Zapatista revolutionary who occupies the city of Cholula which contains 365 churches, one for each day of the year. He falls in love with the fiery beauty Beatriz, played by María Félix (1914–2002), one of the classic beauties of the Mexican cinema. Beatriz is the daughter of the town's richest man, Carlos Peñafiel (José Morcillo) whom Reyes almost executes. The film, uncharacteristically for Fernández, had humor and even some slapstick, especially in a scene where Beatriz hurls a huge firecracker under Reyes's horse. There was even a musical number by the popular trio, Los Panchos, in a serenade scene. Figueroa's camera lovingly caresses Felix's lovely features giving her the full superstar treatment (it was said that in Figueroa's photography, Félix became the 366th monument).

But the film also becomes melodramatic as Reyes wears down Beatriz's resistance, getting her to reject her foreign, presumably American, fiancé, Mr. Roberts (Eugenio Rossi), a bit of nationalistic symbolism. Reyes engages in a debate with the town priest, Father Sierra (Fernando Fernández) over the conflicting objectives of the Revolution and the church — that the Revolution seeks happiness "here on earth" for men while the church should just help them get to heaven. And the none-too-subtle message conveyed by the romance between Reyes and Beatriz is that he represents the emerging mestizo masses and she the creole or white upper classes. Their conflict mirrors the revolutionary conflict and her eventual submissive acceptance of him represents the triumph of the Revolution.[12]

Pedro Armendáriz became to the Mexican Revolution what John Wayne symbolized to the winning of the West. He worked extensively with the Fernández/Figueroa team in their most creative period, but also made many other films. He

María Félix makes a point with the help of Benito Juárez in Emilio Fernández's *Río Escondido* (1947) (Cineteca).

appeared in several Hollywood films, many directed by John Ford, principally in *The Fugitive* (1947), *Three Godfathers* (1949), and *Fort Apache* (1948). His last Hollywood film was *From Russia with Love* (1963), in which he played the Turkish security officer opposite Sean Connery's James Bond.[13]

Río Escondido tells the story of Rosaura Salazar (María Félix), a dedicated and patriotic schoolteacher who is given her assignment personally by the president, Miguel Alemán (played by an actor only shown in silhouetted rear shots). Fernández gives himself over completely to the most blatant and maudlin *patrioterismo* or jingoism as he shows Rosaura (appropriately wearing a *rebozo*) rushing to her appointment at the Presidential Palace for which she is already late. As she ascends the stairs in front of Diego Rivera's famous mural, an off-screen voice identifies itself as the "bell of Dolores" and sternly recounts for Rosaura's benefit the agonized yet glorious history of Mexico as reflected in the mural; then the voice hurries Rosaura along to her appointment.[14]

Although the president has already seen the large group of schoolteachers, he has Rosaura sent in to him for a private interview, in the process making a group of ministers and doctors wait. Rosaura is on the president's list of "outstanding" teachers and he tells her that this is the reason he has summoned her and her colleagues to personally give them their assignments. He recounts for her Mexico's problems — ignorance, disease, and illiteracy — and ominously refers to "*malos mexicanos*" who oppose the new administration's plans for reform; a tear trickles down Rosaura's cheek.

The president assigns her to the town of Río Escondido and instructs her to write to him personally and report on her progress. As she leaves the president's chambers, Rosaura is knocked to the floor by the doctors rushing to get in; she is helped up by her old teacher *don* Felipe (Arturo Soto Rangel) and Felipe Navarro (Fernando Fernández), a young, just-graduated doctor. *Don* Felipe, knowing of her heart condition, does not think she is well enough to teach in a rural area, but she convinces him not to inform the authorities.

Rosaura arrives at Río Escondido, a desolate, poverty-stricken community tyrannized by one of the *malos mexicanos* alluded to by the president—the cacique Regino Sandoval (Carlos López Moctezuma), an ex-*villista* gone bad. Rosaura shows her pluck by courageously defying Regino and his murderous henchmen. He is unsuccessful in forcing her to become his mistress, as he had done with the previous schoolteacher. She calls Felipe back from the village to which he had been assigned to combat a smallpox epidemic in Río Escondido.

Rosaura and Felipe force Regino to fix up the school and have the townspeople vaccinated in exchange for medical treatment for he has also fallen ill. The village priest (Domingo Soler), heretofore powerless against the cacique, gains heart from Rosaura and Felipe's courageous example and helps to gather the villagers for vaccination. In the repaired school building, Rosaura exhorts the boys and girls: "Learn so you can regenerate Río Escondido, Mexico, and the world!" She lectures them about "dark forces" in Mexico, especially ignorance; she points to Juárez's picture as an example of Mexico's (and the Indians') ability to reach the heights. "But what am I saying?" she interrupts herself. "We have to start where Juárez did—with the first letter of the alphabet."

Regino feels his power over the villagers slipping away. One night, after drinking heavily, he goes to Rosaura's school where she also sleeps; he attempts to rape her as his men wait outside. A shot rings out from within; Regino staggers from the building with Rosaura following, blasting away at him with a rifle. His men move menacingly toward her but are attacked by torch-wielding Indians and massacred.

Rosaura, hysterical, collapses. She is seriously ill but insists on dictating her report to the president, which Felipe takes down. Her condition worsens and she is obviously dying; Felipe attempts to teach the village children but concludes that "special ability" is needed for that. A horseman delivers a letter for Rosaura; it is the president's reply: "The *patria* is grateful to you...." She dies just as Felipe finishes reading the letter. The final scene shows Rosaura's tombstone inscribed with a tribute.

Río Escondido, unsurprisingly, has elicited both condemnation and praise.[15] "At a distance of almost twenty years," says Ayala Blanco, "*Río Escondido*, the film that best reveals the ideals of Emilio Fernández, resembles a sculpture, solitary and unmoving."[16] Gabriel Figueroa's photographic preciosity incorporated all of the Eisensteinian techniques: low-angle long shots in silhouette that emphasize the stark landscape and sky and the smallness of the human figures before them; the closeups of Indian faces and shrouded women; and the "dead tree framing" in which long shots are composed between the gnarled branches of a dried-up tree.

All of this in addition to the truculent railing against "dark forces" and "bad Mexicans" by the characters—in reality symbols rather than actual people—were sure to cause widespread annoyance as well as admiration. *Río Escondido* received the Ariel in 1949 for the best Mexican film; Fernández and Figueroa were named, respectively, best director and best photographer. Figueroa also received the award for best pho-

Emilio Fernández's *Salón México* (1947) was uncharacteristically (for him) set in an urban
film noir setting. Beloved movie villain Miguel Inclán, in perhaps his only sympathetic role,
played a good-hearted policeman who falls in love with Marga López, a prostitute and dance-
hall girl. Brutalized by her pimp (Rodolfo Acosta), she kills him with a pair of scissors, but
he manages to shoot her to death before dying (Cineteca).

tography at the Prague Film Festival in 1948 and Fernández received an honorable
mention for direction. In that same year, it was awarded the prize for best photography at Madrid.[17]

Another major 1947 film that combined in a disconcerting way elements of
musical comedy, melodrama, and stark, brutal realism was Ismael Rodríguez's *Nosotros
los pobres* ("We the Poor"). Rodríguez, who had been in films since the 1930s,[18] directed
a sprightly and appealing *comedia ranchera* in 1946, *Los tres García* ("The Three Garcias"), and quickly followed it up with a sequel, *Vuelven los García* ("The Garcias
Return"). *Nosotros los pobres* was Rodríguez's most popular film. Although it won no
prizes, it remained for many years Mexico's all-time leader in box-office receipts and
is often shown on television.

Nosotros los pobres is an emotionally drawing experience as it relates the misadventures of Pepe el Toro (Pedro Infante), his sister Chachita (Evita Muñoz), and his
sweetheart Celia (Blanca Estela Pavón). The plot is too complex to even attempt to
summarize here, but suffice it to say that Rodríguez establishes that poverty is a hellish
condition in spite of the nobility of the poor, or at least of some of them. Miguel

Inclán (1900–1956) as Pilar turns in one of his most hateful roles; not only does his theft of four hundred pesos from Pepe, which is the direct cause of the latter's tragic contretemps, go unpunished, but, dazed by marijuana, he brutally beats Pepe's totally paralyzed mother.

Such scenes of violence, another being Pepe's fight in prison with three hoodlums who had framed him and during which he gouges out the eye of one, are skillfully offset by musical numbers or comedy sequences. An additional aspect of *Nosotros los pobres* worth mentioning is that it continued Galindo's innovation from *Campeón sin corona* ("Champion Without a Crown") of employing authentic street dialogue from the slums of Mexico City.[19] The public's enthusiastic reception of this film encouraged Rodríguez to follow it in 1948 with a sequel, *Ustedes los ricos* ("You the Rich"), in which the fortunes of Pepe el Toro and Celia, now married, are further scrutinized.

The trend toward serious urban drama, however, was best exemplified in the films of Alejandro Galindo (1906–1999).[20] His *Campeón sin sorona* (1945) sensitively told the story of Roberto "Kid" Terranova (David Silva), a talented boxer from the slums who lacks the self-confidence to be a champion. Significantly, "Kid" Terranova is cowed psychologically by a Mexican-American boxer, Joe Ronda (Víctor Parra), who spouts English at him during their match. This theme — the inferiority complex of the Mexican — is a favorite of Galindo's and it is a subject he would continue to explore in the years ahead. In 1947 Galindo directed *El muchacho alegre* ("The Cheerful Lad") for Raúl de Anda; here he took the elements of a standard rural melodrama and transcended its limitations with a superior film.

Returning to his true genre in 1948, Galindo in *¡Esquina bajan!* ("Corner, Getting Off!") examined the world of unionized workers, in this case, bus drivers. Comparing Galindo's approach to social problems with that of Rodríguez in *Nosotros los pobres* and *Ustedes los ricos*, García Riera stated:

> The poor of ... Rodríguez were condemned to solitary impotence because their idea of solidarity did not go beyond the narrow limits of sentimentalism and because their secret aspiration was to become petty bourgeois; Galindo's poor, on the other hand, recognized their social condition to dignify their humble status. Ismael Rodríguez talked of the poor while Galindo concerned himself with the workers; Karl Marx undoubtedly would have been much more in accord with the latter.[21]

In *Una familia de tantas* ("An Average Family," 1948), the middle-class father, Rodrigo Cataño (Fernando Soler), seeks by means of an absolute and tyrannical control over his family to shut out society and maintain his home as an oasis of feudal, Porfirian order amid the turmoil of the world beyond. But unlike Bustillo Oro in *Cuando los hijos se van*, Galindo recognizes that Mexico has changed and that the new, unsettling values cannot be kept out. Rodrigo's stern control is disturbed when Roberto del Hierro (David Silva), a vacuum cleaner salesman representing the "Bright O'Home" line (and symbolically the encroaching "American way of life"), aggressively introduces his product into the Cataño home. Fast-talking, intelligent, and ambitious, Roberto represents the upwardly mobile middle-class created by the Revolution and World War II, the very people most despised by a Porfirian gentleman. Yet he is helpless against Roberto who easily convinces him to purchase first the vacuum cleaner and later a refrigerator. Rodrigo's oldest daughter Maru (Martha Roth) is captivated by Roberto and they fall in love. When Roberto announces to Rodrigo that he and Maru want to marry, the old man is furious that they have initiated a relationship without his permission. Maru defies her father and marries Roberto; on her wedding day no one in her family is on hand, having been forbidden by Rodrigo to attend.[22]

The oft-made charge that the Mexican cinema has been largely alienated from reality cannot be made against Galindo. As in *Una familia de tantas*, he always sought to focus on the underlying tensions of society — to the extent possible, of course, within a capitalistic industrial system. A self-proclaimed "leftist,"[23] Galindo was much franker than his contemporaries in scrutinizing the contradictions of Mexican life.

For instance, his approach to racial tensions in his country was quite unlike that of Fernández who dealt with such a complex subject simply by idealizing Indian culture. Galindo took a much more sophisticated approach in that he was mindful of the subtler tensions between creoles and mestizos in a middle-class ambience. This is a subject that most Mexicans prefer to ignore (or rather sublimate), categorically stating that there is no racial prejudice in their country. Galindo finally made a film in which this problem was the central theme; the picture was *El juicio de Martín Cortés* ("The Trial of Martín Cortés," 1973) which was almost totally ignored, a snubbing that the director attributed to his countrymen's reluctance to face up to their racial problems.[24] In technique, his camera movements were competent yet unobtrusive, unlike Fernández whose elaborate setups often distract the viewer's attention. Galindo himself dismissed the concern with camera technique as "of no importance."[25]

In the later 1940s appeared the only serious threat to Cantinflas's hegemony. This was Germán Valdez "Tin-Tan" (1919–1973), a fresh, imaginative music-hall comic. His humor was quite unlike Cantinflas's, being expressed rather in a spontaneous, often hysterical style; also Tin-Tan was an accomplished song-and-dance man. Born in Mexico City, Tin-Tan moved with his family to Ciudad Juárez in 1931 and from the age of twelve he resided in that border city. He was a radio announcer until he joined the company of the ventriloquist Paco Miller and returned to the capital, where he appeared on the same music-hall programs with Cantinflas. Tin-Tan's specialty at this time was the *pachuco* character he had created, influenced by his proximity to North American culture during his years of residence in Juárez, as well as by the entire milieu of Mexico's border areas. Tin-Tan appeared in the typical pachuco costume, or as it was known in the United States, the "zoot-suit" — wide-brimmed hat with a tremendous feather stuck in the brim, baggy pants, and single-buttoned long jacket.[26]

Tin-Tan also sprinkled English phrases throughout his dialogue in the manner of the Juárez area, but even more so, as Mexican-American pachucos were wont to do. Not that Mexico City audiences were that familiar with the linguistic practices of *pochos* (an Americanized, or "gringoized" Mexican, i.e., a Mexican-American, used in a condescending or derogatory manner), but there does exist a bias of long standing against the northern tier of states — Chihuahua, Sonora, Tamaulipas, Nuevo León, and Baja California. Residents of central Mexico have tended to disdain northerners

Germán Valdez "Tin-Tan" rhumbas with Yolanda Montes "Tongolele" in *El rey del barrio* (1949) (Pelmex).

as being uncultured, boorish, and, perhaps worst of all, semi–Americanized. This attitude increases in intensity when applied to Mexican-Americans. Therefore, although Tin-Tan's pachuco routine was initially accepted for its novelty, he was eventually obliged to change the character, molding it into that of a street-wise native of the Federal District. Yet, Tin-Tan was never a *pelado*, a representative of the lowest class as Cantinflas was; his portrayals were usually of an ambitious, upwardly mobile huckster, as in *Calabacitas tiernas* ("Tender Little Pumpkins,"1948) and *especially El rey del barrio* ("The King of the Neighborhood," 1949). Tin-Tan's talent, his art one might safely say, in later years happily received the recognition it long deserved:

> Perhaps it could be said that this comic is superior to "Cantinflas," since in his "pachuco" role he reflected an entire phenomenology of transculturation, an entire historical problem based on Mexican-U.S. relations. Tin-Tan's linguistic *pochismo*, his demythicizing character, antisolemn and iconoclastic, place this unforgettable artist as unique in his genre.[27]

Such widely divergent talents as Galindo and Tin-Tan were clearly signs of an exciting and creative vigor in the late 1940s. "El Indio" Fernández, although his work was beginning to bog down in clichés, still was capable of lyrical beauty if not dramatic power as in *Enamorada*. Yet even though Mexican cinema was to achieve an almost spectacular success in purely quantitative terms, its aesthetic achievements — those not infrequent moments of true cinematic art it had been able to achieve — were to be suffocated by the commercial demands of a constantly more structured industry. Thus "formula" or "package" pictures were steadily more in demand — "family" melodramas, *comedias rancheras*, and comedies, all quite endemic to Mexican cinema since the 1930s. However, *alemanismo* generated something new: the *cabaretera* films.

Tin-Tan in *Hay muertos que no hacen ruido* (1946) (Pelmex).

The prostitute had been an early theme in Mexican films since the silent era and the early talkies; the three versions of *Santa, La mujer del puerto, La mancha de sangre* ("The Blood Stain," 1937), and others. But the excitement and anxieties of the Alemán era injected a new restlessness into Mexican urban society. The emerging classes of businessmen, technocrats, bureaucrats, and wheeler-dealers sought legitimacy in traditional middle-

Tin-Tan in *Tres lecciones de amor* (1958) (Azteca Films).

class values and thus equity with the remnants of the Porfirian creole elite.

The new elites, however, lacked the ingrained conservatism of their forebears and their lack of total commitment to the old ethical and sexual codes is interestingly reflected in the wave of *cabaretera* films of this period. The settings for these motion pictures were the cheap night clubs of the capital and their luckless *ficheras* or B-girls. As representations of a society in the throes of rapid economic and social change, these films often reflected the tensions of postwar Mexico. If the *comedia ranchera* stood for traditional values, the *cabareteras* dramatized the breakdown of those values. In the first place, the girls found themselves there because of personal or economic adversity. Lacking the skills demanded by an increasingly complex economy and further restrained by a male-dominated society, the girls turned to a traditional profession. In the age-old Mexican and Latin American dichotomy, if they could not be "good" women then they must perforce be "bad." But the melodramatic formula (or middle-class ethic) of the prostitute "with the heart of gold" was usually employed in most of these films to reinforce the underlying moral values.

The urban night spot, in its surrogate role as the city in microcosm, was also a conduit for foreign influences. The music especially symbolized this. Most of it was Afro-Cuban — danzones, rhumbas, congas, mambos, cha-chas — musical forms with a high level of erotic suggestiveness which in turn highlighted the freer sexual standards of postwar urban life.[28]

This musical foundation led to the popularization of a number of Cuban performers, the principal ones being Rosa Carmina, María Antonieta Pons, and Ninón Sevilla. The latter was undoubtedly the queen of the *cabareteras*. She was capable of exuding a child-like naïveté as well as cheap eroticism, and her angry outbursts were almost legendary. Ninón Sevilla appeared in many *cabaretera* films in the 1940s and

The musical moods of Ninón Sevilla in Alberto Gout's *Adventurera* (1949): Her "Persian Market" production number (Rogelio Agrasánchez, Jr. Film Archive).

Ninón with an Afro-Cuban ensemble (Rogelio Agrasánchez, Jr. Film Archive).

1950s but her classic pictures are undoubtedly *Sensualidad* ("Sensuality," 1950) and *Aventurera* ("Adventuress," 1952). In *Sensualidad*, an adaptation of Josef von Sternberg's *The Blue Angel* (1930), she was a ruthless, amoral B-girl who seduces a repressed, middle-aged married age (Fernando Soler).

Aventurera has been lauded as the epitome of the genre, transcending its melodramatic strictures. Directed by Alberto Gout and written by Alvaro Custodio, the film treated middle-class morality as a hypocritical sham and represented Mexican society as being thoroughly corrupt. Elena (Ninón Sevilla), a schoolgirl in Chihuahua City, lives an apparently happy family life in a comfortable bourgeois home. One day she returns home unexpectedly and surprises her mother in a passionate embrace with another man; Elena flees the house in shock and disgust. Returning later she finds her father despondently holding a note from his wife who has run away with the man she "truly loves." Elena's father puts a bullet through his head shortly thereafter.

Elena then goes to Ciudad Juárez to look for a secretarial job. At every job she becomes the object of lustful attentions by her employers, which she virtuously rejects. Jobless and disheartened, she runs into Lucio (Tito Junco), a ne'er-do-well admirer from Chihuahua. He offers to get her a job with a friend of his and takes her to a nightclub where he plies her with champagne. Inebriated, she finally is taken to meet her "employer," Rosaura (Andrea Palma). Elena is given a drugged cup of tea, passes out, and is taken to a bedroom where she is made available while still unconscious

Ninón with the Trío Los Panchos (Rogelio Agrasánchez, Jr. Film Archive).

to an undetermined number of men. When she wakens, she learns the truth of her situation — that she is bound to Rosaura's employment.

Elena eventually becomes a star of the nightclub (her feature number is a mildly suggestive dance to the strains of "In a Persian Market"), although troublesome and subject to furious outbursts. One night she sees her mother's lover and viciously attacks him. Rosaura has had enough and orders her henchman *El Rengo* (Miguel Inclán) to scar Elena's face; Lucio intercedes but Elena stops him from killing El Rengo. Elena then becomes a driver for Lucio's gang while they break into a jewelry store; however, the police are waiting for them, having been tipped off by a disgruntled member of Lucio's gang. Lucio is captured but Elena manages to escape. She goes to Mexico City where in no time at all she again becomes a nightclub star. She captivates Mario (Rubén Rojo), a law student and scion of one of Guadalajara's oldest families. Elena accepts his offer of marriage after the same hoodlum that had betrayed Lucio attempts to blackmail her.

Once in Guadalajara, Elena discovers that Mario's "aristocratic" mother is none other than Rosaura, the notorious Juárez madam. From this point on, the film becomes progressively more vicious as Elena does her utmost to humiliate and disgrace Rosaura before the cream of Guadalajara society. Mario, of course, has no idea of his mother's secret business activities and is at a loss to explain Elena's behavior and the progressively more open hostility between his mother and his wife. Nonetheless, he faithfully sticks by Elena who has already told Rosaura that she will marry her son to get revenge. One night when Mario is working late, Rosaura surprises Elena attempting to seduce Mario's younger brother; the ensuing argument between the two women results in Rosaura physically attacking Elena. Mario arrives home just in time to catch his mother strangling his wife. Rosaura then leaves on one of her periodic "business" trips.

Elena leaves Mario and also goes to Juárez where her mother is seriously ill in a hospital. Elena coldly refuses to forgive her mother and watches her die. In the meantime, Rosaura has instructed *El Rengo* to kill Elena but he cannot go through with it because he is in love with her. Mario also arrives in Juárez in search of Elena who takes him to Rosaura's brothel-cabaret and leaves the shocked mother and son together. In the meantime, Lucio has escaped from prison and wants Elena to cross the border with him to the United States. Mario appears again and confronts Lucio who beats him up; before Lucio can kill Elena, however, El Rengo stabs Lucio to death. Elena and Mario are now free to find happiness together.

Clearly *Aventurera* went far beyond the usual parameters of the *cabaretera* melodrama, allowing its "heroine" to vent her most ruthless instincts freely without eventual punishment. In the course of Elena's misadventures, Mexican middle and upper-class society came in for a severe drubbing. The naïve happiness of Elena with her parents in the opening scenes is soon shattered by her mother's infidelity; but the mother is also a woman trapped in a stifling provincial atmosphere, living with a cloyingly adoring husband for whom she has lost all feeling. In true melodramatic fashion, the mother pays dearly for her reckless grasp at happiness, earning the undying hatred of her daughter and, perhaps worse, unwittingly converting Elena into a cruel, unfeeling person who can look upon others only as objects to be manipulated. And the linking of Juárez's most corrupt underworld activities with Mexico's most conservative, aristocratic, and pro–Catholic elements — Guadalajara's elite — is a shattering commentary on the cynical duality of society: The most arrogant and privileged groups enjoy their status by the gross exploitation of those less fortunate.

In other words, an exclusive, "good" family of Guadalajara, the country's bastion of conservative, traditional, moral values, is maintained by the illicit money from a sordid brothel (the oldest and most blatant form of economic exploitation as well as sexism) in a vice center like Juárez, a city that itself lies uncertainly suspended between two antagonistic cultures. In truth, García Riera comments that the Gout-Custodio-Sevilla trio never managed in their other films to attain the "surprising virulence of *Aventurera*, truly an exceptional achievement of the Mexican cinema."[29]

Thus if the *cabaretera* film was the "cinema par excellence" of *alemanismo*, the genre managed at times to express a devastating indictment of Mexican life.[30] It can even be said that the unabashed greed given free rein by Alemán's ambitious developmental regime created severe societal stresses that found expression in some of the most interesting films ever made in Mexico before outright commercial "packages" came to predominate in the late 1950s and 1960s.

For instance, a minor Fernández/Figueroa vehicle like *Siempre tuya* ("Always

Yours," 1950) made some telling points. The first part of the film has some biting social commentary: tenant farmer Jorge Negrete and his wife Gloria Marín are standing disconsolately in the middle of their barren land: a five-year drought (the same amount of time that Marín has been barren, in a touch of "El Indio's" typical symbolism) has ruined them. The dust swirls about the couple as the landlord rides up on a horse and tells them that he too is bankrupt, that they will all have to move on. Negrete considers going to the United States as a bracero but, being a good Mexican, he dismisses the notion. Instead he and Marín move to a shantytown in Mexico City. When the owners decide to raze the shacks, the people, in a display of *lumpen* solidarity, defy the authorities. When they are arrested, a lawyer berates the property owners "for fearing communism but doing more to bring it on than the communists themselves."

The second half of the film degenerates into musical melodrama: Negrete wins a singing contest on a radio show (interpreting "México lindo y querido"), immediately becomes a star, and is thrust into the hypocrisy and corruption of high society. Gloria Marín, however, knows that her husband will eventually see through the false glamour of his superficial new acquaintances and return to her. He does.[31]

In 1953 Alejandro Galindo filmed one of his most outspoken films, *Espaldas mojadas* ("Wetbacks"). Making it to "convince Mexicans not to go to the United States,"[32] Galindo took on the entire gamut of social and economic problems besetting Mexico and even dedicated considerable attention to the status of Mexican-Americans.

The realism of the film was heightened by Galindo's use of American actors speaking English dialogue. The problem of Mexican illegal emigration has perhaps never been set forth so well, although at times a mite sensationally, in a commercial film. For instance, Galindo has guard towers on the American side of the Río Grande which scan the water with searchlights. When any individual or group is spotted swimming across, a siren shatters the night silence and the border patrol begins firing, shooting to kill.

Although the representation of the United States-Mexico border in *Espaldas mojadas* is more typical of the later Berlin Wall than of anything that ever existed on the border between the two countries, Galindo's intent here was probably not so much anti–American as didactic — to discourage his countrymen from entering the United States illegally. In view of the violence that has periodically flared up along the border, and which continues today, occasionally to an alarming degree, it can be said that in essence Galindo's view is metaphorically correct: the murderous guard towers represent the hostility of American society toward the individuals driven away by the poverty and indifference of their own country. Yet there was enough antipathy expressed toward the United States to make the Dirección de Cinematografía fretful and *Espaldas mojadas* was not released until 1955.

The film opens with a view of Ciudad Juárez, here described as a stalwart cultural frontier; a voice-over declares testily that "on this side of the Río Bravo it is *still* Mexico, where Spanish is *still* spoken and songs are sung to the Virgin of Guadalupe ... on the other side of the Río Grande, as the Americans call it, are skyscrapers and everyone owns a car." A country, continues the narrator, that "forty years of movies have presented as a place where everyone is happy."

Alejandro Galindo (left) directing David Silva and Martha Valdés in *Espaldas mojadas* (1953) (Rogelio Agrasánchez, Jr. Archives).

After the opening remarks, we see Rafael (David Silva) walking along a Juárez street. At the bracero hiring hall, he explains that he is a heavy equipment operator; the clerk tells him that for Mexicans there is only fieldwork. Rafael has no passport and is turned away. He gets involved with the "coyote" Frank Mendoza (José Elías Moreno) who is illegally contracting workers for Mister Sterling (Víctor Parra). Rafael crosses the Río Grande with a group of braceros that night, managing to survive the fire from the American watchtowers, although a new friend of his is killed.

The rest of the film traces Rafael's life as an illegal alien in the United States, constantly on the move, fearful of being discovered. He is at the mercy of exploiters like Mister Sterling who pay him substandard wages and take out all manner of "deductions." In his odyssey he meets Luis Villarreal alias Louie Royalville (Oscar Pulido), a picaresque and thoroughly cynical hobo. At one point when Luis has been berating the capitalist system, Rafael remarks that "you sound like a communist." Luis vehemently denies this, saying that under communism everybody is required to work and he could never abide such a system.

Rafael gets work with a railroad gang bossed by Sterling. After an altercation with him — Sterling snarls, in English: "Don't touch me, you dirty Mexican greaser" — Rafael becomes a fugitive. He arrives at a roadside café where María del Consuelo (Martha Valdés) works as a waitress. He had met her briefly earlier in the film just

Preparing to cross the Rio Grande in *Espaldas mojadas*.

after he crossed over from Mexico. She recognizes Rafael and hides him when a policeman comes in who utters the classic line: "You seen a Mexican with a brown leather
jacket? Looks more like a wop than a Mexican." After the officer leaves, María tells
Rafael of her unhappiness: "I'm not Mexican, I'm a *pocha*. We're worse off than
blacks — they stick together and are not pulled toward another country. The Mexicans don't like us and the gringos look down on us." Rafael asks her if she'll return
to Mexico and marry him. She agrees and they plan to meet in Juárez.

Rafael has to return to Mexico the same way he left it, swimming the river at
night. Ironically, he is picked up by a Mexican border patrol the moment he sets foot
on the other side. In an uneven scene, made so by Galindo's attempt to pack too
much "message" into it, Rafael protests to the border patrol officer that he is indeed
a Mexican, pointing to his swarthy skin; the officer says that that is no proof, that
there are many dark-complexioned people in the world — *pochos*, Greeks, Italians.
"When will you people realize," continues the officer, "the trouble that you cause by
crossing illegally? Have you no dignity?" "Dignity?" asks Rafael angrily. "We're hun-
gry, that's the reason." He talks about abuses in Mexico but pleads to be allowed to
stay.

Rafael goes to the Juárez cantina where he is to meet María. Coincidentally, he
runs into Sterling who had gone there to cancel a contract with Frank Mendoza

Fight in the Juárez cantina, Mr. Sterling (Víctor Parra) getting the worst of it from Rafael (David Silva).

because the U.S. government was investigating his use of illegal aliens. A fight ensues; the others suggest that instead of killing him there, they take Sterling and dump him in the river. Sterling is shot to death by the American border guards while being forced to swim across. Another man tells Rafael: "Neither you nor we killed him. It was he who stupidly tried to swim to the other side."

Not since *El compadre Mendoza* and *Vámonos con Pancho Villa* had a Mexican filmmaker made such an overtly political film and, more importantly, a motion picture that dealt frankly with one of the country's most serious social problems. In spite of certain technical flaws — the clumsy use of back-projections and stock shots, and some uneven direction—*Espaldas mojadas* remains a powerful and generally well-made film.

In 1953 Galindo also made *Los Fernández de Peralvillo* ("The Fernandezes of Peralvillo") again starring David Silva and Víctor Parra. Here Galindo takes a hard look at unscrupulous business practices and the class system. This film, too, is an uncompromising look at a slice of Mexican reality. Interestingly, as in *Una familia de tantas*, the principal character played by Víctor Parra is also a door-to-door salesman of American domestic products. Here, though, the salesman is no harbinger of

Alejandro Galindo's *Los Fernández de Peralvillo* (1953) with (left to right), Víctor Parra, Andrés Soler, Leonor Llausás, and Sara García (Cineteca).

change, of the "American Way of Life." He is a bitter, defeated man, humiliated by housewives, building custodians, and his own family. The only way out of his despair is provided by an old friend, David Silva, who brings him into a crooked consortium for the importation and distribution of medicines. Parra, thoroughly corrupted, finally implicates his friend and other associate in a fraudulent business deal. Silva, now a desperate fugitive from the law, shoots Parra down in the middle of the street. Another noteworthy aspect of this film is the acting of Adalberto Martínez "Resortes," a fine comic actor who was to work often with Galindo.

After the fiasco of *Gran Casino*, Luis Buñuel made only one film in the next two-and-a-half years. This was *El gran calavera* ("The Great Madcap," 1949), a standard melodramatic vehicle coproduced by Oscar Dancigers and Fernando Soler who also starred in the film. This light comedy concerns Ramiro (Fernando Soler), a dissolute rich widower, who is led to believe by his family that his behavior has ruined them financially; when he learns the truth, Ramiro in turn tricks his family into thinking that they are indeed bankrupt. The result is that all learn to appreciate one another and to value hard, honest work. Buñuel was able to inject his particular brand of humor at the expense of middle-class ideals, but subtly enough so that the general public still enjoyed the movie. Worth noting is that the final scenes in the church in Mike Nichols's *The Graduate* (1967) seem to be directly inspired by the denouement in *El gran calavera*, where Ramiro disrupts his daughter's wedding by using a large crucifix to ward off the irate guests.[33]

The commercial success of *El gran calavera* enabled Buñuel to make his masterpiece, *Los olvidados/The Young and the Damned* (1950). For almost three years between *Gran Casino* and *El gran calavera*, Buñuel did not work. During that period of forced idleness, he traveled throughout Mexico and was "impressed with the mis-

Luis Buñuel's *El gran calavera* (1949) with Fernando Soler (middle) (Procinemex).

ery of many of its inhabitants." The result was *Los olvidados*, a stark, realistic portrayal of the brutal existence of slum children in Mexico City.[34]

In *Los olvidados*, Buñuel visualized poverty in a radically different way from the traditional forms of Mexican melodrama. Buñuel's street children are not "ennobled" by their desperate struggle for survival; they are in fact ruthless predators who are no better than their equally unromanticized victims. To Mexican audiences, accustomed to the sentimentalized poor of Rodríguez's *Nosotros los pobres*, *Los olvidados* was an unsettling experience and the film initially was not a commercial success, even though its merit was recognized at once.[35]

Buñuel went on to make eighteen more films in Mexico, and to many non–Mexicans, especially in the United States, he was and still is the only name that comes to mind when Mexican filmmaking is mentioned.[36] In spite of his renown, the effect of Buñuel's work on the Mexican film industry was negligible. His only protegé was Luis Alcoriza who collaborated on the script of *Los olvidados* and several other Buñuel films.

But few Mexican directors sought to emulate the Buñuel style, although his colleagues have been justifiably proud that the "master's" art matured in Mexico, which made it possible for him to go to Europe and make such celebrated films as *Diary of a Chambermaid* (1964), *Belle de Jour* (*Beauty of the Day*) (1966), *The Milky Way* (1968), *Tristana* (1969), *The Discreet Charm of the Bourgeoisie* (1974), and *That Obscure Object of Desire* (1978).

Thus in the years that Buñuel was making films like *Ensayo de un crimen/The Criminal Life of Archibaldo de la Cruz* (1955), *Nazarín* (1958), *Viridiana* (1961), *El ángel exterminador/Exterminating Angel* (1962), and *Simón del desierto/Simon of the Desert* (1965), Mexican filmmaking was falling back more and more on steadily deteriorating melodramatic formula pictures. Undoubtedly it was Buñuel who gave the Mexican cinema whatever vitality it had left in the late 1950s and early 1960s while the creativity of directors like Fernández and Galindo was being suffocated by an increasingly more structured industry. And it was Buñuel's work that managed to keep international attention on Mexican filmmaking.

For instance, *Ensayo de un crimen* (1955) was the first of Buñuel's Mexican films to demonstrate his surrealistic humor toward bourgeois conventions. The character of Archibaldo de la Cruz (Ernesto Alonso) is quite similar to the bemused aristocrats played years later by Fernando Rey in *The Discreet Charm of the Bourgeoisie* and *That Obscure Object of Desire*. Archibaldo believes that he was responsible when a child for

Silvia Pinal and Claudio Brook in Buñuel's *Simón del desierto* (1954).

Buñuel's *Ensayo de un crimen* (1955) with Ernesto Alonso and Miroslava (Pelmex).

his governess's death. As an adult he is relating the story to a nun in a hospital, and when he appears to threaten her, she rushes out, falls down an elevator shaft, and is killed. Archibaldo is convinced that he caused the nun's death and tells the police that it was not his first crime.

Archibaldo relates his plans to murder three women: Patricia (Rita Macedo), Carlota (Ariadna Welter), and Lavinia (Miroslava). In a flashback, the film traces Archibaldo's frustrating relationships with the vulgar yet provocative Patricia, the "pure" and religious Carlota whom he intends to marry, and the beautiful model and tourist guide Lavinia. Archibaldo makes elaborate plans to murder Patricia with a razor but his schemes go awry when she commits suicide after a quarrel with her lover. On another occasion his plot to kill Lavinia is foiled when she brings in a group of American tourists to gape at Archibaldo's colonial mansion. Meanwhile Carlota's lover, the architect Alejandro (Rodolfo Landa), desperate at the thought of losing her to Archibaldo, sends him an anonymous note about Carlota's faithlessness. Archibaldo is unfazed since he plans to murder Carlota anyway after they are married. But Alejandro, insane with jealousy, shoots Carlota while she is at a fitting for her wedding dress.

The flashback ends and the police inspector absolves Archibaldo of any respon-

Luis Buñuel (seated at left) on the set of *Ensayo de un crimen*. The others are (standing from left to right) an unidentified friend, Luis' wife Jeanne Buñuel, the mannequin, Miroslava, José Ignacio Mantecón, and Rafael Buñuel, Luis' son. Seated at the right is Eduardo Ugarte, who worked on the script with Buñuel (Pelmex).

sibility for the two women's deaths. The inspector tells Archibaldo that he cannot be prosecuted for just thinking of murdering someone, and advises him to use an electric razor from now on. Later, in Chapultepec Park, Archibaldo hurls a music box into the lake. He had owned it when he was a child but lost the toy when his parents' house was looted during the Revolution. By chance discovering the music box in an antique store, Archibaldo had met Lavinia at the time. By once again owning the music box, his childhood guilt at his governess's death had revived and Archibaldo began to fancy himself a murderer. In casting away the music box, he also frees himself from the psychological fetters that bound him to a guilt-ridden past. Archibaldo then runs into Lavinia who tells him that she has decided not to marry her fiancé, and they walk off happily together.[37]

In the 1950s, Luis Buñuel also made *Subida al cielo* ("Ascent to Heaven,") released in the U.S. as *Mexican Bus Ride* (1951); *El bruto* ("The Brute"), *Adventures of Robinson Crusoe,* and *El/ This Strange Passion* (all 1952*); Abismos de pasión* ("Abysses of Passion"} and *La ilusión viaja en tranvía/Illusion Travels on a Streetcar* (1953). *Subida al cielo* is on the surface a lighthearted tale about a group of bus passengers in the state of Guerrero, but the film is also an allegory of the story of Adam and Eve in which Buñuel aims his customary barbs at religion and society. *El bruto*, starring Pedro Armendáriz and Katy Jurado, is a realistic, violent tale set in an urban slum. Unlike *Los olvidados*, in which Buñuel portrayed the *lumpenproletariat*, *El bruto* deals with workers who exhibit a well-defined class consciousness within the melodramatic context of the film. *The Adventures of Robinson Crusoe*, made in English, was the first Mexican film by Buñuel that became an international commercial success. Curiously, it was not premiered in Mexico until three years after it had been seen throughout the world.

El, one of the *buñuelistas'* cult films, traces the descent into paranoia and sexual obsession of a devout Catholic aristocrat (Arturo de Córdova). Buñuel humorously examines the shadowy boundaries between madness, sexual desire, and religious fervor, a theme he would return to again years later in *Viridiana*. *Abismos de pasión* was an adaptation of *Wuthering Heights*, and *La ilusión viaja en tranvía* was a "proletarian" comedy of two streetcar conductors who steal a trolley and offer free rides to the public.[38]

Others besides Buñuel occasionally attempted "quality" cinema. A noteworthy effort was *Raíces* ("Roots," 1953), a film about Indians that sought to break the Fernández/Eisenstinian mold. Produced by a television executive, Manuel Barbachano Ponce, and directed by Benito Alazraki, *Raíces* was based on four stories: "Las vacas"

Arturo de Córdova in Buñuel's *El* (1952) (Cineteca).

Beatriz Flores and Juan de la Cruz as the Otomí couple in Benito Alazraki's *Raíces* (1953) (Pelmex).

depicts the struggle for survival of a poverty-stricken Otomí couple. In "Nuestra señora," Jane, an American anthropology student, comes to the conclusion that the Chamulas are savages because one of them baptizes his son with the name of the first "animal" to pass in front of his house — Bicicleta ("Bicycle"). She returns to Chiapas some time later and changes her opinion after she finds the Indians worshipping a copy of *La Gioconda* that had been stolen from her. "El tuerto" tells of a one-eyed body who is tormented by the other children. His mother takes him to a witch-doctor to be cured, but a firecracker accident blinds his other eye. He is now happy because blind people are respected. "La potranca" relates the efforts of a foreign anthropologist in Veracruz to bed a young Indian girl. When he attempts to buy her from her father, the latter agrees as long as the anthropologist gives his own wife in exchange. Although unevenly paced, *Raíces* had enough anthropological and "exotic" value and skillful camerawork to elicit generally favorable comments from European critics.[39]

In December 1952 Adolfo Ruiz Cortines, a scrupulously honest, conservative bureaucrat, was elected president of Mexico. His administration was sure to inspire a less hectic style into Mexican life than that of his flamboyant predecessor. Symbolic of this was the virtual disappearance of *cabaretera* films.[40] The new director of the

Alicia del Lago in *Raíces* (Pelmex).

Banco Cinematográfico, Eduardo Garduño, attempted to reorganize distribution by proposing the creation of six new firms for this purpose to be backed solely by Mexican producers. One goal of this proposed reorganization was to eliminate the problem of *enlatamiento* ("canning" or withholding a new film from circulation); new Mexican films could not be scheduled for public showing soon after completion because of the limited exhibition facilities and the competition of foreign films. The "Garduño Plan" also sought to limit the importation of foreign movies to 150 a year. The exhibitors (who were completely under the Jenkins thumb, especially after ex-president Abelardo Rodríguez sold his chain of movie theaters to the Jenkins group) were opposed to the scheme since it would force them to dedicate more screening time to less profitable Mexican pictures. This controversy, along with a strike against the movie studios and a dispute between Jorge Negrete and Mario Moreno for the leadership of the Asociación Nacional de Actores (ANDA), paralyzed the industry adding to the traditional uncertainty of business groups toward a new administration.

In 1954, 346 foreign films, mostly American, were shown in Mexico City and only 22 new Mexican films were released, even though national studios had turned out 82 movies in 1953 and 118 in 1954. This, however, was an unusual year and the number of Mexican films released in other years was more typical and in fact showed a very slight increase. But the withholding from commercial release of new movies made it more difficult for producers to recover their investments and consequently the amount of interest paid to the Banco increased, making their dependence on that state agency that much the greater. Finally on January 1, 1954, the Banco announced its reorganization plan by assigning distribution to three large companies it created: Películas Nacionales for distribution in the national territory; Películas Mexicanas for Latin America, Spain, and Portugal; and Cinematográfia Mexicana Exportadora (Cimex) for the rest of the world. Capitalization for these companies was provided in part by the producers themselves who were assessed 8 percent of their gross income to Películas Nacionales and Películas Mexicanas and 2 percent for Cimex.[41]

But growing state intervention simply increased the commercialist nature of the movie industry and production reflected the growing conservativsm of the middle class. For instance, more than half of the 1954 films were melodramas dealing with middle-class tribulations[42] and over thirty comedies were based on a new dance craze, the cha-cha. More and costlier movies were made in color and Cinemascope was introduced.[43] There was a greater number of coproductions with other countries — France, Spain, Cuba, and Venezuela. And Mexican filmmakers, seeking lower costs and more favorable working conditions, filmed outside of the country more than ever before. Even dictator Fulgencio Batista offered Mexican producers attractive terms in an effort to lure them to Cuba: 33 percent of the film's cost and generous tax exemptions.[44]

TABLE 1
NUMBER OF FILMS PREMIERED IN THE FEDERAL
DISTRICT, 1953–1958

Origin	1953	1954	1955	1956	1957	1958
U.S.	226	251	206	230	188	183
Mexican	87	22	85	84	86	100
French	21	33	39	36	23	33
Spanish	14	13	6	9	12	14
Italian	11	28	29	21	8	14
British	9	3	4	1	–	–
Argentine	3	2	2	5	–	4
German	2	3	2	2	4	9
Soviet	1	11	–	6	1	3
Others	5	2	4	1	9	5
Total	379	368	377	395	331	375

Source: Heuer, *La industria cinematográfica*, p. 63

The trend of Mexican cinema in the late 1950s was to make more "spectacular" films in color, to utilize new techniques such as Cinemascope, and to inject a rather hesitant eroticism into standard melodramas by the display of nudity. This policy was designed, on the one hand, to draw domestic audiences away from television

Left to right: Jorge Negrete, Carmelita González, and Pedro Infante in *Dos tipos de cuidado* (Azteca Films, 1952).

and, on the other, to make Mexican movies more competitive on the international scene.[45]

The basic problem was that as films became costlier and had to be produced on an assembly-line basis, there was ever-greater reliance on "formulas"—*comedias rancheras*; films based on dance fads—cha-cha, charleston, rock and roll; comedies; lacrimogenic melodramas; horror vehicles à la Hollywood; American-style westerns; and "super-hero" adventures in which masked cowboys or wrestlers took on a variety of evildoers and monsters. Quality plummeted but production increased. With the opening of the América studios in which all personnel belonged to STIC, the production of serials and, illegally, full-length films made originally as serials, increased. Thus "regular" productions were those movies made by STPC personnel at either the Churubusco or San Angel Inn facilities; regular films were also classified into "two-week" and "three-week" productions with restrictions on performers and running time.[46]

For instance, the all-time high in production was reached in 1958 with 138 films—116 "regular," 16 episodes, and 6 coproductions filmed outside Mexico. However, the year's only distinguished films were Buñuel's *Nazarín* and, to a much lesser degree, Ismael Rodríguez's "epic" of the Revolution, *La Cucaracha* with Dolores del

The veteran actors and brothers, Andrés Soler (left) and Fernando Soler in Alberto Gout's *Sensualidad* (1951). Two other brothers, Domingo Soler and Julián Soler, round out this distinguished cinematic family (Azteca Films).

Río, María Félix, and Emilio Fernández.[47] As if to signal the passing of Mexican cinema's brightest era, Jorge Negrete died of a liver ailment in a Los Angeles hospital on December 5, 1953, Pedro Infante perished in a private airplane accident on April 15, 1957, and Fernando de Fuentes died in July 1958 at the age of sixty-four. Also indicative of the state of cinema was the suspension in 1958 of the Arieles, the annual awards of the Academia Mexicana de Ciencias y Artes Cinematográficas. They were reinstated in 1972.

The evident qualitative if not yet quantitative crisis of the Mexican movie industry also aroused concern among the country's intelligentsia, especially in the universities. There had existed film clubs in Mexico since 1931 for the dissemination and serious discussion of worthwhile films from all over the world. The Cine Club de México was founded on July 26, 1950, and functioned throughout the decade, including Mexican films in its programs. The Federación Mexicana de Cine Clubs was created in September 1955 by various university-based and independent film clubs. These film clubs' activities were an important factor in the quest for quality filmmaking and in the formation of young filmmakers. Although their activities were necessarily restricted to a small minority, the film clubs would make an important contribution to the dialogue that was to emerge in the late 1960s.[48]

5

Decline, Renovation, and the
Return of Commercialism:
1960–1980

In 1958 Adolfo López Mateos was designated the PRI (Partido Revolucionario Institucional) candidate for president. During his administration (1958–1964), the film industry was to enter upon its darkest days. The new director of the Banco Cinematográfico, Federico Heuer, in an assessment of the film industry and the Banco's role in it, declared that "had the Banco ... not existed, the result would have been that all Mexican cinematic production would have fallen into the hands of foreign investors."[1]

Although many thought that the Banco's main purpose was to sustain a group of well–connected Mexican capitalists rather than to keep out foreigners from the film industry, it can be argued with equal force that growing state intervention had indeed preserved the industry, even if precariously, and prevented Hollywood producers and distributors from monopolizing filmmaking and exhibition in Mexico and the rest of Latin America. But producers of nonexistent social vision in combination with nervously conservative officials were to render the film industry almost totally unreflective of the problems and tensions of Mexican society.

The industry lost its most significant international voice when Luis Buñuel began making more of his pictures outside of the country, mostly in France. Others, like Alejandro Galindo, were reduced to turning out stock melodramas. Emilio Fernández was eventually boycotted by the producers and he lashed out bitterly at the industry, at one point claiming that it was run by Jews.[2] All in all, the outlook for the 1960s was anything but bright.

Under the administrations of López Mateos and Gustavo Díaz Ordaz (1964–1970), Mexico's contradictions reached unprecedented proportions. On the one hand, the continuing developmental policies resulted in impressive and continuous economic growth; on the other, this growth was made possible by protectionist measures that rewarded a small class of capitalists and entrepreneurs as well as officials of state enterprises. The result was a small and slowly expanding middle class concentrated largely in Mexico City but also to be found in other industrial urban centers like Querétaro, Guadalajara, Puebla, and Monterrey, and a huge unemployed and underemployed population that flocked to these and other centers in search of scarce jobs. Driven by want from their unproductive land and unable to find employment on vast, irrigated mechanized farms in the north, millions of these people found that the sophisticated, automated industrial technology of the cities could only absorb a small percentage of the jobless rural and urban population. Many of them gravitated to the northern border towns and thence into the United States, as Galindo had already dramatized in *Espaldas mojadas*.[3]

Yet these massive population movements and dislocations and the resultant societal tensions were largely ignored by the film industry which adhered more tenaciously than ever to its timeworn formula movies. Rising costs and collapsing foreign markets made the producers respond to the crisis in simple economic terms. Thus in a memorandum to the Secretary of Gobernación, the Dirección General de Cinematografía, and the STPC on August 17, 1962, the Asociación de Productores denounced the STPC's call for nationalization of the movie industry as a "magic formula to solve any and all problems." The statement went on to say that all that was needed was to cut the artificially high production costs (which were the fault of the STPC) and to maintain and increase the pace of production.[4] The government had previously stated its position, asserting that the "solution did not focus on resolving the problems of the industry, but rather of the producers.... We cannot aspire to improve the returns on Mexican films either in the domestic or foreign markets as long as their quality is not improved."[5]

The producers responded to this crisis by increasing production at the América studios which were staffed by STIC personnel and where costs were considerably lower. The films turned out there were ostensibly serials designed for television; however, their marketability on that medium was so restricted that the producers turned to combining the separate serials into one or more full-length features that were released to neighborhood theaters. One of these, which spawned a never-ending series that continued for decades, was *Santo contra el cerébro diabólico* ("Santo versus the Diabolic Brain," 1961) (El Santo was a popular wrestler); it made 125,000 pesos at its premiere in spite of its atrocious quality.[6]

Another gambit of the producers to avoid high costs was to film outside of Mexico where expenses were lower. An additional advantage of foreign filming was that by using those locales and local actors, the movies thus produced might recoup the evanescing Latin American markets. Two examples of these coproductions were *Rumbo a Brasilia* ("Enroute to Brasilia," 1960) and *Los expatriados* ("The Expatriates," 1963). In the former, a Mexican engineer (Antonio Aguilar), who is assisting in the construction of the highway to the new Brazilian capital, becomes romantically involved with a Brazilian girl (Angela María da Cunha). Together they help Paulo (Antonio Carlos Pereira), a young black boy, attain his objective of seeing the president to ask for help for his flood-devastated village.[7] *Los expatriados* was made in Puerto Rico and starred Luis Aguilar and Mapy Cortés, the veteran Puerto Rican-born actress. The film related the trials and tribulations of young Puerto Ricans who emigrated to New York. Obviously inspired by *West Side Story*, it transmitted its message by means of a plentitude of musical numbers.[8]

(Left to right), "El Santo," Emilio Garibay, and Fernando Casanova in *Santo contra el cerébro diabólico* (1961) (Azteca Films).

Mexican filmmakers ranged widely in the effort to find a profitable coproduction formula — they went to Puerto Rico, Colombia, Ecuador, Guatemala, and Venezuela. But such peripatetic recourses could not reverse the painfully clear trend: the markets for Mexican movies in Latin America and the United States were disintegrating. Economic and political problems in the various countries, stricter currency controls, and a general rejection by the publics of the steadily worsening Mexican product took their toll and the results can be seen in table 2.

TABLE 2
MEXICAN FILM PRODUCTION, 1958–1963

Year	"Regular" (STPC)	Serials (STIC)	Coprods	Indpnt	Total
1958a	116	16	6	–	138
1959b	84	21	8	–	113
1960c	90	22	1	1	114
1961d	48	14	6	3	71
1962e	56	24	1	1	82
1963f	41	30	10	–	81

Source: a *Historia*, 7: 8; b Ibid., p. 201; c Ibid., p. 325; d Ibid., 8:8; e Ibid., pp. 210–346; f Ibid., p. 348.

Augusto Benedico and "El Santo" in *Santo contra el cerébro diabólico* (Azteca Films).

The revolution in Cuba had eliminated that formerly important market since Fidel Castro's blueprint for a new society hardly included run-of-the-mill Mexican films. However, the new leaders of Cuba well realized the educational and political value of motion pictures and purposefully set out to create a new cinema that shortly would be eliciting the world's plaudits. Interestingly, one of the first efforts of this new Cuban cinema followed in the footsteps of the traditional coproduction relationship with Mexico: this was *Cuba baila* ("Cuba Dances," 1959), a joint effort between the newly formed ICAIC (Instituto Cubano de Artes e Industria Cinematográficas) and Manuel Barbachano Ponce, producer of *Raíces*.[9] A member of Barbachano Ponce's team, José Miguel (Jomi) García Ascot, unable to breach the STPC's Directors' Guild which as always remained shut tight to new talent, returned to Cuba to work on *Cuba 58*, a full-length feature in three segments. García Ascot directed two of the segements: "Un día de trabajo" (A Day of Work) and "Los novios." (The Sweethearts)[10]

Jomí García Ascot was a member of the Nuevo Cine group, an assemblage of young, generally leftist, critics, scholars, and aspirant filmmakers. The group arose from a series of conferences held in 1960 attended by such luminaries as Luis Buñuel, Luis Alcoriza, Carlos Fuentes, and the painter José Luis Cuevas. Although these individuals did not form part of Nuevo Cine, those who did went on to publish a magazine,

From left, Toshiro Mifune and Columba Domínguez in Ismael Rodríguez's *Animas Trujano* (1961). The eminent Japanese actor played a drunken and abusive Oaxacan Indian who aspires to be mayordomo of his village (Azteca Films).

Nuevo Cine, which in the seven issues brought out (April 1961–August 1962) carried on a lively debate with the "establishment" filmmakers and journalists and called for a renovation of Mexican cinema. The editorial board consisted of Emilio García Riera, José de la Colina, Salvador Elizondo, Jomí García Ascot, and Carlos Monsiváis. Others who became part of Nuevo Cine were: Rafael Corkidi, Paul Ledúc, Manuel Michel, Manuel González Casanova, José María Sbert, Tomás Pérez Turrent, Jorge Ayala Blanco, and Salomón Laiter, among a number of other individuals who were to become better known in the coming years.[11]

Even though the movie industry was stagnant and close to bankruptcy, there were hopeful signs in the early 1960s that filmmaking at some time in the future might yet be put on a more rational basis. For instance, ever since a long-forgotten effort during the Carranza presidency there had been no training facilities for young filmmakers. The STPC had never attempted to provide such instruction because the Directors' Guild was interested only in protecting the prerogatives of its members. Fernández, Galindo, Gavaldón, Bustillo Oro, and all the others had learned their craft

Ana Bertha Lepe and an unidentified actor in *Santo contra el cerébro diabólico* (Azteca Films).

in the early days when the industry was still open to all comers. Some, like Buñuel, received their training in Europe; others, like René Cardona and Tito Davison, in Hollywood's Hispanic movies or elsewhere in Latin America.

Aside from the cine-clubs or film societies, there was no place in Mexico where established or would-be directors could study in detail the works of the world's great filmmakers. But it was unlikely that a film repository would be established because of official indifference; and most producers cared not a whit for cinema as art or for its social or historical significance. Carmen Toscano, daughter of the pioneer filmmaker, organized a film archive in 1963 wholly on the basis of private contributions. It was called the Cinemateca de México. The organization petitioned President López Mateos for a subsidy and quarters in which to locate the archive. A part of the old Ciudadela building was turned over to Carmen Toscano but due to its decrepit state another location had to be found. The Cinemateca was finally placed on the third floor of the old Palace of Communications. In December 1964, shortly after Gustavo Díaz Ordaz was inaugurated president, the Cinemateca was forced to vacate its premises.[12]

Not all cinematic developments in the first half of the decade were as unpromising. A hopeful sign was the establishment in 1963 of a cinema department at the

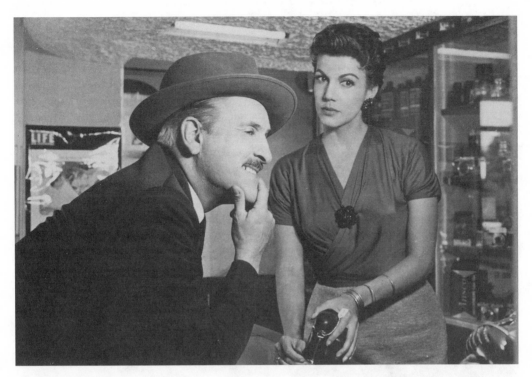

Arturo de Córdova and Elda Peralta in Rogelio A. González's *El esqueleto de lat señora Morales* (1960), a black comedy written by Luis Alcoriza (Azteca Films).

National Autonomous University of Mexico (UNAM); this department was called the Centro Universitario de Estudios Cinematográficos (CUEC) and was under the direction of Manuel González Casanova, one of the Nuevo Cine group.[13] Another encouraging development was the directorial debut of Buñuel's close associate and friend Luis Alcoriza with *Los jóvenes* ("The Youths," 1960). This film was a cut above the average movie about "rebellious" middle-class youth popular in this period, and Alcoriza in the following years was to turn out a number of well-made and provocative films.

García Ascot made *En el balcón vacío* ("On the Empty Balcony," 1961), an independent production that in spite of being refused distribution by the official channels was a great international success. Collecting money from friends, García Ascot gathered enough funds to buy a 16mm camera. A script was written by Emilio García Riera in three months of "long nocturnal sessions."[14] The filming itself took one year because they could only work on weekends since all the members of the crew had full-time jobs.

The film was based on the childhood memories of a woman (García Ascot's wife) wrenched from her native Spain by the Civil War. Even though she has reached adulthood in Mexico, the trauma of flight from her home many years before remains vividly in her consciousness. *El balcón*, as its makers called it, skillfully managed to see such shattering events through the sensitive eyes of a woman projecting herself back to her childhood and re-creating the little girl's (Nuri Pereña) sense of fear and

Nuri Peña in Jomí García Ascot's *En el balcón vacío* (1961) (Cineteca).

wonder as she observes the concerned adults about her making secretive preparations for flight. *En el balcón vacío* was invited to be shown at the Locarno Film Festival in 1962 where it was awarded the International Film Critics' Prize and won universal and enthusiastic praise while the official Mexican entries were all but ignored.[15]

Internationally, the best-known Mexican film of this period is Buñuel's *Viridiana* (1961). More accurately it was a Mexican-Spanish production since it was shot entirely in Spain and coproduced by Gustavo Alatriste and Uninci Films of Madrid. It starred the popular Mexican actress Silvia Pinal in the title role of the religion-obsessed girl who thinks she has been raped by her uncle, *don* Jaime (Fernando Rey, best-known to American audiences as the French drug trafficker in *The French Connection* [1971] and in Buñuel's French films).

In *Viridiana*, Buñuel developed all his favorite anti–Catholic and anti-bourgeois themes within a somber setting. The film was a huge artistic and economic success, except of course in Spain where it was not unexpectedly banned.[16] In 1962 Buñuel filmed *El ángel exterminador* in Mexico, which concerns a bizarre dinner party in which the guests, for no apparent reason, find themselves unable to leave their host's mansion. Alatriste was the producer and he again backed Buñuel in the latter's last Mexican film, the short feature *Simón del desierto* (1965). In 1965, Buñuel transferred all his filmmaking activities to Europe.

Buñuel's close friend and protégé, Luis Alcoriza, directed *Tlayucan* (1961), a study of small-town life which displayed Buñuelian symbolic techniques, such as the juxtaposing of a young couple with hogs in a comparison of their eating habits. In 1962, Alcoriza made *Tiburoneros* ("Shark Fishermen"), the story of Aurelio (Julio Aldama), a businessman who has chosen to forsake urban cares for the simplicity of a shark fisherman's life on the coast of Tabasco. The familiar theme was handled by Alcoriza with sensitivity and realism making the film stand out among the run-of-the-mill products being churned out by Mexican studios.[17] This "new" director gave promise of being a major talent, capable of making distinguished films if given the opportunity.[18]

However, one director like Alcoriza was not about to renovate the film industry. The STPC looked on with increasing frustration as the producers took ever greater advantage of the lower costs of filming at the América studios and the use of STIC personnel. As a consequence, the STPC membership confronted a serious unemployment problem as the production of "regular" films declined steeply.

In an effort to break the industry's impasse and influenced by the work of young university-based filmmakers, the STPC announced in August 1964 the First Contest of Experimental Cinema. All those aspirant cameramen, scriptwriters, actors, musi-

Julio Aldama in Luis Alcoriza's *Tiburoneros* (1962) (Azteca Films).

Julio Aldama in *Tiburoneros* (Azteca Films).

cians, and directors who would not or could not enter the industry got together and sought financing from friends, their own savings, or independent producers.[19] Thirty-two groups signed up when the contest officially opened, but by the time the films were delivered the following year, only twelve groups were represented with an equal number of 35mm full-length motion pictures.[20]

The entries were judged in July 1965 by a jury of thirteen persons representing the industry, various cultural institutions, and critics. First prize was awarded to Rubén Gámez's *La fórmula secreta* ("The Secret Formula"), a cruelly humorous probing of the Mexican's "lack of identity with himself."[21] It consists of a series of vignettes, some surrealistic, like the one showing a blood transfusion using Coca-Cola, and others brutally realistic, like the scene of the slaughter of a steer to the strains of spiritually inspiring music.

Second prize was given to *En este pueblo no hay ladrones* ("In this Town There are no Thieves") by Alberto Isaac. Adapted by Isaac and García Riera from a story by the famous Colombian writer, Gabriel García Márquez, the film traces the experiences of Dámaso (Julián Pastor), a small-town ne'er-do-well. One night he breaks into the tavern and steals the town's only billiard balls. However, once he has taken them, Dámaso realizes that the tedium of life in the village is completely unbearable without even the opportunity of playing billiards. He returns the balls but is caught.

A scene from Alberto Isaac's *En este pueblo no hay ladrones* (1965) (Azteca Films).

The merit of the film is in the directness of its cinematic language, although its slow pace is at times unnerving. The style if generally well adapted to the subject: the social examination of a small, poverty-stricken town where nothing ever happens. Dámaso is seemingly the only resident who dreams of better things, but is finally overcome by the stultifying inactivity of the town.[22]

The STPC film contest was obviously not a major event in international film history nor even in the Mexican cinematic milieu. It did not cause great excitement among the old-line producers who certainly did not perceive Gámez, Isaac, or any of the other directors as portending any "new wave." But the fact that such a competition took place at all and that it was sponsored by one of the industry" most sacrosanct institutions was significant and it pointed to the possibilities inherent in the future. A number of the individuals participating in the contest were in a few short years to become part of the industry.[23] The competition also symbolized the recognition by the STPC of the growing importance of independent, university-based filmmakers who had heretofore been engaged in literary pursuits, experimental theater, or film criticism, among these being Juan Guerrero, Salomón Laiter, Manuel Michel, Alberto Isaac, and Juan José Gurrola.[24]

The STPC was also no doubt well aware of the struggling independent cinema, especially after the international success of García Ascot's *En el balcón vacío* in spite of a boycott of the film by the official distributors and exhibitors. A number of talented people — directors, writers, photographers — were obviously being excluded by the cinematic unions' closed door policies, and the STPC itself was one of the chief culprits in this situation. But now that severe unemployment was widespread in the Mexican film industry, the STPC's voice was added to the many others that for years had been urging reform and renovation. Even though the Banco Cinematográfico in 1960 had bought out the Jenkins group's Operadora de Teatros theater chain, and also become the major stockholder in the Churubusco studios,[25] the same commercialist-minded elements still dominated decision making throughout the official film hierarchy. Thus independent films could not be exhibited in the commercial theater chains but were restricted to the film clubs and private "art" houses, making it impossible for producers of such films to recoup their costs, much less make a profit.[26]

Official protectionist policies failed to satisfy the producers, however. As Tomás Pérez Turrent summarized the situation in the late 1960s and early 1970s:

> Traditionally, these producers operated on credit from the National Cinematographic Bank…, inflating their budgets to such an extent that the loan, theoretically designed only to cover a percentage of the total cost, was enough or almost enough to pay for the whole film. To this was added advance royalties for distribution to some South American countries, and thus bad quality cinema became a sure-fire business with few risks. [27]

The tension in Mexican film circles in the late 1960s was generated by the conflict between the entrenched bureaucratic/business groups in the official agencies and the leftist, intellectual, restless "outsiders" being shaped by the universities. Aware of their country's problems and inequities, concerned by the cultural influence being exerted by Hollywood, these young filmmakers and scholar-critics longed for a cinema that would deal honestly with Mexican reality. They were familiar with the best of world cinema — Italian neo-realism, the French new wave, the new American filmmakers — and consequently the Mexican "packaged" cinema degenerated in their eyes to an "artistically irrelevant enemy."[28] They looked toward the "new" Latin American cinema, the now quiescent Brazilian Cinema Novo and the exciting and vigorous Cuban filmmakers, as well as to experimentation by such independent filmmakers as the Chilean Miguel Littín and the Bolivians Jorge Sanjinés and Antonio Eguino.[29]

On a larger scale, a restless resentment was growing among the country's youth, especially in the universities. In 1968 Mexico had been chosen as the site for that year's Summer Olympics, the first Latin American country to be so honored. The country's official and business circles saw it as an international recognition of Mexico's improved status in the Western family of nations, an acknowledgement that the world no longer looked upon Mexico as a "backward" Latin American republic but rather as a progressive, modern state. However, on the eve of the Olympics, massive demonstrations were organized against the administration of Díaz Ordaz. The results led to the greatest tragedy in the history of Mexico since the Revolution and to a bitter schism between the generations.

One of the origins of the student movement was resentment that a quarter-century of rapid economic growth was benefiting only a tiny minority of politicians, bankers, and businessmen. There was also growing middle-class irritation over the way the administration of President Gustavo Díaz Ordaz censored movies, books and newspapers, persecuted independent intellectuals, and summarily jailed outspoken opponents. In the eyes of many Mexicans, the system had become both economically and politically repressive.[30]

The students continued their ever-larger demonstrations, the date for the Olympics drawing closer. Díaz Ordaz and his minister of Gobernación, Luis Echeverría Alvarez, seeing Mexico's international prestige on the line, panicked — or perhaps decided to nip this opposition in the bud. The army was sent against the students and many innocent bystanders at the Plaza of the Three Cultures in Tlatelolco. In a night of blood and horror, over three hundred persons were shot down and hundreds more wounded. The carnage was little noted at the Olympic Village and fleetingly reported by the world press,[31] with the honorable exception of the Italian journalist Oriana Fallaci, who was caught in the midst of the massacre.[32]

Nineteen-sixty-eight was a pivotal year in modern Mexican history: the economic, political, and social tensions that had been building up since the 1930s exploded in this bloody confrontation. Many students became radicalized by the experience and some small, localized guerrilla movements were spawned. Some Marxist students tried to politicize the peasantry, although perhaps the best-known organizer of the peasants was Lucio Cabañas, a rural schoolteacher. When organizing efforts failed to produce the desired effect among the peasantry, some groups turned to urban terrorism. But more important than such sporadic violence, which had little direct effect on Mexico's political events, was an angry undercurrent persisting in Mexican society, especially among the youth.

The events of Tlatelolco gave a greater urgency to the antiestablishment filmmakers and, according to Ayala Blanco, a stronger independent cinema "arose on the heels of the politicization of certain middle-class nuclei as a consequence of the student movement of 1968."[33] But in the existing political climate, independent filmmakers, even if they could obtain financing from individuals or from university sources, still were up against the stone wall of official distributors and exhibitors. Thus it is not surprising that one of these "new" filmmakers, Alberto Isaac, directed the officially sponsored *Olimpiada en México* ("Olympiad in Mexico," 1968) and enlisted the services of other young filmmakers like Rafael Corkidi, Paul Ledúc, and Felipe Cazals who "had no scruples in collaborating" in the project.[34] The film itself, which was the "most favored, best-organized, and costliest made during the presidential term of Díaz Ordaz," was the subject of much controversy.[35]

On the other hand, the Centro Universitario de Estudios Cinematográficos (CUEC) at UNAM made its own unique contribution to the student movement of 1968. Being a small, relatively unknown department of the National University and located far from the centers of student activism, CUEC went unnoticed by the authorities. Its members decided to record the student movement on film, utilizing the raw film allocated to the department for its coursework. Leobardo López Aretche directed the project with the assistance of Alfredo Joskowics. So, while other departments and faculties in the institutions of higher learning throughout the Federal District and some of the states were being taken over by student revolutionary committees, the members of CUEC took action in the most effective way they knew: with their cam-

Rodolfo Landa (center) in *El tesoro de Pancho Villa* (1954). In 1971, under his own name of Rodolfo Echeverría, he was appointed director of the Banco Nacional Cinematográfico (Azteca Films).

eras. According to Ayala Blanco, *El grito* ("The Cry," 1968) is "the only objective record that exists of any popular movement that occurred in the last thirty years of national life ... [it] is in the final analysis, the most complete and coherent filmic record that exists of the Movement, seen from the inside and contrary to the calumnies spread by the rest of the mass media."[36]

The bitterness arising from the bloody events of October 1968 and the subsequent wholesale arrests of student activists and left-wing intellectuals were still widespread when Luis Echeverría Alvarez assumed the presidential office in December 1970. Since he had been head of Gobernación under Díaz Ordaz, many considered him directly responsible for having unleashed the army on the students and their sympathizers. Echeverría was never to overcome this suspicion on the part of the Mexican left, in spite of his openly pro-left and "Third Worldist" foreign policy. Although the ideological stance of his administration is beyond the scope of this study, it is necessary to be aware of it when observing the repercussions it had on the film industry. Unlike Díaz Ordaz, Echeverría was quite interested in films.[37] His brother had for many years been a well-known actor as well as Jorge Negrete's successor as head of ANDA.[38] In fact, Echeverría appointed Rodolfo Echeverría to head the Banco Cinematográfico and it was under the latter's direction that the state became directly involved in filmmaking to the almost total exclusion of the private producers.

In its cinematic policies, as well as in all other aspects of its program, the Echeverría administration was highly controversial. The radical left remained skeptical, even hostile, while the business community denounced the president as a Communist. Certainly there had not been a so apparently leftist administration since Cárdenas[39] or such an economically activist one since Alemán.[40]

On January 21, 1971, Rodolfo Echeverría proposed a "Plan for the Restructure of the Mexican Film Industry" in order to "renovate objectives and means during the six-year period so as to change the image of the national cinema, so deteriorated and maligned at the beginning of the decade."[41] In 1971, the state owned outright the Banco Cinematográfico, the theater chain Compañía Operadora de Teatros, and the Churubusco studios; of mixed public and private ownership were the distributors Películas Mexicanas and Cimex, and the promotional firm, Procinemex. Rodolfo Echeverría declared that "although this group of firms seemed to be sufficient to maintain the film industry in a state of equilibrium, their financial status was precarious."[42] Besides, the entire structure was maintained by the government "at high cost" primarily for the benefit of "a group of industrial or private producers — in their majority guided exclusively by the criteria of rapid recuperation and maximum rentability — who produced a commercialist cinema and took advantage of the established mechanisms, from the financing to the exhibition facilities provided by state firms." The result, Echeverría concluded, was a "false product, deformed and rejected by numerous domestic and foreign social sectors."[43]

Some significant accomplishments between 1970 and 1976 were the creation of a filmmaking school, the Centro de Capacitación Cinematográfica (CCC) — a dream of many cineasts since the days of silent movies in Mexico[44] — and nearby, the conversion of two Churubusco sound stages into the Cineteca Nacional, another long-deferred dream finally fulfilled. Here the historically important task of obtaining and preserving prints of commercial Mexican film production was finally undertaken with the full backing and resources of the federal government. In addition, copies of a wide assortment of foreign films were obtained for the benefit of young filmmakers and film students, both Mexican and foreign. The Cineteca consisted of two theaters open to the public, Sala Fernando de Fuentes and Salón Rojo; one 35mm private screening room, Salvador Toscano, for staff use and accredited researchers; and three private 16mm screening rooms.[45] In 1974, the Cineteca's holdings consisted of 1,476 films, including both 35mm and 16mm, full-length and short; by 1976 there were 2,500 films in its archives.[46] By 1976, the state was sole owner of the América studios, Procinemex, Películas Nacionales (which absorbed Cimex), and the only remaining privately owned theater chain, Cadena de Oro, in addition to many other individually owned movie houses as well as a number of new ones built by the Banco.[47]

The most important development of the Echeverría *sexenio* was the direct participation of the state in the production of films through three production companies. These were: Corporación Nacional Cinematográfica (CONACINE); Corporación Nacional Cinematográfica de Trabajadores y Estado I (CONACITE I); and Corporación Nacional Cinematográfica de Trabajadores y Estado II (CONACITE II). CONACINE was created in October 1974 as a branch of the Banco Cinematográfico and it served as a model for CONACITE I (June 19, 1975) and CONACITE II (May 8, 1975).

The Banco had been coproducing films with Churubusco-Azteca studios ever since the latter's nationalization in 1960, but the system was cumbersome and the decision was made to regulate production through these officially created companies. Besides, the almost total suspension of private moviemaking since the Banco's curtailment of credit to the producers necessitated the state's intervention if only to assure work for the thousands of skilled workers in the industry. In fact, thirty-nine films coproduced by the Banco and Churubusco between April 1971 and the time of CONACINE's creation were immediately turned over to the latter.[48] The activities of CONACINE and CONACITE I were similar, that is, they both functioned as sole producers or as coproducers with film workers, private investors, and foreign producers. CONACITE II worked exclusively with STIC and América studios.

Total production, both "regular" and "serials," totaled seventy-two films in 1970 (before the inauguration of Luis Echeverría).[49] In 1971, the figure was also seventy-two not including nine independent fill-length features and seven films made abroad. However, in comparison to the previous year's output, which was singularly undistinguished, 1971 saw the appearance of a number of interesting films such as Felipe Cazals's *El jardín de tía Isabel* ("The Garden of Aunt Elizabeth"), Rafael Corkidi's *Angeles y querubines* ("Angels and Cherubim"), Luis Alcoriza's *Mecánica nacional* ("National Mechanics"), Juan López Moctezuma's *La mansión de la locura* ("Mansion of Madness"), Paul Ledúc's *Reed: México insurgente* ("Reed: Insurgent Mexico"), Gustavo Alatriste's *QRR* (*Quién resulta responsible*) ("Who is responsible"), and Alfredo Joskowics's *Crates* and *El cambio* ("The Change"). Of course, there were still plenty of "package" films such as Miguel M. Delgado's *Santo vs. la hija de Frankenstein* ("Santo versus Frankenstein's Daughter") in addition to the regular fare of *comedias rancheras*, tearjerking melodramas, and "westerns."[50]

In 1972, the figure rose to seventy-five full-length features in addition to twelve "official" films such as *Cartas del Japón* ("Letters from Japan"), about a Mexican engineering student in Japan, *Historia del P.R.I.* ("History of the P.R.I."), *Tarahumara — Drama del pueblo* ("Tarahumara — Drama of the People"), and *Compañero presidente* ("Comrade President"), a documentary of Echeverría's visit to Chile. Although commercial production included such standbys as *Bikinis y rock* and *Capulina vs las momias* ("Capulina versus the Mummies"), there were also superior films like Arturo Ripstein's *El castillo de la pureza* ("Castle of Purity"), Gonzalo Martínez Ortega's *El principio* ("The Beginning"), José Estrada's *El profeta Mimí* ("The Prophet Mimi"), Alberto Isaac's *El rincón de las vírgenes* ("The Virgins' Nook"), Alejandro Jodorowski's *La montaña sagrada* ("The Sacred Mountain"), Mauricio Walerstein's *Cuando quiero llorar no lloro* ("When I want to Cry, I Can't"), and *Fe, esperanza y caridad* ("Faith, Hope, and Charity"), a film in three segments directed respectively by Alberto Bojórquez, Luis Alcoriza, and Jorge Fons.[51] These films were generally well received by the critics and, even if some were flawed, did at least explore new directions previously unsought by Mexican filmmakers; more importantly they were made by new directors supported directly by the Banco Cinematográfico through its production companies, an arrangement deeply resented by the old-line producers and directors.[52] Table 3 gives an idea of the scope of state participation in the film industry and the resultant lack of activity on the part of private producers.[53]

Top: Arturo Ripstein's *El castillo de la pureza* (1972) with (left to right) Arturo Beristain, Gladys Bermejo, Diana Bracho, Claudio Brook, and Rita Macedo. *Bottom:* Claudio Brook and Rita Macedo in *El castillo de la pureza* (Cineteca).

A scene from Alberto Isaac's *El rincón de las vírgenes* (1972) with Emilio Fernández and Alfonso Arau (Procinemex).

TABLE 3
MEXICAN FILM PRODUCTION, 1971–1976

Year	Banco &Private	Private	State prod	Total
1971a	63	7	5	75
1972b	34	8	20	62
1973c	26	4	20	50
1974d	23	10	21	54
1975e	13	7	23	43
1976f	–	5	37	42

Sources: a *Informe general*, p. 46; b Ibid, p. 49; c Ibid., p. 52; d Ibid., p. 55; e Ibid., p. 58; f Ibid., pp. 59–60 and *Excelsior*, January 19, 1977, Section Cine, Teatro, Radio y TV, p. 5.

The decline in production was a serious matter and was undoubtedly exacerbated by the Echeverría policies. True, better movies were made by young, often leftist directors but this was small comfort to the industry as a whole. Echoing the opinions of his conservative-minded colleagues, one long-time film executive placed the blame entirely on the Echeverría brothers, saying that the Mexican cinema from 1971 to 1976 was "tendentious ... and up to a certain point, procommunist." He blamed the Banco Cinematográfico for withdrawing credit facilities from the private producers and forcing them to use their own capital or seek backing from other sources. He concluded that under President Echeverría and his brother, filmmaking had a "communist slant, totally to please (Echeverría)"; that a film's commercial potential was of "no importance" and public funds were invested "to line pockets," presumably those of the Echeverrías and their cronies. As to films with a political or social message, this executive felt that Mexico's problems "are not political ... we go to the movies for entertainment.... Of what use could a Marxist idea be to the people?"[54]

While many of the preceding remarks are true, others are not entirely accurate. Production had been falling off since 1960 due to the effects of constantly diminishing quality and the producers' desire for quick profits on minimal personal investment.[55] Public monies accomplished this, since films were being financed up to 80 percent by the Banco Cinematográfico. Inflating the budgets was also common practice, so that the Banco's "80 percent" share actually paid for the entire film and left some over for the producer to pocket. This system was leading the industry from stagnation to ruin, a truth that did not require a great deal of insight to discern. The Echeverrías recognized the problem and tried to do something about it by backing new directors, as well as veteran ones, in officially financed films. Such films as Alcoriza's *Mecánica nacional* (1971), Alfonso Arau's *Calzonzín inspector* (1973), and Alberto Isaac's *Tívoli* (1974) were also more expensive, a fact that fueled the charges of massive corruption in the official film establishment. Such charges might very well have been true, since the system of official corruption was nothing new in Mexico. However, the money spent on these and other films was evident in their superior production values. The infusion of new blood in the directorial ranks was discernible from the controversial themes that these films took on and presented in a realistic, often raw, manner.

A precursor of such films was Alejandro Jodorowski's *El topo* ("The Mole, 1970), a confused, occasionally brilliant mélange of Eastern metaphysics and satire of the western genre. It also incorporated surrealist techniques borrowed from Buñuel and Fellini but lacked their humanism. Jodorowski's satire is heavy-handed and often sado-masochistic. The film was independently produced and for years was not screened in Mexico; however, it proved a great success on the underground film circuit in the United States and Europe. Jodorowski himself is Chilean by birth and has been better known in Mexico for his work in experimental theater.[56]

In 1967 he had made *Fando y Lis*, his first film, based on a work of the same name by Fernando Arrabal. With his cameraman, Rafael Corkidi, Jodorowski filled the screen with images of sado-masochistic and deviant sexual symbolism in an attempt to express his personal view of the universe. *Fando y Lis*, *El topo*, and *La montaña sagrada* proved heavy for popular tastes, but the possibilities that they illustrated

Top: Carmen Salinas and Alfonso Arau in *Calzonzín inspector* (1973) (Azteca Films).
Bottom: Alfonso Arau (center) starred in and directed *Calzonzín inspector*.

of making a filmic statement through the combined use of realism and surrealism was not lost on other filmmakers. True, the technique was hardly new: Buñuel had experimented with it in *Un Chien andalou*, as had many French avant-gardists and German expressionists in the 1920s. But Jodorowski's films showed how such techniques could be used to interpret the tensions and malaise of contemporary Mexican society, something that had not even been attempted since Bustillo Oro's rather timid experiment in *Dos monjes* ("Two Monks," 1934) or De Fuentes's *El fantasma del convento* ("The Phantom of the Convent," 1934).[57]

If a summarization can be made of the direction taken by Mexican cinema in the 1970s, it is that the new directors — Isaac, Cazals, Fons, Arau, Corkidi, Ledúc, and many others — were allowed the freedom to interpret controversial political and social themes. Some established directors like Galindo and Alcoriza took advantage of this climate to also make their own statements. In this they were assured by President Echeverría that they were "at liberty to bring whatever theme they wished to the screen, be it social or political."[58] There was disagreement whether a "new" Mexican cinema in reality existed. Alcoriza compared his colleagues with the initiators of the Brazilian Cine Novo and concluded that no such movement existed in Mexico.[59] Eduardo Maldonado, an independent filmmaker, opined: "None of the films which have been made within the new Mexican cinema truly respond to the necessity of analysis and critical interpretation that is required by the current social reality of Mexico."[60]

Any attempt here to analyze meaningfully all the important Mexican films made in 1971–1976 is impossible. The choice of the few films discussed is dictated entirely by the fact that this writer happens to be familiar with them and does not imply that, in his judgment, they were superior to others. Also, to discuss thoroughly the complex cinematic, cultural, and literary influences operative on Mexican filmmakers is too extensive an undertaking for this brief survey.[61]

Mecánica nacional (1971) was Luis Alcoriza's (1918–1992) most popular film, and his most outspoken.[62] Focusing on the urban lower middle class and their uncertain suspension between traditional, rural values and the anomie of a rapidly growing, modern metropolis, Alcoriza aimed devastating barbs at this group. He employed a number of well-known performers in roles that were veritable antitheses of their popular images. Manolo Fábregas, grandson of the famed Virginia Fábregas, and one of Mexico's best-known actor-producer-directors, played the role of Eufemio, a crude, stupidly *macho* garage owner.[63] The popular *ranchera* songstress Lucha Villa was Chabela, his equally crude wife, and the quintessential mother-figure, Sara García, did a grotesque parody of herself as Eufemio's mother.

Eufemio, his wife, mother, family, and friends set out in a holiday mood to catch the end of an Acapulco-to-Mexico City auto race. The women prepare vast quantities of food since the plan is to spend the night at an area near the finish line so as to observe the end of the race early in the morning. They set out in a caravan through huge traffic jams; a lot of horn-blowing and insults are exchanged with other drivers. The mass of cars finally arrives at an open spot and jams itself into the area so tightly as to make further movement impossible. The occupants of the automobiles, joined by swaggering motorcyclists, proceed to await the dawn by eating, drink-

Manolo Fábregas and Pancho Córdova (second and third from left) in Luis Alcoriza's *Mecánica nacional* (1971) (Pelmex).

ing, and indulging in as much sex as possible. Eufemio's mother gorges herself all night long until she is stricken by a massive attack of indigestion. The cars are so packed in that it is impossible to go for a doctor; finally one motorcyclist volunteers to go, but too late to save granny. She is laid out as if at a wake with her family and friends grieving around her. However, the announcement that the race cars are nearing the finish line draws the mourners away, including Eufemio and his family; granny's corpse is left alone in the midst of a sea of autos and litter, with just a dog picking at the garbage for company. The final indignity occurs as the weary racing fans start for home. Eufemio props his mother up on the front seat. When he gets caught in the middle of the inevitable traffic jam, word gets out that there is a corpse in Eufemio's car and soon hundreds of people leave their cars to gape at the body. A high-angle panoramic shot recedes from the mass of cars and people to the strains of a lusty *ranchera*.

Alcoriza had a Buñuelian disdain for bourgeois society in general and in *Mecánica nacional* he ruthlessly satirized the new Mexican middle class, those people who had recently begun to share in the country's economic "miracle" but in the process lost whatever cultural integrity they once had. To emphasize this, he shows two American girls who somehow joined the unruly group, exclaiming in English, "Why, there's nothing Mexican here!" Throughout the film, a young couple in white sports outfits

A scene from *Mecánica nacional* (Pelmex).

and driving a white sports car is repeatedly shown in brief segments. All they do is gorge themselves with paella, omelets, and various other dishes of Spanish cuisine until their at first spotless white outfits and car become a multicolored mosaic of food stains. *Mecánical nacional* was Alcoriza's interpretation of the structure of contemporary Mexican society — materialistic, uncultured, irrational, while responding in a semiconscious way to certain half-remembered folkways. A searing commentary, but evidently a popular one since the Mexican public flocked to the movie.[64]

Alcoriza's depiction of the "common man" was a far cry from the affectionate paternalism of Rodríguez in *Nosotros los pobres* and *Ustedes los ricos*, or even Galindo's expressions of working-class solidarity in *¡Esquina bajan!* of some twenty-odd years before. While Rodríguez idealized the poor in a static social system and Galindo showed the working class as intelligent and motivated if not radical, Alcoriza sees the children of the *lumpenproletariat* of the 1940s as being completely coopted by the worst of petty bourgeois values. Clearly no new Mexican revolution is possible from such as Eufemio or, even more tellingly, from the shallow, sybaritic young people of *Mecánica nacional*. Alcoriza seems to be saying that it was people such as these that looked unemotionally upon the Tlatelolco massacre and quickly shrugged it off. Fifty years of the official Revolution had succeeded admirably in depoliticizing an entire generation and convincing it that the consumer society was its inevitable destiny.

The theme of disillusion with Mexican society in the wake of Tlatelolco was continued in Alfredo Joskowics's *Crates* (1970), produced by CUEC, and *El cambio* (1971), produced by UNAM's Department of Cinematic Activities. *Crates* dealt with the difficulties that the militant students of 1968 had in trying to pick up the pieces of their lives in the face of government repression and society's indifference.[65] In *El cambio*, "dropping out" is what its young protagonists, an artist and a photographer, opt for. Disgusted by the materialism of urban life, the two young men escape to an unspecified seacoast. They build a shack on the beach and are soon joined by their girlfriends. For a while they enjoy a simple, bucolic existence, but soon the real world intrudes upon their reverie. Waste from a local factory is poisoning the fish in the surrounding waters, threatening the fishermen's livelihood. When the company's bulldozer flattens their shack, the young men decide to take up the local people's fight. They collect the sludge from the factory in pails and, at a banquet in honor of the company representative, hurl the liquid waste all over him and the local dignitaries. The youths run from the banquet laughing hysterically, naively seeing their act as no more harmful than a prank, albeit politically significant. The local lawman sees it

Felipe Cazals's *Canoa* (1975) (Cineteca).

quite differently—he hunts down the two city youths and shoots them down in cold blood. Clearly an allegory of Tlatelolco, *El cambio* is also a bitter commentary on the futility of meaningful change in Mexico.[66]

The most powerful and unsettling statement on the bloody repression of 1968 was to come in the 1975 CONACINE-produced *Canoa* directed by Felipe Cazals. The title refers to the village of San Miguel Canoa, a small community of seven thousand inhabitants twelve kilometers from Puebla. On September 14, 1968, five young employees of the University of Puebla arrived in Canoa intending to climb the nearby Malinche peak, a dormant volcano. A downpour forced them to seek lodging in the town. They were turned away everywhere by the hostile villagers until Lúcas García offered them his hospitality. During the night a mob of over a thousand townspeople formed, went to Lúcas's house, killed him, and dragged away the five young Puebla men. Two were murdered and the remaining three were savagely beaten, one having three fingers cut off by a machete blow. The mob was about to pour gasoline on the three remaining men and burn them alive when the army and Red Cross intervened. These events occurred in the tension-filled days preceding the Tlatelolco killings and they became the basis for a powerful film by Felipe Cazals, one of the new young directors who was able to work thanks to the Echeverría regime.[67]

Cazals structured *Canoa* in a documentary style with titles giving the dates, and then hours, of the events about to be depicted. In addition, a villager speaks directly to the audience giving socioeconomic data on the town. Thus the film provides a background and attempts an explication of the townspeople's behavior. Economic hardship, illiteracy, a lack of skills necessary in the increasingly technological Mexican economy, ancient superstitions, and official indifference all served to make San Miguel Canoa an isolated community, even though it was but a short distance from Puebla, one of the largest and most heavily industrialized cities in the country. An autocratic and obscurantist priest, aided by a fanatical lay organization, maintained strict control over most of the town, including the constabulary. The priest had convinced the townspeople that they were threatened by Communist revolutionaries from outside, and in fact shortly before the events described in the film a group of militant students from Puebla had been in the town trying to politicize the people. Thus when the five unsuspecting and completely apolitical university employees arrived in the town with nothing more in mind than an innocent weekend outing, it was a simple matter for the townspeople to suspect them of being Communist agitators "who are trying to place a black and red flag in the church."

Cazals develops his film against the backdrop of the momentous demonstrations in Mexico City. While the five university employees are making plans for their mountaineering outing, a radio commentator attacks the student movement, declaring "peace and progress means the Olympics." One of the employees feels that they should show solidarity with the students; his friend dismisses the idea, saying that they, as workers, have nothing to do with the movement.

Canoa is a skillfully crafted film, as well as a remarkable one in the Mexican context. It is nothing short of miraculous that the regime would permit, much less produce, such a statement on the events of 1968, especially so since at the time the incumbent president was widely thought to have been directly responsible for the

Felipe Cazals's *El apando* (1975) (Cineteca).

army's attack on the demonstrators. Of all the "new" Mexican cinema, *Canoa* is perhaps the finest example of the government's commitment — for whatever political agenda — to greater freedom for artists and intellectuals.

In 1975, Cazals also made *El apando* adapted from a novella by José Revueltas on prison life, which the latter based on observations he made during his own imprisonment. This is also a powerful, brutal film although not as well structured as *Canoa*. Nonetheless it is a compelling account of the degradation wrought by an unfeeling penal system. Three prisoners use their wives and the aged mother of one of them to smuggle drugs into the penitentiary. They are caught and the men placed in solitary confinement (*el apando*). At the end, they turn on their captors and are finally subdued in an extremely brutal sequence. *El apando* is most impressive in its images of prison life — the hopelessness, the corruption, the brutality — all presented in a starkly realistic manner.[68]

Emilio "El Indio" Fernández in 1976 (CONACINE and Procinemex).

Although young directors like Cazals were experimenting with topics and techniques new to Mexican cinema, it should not be forgotten that the old directors were still around. Emilio "El Indio" Fernández, his most creative days long past, overcame a boycott against him by most producers to make a few films like *La Choca* (1973) and *Zona roja* ("Red Zone") (1975). A shooting on a film location in Coahuila which resulted in the death of a young man for a time seemed to jeopardize what remained of his career.[69]

By the 1970s, Alejandro Galindo was the most respected of the old generation. His populist films of the 1940s and 1950s were still admired by the younger critics and filmmakers as being the most socially relevant cinema of the "old" Mexican film industry. But times changed for Galindo as they did for Fernández, Ismael Rodríguez, Gavaldón, and all the other veteran directors. The necessity of earning a living had obliged him to direct adaptations of television soap operas like *Simplemente vivir* ("Simply to Live," 1970) or children's movies like *Pepito y la lámpara maravillosa* ("Little Joe and the Marvelous Lamp," 1971). He made a populist comedy in his old style, *Tacos al carbón* ("Barbecued Tacos," 1971), which was generally considered anachronistic.

In 1973 Galindo made two films of which he was especially proud even though the critics did not share his opinion—*El juicio de Martín* Cortés ("The Trial of Martín Cortés") and *Ante el cadaver de un líder* ("Before the Corpse of a Leader"). The latter was a black comedy in which the chief protagonist is the corpse of a labor leader discovered in a cheap hotel. His death is due to natural causes, but once the news gets out, the room becomes a gathering point for the labor leader's friends, associates, and two women each claiming to be his legitimate wife. The official investiga-

A scene from Alejandro Galindo's *El juicio de Martín Cortés* (1973), Gonzalo Vega at left (Azteca Films).

Gonzalo Vega (foreground) in *El juicio de Martín Cortés* (Procinemex).

tion of the death is complicated by union delegations accompanied by brass bands paying their final respects in the midst of much speech — making, a rival union official making political capital of the situation, and a taco vendor setting up shop in the hotel room.

More interesting is Galindo's *El juicio de Martín Cortés*, a subject he had been considering for some years. Martín Cortés was the illegitimate mestizo son of Hernando Cortés, conqueror of the Aztecs, by Malinche, the Indian woman who was his invaluable interpreter as well as mistress. There was also a *don* Martín, Cortés's legitimate son by a well-born Spanish woman. In the mestizo Martín's story, Galindo saw the fundamental dilemma of Mexican society: half Indian and half European, Martín was suspended between two worlds, neither belonging fully to nor being accepted by either.

In *El juicio de Martín Cortés*, the action unfolds on a theater stage where a play on Martín Cortés had been presented. It seems that the actor who was playing Martín (Gonzalo Vega) identified so completely with his role that during the premiere performance he actually killed the actor playing don Martín. The police arrive at the theater with "Martín" to conduct the investigation. It is decided to perform the play for the police investigator's (David Reynoso) benefit. The film thus proceeds as a "play within a play" with the play's director and the playwright describing the historical

Another scene from *El juicio de Martín Cortés* (Azteca Films).

background of each scene about to be performed. As the play progresses, the tragedy of Martín Cortés, the mestizo, has a deep effect on the spectators. It is clear, at least according to Galindo, that deep racial antagonisms still tear at Mexican society. Even the police inspector, who at the beginning had declared that racial feeling could not be acceptable as a motive because "In Mexico there is no prejudice," becomes so emotionally involved with the play that by the time the pivotal scene comes up — in which Martín attacks his half-brother — he leaps to his feet yelling "Kill him! Kill him!" The police inspector is so shaken by his own display of a racial hatred he had not thought existed within him that he disqualifies himself from the case on "the grounds of being a mestizo." In Galindo's final, sardonic comment, a mestizo reporter in the audience is wakened at play's end — he had slept through the entire performance.

The film was not well received and was panned by some critics.[70] Galindo insists that Mexicans, though professing officially to be proud of their origins, really look upon themselves as the bastard off-spring of a symbolic rape. Some students in Veracruz, the director relates, upon being told that the film was the story of the "first Mexican in history," responded "Ah ... then he was the first son of a bitch."[71] Whatever the truth behind the nonacceptance of *El juicio de Martín Cortés*, it is a provocative and well-made, albeit somewhat complicated, work, possibly the only Mexican film that has attempted to explore the complex emotions underlying Mexico's racial composition. It might be that Galindo is right: perhaps Mexicans by and large do not wish to reflect on the problem, or even to admit that one may exist. If so, it is no surprise that *El juicio de Martín Cortés* was a commercial and critical failure. It may very well remain the only Mexican film to ever deal overtly with the country's racism.

Although the racial prejudice among Mexicans dealt with in *El juicio de Martín Cortés* did not have box-office appeal, films concerned with other types of social and political themes continued to be favored by the public. Gustavo Alatriste scored a resounding success with *México, México, ra, ra, ra* (1974), an outrageous satire of Mexican society that was enjoying a successful revival in late 1977.[72] Alberto Isaac dealt with censorship and the unfettered urban development of the 1950s in *Tívoli* (1974), which concerns the closing down by the Federal District authorities of a popular burlesque theater.[73]

Tívoli may be placed in the genre of *cabaretera* films although the action unfolds in a burlesque theater. The main thrust of the plot deals with a city administration working hand-in-glove with developers seeking to profit from Mexico City's rapid growth. The Tívoli Theater lies in the path of a grandiose urban renewal project and

A scene from Alberto Isaac's *Tívoli* (1974) (Cineteca).

the authorities decide to close it down. The main protagonist is a burlesque comic, played by Alfonso Arau, who leads his fellow performers in a futile struggle to save their theater. The film is also an exercise in nostalgia, since all the musical and comic routines are faithful recreations of those popular in the 1950s, and many of them had been performed by Arau when he worked in burlesque at that time.

Tívoli sparked a new generation of the *cabaretera* films, according to Arau. Among these movies are *Las ficheras* ("The B Girls," 1976) and *Muñecas de media noche* ("Midnight Dolls," 1979) which featured physically attractive but superficial performers such as Sasha Montenegro and Jorge Rivero. These films demonstrate the utter decadence of the genre: while Alberto Gout's *Aventurera* (1949) was imbued with both eroticism and social commentary, the new crop of cabareteras featured female nudity, soft-core sex, and puerile music-hall jokes. In spite of such flaws, these movies were immensely popular

Lyn May (left) and Alfonso Arau (right) in *Tivoli* (Azteca Films).

and garnered handsome profits; for instance, *Las ficheras* was being shown simultaneously in twelve first-run movie houses in Mexico City in the summer of 1977.

However, the cabaretera/prostitute genre in the 1970s was not all cheap eroticism. Felipe Cazals combined social commentary with realism in *Las Poquianchis* (1977), a disturbing film dealing with a true-life incident. Three sisters, "Las Poquianchis," kidnapped or bought young girls from poverty-stricken rural families to stock their brothel. Worse still, they resorted to murder to maintain control over the unfortunate women. In the late 1960s, the authorities finally broke up the notorious prostitution ring, although too late for many girls who had been murdered — or others who had been forced to become killers.[74]

Actas de Marusia ("Letters from Marusia," 1975), a major CONACINE production, received favorable attention from European critics, partly as a result of extensive international promotion, and was the only recent Mexican film to generate significant foreign interest.[75] The widely favorable response was also elicited by the fact that the director of the film was Miguel Littín, the famous Chilean filmmaker, creator of *El chacal de Nahueltoro* ("The Jackal of Nahueltoro," 1969) and *La tierra prometida* ("The Promised Land," 1973), who had fled for his life from the bloody coup that took the life of President Salvador Allende on September 11, 1973. Since President Echeverría was a close personal friend of the Marxist Chilean chief executive, Mexico generously opened its doors to many refugees from the Pinochet junta.[76]

A scene from *Las ficheras* (1977). At the center is Jorge Rivero with his arm around Sasha Montenegro. Lyn May is next to him (Azteca Films).

Littín was a prize catch for the Mexican movie industry, since he was internationally known and admired, especially in Europe where a good many filmmakers and critics are leftist.

    Associated with Littín's name, a Mexican film would be more likely to be noticed. And it was. *Actas de Marusia* was entered at the Cannes Film Festival where, Littín claimed, it came within one vote of being named best film.[77] It was also Mexico's entry for best foreign film in Hollywood's Academy Awards presentations, but it received scant notice from American critics. *Actas de Marusia* did well in Mexico, setting box-office records for a Mexican film.[78] The motion picture tells of a strike in Chile in 1907 against a European-owned mine. The army was called in to quell the strike and the entire town of Marusia was massacred with the exception of two miners who escaped to tell the tale. It was filmed in northern Mexico with six hundred extras, many of them nonprofessionals.[79]

    The Echeverría government's identification with international radical causes facilitated the resumption of coproductions with Cuba. *Mina: Viento de libertad* ("Mina: Wind of Liberty," 1976) was a CONACITE I/ICAIC coproduction directed by the Spaniard Antonio Eceiza. However, *Caribe, estrella y águila* ("The Caribbean, Star and Eagle"), a documentary that Alfonso Arau made to coincide with Echeverría's state visit to Cuba in 1975, was not released. The Dirección General de Cinematografía, the censoring agency, apparently felt that it would exacerbate political

A scene from Miguel Littín's *Actas de Marusia* (1977).

divisions within Mexico, where there was already much criticism of Echeverría's policies. Of course, since the Dirección General was unlikely to act on its own authority on such a politically sensitive issue, it was evident that the government wished to limit the degree to which it was identified with the international left.[80]

The Chicano movement in the United States was another subject seen as profitable by Mexican filmmakers in the 1970s. Mexican-American characters had occasionally appeared in Mexican films throughout the industry's history, albeit generally in secondary roles. Surprisingly, in view of the large Mexican-American moviegoing public, films dealing with subjects directly relating to their experience had been few and far between. Galindo, in *Espaldas mojadas*, was one of the first directors to deal at length and sensitively with the problems of Mexican Americans, but other filmmakers showed scant interest in the subject. The reason seems to be many-sided. There was the traditional Mexican disdain for *pochos* and the very real danger that a movie entirely devoted to Mexican Americans would not be commercially successful in Mexico and certainly not so in the rest of Latin America.

Spurred on by the black civil rights movement in the United States, ethnic and racial activism spread to other groups including Mexican Americans, some of whom, usually the younger and more militant ones, adopted the label of "Chicano." The Chicano movement gained strength first in the universities and then among some of the general Mexican-American populace. News of this new militancy on the part of

Mexican Americans filtered back to Mexico and aroused some sympathy on the part of leftist activists, since many Chicano militants also professed radical ideas. In time, some producers felt that commercial exploitation of the subject would be feasible. Pepito Romay directed the fist "Chicano" film, *De sangre chicana* ("Of Chicano Blood." 1973), which he claimed did very well in Los Angeles.[81] A few other movies followed: *Soy chicano y mexicano* ("I Am Chicano and Mexican," 1974), *Soy chicano y justiciero* ("I Am Chicano and a Seeker of Justice," 1974), *Chicano grueso calibre* ("Chicano Heavy Caliber," 1975), and *Chicano* (1975). Their small number indicates that they did not prove to be quite as popular with Mexican-American audiences as their producers expected they would be. Perhaps Mexican filmmakers had little understanding of the nature of the Mexican-American population in the United States.[82] Carlos Monsiváis characterized these films as a "series of catastrophes" motivated by the "growing importance and prosperity of the Chicano public."[83]

In spite of the opportunistic approach to the subject of Chicanos or Mexican Americans in general by the state-controlled Mexican cinema, the Chicano films suggested a type of coproducing with U.S. filmmakers in which Mexicans might make a contribution. In late 1977 and early 1978 Alfonso Arau was in the United States shooting *The Promised Dream*, a film on Mexican illegal workers but which never materialized.[84] A distinguished precedent was the 1953 independent film, *The Salt of the Earth*, produced by the Mineworkers' Union, which concerned a strike in Silver City, New Mexico. The cast included a Mexican actress, Rosaura Revueltas, who was deported from the United States for her association with the controversial film.[85]

Actually, there had always been some cooperation between the American and Mexican film industries. The fad for Mexico that lingered on for a few years after World War II resulted in a spate of generally mediocre Hollywood movies filmed in Mexico in the late 1940s and 1950s like *Sombrero* (1953), *The Bullfighter and the Lady* (1951), and the crowning disaster, *Pepe* (1960), Cantinflas's only starring role in a Hollywood movie.[86] Yet such foreign filming in Mexico provided much-needed work for Mexican technicians and extras, especially in the 1960s and 1970s when Mexican production fell off so sharply.[87] In the 1980s serious overpopulation and economic pressures drove millions of Mexicans to the United States. Cooperation between Mexican and American filmmakers might have resulted in motion pictures that would have fulfilled a vital role in informing the citizens of both countries of the mutual responsibility they shared in resolving these and other problems. To this end, perhaps the Mexican "Chicano" films as well as Hollywood westerns made in Mexico and showing it as a perennially undeveloped and violent land, at least demonstrated the need for something better.

Interestingly, the one "Chicano" film that did have artistic merit was written and directed by an American of Mexican descent — Jesús Salvador Treviño. The film was *Raíces de sangre* ("Roots of Blood," 1976) produced by CONACINE and filmed on location in Mexicali. It relates the efforts of Mexican Americans and Mexicans to form an international labor union to represent workers employed in *maquiladoras*, the largely American-owned assembly plants along the border. The film was well-made with realistically drawn characters and the cast included both Mexican-American and Mexican performers. However, since *Raíces de sangre* reflected Treviño's militant Chicano philosophy, commercial distributors shied away from the film and it was generally screened only within the university circuits in both Mexico and the United States.[88]

By the middle of the 1970s the Mexican film industry was in a precarious but still promising condition. The policies of Luis and Rodolfo Echeverría had brought mixed blessings. On the negative side, production of feature-length films was down to the lowest point since the 1930s. The frantic scrambling for the little work available had perpetuated the rivalry between the Churubusco and América studios even though both were government owned. This rivalry was fueled by the old bitter competition between the two cinema workers' unions — the STPC and the STIC — which continued unabated.[89] In the first half of the 1970s the industry was nationalized,[90] and among the most positive results of this was that the directors' ranks were opened to new talent, and films dealing with heretofore prohibited social and political themes were made. For many of these achievements, Rodolfo Echeverría (d. 2004), as director of the Banco Nacional Cinematográfico, was responsible. In addition to opening new directions for the industry, Echeverría traveled widely in the United States and Europe promoting his country's films and succeeding in awakening some international interest in Mexican motion pictures.[91]

The new administration of José López Portillo (1976–1982) reversed the cinematic policies of the Echeverría *sexenio*, although some films like Julián Pastor's *La casta divina* ("The Divine Caste," 1977) overlapped into the new administration. The transfer of power began, innocuously enough, with the customary resignations of

Ignacio López Tarso sounds off in Julián Pastor's *La casta divina* (1977), which depicts the Yucatecan aristocracy on the eve of the 1910 Revolution (Azteca Films).

Echeverría appointees; thus Rodolfo Echeverría handed over his post as head of the
Banco Cinematográfico to Hiram García Borja.[92]

López Portillo named his sister, Margarita López Portillo, as head of the Direc-
torate of Radio, Television, and Cinema (DRTC), a newly formed agency for the coordination of all government-owned production activities in the electronic mass media.[93]
As regarded the film industry, this was the first step in the implementation of López
Portillo's overall economic program to encourage private enterprise and discard
government-owned enterprises that were wasteful and inefficient. In the movie industry this meant the retreat of the State from direct participation in filmmaking and
the return of private producers.

Shortly after Ramón Charles, a self-declared enemy of official filmmaking, was
made the DRTC's chief counsel in early 1979, the Banco Cinematográfico was dissolved, its functions transferred to the DRTC, and its top officers, including García
Borja, charged with fraud and corruption. Reflecting the new state of affairs, the
Centro de Capacitación Cinematográfica (CCC) seemed to be facing imminent
demise as an independent film school.[94] Murky, semiofficial statements threatened
the CCC with merger with Churubusco studios or CUEC. In the midst of all this,
Bosco Arochi, head of Churubusco, was jailed on charges of fraud as were Fernando
Macotela, the studio's Director of Cinematography, and Jorge Hernández Campos of CONACINE, among others.[95] And in July 1979 CONACITE I was dissolved.[96]

These moves were the result of a sweeping reorganization of the film industry
in favor of the private sector initiated by Margarita López Portillo as early as July
1977. Her policies naturally caused alarm and resentment among those filmmakers
who favored a state-financed cinema of leftist-oriented social commentary — García
Riera reportedly called for a directors' strike to force the government to "respect ...
freedom of expression."[97] But such militancy aroused little support from filmmakers
who depended on the film bureaucracy for whatever work opportunities existed.

Regarding the above problems, Margarita López Portillo stated: "Any line of
social films is acceptable if they are made with talent. There exists a group of young
directors who work in cooperatives producing good things that debate problems of
political or bourgeois life — they do it well. I have faith in them, I am moved that
they want to change the world. Who has not dreamed of doing that at the age of 25
or 30?"[98] A propos censorship — "I detest the word 'censorship' — why not say 'supervision?'"[99] And continuing: "We will avoid the presentation of coarse themes that
poison the mind.... The people have the right to be respected."[100] And on official
filmmaking: "The State will not retreat from production because it will meet its
responsibility of producing a cinema that orients, educates, and entertains."[101]

Although such statements were hardly reassuring to antiestablishment filmmakers, it must be pointed out that the Mexican film industry had always been a business that had to make money to survive. When the state stepped in, as in the
Echeverría years, it was to try to revive a faltering industry as much as to use it to
bolster the regime. Luis and Rodolfo Echeverría encouraged a franker and more committed cinema because they believe that in this way Mexican films could find new
international markets. However, leftists apparently were neither a profitable nor

numerous movie audience and by 1976 Mexican production was at its lowest point since the mid–1930s.

After 1977 the financial health of the film industry improved, even though the organizational problems of 1977–78 caused a 13 percent drop in production.[102] However, the outgoing president of the National Chamber of the Cinematic Industry, Manuel Ampudia Girón, reported that "since 1977, average production has increased to 86 films per year ... an average rate of increase of 32.7% compared with the 1971–1976 period." As a result, from a total of 20, 602 workers in the film industry in 1977, "there was a 5% increase in 1978 [and in 1979], 18.2%—in only two years the number of workers has increased to 25,600.... The fastest growing sector was exhibition, accounting in 1979 for 75.4% of total industry employment; production employed 20.9% and distribution 3.7%. In 1978 private investment increased by 58%; in production this translated to an increase of 84%. By 1979, total investment in the movie industry amounted to almost 69 million dollars. Foreign receipts increased in 1977–1980 by 35.6%, from 10.4 to 14.1 million dollars. In the meantime real production costs, taking inflation into account, decreased by 60% in state-financed films in comparison with 1975 costs; private producers reduced their costs by 35% in this same period."[103]

This improvement in the film industry's financial ledger was achieved by a commercialist thrust that exploited traditional genres, soft-core sex, and whatever timely topics could be quickly taken advantage of. There was also a renewed emphasis on coproducing, a system that lessens somewhat the financial risk for the individual producer and assures distribution in the coproducing countries. Illustrative of the direction of Mexican cinema at the time was the election in 1980 of Guillermo Calderón Stell as the president of the National Chamber of the Cinematic Industry, an association of private producers founded in 1942 which became considerably more visible after 1977; Calderón Stell was the producer of successful *cabaretera* movies such as *Las ficheras* and *Muñecas de media noche*.

RE-AL Productions was described by *Variety* as "about the biggest Mexican producer making a product geared to the world market." René Cardona, Jr. wrote and directed *Guyana, The Crime of the Century* (1979) as well as an earlier film, *Survival* (1975), based on the crash in the Andes of a Uruguayan plane whose survivors, a rugby team originally headed for a match in Chile, had to resort to cannibalism while waiting to be rescued. *Hostages* (1980) was loosely based on the American hostage situation in Iran. Both *Guyana* and *Hostages* used recognized American actors well past their prime to ensure the widest international distribution. *Guyana*, for instance, starred Stuart Whitman, Joseph Cotten, and Yvonne de Carlo along with an international cast.[104]

Another significant development was the entrance of the giant conglomerate Televisa, S.A. into the film arena. Already exercising a near-monopoly on Mexican commercial television, Televisa initiated the television Spanish International Network (SIN) in the United States and retained a 75 percent controlling interest. In 1980, its film production and distribution subsidiary, Televicine Distribution International Corporation, bought out the Spanish Theatrical Division of Columbia Pictures. Columbia's disposal of this operation, which held 40 percent of the United States

Spanish-language market, signaled a new domination of the American Spanish-language movie and television market by Mexican interests. (Azteca Films, a Los Angeles-based distribution firm owned by the Mexican government, already had some 50 percent of the market.) Columbia turned over its entire Spanish-language film library of five hundred motion pictures to Televicine, as well as licensing its United States subdistrict rights to Cantinflas comedies which it produced and distributed worldwide.[105]

Televicine apparently was convinced of the market potential of the United States market by the box-office success of such movies as *El changle* (*changle* is Mexican slang for "shoe"; the reference here is to the footwear used by soccer players) and *La ilegal* ("The Illegal Alien Woman") (both 1980), which took in receipts of more than one million dollars apiece shortly after being released in this country. The United States Hispanic market was estimated at 25 million people and represented 40 percent of Mexico's film export sales. There were about 450 Spanish-language theaters in the United States that brought in $45 million a year.[106] These figures attracted the giant Televisa, through its filmmaking arm, Televicine, to the American scene in production and distribution for both theaters and television.[107]

The administration of José López Portillo played itself out amidst charges of gross mismanagement of the economy and unprecedented corruption.[108] As is well known, when Mexico's vast oil reserves were announced to the world at the beginning of the López Portillo *sexenio*, the country entered a period of such economic expansion that many Mexicans and foreigners felt that Mexico might finally join the ranks of developed nations. Foreign bankers backed up their confidence in the country's future with billions of dollars worth of loans, both to the Mexican government and to private firms. The dream burst with the collapse of oil prices in 1982. Mexico announced it could not service its foreign debt, thereby initiating an international financial crisis.

For the film industry, the national economic disaster led to further retrenching by the remaining state production companies although, as has been described above, Margarita López Portillo's reorganization of the film industry was initiated while the country was still riding the oil boom. The economic setback simply gave greater impetus to the ascendancy of private producers, one of whom implied the irrelevance of quality films to Mexican audiences thus: "The so-called art cinema is accepted and supposedly enjoyed by a select minority or elite, whose capacity to judge and profoundly analyze a film in all its different phases is the result of a long process of culturization, of refined taste, and a sophisticated mentality."[109]

The mass audience within Mexico (and the Mexican-Americans in the United States) had not yet developed such a capacity to enjoy quality cinema, or at least in the judgment of the businessmen who ran the movie industry it had not. If, as Marxists say, film can be used as a weapon to awaken the progressive instincts of a people and mobilize them toward meaningful social change or even revolution, a commercial movie industry was not about to knowingly encourage such a cinema. Margarita López Portillo's patronizing remarks about idealistic young filmmakers were ample evidence of official thinking regarding such a cinema and a reflection of the bitter taste that the Echeverría experiment left in much of the film community. The auteur cinema was left to the young filmmakers in the universities and film clubs during the López Portillo *sexenio*.

The figurative disaster that the López Portillo policies represented for quality filmmaking turned into a literal one with a tragic event: the destruction of the Cineteca Nacional on March 24, 1982. A fire believed to have started with an explosion in the Wings Restaurant located on the ground floor of the Cineteca completely gutted the three-story building with the loss of six lives and the destruction of over 6000 films and two cinemas. A specialized library of film books, thousands of documents, film records, scripts, and photographs were all consumed in the flames.

Although the fire was most probably of accidental origin, under the prevailing bitterness accusations of sabotage were inevitable. Margarita López Portillo defensively stated that "for two years I had been warning of the danger that the stored filmic materials represented."[110] She said she had asked that the storage vaults be lined with fireproof materials but that her request for 25 million pesos (about one million dollars) was denied by "high authorities" because of the country's precarious economic situation.

A chorus of indignation greeted her statement. Film scholar Jorge Ayala Blanco, director Marcela Fernández Violante, and historian Emilio García Riera among others decried the government's lack of interest in preserving the precious national heritage represented by the Cineteca. "How could they say there was no money while 40 million pesos [$1,600,000] was spent on a coproduction like *Campanas rojas* ["The Red Bells"]," exclaimed filmmaker Matilde Landeta.

Landeta's allusion was to an 80-million-peso Mexican-Soviet coproduction premiered with much fanfare on March 19, 1982, in twenty-five theaters of the Federal District. Directed by Sergei Bondarchuk (*War and Peace, Waterloo*) with his usual emphasis on epic battle scenes, the film itself was "pure and simple, an average motion picture, which barely manages to be decorous and acceptable, but are these sufficient reasons to justify the investment of millions?"[111] *Campanas rojas* is "allegedly about U.S. journalist John Reed's experiences during the Mexican Revolution" commented scholar/critic John Mosier. Referring to Salvador Toscano's footage which was collected by his daughter Carmen into a significant documentary and to Paul Ledúc's low-budget but excellent *Reed: México insurgente*, Mosier noted that "Bondarchuk does not seem to have seen any of these films.... Any resemblance between his Mexico and the real one appears purely accidental ... [and] marred by the presence of contemporary power lines and beer bottles."[112]

In spite of a litany of disasters and failed attempts, some filmmakers doggedly kept alive the tradition of good cinema in Mexico even though their efforts were hard put to compete against domestic *churros* and foreign, principally American, films.

Llámenme Mike ("Call Me Mike," 1979), was finally premiered in the otherwise dismal month of March, albeit in few and hard-to-find theaters "on the periphery" of Mexico City. Despite the niggardly distribution and promotion, the quality of this film by Alfredo Gurrola soon transcended its unfavorable exhibition conditions. It was an unusual case, "not only because it was a good Mexican film, released three years after it was made, but because it was also an excellent example of what can be done with a foreign genre — in this case the thriller — whose elements cannot be incorporated but still utilized in an intelligent way to make a good parody."[113]

Alejandro Parodi and Sasha Montenegro in Alfredo Gurrola's *Llámenme Mike* (1979) (Estudios América).

There was never really a Mexican *film noir* although some laudable attempts had been made, notably Alejandro Galino's *Mientras México duerme* ("While Mexico Sleeps," 1938), Julio Bracho's *Distinto amanecer* ("A Different Dawn," 1943) and José Bohr's *Mariguana, el mónstruo verde* ("Marijuana, the Green Monster," 1935).

But *Llámenme Mike* had some characteristics of the genre. The main character Miguelito (Alejandro Parodi), a narcotics cop, is an avid reader of Mickey Spillane's Mike Hammer novels. As a hapless victim of circumstances in a corrupt agency, Miguelito is thrown into a jail cell full of drug traffickers he had jailed himself. Beaten to the point of death, he is miraculously saved by a team of doctors. During the surgery, Miguelito undergoes a transformation becoming, in his own mind, his idol Mike Hammer. *"Llámenme Mike,"* he insists to everyone, until he's committed to a mental hospital from which he eventually escapes. Thinking himself the victim of an international Communist conspiracy, "Mike" embarks on a one-man crusade to destroy a gang of drug dealers against whom the police are helpless. Tellingly, they are headed by a character very similar to "Negro" Durazo, the spectacularly corrupt Mexico City police chief appointed by José López Portillo. The principal virtue of director Alfredo Gurrola and his screenwriter Jorge Patiño is that they transcend the Hammer mystique with a healthy dose of humor.

Gurrola and Patiño followed their artistic if not commercial success *Llámenme Mike* with *Días de combate* ("Days of Combat," 1979), also released three years after

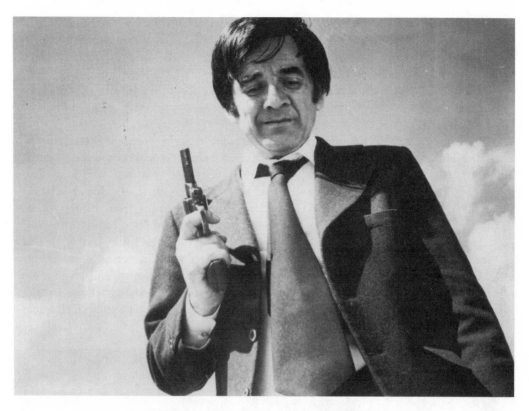

Alejandro Parodi in *Llámenme Mike* (Pelmex).

its completion. Based on a novel of the same title by Paco Ignacio Taibo II, the film introduces Hector Belascoarán Shayne (Pedro Armendáriz, Jr.), an engineer who abandons his profession to become a private detective. A plumber with whom he shares an office exclaims incredulously, "A private eye? In Mexico? You're crazy — I, on the other hand, have work."

Belascoarán is obsessed with capturing a strangler who is causing panic in Mexico City. Thanks to his detailed knowledge of famous stranglers of history, he is invited to appear on a television quiz show, and from that moment on he establishes a strange rapport with the murderer who writes him "...without me you're nothing, nothing, Belascoarán Shayne."

Cosa fácil ("Easy Thing," 1982), the second adventure of Hector Belascoarán Shayne, again played by Pedro Armendáriz, Jr., combines three distinct cases and plays with them in an intelligent manner. "Within the detective novel," explains Shayne, "every time that three cases were combined they would blend together until, at a certain instant as if by magic, when one was solved, the other two were also. I wanted to demonstrate the absurdity of the statement, what possible links could possibly exist between the death of Emiliano Zapata, the murder of a homosexual engineer, and the kidnapping of a showgirls' daughter?"[114] And, true, there is no apparent connection aside from the fact that all three incidents occurred in Mexico. As in the best detective fiction, Gurrola uses the genre to reveal the grave ills of society, its violence, corruption, and injustice.

A series in quick succession of three such outstanding state-financed films — *Llámenme Mike, Días de combate*, and *Cosa fácil*— by a talented director-writer team struck a bright note in an otherwise discouraging cinematic scene, particularly since both were graduates of the Centro Universitario de Estudios Cinematográficos (CUEC), UNAM's distinguished film school giving proof that some of the country's best young talent was being developed and given an opportunity to make films by the State.

Another bright spot on the cinematic scene was the independent filmmaker Jaime Humberto Hermosillo with his tenth feature film *María de mi corazón* ("Maria, My Love," 1982), adapted from a story by Gabriel García Márquez.[115] Filmed in 16mm, the film tells the bittersweet love story of a novice thief, Hector (Héctor Bonilla) and his former lover, María (María Rojo). Returning from a burglary, he finds María asleep in his apartment. She had just been stood up at her wedding and Hector was the only person she could think of going to. They fall in love again and marry. María uses her skills in magic to form an act with Hector as her assistant. María is a carefree soul who overwhelms Hector with her optimism and love of life. One day, however, María's van breaks down on the highway while she's on her way to join Hector in Veracruz for a performance. It is the middle of the night in a tor-

María Rojo and Hector Bonilla are the bride and groom in Jaime Humberto Hermosillo's *María de mi corazón* (1982) (Clasa Films Mundiales).

María Rojo and Hector Bonilla in *María de mi corazón* (Clasa Films Mundiales).

rential rain; finally a bus stops for her. It carries a strangely silent and sullen load of passengers. When the bus stops and the passengers get off, María realizes it has arrived at a mental hospital. She tries to use a phone but the nurses think she is one of the patients. The more María protests her sanity and insists on using a phone, the more obsessive she appears. One night she finally gets a call through to Hector but he hangs up on her, thinking she had walked out on him again as she had once before.

Hector, in the meantime, had sought out María's ex-fiancé who tells him of her erratic behavior. When a staff member from the hospital finds him, Hector thinks that María is really mentally ill. He visits her (dressed in his magician's tuxedo, as she had imagined he would) but makes no attempt to have her released. María becomes hysterical when he leaves. Is María really insane or has her unconventional and independent behavior been misinterpreted by society and by Hector? Or are the lovers being manipulated by a fate totally beyond their control? In this film, as Tomás Pérez-Turrent wrote, Hermosillo "once again ... demonstrates his unique powers of observation of the [behavior], customs, myths and values of the Mexican middle class, caught in their everyday moods ... at the same time, while appraising this seemingly banal everydayness, Hermosillo is also capable of penetrating beyond it to the fantastic, without any barrier to separate it from reality."[116]

Toward the end of 1982, a uniquely Mexican film tradition came to an end. "El Santo," the gold-masked wrestler who always kept his true identity secret, announced his retirement from the screen with his last film, *El Santo contra el asesino de la televisión* ("Santo Versus the Television Assasssin"). Santo was the Mexican superhero par excellence and his filmography exceeded by far that of Tarzan, James Bond, or Superman — more than fifty films in twenty-four years. "Symbol of justice, tireless collaborator with the well-meaning but inept metropolitan police, Interpol's agent in Mexico, sometime inventor of simple but effective crime-fighting devices, virtuous sportsman (he doesn't drink or smoke), a gentleman admired by the so-called weaker sex to whom he never submits, Santo is that and much more."[117]

Throughout his film career, Santo would combat all manner of monsters, vampires, werewolves, witches, newly resuscitated vampires, mummies (preferably from Guanajuato); he would struggle against extraterrestrials (Martians or assassins from other worlds) or against mad scientists, maniacal stranglers, evil geniuses, graverobbers, international smugglers, kidnappers, secret bands of assassins, the underworld, and other unusual delinquents. Santo was lord and master of all the cardboard sets through which he battled assorted villains, using the latest plastic toys with flashing lights as if they were ultramodern devices. The king of kitsch and unintentional humor, Santo became a wholesome camp figure with a huge following among both adults and children. His films reinforced each other over the years, amounting to a single Mexican-style fairy tale of good versus evil played out on the wrestling mat.[118]

Santo inspired a multitude of other wrestling superheroes who never quite gained the public's acceptance as he did. No sooner had Santo's retirement been announced than a film tribute to him appeared: José Buil's *Adiós, adiós, ídolo mío* ("Farewell, Farewell My Idol"). An aging and arthritic Santo lives on his pension with his faithful servant and her little girl who dresses as Batman. The producers who grew rich from his films disdain him because he's "old and fat." The public, which once adored him, now prefers Superman, Wonder Woman, and the other transnational superheroes that infest the media.[119]

Nonetheless Mexican film production in the closing days of Margarita López Portillo's tenure was in a sorry state. So troubling was the situation that the great photographer Gabriel Figueroa spoke out bitterly during an awards ceremony for independent filmmakers: "The cinema of B-girls, prostitutes, and obscene language should be exhibited only after midnight. The current *sexenio* has been the most disastrous for the national film industry, because all the themes were oriented toward that type of story. Undoubtedly, the future of the commercial Mexican cinema has to take more positive directions, since it is not possible to continue any longer with such themes, which have only succeeded in further reducing the markets for our films."[120]

Tomás Pérez-Turrent echoed Figueroa's statements: "Mexican cinema has not reached such a low level in several decades. Cheap cinema, with no artistic or cultural ambitions, a repetition of the oldest and most time-worn formulas, subpornography, facile folklore, routine melodramas, films aimed at manipulating the emotions and frustrations of the lower strata of the population and the nostalgia of Mexicans and of those of Mexican descent in the United States (presently the so-called Spanish markets of the United States are fundamental to the financial stability of the film industry)." And Pérez-Turrent concluded, echoing the director Antonio Bardem's famous phrase about Spanish cinema at the Salamanca talks of 1955, "the resulting cinema is industrially feeble, socially useless, culturally nil, and aesthetically impoverished."[121]

It was apparent to all that the cinema industry was aesthetically very ill and there was no shortage of physicians offering remedies to the patient.[122] However, close to one hundred films were made in 1982 providing steady employment for studio workers. The role of the state as a cultural arbiter was much discussed: what type of official intervention would be prudent in a situation like that existing in 1982 when "quality" state-sponsored film production was practically nil and movies of abysmal quality made by private producers were thriving?

The advice was of course being proffered for the incoming administration of Miguel de la Madrid, but the film industry had a low priority in the agenda of a government that faced the most acute economic crisis in fifty years. The state, ideally, should guarantee jobs for workers in the industry and, at the same time, exert a counter influence when commercialism and popular fads result in a surplus of undesirable film topics. It was proposed that legislation should also guarantee work for filmmakers trained in the state's own training centers such as CUEC and the Centro de Capacitación Cinematográfica (CCC). "Training a filmmaker is more costly than training a cardiologist and all the money spent on this training will be thrown out the window if the filmmaker cannot find work in the industry."[123]

These were some of the sweeping proposals for a new cinematic law that many thought was long overdue and should be enacted under the new administration. The existing cinematic law dated from 1949 and its most famous provision, that theaters throughout Mexico should screen national films 50 percent of the time, had been almost wholly ignored from the moment it became law. A new law (never legislated under De la Madrid) would seemingly provide "cradle to grave" security for Mexican filmmakers; censorship would protect public morals and family values but not arbitrarily prohibit themes of political or social criticism; clean, comfortable theaters would be guaranteed for the showing of Mexican films as well as adequate promotion.[124]

Other ideas that began to surface at this time were how to utilize television and the mass audience it commanded as a medium for disseminating the cinema. Related to this was the unanticipated videocassette revolution which in the coming years spread throughout Mexico as it would in many other countries.[125] Another idea advanced at this time was to create a secretariat or ministry of culture under which all cinematic activities would be placed.

As the inauguration of Miguel de la Madrid approached, there was apprehension at the uncertain future faced by a nation in financial crisis. But in the film community there was hope — as there always is at the beginning of a new *sexenio*— for new policies, new ideas, and perhaps new opportunities.

Lamented Salomón Laiter, as so many others had, "We are a people rich in cultural traditions. Why are they not reflected in our film theaters?"[126]

6

"To Rebuild a Ruined Cinema in a Ruined Country": 1981–1989

Alberto Isaac uttered those unsettling words on what was actually a rather optimistic occasion: his appointment on March 25, 1983, as director of the newly created Mexican Cinema Institute (Instituto Mexicano de Cinematografía — IMCINE). Isaac's assumption of the post struck a hopeful chord in a largely disillusioned film community which hoped that, by turning over the reins of the official film agency to one of Mexico's most respected directors instead of to a career bureaucrat, a sea change had occurred in the official attitude toward the film industry. Coming on the heels of Margarita López Portillo's disastrous tenure during the previous administration, it was hoped that the new *sexenio* of Miguel de la Madrid would open the way to the long-awaited resurgence of quality cinema.

Isaac, director of over fifty short features and eight full-length films, among them *Tívoli* and *El rincón de las vírgenes*, had been blacklisted by the previous administration for publicly criticizing the investment of half a million dollars in the U.S. production of *Superman*. An infuriated Margarita López Portillo forced him out of his post as director of the Organización Editorial Mexicana. "I paid dearly ... I was totally boycotted," explained Isaac. "They threw me out in the street, I lost two films, one already under contract and the other verbally agreed to; I lost my jobs on *El Sol* and *Esto*."[1]

Isaac's experience was the most extreme instance of what other directors who had established distinguished reputations between 1970 and 1976 had had to go through in the post–Echeverría period. Only Arturo Ripstein managed to continue making films with some regularity while others, such as Felipe Cazals, "[had] been obliged to make films in three weeks, productions of no interest, dedicated to some singing idol; others [worked] for television; and others [made television commercials]."[2]

The new Mexican Cinema Institute brought under its fold the state production companies CONACINE and CONACITE II, the documentary film center, the

Churubusco-Azteca and América studios, the State-owned promotion, distribution, and exhibition companies, and the film school, Centro de Capacitación Cinematográfica (CCC). At the time of his appointment, Isaac was optimistic that this reorganization signaled the beginning of renewed official support for the film industry.

However, within a year, Isaac had resigned to return to what he liked to do best — directing films, but the frustration of dealing with a bureaucracy in the throes of economic crisis was also a contributing factor. His principal achievement was to organize the Third Contest of Experimental Cinema in 1985[3] which served to reveal the talents of Alberto Cortés with *Amor a la vuelta de la esquina* ("Love Around the Corner") in which he demythifies the genre of the cinema of prostitutes, and Diego López's political melodrama *Crónica de familia* ("Family Chronicle"). Shortly

Alberto Isaac (1925–1998)

after this event, Isaac resigned over a jurisdictional conflict with the State exhibition agency COTSA (Compañía Operadora de Teatros, S.A.), and his successor Enrique Soto Izquierdo failed to continue Isaac's policy of seeking new avenues of dissemination for the cinema.[4]

Still, some filmmakers expressed optimism for the new *sexenio*, even if only because the film industry's condition had deteriorated to such an extent that any change had to be for the better. Said Sergio Olhovich: "The economic crisis should have a favorable effect on the film industry. We have first-class ... directors, writers, actors — we have an impressive capability for exhibition, over 2,500 theaters throughout the country, both commercial and art houses, in addition to excellent laboratories."[5]

Another director, José Estrada, was more guarded: "I think the panorama is quite bleak ... I suspect there won't be much funds to play around with for cinema.... Therefore we filmmakers will have to dream up new projects involving novel production schemes."[6] Olhovich stated, "A strong nation should not fear creative works. One film is not going to cause a revolution.... Another important goal is to decentralize production; films should be made all over the country so new filmmakers can be trained outside of the capital." But the most important goal, continued Olhovich, was to "consolidate a cinematic policy that would be independent of political changes every six years."[7]

One way of achieving this, according to Estrada, was to remove the film industry from under the jurisdiction of the Secretaría de Gobernación (equivalent to the U.S. Department of the Interior). "The very fact that the cinema is governed by that ministry, which is charged with internal security, means that they approach filmmaking as a potentially subversive activity, converting Gobernación into a police agency.... We'll have to lobby to have the Dirección de Cinematografía transferred to the Ministry of Education so that the cinema can finally be administered as a cultural activity."[8] Although this was not to occur under the administration of Miguel de la Madrid, IMCINE, charged with fomenting quality cinema, would finally be merged in early 1989 with a newly created Council for Culture and the Arts under the Ministry of Public Education.

Symbolizing the gap between the present state of Mexican cinema and what it had once been was the loss of two of its most distinguished figures. On April 11, 1983, Dolores del Río died in La Jolla, California, of chronic hepatitis. Although only 19 of her 56 films were Mexican, Dolores del Río's collaboration with Emilio "El Indio" Fernández, Gabriel Figueroa, and Pedro Armendáriz resulted in two classic works of Mexican cinema, *Flor silvestre* and *María Candelaria* (both 1943), and a long list of distinguished subsequent films. Her influence was "very great and much time would pass before another star of her magnitude would arise. Her death [deprived] Mexican cinema of one of the great figures that gave it an international reputation during its golden age." Her last film was *The Children of Sanchez* (1978) in which she costarred with Anthony Quinn; afterward she dedicated all her time to working with disadvantaged children.[9]

The second great loss to the Mexican and international film world was the death at the age of 83 of Luis Buñuel on July 29, 1983, in Mexico City. Buñuel's Mexican films have been discussed earlier and in many other books and articles, and certainly no final assessment is called for here. More appropriate, perhaps, would be some thoughts on the relationship between Buñuel and his adoptive country. According to British critic Michael Wood, Buñuel, in spite of his Mexican citizenship, was "not really a Mexican ... one cannot become a Mexican ... [it] is a shy, secret country, and even the eloquent diagnoses of its quirks and ills by gifted natives like Octavio Paz and Carlos Fuentes tend to deepen the mystery rather than abolish it. For this reason it is essential to avoid all bland conclusions on the subject." As Wood wrote:

> Mexico gave Buñuel a home when he needed one, reunited him with friends, returned him to his language, and offered him more of those stark, dry landscapes which are so much a part of his visual kingdom. The rocks of Majorca modulate into Mexican boulders; the aridity of *Land Without Bread* stalks the villages of *Nazarín*. But above all, perhaps, Mexico [allowed] Buñuel to practice being no one, like Odysseus, and nourished his secret personality and his ability to be everywhere, like those nameless streets. Mexico represents neither a displaced Spain nor a cozy cosmopolitanism. It is the perfect, strenuous, uninvaded exile which opens out on to nothing less than the infinite particulars of the world.[10]

And Buñuel himself commented:

> It must also be said that Mexico is a genuine country whose inhabitants are animated by one impulse, a desire for learning and to better themselves, that is rarely encountered

elsewhere. Add to that an extreme amiability, friendship, and hospitality that have made of Mexico, from the Spanish Civil War to Pinochet's coup d'etat in Chile, a country of safe haven.[11]

It is perhaps these qualities of the Mexican people, which have not always gone unnoticed by foreign observers, that will enable the society to ameliorate if not totally solve its numerous problems. And the film community, as a microcosm of the attitudes, opinions, ideologies, and problems facing the nation as a whole, continued to vigorously debate questions of national identity, morality, and purpose in the pages of periodicals, in assorted gatherings, and through films themselves. As one observer commented, "The situation of Mexican cinema is similar to that which exists in the country, and we will extricate ourselves from that trap only on the basis of work and the cooperation of everyone."[12]

State production, which had been reduced to just four films in 1982, the last year of the López Portillo administration, showed an encouraging increase in 1983–84. Still, the attempt to gain international prestige and commercial success remained elusive: *Antonieta*, coproduced with Spain and directed by Carlos Saura, "failed completely"[13] just as *Campanas rojas* had in 1982.

Independent filmmaking, however, increased: thirteen films were made in 1982, among them *El día que murió Pedro Infante* ("The Day Pedro Infante Died") by Claudio Isaac (Alberto Isaac's son) and *Nocaut* ("Knockout") by José Luis García Agraz. Although the State produced little, "partly because of the country's economic crisis, and partly as a continuation of the tendencies of the previous administration," it was showing an inclination to sponsor films produced outside of the industry such as *Nocaut* and the highly praised *Vidas errantes* ("Wandering Lives," 1983) by CCC graduate Juan de la Riva.[14]

Claudio Isaac's loosely biographical and intensely personal *El día que murió Pedro Infante* is an unpretentious but well-crafted film that follows the personal and professional frustrations of a young writer. The title stems from the fact that the principal character, Pablo (Humberto Zurita), was born in 1957 on the day that Pedro Infante, the popular movie and singing idol, was killed in a plane crash. Reportedly, the title attracted many people who were then disappointed to discover that the story had nothing to do with Pedro Infante (except for a few brief newsreel sequences of his funeral, in the film's last scene). The film is about Pablo's efforts to publish his second novel while attempting to rekindle a love affair with Teresita (Beatriz Marín). In neither endeavor is he successful. The State-supported firm which had published his first novel now has a new management emplaced by the new government; the editor (Pedro Armendáriz, Jr.) is a bureaucrat incapable of understanding the novel's philosophical implications. Instead he suggests that the writer produce a work based on a theme and outline provided by the editor—a proposal that is contemptuously rejected by the young writer. This simple yet sensitively done film manages to express the frustrations and ennui of educated middle-class youths in a society that offers them few choices.

Nocaut was a promising first effort that told the story of Rodrigo (Gonzalo Vega), a boxer who murders his promoter, a notorious drug dealer. At the urging of Beltrán

(Wolf Rivinskis), the promoter/gangster, he had given up a slot on the Olympic squad to turn professional. Rodrigo's resentment is more than justified. Beltrán's insistence that Rodrigo fight without allowing an eye injury to heal effectively ruins the young pugilist's career and he is then reduced to throwing fights. Done in *film noir* technique, the film unfolds in two temporal currents: in the present, as Rodrigo tries to elude pursuing thugs and police, and in the past, reconstructing in flashbacks the events that have led to his present predicament.

For forty-eight hours, he desperately seeks to lose himself in Mexico City managing to avoid assorted dangers and betrayals. Rodrigo's luck finally runs out, and he is cornered by the murderous thugs — the final, and deadliest, "*nocaut*." García Agraz "demonstrates an ability to tell a story with verve, to create an atmosphere, enabling Mexico City, especially the city at night, to become an important character in the film.... [He] constructs solid, life-like characters and establishes relations between them with a few strokes."[15] If any criticism can be leveled at the film it is that it is probably longer than it need be, and the flashbacks at times become confusing. However, for a first effort the film was impressive and again demonstrated the caliber of training being offered in the publicly supported film schools, in this case the CUEC.

Vidas errantes (*Wandering Lives*) was also a highly praised first effort by a graduate of the CCC. The favorable reactions it has received from many quarters place *Vidas errantes* among the finest examples of recent Mexican cinema. Although completed in 1984, it was not released commercially until the following year. A joint production between CONACINE and a private cooperative, it was one of the first accomplishments of IMCINE. "A reflection of the cinema, within the cinema," this film relates the life of Francisco (José Carlos Ruiz) and his young assistant, Guillermo (Ignacio Guadalupe). Francisco is a peripatetic film exhibitor who travels the Durango countryside in his van, setting up screenings in the most remote villages. *Vidas errantes* is a tribute to the old Mexican cinema, "considerably superior to the average film of today." Fernando has a deep love for movies and he represents those dedicated souls who disseminated Mexican films to the farthest corners of the country. The tragic scene of the fire that destroys Francisco's impromptu theater "can be considered an allegory of the tragedy of the Cineteca, and a moral that even if the dreams and hopes of an entire life are lost because of one person's carelessness, one always has to rise again and continue the struggle for a better life, and a better cinema."[16]

On January 27, 1984, the new home of the Cineteca Nacional was inaugurated. The attractive facility, formerly a small shopping center with four theaters, was purchased from the Society of Composers and Writers and is located on México-Coyoacán Avenue just north of Río Churubusco. Situated around an inner courtyard that insulates it from the noise, pollution, and traffic of the busy thoroughfare outside, the Cineteca complex consists of the administrative offices of the Dirección de Cinematografía, a library, a bookstore, an archive of photographs (many rescued from the old Cineteca and still bearing burn marks), a gallery for cinema-related exhibits, the Documentation and Research Department, and the four theaters: "Jorge Stahl," for double features and children's programs; "Salvador Toscano," for international film weeks and film retrospectives based on different themes — directors, subjects, actors, and others; "Fernando de Fuentes," for foreign films; and "Arcady Boytler," for advance screenings and revivals of Mexican films.[17]

On January 16, 1987, financial administration of the Cineteca was transferred from the Banco Cinematográfico (itself in the process of being dissolved) to the Banco Nacional de Obras y Servicios (BANOBRAS) in keeping with President de la Madrid's instructions for "maintaining Mexican cinema as a living testament of quality of the national culture, and also as a source of employment that can expand and increase its productivity." At that time, the Cineteca had in its archive (now in securely fireproof vaults) 2,968 films in both 35mm and 16mm of which 60 percent, or 1770, were Mexican. The library had more than seven thousand volumes and six thousand film periodicals. The four theaters had projected, since 1984, an annual average of 4,700 screenings. The Cineteca had also published fourteen monographs and owned some 1800 videos.[18]

Such tangible developments seemed to indicate the beginnings of greater, though still far from copious, official support for a revitalization of the film industry. Earlier, in four conferences held from August 6 to 13 in the Secretaría de Gobernación, all sectors of the industry presented their suggestions and wish lists. Churubusco studios said it needed funds to modernize and maintain its equipment; STPC and STIC pledged to support private producers committed to quality; the producers and distributors complained that their product was screened in the less desirable theaters while foreign films enjoyed the first-class houses; and the cooperatives insisted (again!) that 50 percent of screen time be reserved for national films in all the country's theaters.[19]

In 1985 four films were released that seemed to highlight both the potential of Mexican cinema and the commercialist tradition of profitable *churros* (low-quality potboilers) that showed no sign of going away because of their popularity with the great majority of the Mexican public.

Paul Ledúc's *Frida, naturaleza viva* ("Frida, live nature") produced by Manuel Barbachano Ponce, was a serendipitous combination of accomplished filmmaking with a topic that could readily appeal to sophisticated foreign audiences. As Joan and Dennis West described her in *Cineaste*:

> Frida Kahlo was the intelligent, spirited, and sexy Mexican beauty whose scandalous bisexual love life included the conquest of Trotsky. The flamboyantly dressed, on-again-off-again wife of the legendary Diego Rivera, the extravagant giant of the Mexican muralist movement. A leftist and revolutionary committed to *Mexicanidad* ... and the Mexican Revolution. The heroic survivor of polio, miscarriages and abortions, a crippling and nearly fatal traffic accident, and dozens of surgical operations, who spent much of her life in pain confined to wheelchair or bed. And Latin America's greatest woman artist who, when she died in 1954 at age forty-seven, left a legacy of some two hundred extraordinary paintings including scores of haunting self-portraits.[20]

Certainly a life ready-made for a sensationalized screen adaptation that could very well have been flawed in less capable hands by melodramatic excesses of all kinds. But Paul Ledúc used an approach emphasizing images over dialogue, and each scene is as lovingly elaborated as any of Frida's paintings. Ledúc does not pretend to provide

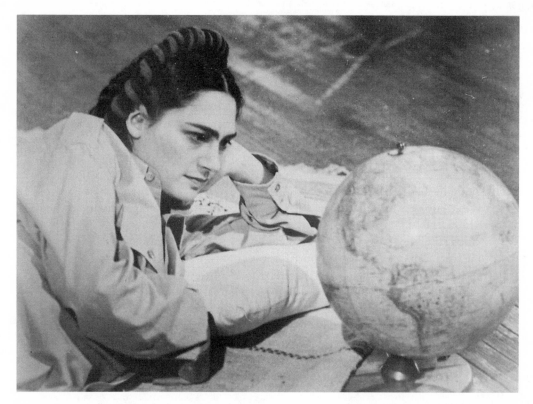

Ofelia Medina in *Frida, naturaleza viva* (1985), directed by Paul Ledúc (Estudios América).

a linear, structured biography of the artist, employing instead impressionistic images to focus on some of the principal themes and events of Frida's life: childhood memories of her father (Claudio Brook) entertaining the young Frida (Valentina Ledúc) and her sister (Cecilia Toussaint) with a puppet show; Frida being carried back from the bus accident that nearly killed her and left her crippled; a nighttime political rally punctuated by *zapatista* songs; a melancholy New Year's Eve party with couples dancing a charming but somber *danzón*; the adult Frida (Ofelia Medina) in her wheelchair bringing a meal to Diego Rivera (Juan José Gurrola) as he works on a mural, and they both burst out in good-natured but very bad operatic singing.

One lively scene (most traditional in terms of sustained dialogue) involves Frida, Diego Rivera, and David Alfaro Siqueiros (Salvador Sánchez) heatedly discussing Trotsky in the lush garden of the Kahlo home in Coyoacán. Siqueiros, just returned from the Spanish Civil War, melodramatically describes a terrible battle in which he participated. The horribly wounded Spanish soldiers "looked up at their Mexican commander" and somewhat incongruously "demanded to know why Mexico had broken ranks with international socialist solidarity and granted asylum to Leon Trotsky [Max Kerlow]," which is really too much for Rivera who tells his fellow artist to stop spouting such *pendejadas* ("bullshit"). With the exception of this scene and others involving Trotsky, in which more French and Russian are spoken than Spanish, dialogue is nonexistent or kept to a bare minimum.

Juan José Gurrola as Diego Rivera in *Frida* (Alejandro Pelayo).

Throughout the film, Angel Goded's camera moves constantly but unobtrusively, making the viewer feel like an unnoticed spectator in the characters' most intimate moments. Originally filmed in 16mm, the film was expertly blown up to 35mm and retains Goded's sharp, clear cinematography. Inexplicably, *Frida* was not entered in the Academy Award nominations for best foreign-language film because when Academy representatives arrived in Mexico to screen the film, some bureaucratic bungling prevented it from being projected for them.[21]

Frida represented Manuel Barbachano Ponce's greatest success since *Nazarín* and other Buñuel films. "It gave me great satisfaction because it was like a dream come true," he exclaimed. "To capture and recreate that marvelous atmosphere of Mexico in the 1930s was Paul Ledúc's greatest achievement."[22]

In addition to portraying internationally renowned artists and political figures, *Frida* also benefited from the publication of an important biography of Frida Kahlo[23] and a major exhibition of her work in the National Gallery in Washington, D.C. This was a rather rare confluence of factors that enhanced the international marketability of a Mexican film, but another film received a warm reception because it tapped quite another kind of transnational interest.

Jaime Humberto Hermosillo's *Doña Herlinda y su hijo* ("Doña Herlinda and Her Son), also produced by Barbachano Ponce, concerns the desire of Rodrigo (Marco Antonio Treviño), a successful Guadalajara pediatrician, to pursue a passionate love affair with Ramón (Gustavo Meza), a young music student. Having trouble finding privacy for their encounters, Rodrigo even schedules an "examination" for Ramón at his office. Rodrigo's mother, Doña Herlinda (Guadalupe de Toro, mother of Guillermo del Toro) is fond of Ramón although she does not let on that she is quite aware of the exact nature of her son's relationship with him. Doña Herlinda, as the matron of an ultra-respectable and prominent family, goes about implementing an elaborate scheme to protect her son from scandal while at the same time getting what she wants — marrying him to Olga (Leticia Lupercio), a socially acceptable girl, and getting a grandchild (to which Ramón is the godfather). Herlinda deftly accomplished her goals by film's end — she is proudly showing her family the plans for a new house with a separate wing for Rodrigo and his wife, a nursery for the baby, and, in the other wing, a studio and apartment for Ramón. "[Doña Herlinda] is an ace manipulator, but in the context of a repressive society her string-pulling seems a sane, humane, and efficient means of spreading happiness. The result is a jolly *ménage à cinq* in which everyone gets a piece of the best of possible worlds."[24]

In fact, Doña Herlinda's achievement of reconciling radically different lifestyles and philosophies and convincing them to coexist under one roof might be seen as a metaphor for the manipulative manner in which the PRI governed Mexico for seventy years. In any event, this gentle, humorous story in which gay love is treated with sensitivity and acceptance found an audience well beyond its borders. Still, the steamy love scenes between Rodrigo and Ramón were somewhat surprising coming from a

Marco Antonio Treviño and Gustavo Meza as the lovers in Jaime Humberto Hermosillo's *Doña Herlinda y su hijo* (1985) (Clasa Films Mundiales).

(Left to right) Gustavo Meza, Leticia Lupercio, Marco Antonio Treviño, and Guadalupe del Toro in *Doña Herlinda y su hijo* (Clasa Films Mundiales).

"shy, secret country" and invited comparison with the Spaniard Pedro Almodóvar's *Ley del deseo* (*Law of Desire*, 1987), a not-so-gentle examination of the obsessiveness of physical desire. A sweetly funny scene depicts Ramón listening to a sad *ranchera* record of lost love and bawling his eyes out. This occurs while Rodrigo is on his honeymoon and Ramón is sure he has lost his lover forever. Here Hermosillo takes the most macho element of traditional Mexican movies — the manly *charro* in a cantina getting drunk while listening to mariachis singing a song of betrayed love — and turns it on its head by having a man cry over another man.

In stark contrast to *Frida* and *Doña Herlinda y su hijo* was *Lola la trailera* ("Lola the Truck Driver") directed by Raúl Fernández. With wooden acting, atrocious dialogue, amateurish photography, and spotty direction, the film nonetheless was a box-office success in both Mexico and the United States: it made $3.5 million ($2.5 million in the United States and "only" $1 million in Mexico) profit on an investment of $150,000 — a powerful rationale to continue making *churros* for the Southwest U.S. Spanish-speaking market.[25]

The very comely Rosa Gloria Chagoyan stars as Lola who becomes a truckdriver (*trailera*) so her murdered father's truck won't be repossessed by his employer, a notorious drug trafficker. Lola falls in love with an undercover cop and together they wipe out the gang (which has gotten the upper hand over the police in a climactic full-fledged battle complete with grenades and helicopter gunships). In the midst of all

Lola and her undercover cop (director and real-life husband Raúl Fernández) (Pelmex).

this is Amapola (Vitola) and her ambulatory brothel — an eighteen-wheeler that converts to a sleazy night club whose star attraction is another undercover (in both senses) agent, policewoman Alondra, played by an aging and expanding Irma Serrano.

 Lola la trailera merged the *fichera* movies with the action genre, usually cops versus drug dealers (*narcotraficantes*). In fact it spelled the end of the former and the beginning of the latter, reflecting the expansion of the drug traffic in Mexico.[26] The film, in spite of its low quality, has some elements atypical of the genre (or several

Rosa Gloria Chagoyan as the title character in *Lola la trailera* (1985) (Pelmex).

genres it encompasses). Lola does enter the extremely macho world of truckdrivers. She succeeds not only professionally (even if she is unable to change a tire and the undercover cop has to do it for her; this can be dismissed as a plot device since the incident leads to their romantic involvement), but also in assisting in the destruction of the drug dealers. Although Alondra is discovered and brutally murdered, Lola herself is never the object of physical or sexual violence (she does come out second best in a fight with a hooker). She seems to continue the María Félix tradition of the "macho woman"— the female who competes with men and excels, manipulating them in the process.

Of much better quality but entirely derivative was *El maleficio 2* ("The Curse 2"). Based on a popular *telenovela* (prime-time TV soap), this slick, expensive Televicine production was inspired by the "satanic" genre of horror films like *The Omen* and *Damian*. It starred the respected actor Ernesto Alonso (who had appeared in Luis Buñuel's *Ensayo de un crimen*) and the singing and *telenovela* star Lucía Méndez. The opening scenes were filmed in New York and other scenes in Venice. The confused plot has Enrique de Martino (Alonso) as an immortal (or at least very long-lived) servant of Satan who seeks a boy whose face he has seen in a painting. The trail leads from New York to Venice and thence back to Mexico City and ends with Gabriel (Eduardo Yáñez), an arrogant, brilliant, and disturbed youth with formidable kinetic powers. (After a quarrel with his sister Marcela [Méndez], he causes part of their house to collapse.) Martino falls in love with Marcela and ponders giving up his power and immortality. However, Gabriel, who is in love with his own sister, is becoming increasingly surly and dangerous, which sets the stage for a confrontation between the two evil, supernatural forces. *El maleficio 2* is interesting as an example of the type of film that some Mexican producers felt they needed to make to compete with U.S. products. It had good special effects, excellent cinematography, and good production values. It was a profitable film and did well in videocassette rentals, both in Mexico and the United States.[27]

El maleficio 2 was also representative of the type of vehicle used by Televicine (Televisa's filmmaking operation) to promote television performers to movie "stardom." Lucía Méndez was only one such example; another was Roberto Gómez Bolaños, "Chespirito," star of a puerile television program of the same name. But the most resounding success of this TV-to-the-big-screen transition was María Elena Velasco, "La India María," literally Mary the Indian. Her 1987 film *Ni de aquí, ni de allá* ("Neither From Here nor From There") was that year's top box-office success.

The character of La India María originally appeared in the early 1970s on Televisa's marathon television variety show "Siempre en Domingo ("Always on Sunday")— a sort of extended Ed Sullivan show where she played brief sketches as host Raúl Velasco's "country cousin," a Mexican version of Minnie Pearl. But her popularity took a quantum leap after she began appearing in films. The character is basically that of a bumpkin, an Indian from a remote village who is naïve, illiterate, and unsophisticated but who possesses a shrewd native intelligence that enables her to win out over an assortment of socially advantaged types like "haughty employers, corrupt politicians, incompetent policemen, smugglers and American tourists," the latter usually a Mr. Peppermint (Pancho Córdova), a trusting soul to whom María sells phony pre–Hispanic curios.[28]

La India María's first film was *Tonta tonta pero no tanto* ("Foolish But Not Too Much," 1971) followed by other successes: *Pobre pero honrada* ("Poor But Honest," 1972), *La madrecita* ("The Little Mother," 1973), *La presidenta municipal* ("The Municipal President," 1974), and *El miedo no anda en burro* ("Fear Does Not Ride a Donkey, 197?).

In *Ni de aquí, ni de allá*, La India María shares the experiences of millions of her countrymen when she emigrates to Los Angeles to work as a domestic. Shot on location in eight weeks for $175,000, the film, which made over one million dollars, was "a tremendous success, even intellectuals went to see it."[29] What these intellectuals saw was an uneven collection of puns, sight gags, and slapstick loosely connected to a story line involving María being hired without proper papers by an American couple and flying to Los Angeles where, in the confusion of the Los Angeles airport, she is immediately separated from her employers and becomes involved with a remarkably incompetent spy, presumably Russian. He chases her (because she's the only witness to a murder he committed), and the FBI chases both of them thinking that María is another agent "disguised as a Mexican." Then ensues a confusing series of chases, jobs, and occasionally wry observations of American life. She is finally caught and deported, and the film imparts the "message" that poverty in one's own country is preferable to earning dollars in the United States. Directed by Velasco herself, the film displayed greater cinematic skills than *Lola la trailera*, faint praise though that be.

The popularity of La India María, who may be considered to have replaced Cantinflas as Mexico's favorite comic figure, occasioned some polemical exchanges. Intellectuals on the left considered the portrayal of the character to be racist — a perpetuation of the stereotype of the socially and mentally retarded Indian which had

María Elena Velasco "La India María" in *Ni de aquí, ni de allá* (1987) (Alejandro Pelayo).

been a staple of Mexican popular culture since the colonial era.[30] Other observers, on the other hand, interpreted her popularity as a reaction against the preponderance of *güeros* (i.e., blondes, fair-complexioned types) in Mexican movies and television, a phenomenon that rarely escapes the notice of many foreign visitors. Most of the latter — especially those from the United States, who carry their own cultural baggage in these matters — will generally conclude that the explanation is due simply to racism, and this is partly but not entirely true.

Alfredo Crevenna (1914–1996) was a German-born director who arrived in Mexico in the mid–1930s and was honored in August 1988 as the most prolific filmmaker in the history of Mexican cinema (well over 100 films). He opined that the *güeros* (both Mexicans and foreigners) who proliferate on television and in print advertisements symbolize that better, and/or more fashionable, life to which many of the people emerging into or struggling to maintain middle-class living standards aspire to. But, said Crevenna, "...you should ask that question of the advertising agencies."[31]

It is also apparent that the question does not seem to be an issue among the great majority of genetically Indian and mestizo Mexicans (it seems to bother some foreigners more). In any event, the film industry has always done a better job of reflecting Mexican social reality than the more recent television, which, like many others around the world, is probably simply trying to look "American," a not inconsequential influence considering Mexico's geographical location.

Whatever the explanation for mass tastes, the success of films like *Ni de aquí, ni de allá* and *Lola la trailera* points up the eternal problem of Mexican and any other cinema — commercial success is predicated on tapping mass tastes, also referred to as "the lowest common denominator." In this chapter, and indeed throughout this book, the emphasis has been on the somewhat subjective term of "quality" filmmaking. Motion pictures like those of La India María, *Lola la trailera*, and Crevenna's own highly successful *5 nacos asaltan Las Vegas* ("Five Nerds Hold Up Las Vegas," 1986) offered the majority of viewers — working-class people with an average of three to eight years of elementary-school education — escapist entertainment that enabled them to forget for an hour and a half their economic and other personal problems. La India María might tangentially reference deeper social problems, but she also made audiences laugh, either at her or with her.

In the 1970s and 1980s the Mexican middle class had by and large given up on Mexican cinema — these spectators flocked to see *Rambo* and *Star Trek* movies and other popular American imports, just like their European and Asian counterparts.[32] A minority with more refined tastes prefered quality American (e.g., Woody Allen films), European, and Japanese cinema. How to win back these middle-class viewers was the dilemma of the Mexican film industry; the "80 percent trash"[33] movies that generated profits for the private producers reflected the majority tastes: *narcotraficante* pictures, often set near the U.S. border, e.g., *El secuestro de Camarena* ("The Abduction of Camarena," 198?), a sensationalist treatment of the infamous case of the American drug agent murdered in Guadalajara by drug dealers with alleged collaboration by corrupt police officers; an incident that strained United States–Mexican relations; *Rosa de la frontera* ("Rose of the Border," 1985); sex comedies relating to certain professions, e.g., *Un macho en el salón de belleza* ("A Man in the Hairdressing

Salon," 1987); *Los mecánicos ardientes* ("The Passionate Mechanics," 1987), and on and on.

One strategy being employed by some Mexican producers was to make films in English, not only to penetrate English-speaking markets (especially the United States), but also to win back Mexican middle-class viewers. One interesting effort along these lines was *Gaby* (1987), the story of a Jewish European refugee who arrived in Mexico as a child. Directed by a Mexican, Luis Mandoki, and starring Liv Ullmann as the adult Gaby and Norma Aleandro, the Argentine actress who starred in *La historia oficial* (*The Official Story*, 1986), as Gaby's nanny. What is evident from the casting is that such films seemed to provide few important roles for Mexican actors simply because very few, if any, were internationally recognized names. Nonetheless, Luciana Cabarga, the film's executive producer, insisted that *Gaby* "is a Mexican film because Mexican money was involved."[34] However, according to Juan López Moctezuma, even though "it was shot in Mexico by a Mexican director, it was done with North American money, but didn't find an audience." In his own effort to tap the most responsive segment of the complex and elusive American market, López Moctezuma in 1987 completed *Welcome María*, coproduced with Mario Moreno, Jr. and starring María Victoria. Bilingual and shot in the streets of Los Angeles, it is about María coming to the United States to find her wetback husband who has stopped writing and sending her money.[35]

Coproductions with the Soviet Union continued, in spite of the resounding failure of *Campanas rojas*. Sergio Olhovich wrote and directed *Esperanza* ("Hope," 1987), the story of a Russian youth (his own grandfather) who emigrates to Mexico during a period when both countries are experiencing revolutionary upheaval. *Esperanza* took eight weeks of shooting in Mexico and fourteen in the U.S.S.R. It was entered in the Rio de Janeiro and Havana film festivals,[36] and it won gold and silver Arieles in several categories.

A particularly violent genre in the 1980s was the "punk" action movies inspired by foreign models, especially the Australian "Mad Max" films. In *Siete en la mira II: La furia de la venganza* ("Seven in the rifle Sight II: The Fury of Revenge," 1986), a bizarre gang of long-haired punks roams a contemporary Mexican countryside seeking a lawman who had killed the gang chief's brother (who rides his motorcycle down from his luxurious Denver home to reassume leadership of his old gang; the source of his wealth is never explained although drug trafficking is likely); they utilize an odd assortment of vehicles, including a pink Cadillac convertible of 1960s vintage. They take over a town in the manner of *The Wild One*, with the difference that they bloodily massacre police and townspeople. Films of this type were a specialty of Producciones Galindo (Pedro Galindo III and Jesús A. Galindo).[37]

This type of movie angered Blanca Guerra, an actress "who is forced to straddle the two extremes of Mexican cinema." She described her reaction every time she visited the United States: "I see the movie posters at the Spanish-language theaters, showing Mexican films, and I realize that there's literally zero respect for the Mexican audience. I think they would go see better films if better films were offered. This is my long-standing complaint with the producers. The least we can expect is that the films have quality, which they usually don't."[38]

Blanca Guerra appeared in *Nocaut* and in Arturo Ripstein's *El imperio de la fortuna* ("The Realm of Fortune," 1986), the latter a three-hour-and-forty-minute remake of Roberto Gavaldón's *El gallo de oro* ("The Golden Cock," 1964). One of the major productions of the late 1980s, it was based on a story by Juan Rulfo. Dionisio Pinzón (Ernesto Gómez Cruz) is a humble news hawker in a provincial town. As the film opens, he is announcing that evening's movie (*Santo vs. el Espectro,* or "Santo versus the Specter") and a lost cow belonging to the church. That night at a fair, Dionisio witnesses a cock fight; taking pity on the losing rooster, he convinces the owner not to kill the badly wounded creature but to give it to him. Dionisio takes the bird home and nurses it back to health by burying it up to its neck — so preoccupied is he with the animal all night that he does not notice his mother dying of a heart attack.

In the morning, he discovers her body on the floor of their ramshackle house. Poignant scenes follow of Dionisio dragging around his mother's corpse wrapped in wood and straw fruitlessly trying to raise money for her burial. He finally buries her in a cornfield. In such scenes does Ripstein provide glimpses of the stark poverty of some rural villages. Wryly, he shows the consequences: Dionisio returning the lost cow to the priest who, instead of a cash reward, blesses him without taking his eyes off a television program. In another scene, the priest announces at mass that he's rented out the church during the fair; then we see gaming tables set up in the parish and the pulpit converted to a lighted stage — from which an untalented singer, "La Caponera" (Blanca Guerra), does painfully bad interpretations of popular songs.

Dionisio's rooster recovers and goes on to win a few fights, enough to catch the attention of Lorenzo Benavídez (Alejandro Parodi), a successful breeder, who is also La Caponera's lover. Dionisio's rooster is finally killed and he buries the bird in a cemetery (in contrast with his mother). He goes to work for Benavídez picking and training roosters. Benavídez, in turn, teaches Dionisio how to play cards. By this time, Dionisio is relatively affluent so he buys a coffin and hires a man to carry it around for him in his village to show off his new prosperity. Unfortunately he is unable to locate his mother's burial place.

Dionisio runs into La Caponera who has left Benavídez; she's impressed by Dionisio's prosperous appearance. They marry and in time a baby girl is born. They return to Benavídez's hacienda and Dionisio challenges his erstwhile employer and teacher to a card game in Benavídez loses everything, including his house. From this point, Dionisio enjoys his greatest success which he believes is due to La Caponera who he insists must be at his side during his all-night gambling sessions. Dionisio's obsession changes him — he treats his wife harshly, as an object, a good-luck charm. She flees with their now teenage daughter, "La Pinzona" (Zaide Silva Gutiérrez), and tries to rejoin her old troupe, but they have a new — and equally untalented–singer. La Caponera offers them her daughter but the girl is just as bad. The two women return to Dionisio's house. During a gambling session, he loses everything, including the house; La Caponera dies in a corner of the room where Dionisio still keeps the coffin he had bought for his mother years before. He goes off to another room and puts a bullet through his head. The last scene shows La Pinzona doing an off-key rendition of a song at another dreary rural fair.

Blanca Guerra and Ernesto Gómez Cruz in Arturo Ripstein's *El imperio de la fortuna* (1986) (Estudios América).

Ripstein seemed to have fallen into a decline after his principal works, *Tiempo de morir* ("A Time to Die," 1965), *El castillo de la pureza* ("The Castle of Purity," 1972), *El Santo Oficio* ("The Holy Office," 1973), *El lugar sin límites* ("The Place Without Limits," 1977), *La viuda negra* ("The Black Widow," 1977), and *Cadena perpétua* ("Life Sentence," 1978), followed by disappointing efforts like *La seducción* ("The Seduction," 1979), *Rastro de muerte* ("Trace of Death," 1981) and *El otro* ("The Other," 1984).[39] "In Mexico there is no such thing as a cinematic career," said Ripstein. "For one to exist it would be necessary to make forty to fifty films as in the past, and of those ten should be exceptional. At the present time, we can only expect to make four or five films, which eliminates the possibility of a career."[40]

El imperio de la fortuna marked a revitalization of Ripstein's talent, and a return to his thematic constant — "the tragic framework, the trajectory of the main character toward an ineluctable destiny which we share as witnesses...." Dionisio sets in motion the plot's dramatic structure: a man to whom the power represented by money disturbs his primitive simplicity converting it into a pride and arrogance that destroy those around him.[41]

Felipe Cazals is another director who made a number of important films in the 1970s — *Canoa*, *El apando* (both 1975), *Las Poquiánchis* (1976) — who was obliged to retreat from the politically and socially oriented cinema he favored. A flawed yet

Blanca Guerra in *El imperio de la fortuna* (IMCINE).

highly significant film made early during the López Portillo period was *El año de la peste* ("Year of the Plague," 1978), in which Cazals deals with the political and economic consequences of an ecological disaster. Freely adapted from Daniel Defoe's *Diary of a Plague Year*, Cazals's film unfolds in a large, unidentified city (though it is obviously Mexico City). A mysterious ailment appears among the population, initially as a bronchial infection among children. A courageous doctor wants to issue a public warning but he is vetoed by the hospital administrator and city and federal authorities who want to avert a panic, particularly so as not to discourage investment and scare away tourists.

With the connivance of the media, the plague is covered up; municipal garbage trucks collect the dead at night and dispose of the bodies in mass burial sites (a modern version of the way in which the dead were collected during medieval pestilences). Some prophetic touches to the film are its warnings of the disastrous ecological consequences of pollution and unrestricted urban growth — especially vis-à-vis Mexico City. At one point in the film, the authorities extend the school winter vacations to minimize the spread of contagion, a step that was actually taken in January 1989 in Mexico City in an attempt to reduce pollution levels.

The plague disappears as mysteriously as it appeared and the authorities issue their official finding; the illness was caused by a stock of toothpaste illegally sold after its expiration date — a touch of Cazals's irony. *El año de la peste* is also significant in that it is the only science-fiction film made in Mexico to date (Santo movies in which he battles invaders from outer space are *not* science-fiction). Cazals was unhappy with the film because, first, it was made in the América studios which at the time were technically inferior to the Churubusco facilities and, second, due to union problems he was forced to start filming anew after two weeks with an entirely new cast.[42]

In the next few years Cazals was obliged to make purely commercial vehicles. In 1982, however, he returned to making films of social and political content with the highly praised *Bajo la metralla* ("Under Fire," 1982). In 1985, he returned to the documentary style he had employed so successfully in *Canoa* with *Los motivos de Luz* ("Luz's Motives"). Based on a real-life incident, the film analyzes the life of Luz (Patricia Reyes Spindola), a slum-dweller who has strangled her four children. At the beginning of the film, Luz is being interrogated by an off-camera male voice; she remembers nothing of her children's deaths, in fact she thinks that her boyfriend Sebastián (Alonso Echanove) and his mother (Ana Ofelia Murguía) are responsible because the latter hated Luz.

A lawyer (Martha Aura) and a psychologist (Delia Casanova) take an interest in Luz's case. What they discover is that Luz is a product of an environment of poverty

Patricia Reyes Spíndola and Alonso Echanove in *Los motivos de Luz* (1985), written and directed by Felipe Cazals (Estudios América).

in which women are abused and exploited. As a girl in her village, she had been seduced by the priest; later she moved to Mexico City where she had a baby by the chauffeur in the house where she worked as a servant; afterward she lived with a policeman who beat her and gave her three more sons. Finally she meets Sebastián during a land takeover action by activists. She becomes obsessed with him to the point of resenting her own children — at one point her oldest boy interrupts Luz while she's trying to have sex with Sebastián; she becomes furious and beats the boy.

Is Luz retarded? (She has visions and hears voices.) Or is she a product of her brutal environment? The psychologist concludes that Luz does not fit the psychological and social profiles of classical theory as developed in Europe and the United States — she decides that Luz lives in a different reality from the rest of us and withdraws from the case. In sum, "the story of Luz is as tragic as that of millions of Mexican women, condemned to subordination, ignorance, and religious fanaticism by a male-dominated society in which the male is worshipped like a god."[43]

In *El tres de copas* ("Three of Hearts," 1986), Felipe Cazals completely changes pace in relating the story of two drifters and soldiers of fortune who are "closer than brothers," Pedro (Alejandro Camacho) and Damián (Humberto Zurita), sons of Irishmen from the San Patricio Battalion which deserted from the American army during the United States-Mexican War (1846–1848). They are ex-guerrilla fighters in

Alejandro Camacho (left) and Humberto Zurita in Cazal's *El tres de copas* (1986) (Estudios América).

Felipe Cazals (center) directing Alejandro Camacho and Humberto Zurita in *El tres de copas* (IMCINE).

Benito Juárez's forces that have been resisting the French-supported regime of Maximilian (1863–1867). On their way back to Nochistlán, they stop off at the Lagos de Moreno fair where they meet a gambler accompanied by his beautiful young mistress Casilda (Gabriela Roel). Both fall in love with her but it is Damián who wins Casilda in a card game and presents her to Pedro. They all return to Nochistlán where they start a successful business. However, Damián is obsessed by his passion for Casilda. He spends his time gambling and one day kills a man who mocks him about the woman. Soon after Casilda leaves town with all their money. The dead man's relatives, the Sánchez clan, attempt to avenge him, but Pedro and Damián kill several of them in a shootout and hurriedly leave town.

Gabriela Roel and Humbero Zurita in *El tres de copas*. (IMCINE).

Pedro and Damián encounter a band of highwaymen, also veterans of the war,

led by Cipriano Melquisidor (Pedro Armendáriz, Jr.) and join them. When Pedro
and Damián discover a buried cache of Winchester rifles hidden during the war
against the French, they double-cross Cipriano and run off with the arms. In a brothel,
they encounter Casilda, but this time she offers herself to Damián whereupon they
run off together after a fight with Cipriano in which they shoot out his eye. Casilda
once more robs Pedro and Damián and escapes. When they return to Nochistlán,
they find Casilda living in their house and running the business. Pedro and Damián
sell the property to an ambitious neighbor, Ponciano Méndez (Enrique Lucero),
including Casilda's share. Furious, she tries to provoke a fight between Pedro and
Damián. However, she is shot in the leg during the altercation, and as Pedro and
Damián ride off they are ambushed by the surviving Sánchez brothers. Pedro dies in
the fight, and a badly wounded Damián rides back into town where a Sánchez widow
kills him with a pair of sewing scissors. The film ends with Casilda marrying Ponciano; she lived a long life, the narrator tells us, and left everything to her twin sons,
Pedro and Damián, who became important figures in the region.

El tres de copas, unlike most of Cazals's work, is a funny film. He intimates that
some of Mexico's most respectable families had similar disreputable beginnings. The
narrator (José Carlos Ruiz) is a 1930s campesino, presumably an employee of Casilda's
sons, Pedro and Damián, but he constantly intrudes into scenes he is narrating; for
instance, in the whorehouse scene he comes through a door and bumps into Cipriano. In the final scene where a pregnant Casilda and Ponciano are walking away from
the camera, when the narrator says that the twins are not Ponciano's, the latter angrily
shuts the gate on the narrator. Zurita and Camacho dress alike in attire reminiscent
of Clint Eastwood in a Sergio Leone spaghetti western; they maintain dead-pan
expressions most of the time. They don't act their roles, rather they model their way
through the film.

Only Pedro Armendáriz, Jr. turns in a lusty, spirited performance. Another joke
by Cazals is the unexplained presence of a boy in twentieth century attire; when the
Sánchez brothers assault Pedro and Damián, it is this boy who shoots down the
remaining ones before they can kill Damián. Is it perhaps his grandson who moves
through time to try to save his ancestor? Cazals offers no explanation; the boy's presence is simply an amusing incongruity. And of course, when Damián rides by the
woman who is calmly crocheting, she suddenly leaps up and kills him with her sewing
scissors. In addition, the film is beautifully photographed by Angel Goded (who also
shot Frida) on location in Tres Marías just outside Mexico City.

Cazals's next film was La furia de un dios (Lo del César) ("The Fury of a God
[Render Unto Caesar," 1987), as different from Tres de copas as the latter was from
Los motivos de Luz. The screenplay was adapted by Tomás Pérez Turrent from the
Albert Camus story, Caligula, but here the power-mad and sex-obsessed Roman
emperor becomes a ruthless capitalist, Claudio O'Reilly (Humberto Zurita), who
inherits an important fish-processing company. He is obsessed with dominating others, economically and sexually (it is suggested that Claudio had incestuous relations
with his sister who has died prior to the events of the film).

Claudio tries to break a fishermen's cooperative with the connivance of a federal bureaucrat (Fernando Balzaretti), and monopolize the fishing industry in that

A scene from Felipe Cazals's *La furia de un dios* (1987) (Estudios América).

part of the country. He berates his board of directors and business partners, characterizing them as weak, greedy fools who leave their money "invested safely in Houston banks and condos in Florida." But Claudio is slipping steadily into madness as he accrues more power; finally the directors arrange to have him murdered and, with the assistance of a corrupt police chief, frame the two leaders of the fishing cooperative with the murder. Again, Angel Goded's masterful photography renders the Yucatán settings in brilliant tones for this tale of corruption among the powerful. *La furia de un dios* was coproduced with Spain's TVE (Televisión Española) which explains the presence of the Spanish actress, Assumpta Serna, in the role of Cecilia, Claudio's wife.

Certainly Felipe Cazals was still one of the most creative and interesting Mexican directors working in the 1980s. He was preoccupied with expanding the thematic possibilities of his country's cinema, as had been other directors, but he seemed to be the filmmaker most intent of offering in each of his films "A story totally different from the previous one, and much less with any resemblance to the tired old formulas."[44]

On August 6, 1986, Emilio "El Indio" Fernández died of heart failure at the age of 82. The foremost exponent of a nationalist and "Indianist" genre, Fernández was Mexico's most internationally known and honored director (as noted above, Luis Buñuel, was not really a Mexican director). At the time of his physical death,

Fernández had been cinematically dead for three decades, since his nationalistic message formed in the postrevolutionary era of the 1940s was considered anachronistic by the younger generation and therefore devoid of commercial possibilities. In recent years, his economic situation worsened to the extent that he was forced to accept small roles in films like *Lola la trailera* (as a narcotics cop) and as a villain in *telenovelas* like "La traición" ("The Betrayal"), in addition to the roles given him by American friends like Sam Peckinpah (*The Wild Bunch, Bring Me the Head of Alfredo Garcia*) and John Huston (*Under the Volcano*). Fernández's legend surpassed the reality and he was its most fervent believer — a cultured, dynamic, yet crude and violent personality, he was a proud and unique man "...unable to adapt to changing times, preferring to die faithful to his ideals, always expecting to direct 'one more great film,' something he never achieved."[45]

But the "golden age" that Fernández personified was just that — a period in the past that came about from the particular historical and social conditions of the time. Mexico in the 1980s was a totally different society with a dynamic, growing population ever more exposed to international currents in culture, technology, economics, and politics. Its people faced a severe economic crisis that also posed additional challenges because the winds of change were blowing through the country's anachronistic political and economic structure. The PRI's formula for economic development and social stability, which had served it and the country well enough for forty years, was foundering.

The population of Mexico City was approaching 20 million — the largest city in the world — and projections placed its growth, if present trends continued, at 32 million by the year 2000 (which it hasn't quite reached). It was also among the most polluted cities in the world (Cairo and São Paulo among the others), with serious consequences for the health of its residents as Cazals's 1978 film *El año de la peste* grimly foretold — an ecological disaster waiting to happen.

And as if this were not enough misfortune, a disastrous earthquake struck the sprawling metropolis in October 1985, causing a still undetermined number of deaths (the official count was about seven thousand; many residents scoffed at this figure, insisting the tally was much higher) and billions of dollars in reconstruction costs. The collapse of the oil boom plunged Mexico into an economic depression that it still had not overcome on the eve of the decade of the 1990s.

Yet in response to these and other pressures the government was taking the first, tentative steps to modernize the economy and diminish dependence on oil exports. In response to public outcry, the authorities were beginning to deal with Mexico City's pollution, although a satisfactory solution was distant. In July 1988 Mexicans went to the polls to elect a new president after the most dramatic campaign in postrevolutionary history; two strong opposition challengers ran energetically against the PRI candidate, Carlos Salinas de Gortari, who finally won with barely 51 percent of the vote.[46] The runner-up was Cuauhtémoc Cárdenas, candidate of the FDN (Frente Democrático Nacional — a coalition of leftist parties), PRI-renegade, and son of the revered Lázaro Cárdenas; the other candidate was Manuel Clouthier of the conservative PAN (Partido Acción Nacional).

One 1987 film that tried to deal with contemporary problems of economic crisis,

The opening scene from Alejandro Pelayo's *Días difíciles* (1987). Left from and behind the priest is Alejandro Parodi. From the right, Blanca Guerra and Fernando Balzaretti (Alejandro Pelayo).

corruption, pollution, and terrorism was Alejandro Pelayo's *Días difíciles* ("Difficult Days"). The setting is Ciudad Leyva, a fictional city in the north (the film was shot on location in the city of Chihuahua). The Castelar family controls the region's most powerful industrial holding company, but their firms are grappling with the financial problems besetting the country as a whole. In addition, one of their still profitable operations, a chemical plant, accidentally releases a cloud of toxic gas that drifts over to a nearby school, necessitating the hospitalization of many children and the evacuation of nearby neighborhoods. Now the Castelar family faces the wrath of the citizens, many of whom are their employees. The labor union demands that pollution-control devices be installed in the plant, a step that the firm is reluctant to take because of the cost involved and the negative effect it would have on the plant's profitability.

Complications mount. The Castelar brothers, Edmundo (Alejandro Parodi) and Ricardo (Fernando Balzaretti), assume management of the firm after the death of their father (the film begins with his funeral) but disagree on how to approach their myriad problems. Edmundo favors a conciliatory approach while Ricardo, pushed on by the hard-line Ezequiel Rodríguez (Luis Manuel Pelayo, the director's father), who heads the association of industrialists, opposes any concessions. Demonstrations break

Another scene from *Días difíciles* (Alejandro Pelayo).

out and a strike is called at the plant. The federal government becomes involved–a senator proposes legislation to force a cleanup of the Castelar plant. In the midst of all this, Edmundo is kidnapped one afternoon. The family endures days of anxiety as they await the kidnappers' demands. Ricardo, now temporarily heading the enterprise, at the urging of Ezequiel refuses to pay ransom. Edmundo's wife, Luisa (Blanca Guerra), goes on television to plead with the kidnappers that they contact her directly; Ricardo, however, calls the station to say that Luisa has no authority to deal with the kidnappers. This in effect seals Edmundo's fate; the kidnappers uncover their faces to him (one is a Castelar employee), thereby passing a death sentence on him. The film ends as it began, with a funeral — this time Edmundo's. But now the family is irrevocably split — Luisa takes her children and leaves Ciudad Leyva abandoning Castelar industries to an uncertain future.

Días difíciles was Pelayo's second film in a trilogy that has as its overall theme the problem of *cacicazgo* — political and/or economic bossism. The first in the trilogy (and his first film) was *La víspera* (*The Prelude*, 1982) about an ex-government minister who has been waiting twelve years for another appointment. As a new government is being inaugurated, he waits for the call that never comes. The third film in the trilogy was *Morir en el golfo* ("To Die in the Gulf, 1990") about a powerful rural landowner.

Other noteworthy films released in 1987 were Servando González's *El último túnel* ("The Last Tunnel"), Luis Alcoriza's *Lo que importa es vivir* ("Living is What Matters"), and Alberto Isaac's *Mariana, Mariana*, the last two "worthy of being taken seriously," according to Juan López Moctezuma.[47]

El último túnel is a rather standard story of father-son conflict, but set in the spectacular Tarahumara country of Chihuahua and dealing with Mexican social complexities. It is also a fictionalized account of the construction of the railroad that connects Chihuahua City with Los Mochis on the Pacific coast and crosses the Sierra Madre Occidental in which the Barranca del Cobre (Copper Canyon) is located. Manuel Iglesias (David Reynoso) is a hard-working, hard-driving railroad construction foreman whose son, Julián (Gerardo Zepeda), has just received an engineering degree. Manuel is called upon to oversee the laying of the rails connecting the mountains with the sea — the last segment of the Chihuahua-al-Pacífico railroad. He looks forward to having Julián work at his side but the young man is not pleased at the prospect; he prefers to stay in Mexico City and open a night club with his friends.

Another interesting plot element that is never developed is that Julián is not Manuel's natural son; not only is he adopted but he is also a Tarahumara Indian. Although Julián seems anxious to deny his background, he speaks fluent Tarahumaran (unusual in that he was raised by a non–Indian father, but he might have grown up in the Tarahumara mountains thus maintaining cultural links with his people — again, a loose end in a vital part of the plot that would do much to explain the relationship between father and son).

David Reynoso (right) in Servando González's *El último túnel* (1987) (Estudios América).

Gerardo Zepeda and Holda Ramírez in *El último túnel* (IMCINE).

In any event, Manuel forces Julián to sign on as a construction engineer for the railroad. The work crews come in contact with the Tarahumaras who live in the region (in fact, two work for Manuel). This leads to Julián being smitten by Anarica (Holda Ramírez), a beautiful young Tarahumaran girl, whom he seduces and impregnates but refuses to marry. When Manuel learns of this, he protects and helps her at childbirth. In the meantime, two work teams have been formed: one, with Manuel in charge, to complete the line through the mountains, and the other under Julián's supervision to lay track through the desert, with both lines to meet at the "last tunnel" before the sea. When Manuel's team is trapped in a cave-in, Julián takes charge of the rescue effort. Predictably, Julián reaches his father in time to effect a reconciliation; he agrees to marry Anarica, thus openly accepting his Indian roots which he had been denying since his student days in Mexico City.

El último túnel did raise some potentially fascinating issues dealing with assimilation; unfortunately, the film never picks up on these topics but prefers instead a melodramatic solution to the conflict between Manuel and Julián. The Tarahumara characters are stereotyped "wise" Indians straight out of stock Hollywood westerns, and shed no light on the complex relations between these reclusive, shy people and the Mexican population that ever more encroaches on their mountain domains. The railroad itself is a dramatic metaphor for the end of centuries of self-imposed isolation, first from the Spanish and then from the Mexican authorities.[48]

Luis Alcoriza's *Lo que importa es vivir* is a well-made film about Candelario (Gonzalo Vega), a handsome young drifter who arrives at a run-down hacienda asking for room and board in exchange for work. The owner, *don* Lázaro (Ernesto Gómez Cruz), is wary of Candelario at first, but eventually the charismatic young man wins his boss's confidence by advising him on improved techniques for taking care of the livestock and working the land. Soon the hacienda is enjoying an unaccustomed prosperity, just as *don* Lázaro's wife Chabela (María Rojo) breaks out of the dullness of

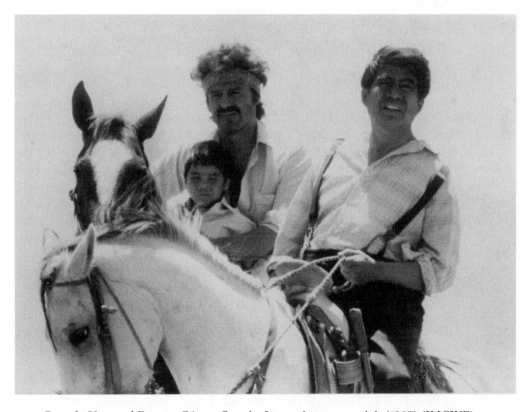

Gonzalo Vega and Ernesto Gómez Cruz in *Lo que importa es vivir* (1987) (IMCINE).

her isolated, rural life by initiating an affair with the handsome Candelario. Other ranchers become frightened at the "progressive" ideas that Candelario is imparting to the peasants and insinuate to *don* Lázaro that his wife is cheating on him. When he rushes out, rifle in hand, to kill Candelario, *don* Lázaro accidentally falls down a cliff, suffering a head injury which leaves him brain-damaged. Eventually Chabela gives birth to Candelario's son, and she and Candelario, who is now running the hacienda, raise their baby and *don* Lázaro as if they were brothers (due to his injury, Lázaro has to be taught everything again, like a child).

The film's most charming scenes are those where *don* Lázaro and his "brother" stand contrite while Candelario chastises them for some youthful transgression. When *don* Lázaro is killed in an accident, Candelario demonstrates sincere grief at the funeral. *Don* Lázaro's death leaves the way open for Candelario and Chabela to marry and acceptance by the town's society. However, Candelario balks at the structured, restraining life that marriage and "respectability" portend, especially having to deal with people who not long before had resented and humiliated him and now look upon him as a potential political and economic asset. While Chabela is in town enjoying a party in their honor, Candelario abandons the ranch with their son "to see the sea," promising to return the boy safely some day.

Mariana, Mariana, directed by Alberto Isaac who took over after José Estrada's untimely death, is an evocative piece about first love and coming of age in a Mexico

Elizabeth Aguilar and Luis Mario Quiroz in Alberto Isaac's *Mariana, Mariana* (1987) (Estudios América).

City very different from the polluted megalopolis of today. At a funeral Carlos (Pedro Armendáriz, Jr.) meets Rosales, whom he has not seen in many years. On the drive back they reminisce about their school days in the 1940s. The film then becomes a long flashback centering around Carlitos (Luis Mario Quiroz) and his infatuation with his best friend Jim's mother, Mariana (Elizabeth Aguilar). It is also about his own family, dominated by his mother (Saby Kamalich), a woman constantly concerned about morals and etiquette who has to cope with Carlitos's older brother's sexual escapades and her husband's extramarital affairs.

But Mariana becomes an obsession for him, until one day he runs away from school to declare his love for her; she gently explains the impossibility of his love and gives him his very chaste, first kiss. In the meantime, Rosales has tattled on Carlitos to the school principal, who goes to his home to tell his mother. Aghast, his parents send him to a psychiatrist (actually two, who spout Freudian babblings and end up arguing with each other), then a priest, and finally oblige him to change schools. Carlitos loses contact with Jim and Mariana, and later he hears from Rosales that she had committed suicide. Mariana was the mistress of an important politician, and after she denounced a group of his corrupt friends at a party, she and her protector fought bitterly after which she killed herself. The bittersweet memory still haunts the adult Carlos even though Rosales insists that those times belong in the past. Carlos agrees, even though he thinks that just as he and Rosales exist now, so did Mariana and Jim, intensely for him.

Angel Goded's photography enhances Isaac's nostalgic recreation of a Mexico that is also very much in the past. The scenes in the school are of interest for the class differences they demonstrate. The school was obviously a rather exclusive private institution whose student body came from upper-middle-class families. Apparently in response to the social and political milieu of the time, a few mestizo and Indian students had been admitted on scholarships, Rosales among them. When they are the objects of some mild racial epithets, the teacher explains to the *niños bien* ("privileged" or "socially advantaged"), Carlitos and Jim, why it is wrong to harbor such feelings. Otherwise, *Mariana, Mariana* is not socially meaningful; it is principally a nostalgic evocation of a lost childhood and the first manifestations of puberty.

Other noteworthy films were *Thanatos* (1984) and *Polvo de luz* ("Dust of Light," 1988) by another new director, Cristián González, who was appointed in January 1989 as head of the Subdirección de Autorizaciones (censorship office) of the Dirección de Cinematografía — in itself an unusual step since never before had a filmmaker been placed in charge of that critical office.

González, who entered CUEC at the age of 20 (and left it a year later), spent three years writing *Thanatos*. The story is based on an escape artist named Sobec who was popular on "Siempre en Domingo." González changed the character to a woman, a divorced mother who runs a pastry shop with her partner, another single woman. She is discovered by a television producer whose career is threatened by low ratings; he names her Thanatos, symbolizing death in Greek mythology, and puts her on television where she becomes a huge hit. However, in her final escape routine she disappears inexplicably. The film, which was produced by STPC, was, in González's words, "more of a teenager picture, of the imagination — in it I wanted to express everything I knew about making a movie." *Thanatos*, while interesting, does not succeed as either a fantasy or a parody, but it must have been a valuable exercise for González, because his second film, *Polvo de luz*, is an impressive achievement.

The film has just three characters, none of whom are given names. A young married couple, Alejandro Camacho and Rebecca Jones (married in real life), arrive by motorboat (the boatman is Agustín Yáñez, who doesn't utter a word in the entire film) at a breathtakingly beautiful island, the setting for an attractive home. (The interiors were filmed in Emilio Fernández's home in Coyoacán; the exteriors at Lake Valsequillo in the State of Puebla.) We soon learn that the man is dying of an incurable disease and the couple have gone to this lovely, isolated spot to spend their last days together. She is an artist and he is a filmmaker, intending to record the remaining days of his life. The deep love he has for his wife causes him anguish when he reflects on the unfairness of his early death, and he lashes out in despair at her in apparent cruelty. Idyllic happiness is punctuated by moments of bitterness until death finally comes and he is put to rest in the lake that surrounds the house.

Polvo de luz is characterized by slow pacing and scenes of great beauty. It was shot by José Ortiz Ramos, a veteran cinematographer (*Nosotros los pobres, Ustedes los ricos*) and the haunting music score, played by a cello, was written by Emiliano Marentes Martínez, a young composer. The film was shot in three and a half weeks for $150,000 (*Thanatos* took nine weeks and cost $50,000). It was screened at film festivals in Colombia and the Soviet Union.

González's views on his own work were illuminating: "The critics don't like me — they say I'm not Mexican. Somebody told me that *Thanatos* was a cold film because I didn't show feeling but I think it had some good things about Mexican mythology; in *Polvo de luz* I tried to change my technique. I wanted to deal with loneliness and tenderness. I learned while doing it — making a film is a magic thing. One can have the best camera and photographer, but the magic moment cannot be repeated. I don't know if it's a good film, but it is unique. I had to work with feelings, so I didn't improvise too much. I discussed the scenes with the actors, and they expressed their views. The crew is also making the same picture and they are very sensitive to how the shooting is progressing. At the end of the first weeks they were very happy — in fact they continued working even though I was unable to pay them that week's salary."

González's views were typical of Mexico's young filmmakers in the 1980s, perhaps imbued with greater significance in view of the crucial position that he held in the State film bureaucracy. He was concerned with recapturing the Mexican middle-class audience and felt that the "only solution is to make movies in English, with American actors" because that is what these viewers are accustomed to seeing — a somewhat surprising and not too popular idea among his colleagues at this time. But it would be acted upon, in part, by a new generation of filmmakers in the late 1990s with great success. On commercial films: And about the mass audience he said, "These films touch the real feelings of people who can't afford other types of entertainment. They have no access to culture, these are people who can't read, who don't wear shoes. They watch movies about violence, drugs, sex comedies — 80 percent of Mexican movies are like this. If a woman is not a prostitute, she's being raped, or willing to have sex on the spur of the moment. Our policy is to try to influence the commercial producers to return to family entertainment."[49]

González's comments pointed up the dilemma of Mexican cinema. From the 1930s through the 1950s, the middle class went to see Mexican films and the generally higher caliber of motion pictures made in that era reflected in part the more elevated culture of their audiences. The deterioration in quality of Mexican films beginning in the late 1950s coincided with the loss of this audience. At that time also Mexican middle-class audiences were discovering an improved Hollywood product and more innovative European films. For whatever the myriad contributory reasons — the death and retirement of the great stars, the change in government policies every six years, a basic cultural transformation of Mexican society (e.g., the youth could not relate to film themes of the 1940s and 1950s and looked to foreign models), economic realities of moviemaking — the commercial product markedly declined in quality. Most quality films of the 1980s were State-supported and made for a tiny minority of the intellectual class who attended films by Cazals, Ripstein, Alcoriza, Isaac, and others.

Alejandro Pelayo also addressed these issues, but foresaw a brighter future for Mexican cinema:

> I'm very optimistic — for the first time in our history there are three generations of filmmakers, each one with something different to say with its own style. Alcoriza is the last of the directors who began their careers in the 1960s, but the CONACINE directors — Cazals, Ripstein, Leduc, Fernández Violante [*Amor nocturno que te vas* ("Evening Love That Fades Away," 1987)] — who started in the 1970s are all still quite active. Then there's the group ranging from thirty to forty years old — Diego López, Alberto Cortés, myself, Busi Cortés [*El secreto de Romelia* ("Romelia's Secret," 1988)]. We generally work through producers' cooperatives, in which we own the films we make. And finally there's an under-thirty group, people who entered the business about ten years ago. Among these are Luis Estrada, son of the late José Estrada, and María Novaro, who has just completed a film, *Lola*, about women which has nothing in common with any previous feminine or feminist cinema.
>
> I'm speaking of Mexican quality cinema, not the other kind. For the latter, it is a problem of demand — while it exists, it'll continue to be made. But as far as quality cinema is concerned, I'm optimistic because a Council for Culture and the Arts has just been formed [January 1989], under the Ministry of Education, which will encompass the cinema for the first time. It will have the same status as the Institute of Fine Arts [Bellas Artes] and the Anthropological Institute. With this development, Mexico will finally have a cultural policy, which we've never had before. With this new organization, I think about ten to twelve quality films a year will be produced, and of these, three or four might be extraordinary, another three of good quality, and the rest less so. Coproducing will figure prominently — for instance Spain's national television network is strongly supporting Mexican and other Latin American cinema.
>
> The problem is that I can exhibit a film like *Días Difíciles*, but the public doesn't go to see it. It's not a problem of exhibition, because my film was premiered in five theaters. The public is simply not interested in the theme.
>
> There are two kinds of viewers: the mass working-class public that goes to see comedies, action, violence, drug smugglers. It coincides somewhat with the undocumented Mexicans in the United States, among whom the most popular stars are La India María and the Almada brothers. The middle-class public, to which my movie

is directed, doesn't come — they prefer to see *Rambo* and other American movies. Thus we have a serious problem, we don't have a public. And if a film doesn't reach a weekly *tope*, a minimum number of ticket sales, then it's withdrawn. Our only hope then is to try to break even in the art circuit, like the Cineteca theaters. That's why official support is very important — the role of IMCINE and the public television channel in promoting our films on television, radio, and in the press. It happened once, under Echeverria — I remember seeing *Canoa* in packed movie houses.

Pelayo also stressed the importance of international promotion, with a strong Mexican presence at film festivals. At this time, the Argentine and Brazilian cinemas were establishing a foothold in the United States and European art house circuits, which was the market that Pelayo thought that Mexican filmmakers should set their sights on:

> We'll never have a mass public as long as our pictures are in Spanish, but we want that "art house" public. I'm optimistic that we'll arrive in the decade of the 1990s because we'll have the cinematic product that'll enable us to reach out to an international public. For a film industry to have this appeal, it has to be profoundly national, like *Babette's Feast*. The only quality Mexican film that's been successful internationally in the last fifty years has been *Frida*. The film has its flaws, it's really just a series of sketches — but it is uniquely Mexican. Even though Mexico is one of the few countries in which really cheap films can be still be made, we still cannot recover our production costs domestically, so we have to export. And we're talking about production costs of $150,000 to $300,000, not millions of dollars. We're experimenting with novel production arrangements — cooperatives, coproductions, television, videocassettes, cable, satellite transmission. In coming years the Argentine and Brazilian cinemas will undergo crises due to inflation and unsettled politics; they don't have younger generations of directors to replace the current ones. And much of their best talent emigrates, to Europe, the United States, and even to Mexico. So, I'm optimistic — I think all of these factors will come together by the middle 1990s, and Mexican cinema will be once again, as it was in the 1940s and the 1970s, the predominant one in Latin America."[50]

Another view, more representative of the filmmakers from the "middle generation," was expressed by Felipe Cazals:

> Predictions are difficult because the future is complex. There is a generational problem because the young directors who are on their way up also have a right to their space. Since the economic space of Mexican filmmaking is very small, the picture for me is very problematic. This is the moment in my professional life in which I best know my craft. Thus I see many complications. My projects, as always, are many — although not one is yet finalized. At present, deciding on a film project is much more difficult for me. I think more about it — much more than in the past. I'm more self-critical now. At the same time, the economic circumstances surrounding film production are much more adverse. One can count on less money, fewer facilities.
>
> Mexican cinema has lost much ground. The situation is most worrisome. We are in a period of reorganization being initiated with a certain amount of good will. But cinema is much more than good will — it needs a lot of support and enthusiasm. To make films, or to help in the making of films, is very difficult from the State's viewpoint. It needs faith and a willingness to spend. There is no norm of action because

talent is the only limitation, there's no other. One has to act in good faith, there must be trust, a willingness to take chances. No one can write a predetermined novel, or paint a predetermined picture — similarly one cannot make film "X" because, on that basis, no creativity is possible. And in Mexico, the film industry is not a priority — well, it is from a cultural point of view. But given the current priorities in this country, cinema is not among the most important.

Therefore the future is very uncertain. I wish I were an incurable optimist. But unfortunately I've been in this business too many years and I know that there is no cinema possible without a constant struggle — one must struggle every day, as if it were the first day. But the moment comes when one is overtaken by fatigue. But I can agree with Pelayo that there is a continuity, that there will be new filmmakers and that Mexican cinema will always exist. But what I would want is an informative and assertive cinema, especially outside of Mexico.[51]

The views set forth by González, Pelayo, and Cazals were generally representative of the majority of serious Mexican filmmakers; such concerns, however, were not shared by the commercial producers who felt that "quality" cinema was a luxury they could not afford and therefore should be the financial responsibility of the state.

Ignacio Durán, the new director of IMCINE as of January 1989, concurred that a new generation of filmmakers had emerged from television, the industry itself, and the state schools:

Talented people in their twenties and early thirties, such as Arturo Velasco, Diego López, and others. The film market in the United States is quite competitive, and we want to penetrate the American market, especially the East, with films for the general public, and not only in theaters but also cable TV and videocassettes. What has happened with television in Spain, France, and Germany, in which the state-owned networks finance films which are first released in theaters and then shown on television, should also be done in Mexico. It is something that would be beneficial for both mediums, and I see it happening in Mexico, not perhaps in the short run but possibly in a few years.

One of the objectives of the industry will be to promote, encourage, and sponsor well-made films, and not just cultural ones, but also those with commercial appeal. It's an endless discussion, but I think that little by little the film producers are coming to terms with the fact that they should change their emphasis. The general public is becoming much more demanding, and wants better material, so the film producer will have to find new ways to combine the two aspects — it has been done in the past, and I don't see why it cannot be done again.[52]

"The Mexican cinema is dying,"[53] glumly declared Jorge Ayala Blanco in the conclusion to his masterful study, *La condición del cine mexicano*. But the reports of its death were greatly exaggerated. In the words of the late Manuel Michel, "...never had a patient survived so robustly such a long illness."[54] But the Mexican cinema was changing rather than dying. It was changing in response to innumerable and complex social, economic, cultural, and political currents both within Mexico and from without. With so many good people concerned about it, was not about to wither away.

First of all, the cinema in Mexico, as in all other countries, expresses the national heritage and the cultural fiber of a people. Alejandro Galindo, the venerable patriarch

of Mexican cinema, stated that "...in those images up there on the screen is where
Mexicans can find their identity."[55] Film industries were changing and in the process
undergoing their own crises in France, Italy, Spain, Britain, Eastern Europe, the
Soviet Union, China, and almost anywhere else.

Alarums were being sounded that "...even the larger cinemas in Europe are today
dominated by American films ... [and] the film industry in Europe is facing its most
serious economic crisis ever.... There is a warning, too, that the abolition of national
aid would amount to the complete disappearance of the European film industry."[56]
In Mexico there were many bright, capable, creative, and motivated people seeking
to resuscitate the cinema in the face of bureaucratic timidity, political pressures, and,
as in the rest of the world, the pervasive cultural influence of American films.

The great filmmakers and performers who created Mexican cinema — Salvador
Toscano, Fernando de Fuentes, Emilio Fernández, Dolores del Río, Pedro Armendáriz,
Gabriel Figueroa, Alejandro Galindo and so many others — molded a great tradition
that contemporary filmmakers seek to build on. The filmmakers of the past examined and interpreted a Mexican society recently emerged from revolution and fratricidal warfare. Aside from the Tlatelolco massacre of 1968, the filmmakers of the 1980s
had no dramatic events more recent than that on which to focus their creative talents; in any event it was difficult to address such issues.

National cinematic revivals, the explosion of new talents who reinterpret a people's historical experience, have often occurred after great national traumas. German
expressionism was a reaction to the disastrous defeat in World War I. The great Soviet
cinema of the 1920s and early 1930s was a product of revolutionary upheaval. Italian neorealism arose from the ashes of fascism and the French *nouvelle vague* from
World War II. The new Spanish cinema surged during and after forty years of Fran-
coist repression; and even Hollywood, which is like no other film industry in the
world, has reacted to domestic and foreign events. Argentine, Brazilian, Chilean,
Cuban, and other Latin American filmmakers have often worked under great personal peril to make socially oriented, committed, and above all, honest cinema.

The Mexico of the 1980s did not experience trauma greater than seeing its currency on the verge of collapse and its foreign debt balloon. Disconcerting certainly,
but hardly comparable to Argentina's "dirty war"— and fortunate because as Cristián
González commented, "If it takes military dictatorship and mass torture to inspire a
good cinema, then I'm glad we don't have it."[57]

To paraphrase Alberto Isaac's statement at the beginning of this chapter, Mexican cinema was not in ruins, and neither was Mexico. As Gabriel Figueroa stated:
"The new filmmakers will have to work very hard to achieve an image of Mexico
worthy of showing to the world."[58]

7

Globalization and New Paths: 1990–2004

The fledgling twenty-first century saw two Mexican films achieve international commercial success and critical acclaim: Alejandro González Iñárritu's *Amores perros* (2000) and Alfonso Cuarón's *Y tu mamá también* (2001). Another Mexican filmmaker, Guillermo del Toro, who had first attracted international attention with *Cronos* (1992), an offbeat vampire movie, established himself in Hollywood with smart, chilling films in the fantasy/horror genre such as *Mimic* (1997), *Blade II* (2002), and *Hellboy* (2004).[1] Another Mexican film that was well received internationally was Carlos Carrera's *El crimen del padre Amaro* (2002). It was Mexico's entry for the Academy Awards and by April 2003 had taken in $5.7 million in the U.S after breaking box-office records in Mexico. The international success of these talented directors reflected the continuing problems and successes of Mexican cinema as it embarked on its third century.[2]

Internationally, the best-known Mexican film personality at the turn of the new century was Salma Hayek. After starring in *Teresa*, a popular Mexican *telenovela*, she arrived on the Hollywood scene in the 1990s and appeared in some high-profile films. A few were well regarded, others less so (*Mi Vida Loca* [1993], *Desperado* [1995], *The Faculty* [1998], *Wild Wild West* [1999], *Dogma* [1999], and *Traffic* [2000]) to note a few. This valuable exposure to the U.S. public and the big Hollywood studios enabled her to venture into producing and directing. In 1994 she appeared in her first Mexican film, the highly praised *El Callejón de los Milagros/Midaq Alley*, in a well-received performance.

Hayek deftly used her celebrity and connections to launch her most ambitious project: the film *Frida*, in which she played the tormented Mexican surrealist painter Frida Kahlo. Directed by Julie Taymor (who directed *Titus* [1999]) and the Broadway production of *The Lion King*), the film also starred Alfred Molina, and featured Ashley Judd, Antonio Banderas, Geoffrey Rush, and Edward Norton. *Frida*, while of course not a Mexican film, was on a Mexican topic rarely touched upon by Hollywood.[3] And it was produced by and starred a Mexican actress, the first of her nationality to achieve prominence in Hollywood since Dolores del Río in the 1920s, Lupe Vélez in the 1930s and 1940s, and Katy Jurado in the 1950s.

After repeated delays, *Frida* was released in November 2002 to generally favorable reviews but initially unimpressive attendance figures. But through Hayek's steady promotion, the film found an audience.[4] *Frida* is an unusual hybrid, combining an art film topic with big-name stars in an attempt to appeal to a broader audience. It has strong performances by Alfred Molina as Diego Rivera and Salma Hayek as Frida Kahlo. The film begins as a standard Hollywood biopic in which Rivera and Kahlo "meet cute" and significant events in their lives are dutifully depicted. However, its tone changes after Frida's bus accident, especially when Julie Taymor employs her stage-nurtured creativity in combining animation with live action to express Frida's emotional anguish and how it contributed to her painting. As one critic observed, "when the movie manages to break free — in bursts of color, imagination, music, sex and over-the-top theatricality — it honors the artist's brave, anarchic spirit."[5] In spite of the inevitable linguistic problems when a film involving foreign characters who are supposed to be speaking their own language is filmed in English, *Frida* largely subsumes such inconsistencies because of the film's many merits.[6] Hayek's best actress Oscar nomination in March 2003 was also significant in that it was the second time a Mexican actor was so honored.[7]

The Hollywood success of Salma Hayek, Alfonso Cuarón, Alejandro González Iñárritu,[8] and Guillermo del Toro, while principally their own personal triumphs, did serve to focus international, and most importantly, American attention on Mexican films. But their decision to further their careers in the United States pointed up the enduring problems of filmmaking in Mexico.

The fortunes of the Mexican film industry have always been closely linked to the country's politics. And the last decade of the 20th century was especially volatile. The controversial election of 1988, in which Carlos Salinas de Gortari was elected president amid charges of widespread electoral fraud, ushered in a troubled decade for the country. Salinas, for most of his *sexenio* the darling of the international financial community, launched economic policies that encouraged massive borrowing and foreign investment leading to a spending binge among the middle class. He lobbied hard to make Mexico the third member of the North American Free Trade Association (NAFTA), thus linking his country's economy ever closer to the United States and, to a lesser degree, Canada.

On January 1, 1994, the date when Mexico joined NAFTA, the Zapatista (EZLN, Ejército Zapatista de Liberación Nacional) uprising in Chiapas cast a dark cloud over the event. Indian rebels launched attacks on government and military facilities in San Cristóbal de Las Casas and other towns. Army troops were rushed to Chiapas and quickly put down the uprising, but not soon enough to avoid a major embarrassment to the Salinas administration before the entire world. The Chiapas attacks were meant to focus international attention on the poverty and exploitation of the indigenous population in that southernmost state. The rebels' most charismatic spokesman was the enigmatic ski-masked, pipe-smoking subcomandante Marcos (real name: Rafael Sebastián Guillén Vicente, a leftist intellectual turned radical militant).[9]

The Salinas administration was also beset by charges of widespread corruption, including the arrest on murder charges of his brother, Raúl, amid lurid stories involving his Spanish mistress, a witch, drug connections, and personal payoffs to him of millions of dollars by Mexico's largest corporations. Salinas's term ended with scandals swirling around him and the still unsolved assassination in Tijuana of Luis Donaldo Colosio, the PRI candidate for president. The low-key (and many said colorless) Ernesto Zedillo, hurriedly brought in to replace the murdered Colosio, narrowly won the election in 1994. Salinas quickly went into self-imposed exile in Ireland, which has no extradition treaty with Mexico. Salinas has the unenviable reputation of being possibly the most despised man in Mexican public life since Antonio López de Santa Anna, the 19th-century strongman who lost Texas.

Ernesto Zedillo (1994–2000), unpopular as he was, did respond to the general public disgust with a blatantly corrupt political system and pushed through electoral reforms. This in no small measure enabled Vicente Fox, a former Coca-Cola executive, governor of Guanajuato, and standard bearer of the conservative, pro-business Partido Acción Nacional (PAN), to win the presidential election of 2000. For the first time in seventy years, an opposition party had beaten the PRI and Mexico was launched on the uncertain but exciting path of democracy.

The euphoria of Fox's stunning electoral victory soon gave way to the realities of the new rough and tumble politics. The PRI, smarting from its defeat, still held a majority in the Congress and was able to block most of Fox's proposed legislative reforms. Crime and the drug trade remained critical problems and major factors in increasing public dissatisfaction with Fox's administration.

A new "equal" relationship with the United States was high on Fox's agenda. In early September 2001, he made a highly visible official trip to the northern neighbor, urging the recently elected George W. Bush to enact broad changes in the status of Mexican illegal immigrants (Fox preferred to refer to them as "undocumented migrants"). In fact, Fox's public speeches in the United States and amiable but forceful insistence with Bush signaled a remarkable change from the traditional low-key approach of previous Mexican presidents to their American counterparts. And his brash, open style was briefly effective: no visit of a Mexican president had ever received so much coverage from the U.S. news media. But any headway that Fox might have been making with the Bush administration was abruptly halted by the terrorist attacks on the World Trade Center and the Pentagon on September 11, 2001. American policy was henceforth centered on the war on terrorism and the military campaigns in Afghanistan and Iraq, thus giving low priority to relations with Mexico.[10] And of course, Mexico's refusal to support the United States invasion of Iraq in April 2003 cooled relations between the two countries, and between Fox and Bush as well.

It is not an easy matter to characterize Mexican films during these years, except that many expressed a new edginess and internationally inspired style as in *Amores perros* and *Y tu mamá también.*[11] Tellingly, they were box-office triumphs in Mexico, the United States, and Europe. These and other films also expressed strong critiques of the nation's political, economic, and social conditions. But Mexican cinema consisted of much more than just these two films during the turbulent decade and *fin de siècle* of 1990 to 2003.

The decade and turn of the century also witnessed the passing of the last major figures of the Golden Age of the 1940s and 1950s. Of Mario Moreno "Cantinflas" (1911–1993),[12] David Wilt commented:

Although Cantinflas is almost unknown in the United States, in Latin America and wherever Spanish is spoken, he remains a beloved figure, a representative of the "common man," who was never afraid to confront authority and speak his mind. He leaves behind a rich heritage which will continue to be enjoyed for many years to come. As one mourner remarked: "Mario Moreno is dead, but Cantinflas lives on in his films."[13]

Others who passed on were Alejandro Galindo (1906–1999),[14] María Félix (1914–2002),[15] Gabriel Figueroa (1907–1997),[16] Tito Guízar (1908–1999),[17] Katy Jurado (1924–2002),[18] and the Argentine-born Libertad Lamarque (1908–2000), "who spent most of her career in Mexico after a run-in with Eva Perón,"[19] among others. Lupita Tovar, the star of *Santa* (1931), Mexico's first talkie, was still alive in the summer of 2005. Her children and grandchildren have been prominent in the Hollywood film industry—an outstanding example of the many links between the American and Mexican film communities.[20] In 2005 the only surviving actor in the United States[21] from the Golden Age was Ricardo Montalbán (b. 1920), who began acting in Mexico in the 1940s but spent the rest of his career in Hollywood.[22]

In the 1990s a modest renaissance began. Significantly, Mexican middle class audiences were slowly being enticed to see their country's movies. This trend was encouraged by a 1989 film, *Rojo amanecer* ("Red Dawn"), which dealt with a heretofore taboo subject: the violent suppression, i.e., massacre, of the student demonstrators in October 1968 during the Mexico City Olympics. Produced by Cinematográfica Sol (Valentín Trujillo and Héctor Bonilla; script by Xavier Robles and Guadalupe Ortega Vargas), the film starred María Rojo and Bonilla as middle class parents trapped with their multigenerational family (retired grandfather, two high-school-age sons, and two primary school children) in a high-rise apartment overlooking the Plaza of the Three Cultures in Tlatelolco. Limited by budget and political considerations, director Jorge Fons effectively used the enclosed space of the apartment to create an atmosphere of menace and terror.[23]

The army's massacre of student and nonstudent demonstrators had never been addressed in a post–1968 Mexican film, although Felipe Cazals indirectly alluded to it in his 1975 *Canoa*. Initially censored, reportedly by the Presidential Military Guard, *Rojo amanecer* was approved for exhibition and became a big box office hit. Perhaps the Salinas administration relented and gave the go-ahead to distribute this film because his government had come to power amid charges of massive electoral fraud. It might have been seeking to bolster its democratic image by approving a film that brought up bitter memories of the bloody repression of 1968, especially since it was in the midst of negotiations for NAFTA. Alex Cox, the American filmmaker who has often worked in Mexico, described it as "the Salinas government [caving] in to popular pressure and [allowing] the public screening of the controversial film.[24]

Rojo amanecer also had its detractors, who accused Jorge Fons of "going to great lengths to minimize the role of the military ... throughout the movie."[25] Such an accusation is baseless because Mexican audiences were very much aware that the army and security forces launched the unprovoked attack on the demonstrators. And if the perpetrators of the massacre of the family in the film were shown in plainclothes no one had the slightest doubt under whose orders they acted. Even if *Rojo amanecer* was an independent production and largely financed privately, it still was subject to government censorship and authorization for public exhibition. Those terrible events "continue to be virgin topics for the national cinema. But that is not a defect of *Rojo amanecer* but of a movie industry that requires much more than one film to redeem itself."[26]

Rojo amanecer demonstrates that filmmaking is also inextricably involved with politics not to mention economics, especially in countries like Mexico where production funds are provided largely by the state. This is the situation in most of the world but even in Hollywood, which is a commercial industry, conservative critics denounce the moral and political "messages" conveyed by movies.[27]

In addition to the politics of the Salinas administration, the complex structure of the Mexican cinematic production bureaucracy continued to present a challenge for novice and veteran filmmakers. Also in the early 1990s, the Mexican economy was being restructured to comply with the requirements for membership in NAFTA, which inevitably affected the film industry.

After 1990, when all cultural production came under the Consejo Nacional de Cultura (CONACULTA), IMCINE encouraged an *auteur* cinema and stopped working with cooperatives because of union pressure. The new IMCINE policy was to not produce directly but to coproduce with filmmakers affiliated with private companies. According to Alejandro Pelayo, this was to conform with the neoliberal policies of the Salinas administration that "the state should not be involved with filmmaking." This was "a good moment for Mexican cinema—five years of a very solid policy that resulted in films such as *Como agua para chocolate, Solo con tu pareja, La mujer de Benjamín, Danzón, Principio y fin, Miroslava* ... under Ignacio Durán, the best administration of IMCINE."[28]

Established directors like Arturo Ripstein were well connected and generally able to continue obtaining financing for their films.[29] He even filmed during the otherwise disastrous López Portillo *sexenio* when he made two of his best films, *El lugar sin límites* and *La viuda negra* (both 1977). Ripstein comes from cinematic aristocracy: his father is a well-known producer and his son is also a director—"Ripstein the father, Ripstein the son, and Ripstein the Holy Ghost" in Jorge Ayala Blanco's amusing quip.[30]

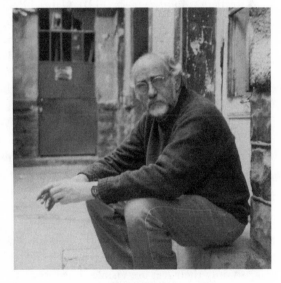

Ripstein's films, like those of Jean-Luc Godard, appeal to a very select audience both inside and outside Mexico. Described as "the master of the feel-bad movie,"[31] his films stand as a contradiction to the standard Mexican family-friendly melodrama. This is

Arturo Ripstein

perhaps partially a legacy from Luis Buñuel, for whom Ripstein worked at the beginning of his career (he was an assistant on the set of *El ángel exterminador* [1962]). But his films lack the whimsy and humor of the great Spanish master. Ripstein's films, by his own admission, "have no audience and no commercial interests to serve."[32] His characters are "marginalized loners burdened with guilt and suffering."[33] His style is characterized by long takes that include two or more actors, more typical of movies from the 1940s to the 1970s, prior to the MTV-inspired fast cuts and close-ups that became current from the 1980s.[34]

In 1991, Ripstein and Paz Alicia Garcíadiego, his wife and collaborator, adapted a 1933 Arcady Boytler movie, *La mujer del puerto*, which starred Domingo Soler and Andrea Palma, as a coproduction with a small American independent company, Chariot 7. The original film was a sordid one of incest and suicide (see Chapter 2). Even though Ripstein's remake was "hardly the stuff of mainstream movies," the Chariot 7 executives thought that *Woman of the Port* "could be a path-breaking Mexican entrant into the international art film market.... There has yet to be a Mexican breakaway hit, and it's due."[35]

To no one's surprise, this typical Ripsteinian exercise in emotional desperation and death was no breakaway hit. In fact it was mostly screened at secondary film festivals and rarely in art houses. Given that Ripstein's films in collaboration with Garcíadiego had become "increasingly pessimistic and nihilistic — to the point where suicide is a recurring option for their characters,"[36] the film had little chance to be a crowd pleaser, especially in the United States. The Mexican international "breakaway hit" was not long in coming, just a year away. It was not made by Ripstein and was just the opposite in every way from his dark visions.

Several noteworthy films were produced in the first years of the decade: Jaime Humberto Hermosillo's *La tarea* (1990), Nicolás Echevarría's *Cabeza de Vaca* (1991), Alfonso Cuarón's *Solo con tu pareja* (1991), Guillermo del Toro's *Cronos* 1992, Dana Rotberg's *Angel de fuego* (1991), Gabriel Retes's *El bulto* 1992; María Novaro's *Danzón* (1991), Juan Mora Catlett's *Retorno a Aztlán* (1992), and the aforementioned "breakaway" hit, Alfonso Arau's *Como agua para chocolate* (1992).

Jaime Humberto Hermosillo, after his successes in the previous decade with *María de mi corazón* (1982) and *Doña Herlinda y su hijo* (1985), continued his independent filmmaking and association with the University of Guadalajara. "Sometimes attacked in his own country, consistently honored in Europe and Canada, and virtually ignored in the United States, Mexico's only openly gay film director has made a career out of satirizing middle-class hypocrisy and debunking bourgeois myths."[37]

In 1990 he filmed an innovative, highly amusing sex comedy called *La tarea*. It starred María Rojo as a woman making preparations to receive an ex-boyfriend, José Alonso (or so Hermosillo would have the audience believe). The idea behind this film is rather simple. Virginia (Rojo) is preparing her *tarea* ("homework") for cinema school. She hides a camcorder under a table to record her attempts to seduce Marcelo (Alonso), a former boyfriend whom she has invited for the evening. For a good part of the film we are unable to see the faces of the actors. The camera is under a table, so only their feet are visible. But lots of things are revealed through their body language, as they come closer together, move around, tap their toes, pull apart and so

José Alonso and María Rojo's leg in Jaime Humberto Hermosillo's *La tarea* (1990) (Agrasánchez).

on. Halfway through the film the camera is discovered and the films (plural: i.e., the "term project" and the film we are watching) undergo a rather dizzying series of changes until it becomes impossible to tell one from another or to clearly distinguish between the term project and the characters' daily lives. And finally, in a surprising and unexpected plot twist, Virginia and Marcelo become Pepe and María, a married couple who contrived the whole charade as a way of spicing up their sex life. The truth is abruptly revealed when their sons come home from school and impatiently knock on the door of the apartment while their parents scurry about making themselves presentable.

This unique film, shot essentially in one take, won a Silver Ariel for Alonso as best actor and a Special Mention at the 1991 Moscow Film Festival — a disgracefully limited recognition for an utterly delightful and novel film. María Rojo continued on her path to becoming the doyenne of Mexican actresses. While not a classic beauty, she exudes an intense sex appeal through the naturalness and genuineness of her interpretations, and she was *very* sexy in *La tarea*. To borrow the words written by Roger Ebert for another actress, which are also very apt to describe Rojo's appeal: "Some people are fortunate to have faces that can be decoded as a sign of good character. This has nothing to do with 'beauty' and more to do with ineffables like smiles and eyes. [She] involves us, implicates us. We don't stand outside her performance and neither does she."[38] Hermosillo and Rojo followed up with a less successful sequel in

1992, *La tarea prohibida*, "a difficult film that was very misunderstood in Mexico, but which was also rejected by most of the public due to its theme [of incest]."[39]

The approaching 500th anniversary of Christopher Columbus's voyage in 1492 sparked a considerable amount of controversy and many official cultural activities. The Socialist government of Spain saw this as an opportunity to celebrate the country's emergence from the thirty-six-year dictatorship of Francisco Franco to full-fledged democracy and membership in NATO and the European Union. But Spanish officials spearheading this effort immediately ran into problems. First of all, "discovery," the term they initially used, upset many in Latin America and the United States, mostly indigenous/Indian/Native American advocacy groups and their supporters. "Discovery" was highly politically incorrect even though 16th century Spanish explorers technically did discover the West Indies and the American mainland since these land masses were previously unknown to them and other Europeans. So Spanish officials then decided to call it an *encuentro* or "encounter" between two worlds.

In any event, in the sphere of film, Spain's state-run television network, Televisión Española, embarked on a coproduction program with Latin American countries, especially Mexico, Cuba, Argentina, and Venezuela, in the immediate years before the official observation of the quincentenary. One of the most interesting and successful films produced under this policy was Nicolás Echevarría's *Cabeza de Vaca* (1991).

Alvar Núñez Cabeza de Vaca (ca. 1490–1557) was the treasurer for the expedition of Pánfilo de Narváez, a wealthy and ambitious adventurer who outfitted a fleet of five ships and a private army of 600 men in Spain to occupy and settle the barely known Florida, which was thought to be an island. When the little armada arrived in the West Indies, it promptly lost two ships to a hurricane off Cuba and half its recruits deserted in Santo Domingo. They finally landed at Tampa Bay and marched inland with no idea of the terrain or peoples. They ran out of food and were attacked by Indians. Narváez led his men in the opposite direction from where the remaining four ships waited for them. By the time the Spaniards reached the Tallahassee area, they were a desperate lot. They built rafts out of trees and horsehide and made sails from their clothing in an attempt to reach Pánuco (now Tampico) on the gulf coast of Mexico. The ships at Tampa Bay waited around for about a year and then returned to Cuba.

Farnesio de Bernal in Nicolás Echevarría's *Cabeza de Vaca* (1991) (Cineteca).

Cabeza de Vaca and three

other men were the only survivors of the expedition. Over eight years (1528–1536) he and his three companions sailed by horsehide raft from northern Florida to the coast of central Texas (near the present-day Galveston), crossed Texas on foot to El Paso, then across northern Mexico to Culiacán on the Sea of Cortez, then southward to Mexico City — a journey of more than 5,000 miles. It is one of the most remarkable accounts of survival in the annals of American exploration.

Echevarría's film is not an accurate historical reconstruction of Cabeza de Vaca's odyssey, nor is it meant to be. It is a symbolic, impressionistic, mystical interpretation — an attempt to uncover the meaning of his experience within the context of the European conquest of the native peoples of the Americas. Cabeza de Vaca was an atypical conquistador — "the conquistador conquered," if you will. He got to know the native peoples because his survival depended on them. But he also developed an understanding and affection for them. After his return to civilization, he urged the Spanish authorities to approach the Indians humanely — only in this way could they be converted to Christianity and be convinced to adopt European civilization.

The film gives the impression that Cabeza de Vaca adopted native mysticism and accomplished miraculous cures. He is shown at times as a Christ-like figure, particularly in a native village more reminiscent of the ancient Middle East than pre–Hispanic Mesoamerica. When he arrives at the village, he is taken to the tomb of a young girl who has recently died. She had been placed in a chamber hewn out of the rock face, similar to Jesus's tomb. Cabeza de Vaca mutters incantations seemingly in a self-induced trance and raises the girl from the dead, as in the New Testament story of Lazarus.

A Native American in *Cabeza de Vaca* (IMCINE).

The four horsemen in *Cabeza de Vaca* (IMCINE).

The film implies that Cabeza de Vaca was the first "cultural mestizo" who adapted his European culture to native American culture in order to survive. The three Spaniards — Cabeza de Vaca, Andrés Dorante, Alonso del Castillo, and Estevanico, a black servant — were trained by their captors to be shamans or healers. But according to Cabeza de Vaca's own account in the *Naufragios*,[40] the published memoir of his experiences, all they did was make the sign of the cross and pray over sick Indians, who immediately said they were cured. There was a good deal of psychological suggestion in these alleged cures.

The Indians responded enthusiastically to these strange-looking men because they believed them to be gods. Also many of their ailments were not serious. In one instance where Cabeza de Vaca was taken to see a dying man, he prayed a bit but said there was no hope. The next day he learned that the man had revived and felt great. Echevarría's filmic portrayal of the girl being brought back to life was a complete fabrication.

Echevarría was a non-too prolific documentary filmmaker when he began the Cabeza de Vaca project. At the beginning, he says, there was "much skepticism" and it took him "more than six years to complete it."[41] In the third year production was about to begin with CONACINE, but "one week before shooting began, it was suspended."[42] Although discouraged and ready to abandon the project, Echevarría persevered.

Iguana, a small independent producer "with very little capital," decided to take on the film and raised funds from IMCINE, Televisión Española, Spain's Comisión del Quinto Centenario, and eventually American Playhouse which "helped us very much and became a coproducer, because the money they gave us was considerable."[43]

Cabeza de Vaca cost $1,300,000, "nothing" for an American film said Echevarría in 1991, "but unfortunately in our country few motion pictures have that kind of budget." He continued:

> Recently our industry has been forced to make films in five weeks, practically without location changes. Those who need to make films cannot escape this pattern because there is no one to give them money or produce them. In this case, the attitude of IMCINE seems to me quite logical, not wanting to produce films entirely with their funding. They provide support, 25 or 30 percent, but the filmmaker has to obtain the rest of the money from other sources, so that the risk is shared and the cinema does not degenerate into what it had always been, based on cronyism and personal connections, which ultimately is the group around the director of IMCINE, or of Conacine, or of RTC [Radio. Television, and Cinema Directory], the only one that made movies.[44]

Echevarría came to this project quite naturally, perhaps even inevitably in view of his background and interests. In response to an interviewer's observation that many scenes seemed filmed by a documentarian of the 1530s, he responded:

> I've been able to do many things as a documentarian, but I couldn't film the most beautiful things I have seen. I lived with the Huichols for two years, with the Coras.[45] ...Instead of going to the university, I spent time in the mountains. That was my passion: the Indians. And above all, not that Indian question at an ethnographic or folkloric level, but at the mystical and the means to achieve ecstasy.... There is a species of fundamentalism, of syncretism between what is basically Christian, and what it is to belong to another religion. In the film I use very simple examples: all that magic at a distance, when the medicine man wounds the giant. They are things that I experienced on a daily basis when I lived in the Huichol mountains.[46]

Cabeza de Vaca was a significant achievement but restricted in some respects primarily because of the limited budget. Even so Echevarría was able to achieve many stunning visual effects, especially the closing scene in which a large group of enslaved Indians carry a huge cross while keeping step with a lone Spanish drummer. Toward the horizon, thunderheads roil over distant mountains

Cabeza de Vaca was played by the veteran Spanish actor Juan Diego, with what one reviewer called "loony passion."[47] His companions were played by Daniel Giménez Cacho as Dorantes, Carlos Castañón as Castillo, and Gerardo Villarreal as Estebanico.

A Mexican reviewer summarized the film:

> Echevarría experiments with the spectacular — without this being his objective — and achieves it; he seeks the sublimation of the magical consciousness of the indigenous shaman and Christian ecstasy and finds it; when he needs to show action, he manages it with surprising results ... but he obsesses too much with biblical references and metaphors [the burning bush, the resurrection, or those four apocalyptic horsemen toward the end].... *Cabeza de Vaca* is a film that can equally irritate or fascinate, and that is a merit within the habitual mediocrity of our cinema.[48]

Foreign reviews were generally laudatory. *Variety* said, "the film is first-rate in every technical department. Every attempt has been made to achieve authenticity.

It's a demanding pic for audiences, but they will be well rewarded with a film that's exotic, mysterious, bizarre ... and dramatic. Certainly *Cabeza de Vaca* is one of the best Mexican films produced in recent years."[49] A Spanish reviewer viewing the film at the Berlin Film Festival was not so enthralled: "The Mexican film *Cabeza de Vaca* is far from satisfactory.... Echevarría ... is incapable of a minimum of verisimilitude. Thus he does not achieve a fiction, but the contrary: a make-believe, a simulation."[50]

In a quite different vein was the 1991 hit *Sólo con tu pareja* ("Only With Your Partner"), the debut feature of Alfonso Cuarón, a young director who would achieve much in subsequent years. Born in Mexico City in 1961, Cuarón as a boy made Super 8 home movies and began taking courses in television production. At the age of 17 he tried to enroll in the Centro de Capacitación Cinematográfica (CCC), the prestigious film school administered by IMCINE, but was turned down because of his age. In 1980 he entered the Centro Universitario de Estudios Cinematográficos (CUEC) at UNAM, where he directed, wrote scripts, and photographed student films. In 1986, Cuarón won an Ariel for best fiction short feature. In conjunction with his studies, he also worked as an assistant on such films as *La víspera* and *Nocaut* (both 1982), *Gaby, una historia verdadera* (1987), *Romero* (U.S., 1989), and *Diplomatic Immunity* (Canada, 1991). This intense work in both films and television culminated with the founding in 1990 of his own production company, Sólo Películas.

Claudia Ramírez and Daniel Giménez Cacho in *Sólo con tu Pareja* (1991) (Cineteca).

In that same year he made his *ópera prima*, *Sólo con tu pareja*, which he wrote with his brother, Carlos Cuarón.[51]

Sólo con tu pareja is about Tomás Tomás (Daniel Giménez Camacho, who was Dorantes in *Cabeza de Vaca*), a successful advertising executive who spends a good part of his life seducing women. One of them, Silvia (Dobrina Liubomirova), is a nurse who works for his doctor and friend Mateo (Luis de Icaza). Angry at being dumped by Tomás, she decides to him give a scare by altering his blood test results to indicate he has AIDS.

He learns this just when he meets Clarisa (Claudia Ramírez), a new neighbor in his apartment building with whom he falls in love and to whom he vows to change his irresponsible and hedonistic life style. However, believing he is terminally ill, Tomás tries to commit suicide by sticking his head in a microwave oven. Clarisa, a Mexicana Airlines stewardess is also despondent because she learns her pilot fiancé is cheating on her with a stewardess from Continental Airlines (berating him for his philandering, she says, "Who's next, Debbie from Delta?"). Both of them decide to commit suicide by jumping off the Torre Latinoamericana, Mexico City's tallest skyscraper. But prior to the happy ending (Tomás learns he doesn't have AIDS, Clarisa realizes she loves him, and they have sex at the very top of the building), a series of

Tomás Tomás has sex with the bride, but he's not the groom (Cineteca).

XXIV MUESTRA INTERNACIONAL DE CINE

DANIEL GIMENEZ CACHO
CLAUDIA RAMIREZ
CLAUDIA FERNANDEZ
LUIS DE ICAZA

SOLO CON TU PAREJA

Dirección ALFONSO CUARON

Tomás Tomás with Silvia the nurse (Dobrina Liubomirova) (Cineteca).

skillfully timed comedy sequences made *Sólo con tu pareja* a big hit with Mexican audiences.

Nelson Carro, a leading Mexican critic, remarked that this film "raised the expectations of a public that rarely goes to see Mexican films, but lately has been attracted by certain movies that present a novel and different image than is usually shown by Mexican cinema."[52]

Carlos Cuarón based his screenplay on the famous story of Don Juan, the famous 16th century Spanish libertine, although his version follows more closely José Zorrilla y Moral's 1844 version in which Don Juan achieves repentance and salvation instead of being dragged down to hell by a horrific stone ghost as in Tirso de Molina's original *El burlador de Sevilla*.

According to Nelson Carro, *Sólo con tu pareja* is "a realistic portrait of a Mexican *yuppie*: that portrayal of the complications of people without problems has an ambience of believable sets, in apartments furnished in accordance with the characters' traits (and not, as in much of Mexican cinema, according to the director's limitations)."[53] He observes that the film is often reminiscent of a Blake Edwards comedy in the way that it works with "certain sexual stereotypes and in his effective handling of *gags*."[54] Carro emphasizes that "it is important to clarify that [the film] is not about

AIDS, which is nothing more than a pretext to launch the story; perhaps the way in which the disease has grown rapidly has accentuated the sensitivity of certain groups."[55]

Reportedly, U.S. distributors shied away from *Sólo con tu pareja* because it used AIDS as a comic plot device. Cuarón himself remarked that the film was *enlatada* (literally "remained in the can," i.e., not released) for two years for reasons "somewhat unknown."[56] Asked if this was the reason that he and his cameraman, Emmanuel Lubezki, went to work in the United States after the success of *Sólo con tu pareja* in Mexico, Cuarón replied that they had already established American contacts prior to the film's release.[57] When the film opened in 1991, it coincided with a worldwide homage to Mozart whose music is used in the sound track, and the explosion of the AIDS epidemic which, up to the prior year, was still not a major public health issue. In fact the film's title, *Sólo con tu pareja*, had been adopted by the government health services as the official slogan to raise consciousness about the disease among the Mexican public.

"In the manner of a Mozart *divertimento*," the film "knows how to repeatedly interrupt the light tone of the narrative to insert momentary intrusions in which [it] fully confronts the loneliness of its characters. The comic tone then appears as the most delirious response to the tragedy."[58] It was this technique that Cuarón used again to great success in his 2001 megahit, *Y tu mamá también*.

A Mexican film that traveled very well indeed was Guillermo del Toro's *Cronos* (1992). Del Toro (b. 1964) has a deceptively teddy bearish appearance but has always been addicted to fantasy and horror. He has said that "he cannot imagine himself directing anything but a movie in which, for example, the sexual organs of a gigantic insect explode in the face of the beautiful heroine. For me, terror is not gratuitous; in my films, the special effects do not overwhelm the pain of the character."[59]

Cronos, his first full-length film, was a vampire tale set in contemporary Mexico City. It won the Grand Prize during Critics' Week at the 1993 Cannes Film Festival and nine Golden Ariels in Mexico. At $2 million, it was the second-highest budgeted film in Mexican cinema history (the first was *Como agua para chocolate*, made that same year).[60]

Del Toro's film was not unrelated to a previous Mexican tradition of horror movies. Up to the late 1950s and 1960s, the principal scary movie made in Mexico remained Fernando de Fuentes's *El fantasma del convento* (1934). From there, David Wilt traces the trajectory of the Mexican horror genre:

> Although a few local characters — La Llorona and the Aztec mummy, for example — have been featured in Mexican fantasy cinema, the most popular film menace south of the border is actually a Transylvanian import, by way of Hollywood: the vampire. In the 35 years from *El Vampiro* [1957] to *Cronos* [1992], vampires have appeared in nearly four dozen Mexican films.[61]

Del Toro had an early start in filmmaking: At the age of seven he shot his first films with a Super 8 camera. In secondary school, he borrowed another Super 8 camera and made his first short film, *Matilde* (1983), followed by other shorts and animated films. His predilection for the horror genre was inspired by comics such as

Batman and Spider Man as well as the horror movies from Universal and Hammer studios. In 1982 he founded his own special effects company, Necropia. He was an assistant producer on two Jaime Humberto Hermosillo movies: *El corazón de la noche* (1983) and *Doña Herlinda y su hijo* (1984). In 1985, Del Toro studied special effects in New York with Dick Smith, who created the gruesome images in *The Exorcist* and *Death Becomes Her.* Returning to Mexico, he was responsible for the artistic design on several films, including *Cabeza de Vaca.*[62]

So Del Toro was quite ready to embark on his first solo feature. He raised seed money by various means, including putting up his house as collateral for a loan. As he told his wife, "Look, there are two options: or we live under a roof without a movie, or we live without a roof but with a movie.... We invested everything we had, absolutely everything."[63] Other producers eventually came aboard to shore up the Del Toros's roof, including IMCINE, the Fondo de Fomento a la Calidad Cinematográfica, Alejandro Springall, Iguana Producciones, the University of Guadalajara, and Ventana Films.

The Cronos device is both an elegant and forbidding object, looking like a scarab beetle from Fabergé. It was invented by an alchemist in Italy who flees to colonial Mexico to elude the Inquisition. In 1937, his strangely white-skinned corpse is found in the rubble of a collapsed building after an earthquake. In his apartment, the police encounter a horrifying scene: corpses drained of their blood hanging from the ceiling. The Cronos device disappears only to turn up many years later encased in the statue of an archangel in the antique shop of Jesús Gris (the Argentine actor Federico Luppi). The antique dealer's name translates as "Gray Jesus"—one of the many religious allusions in the film.

The Cronos device gives immortality to whomever allows it to dig its metal claws into the skin. But it also gives that person a desperate craving for human blood. And desperate Jesús Gris becomes in a couple of stomach-turning scenes—he laps up blood droplets from the floor of a nightclub restroom after a patron has a nosebleed, and he drinks blood from the shattered skull of his nemesis, Dieter de la Guardia (Claudio Brook). Not for del Toro the elegant, erotic vampires of the classic Hollywood or Hammer horror films. He wished to "reinvent a vampire legend from a new perspective that would allow me to show the vampire in the light of everyday life."[64] His vampire is an initially gentle, unromantic wretch entrapped by an evil he scarcely comprehends.

De la Guardia is a dying industrialist who will do anything to obtain Cronos so as to prolong his own life. He dispatches his nephew Angel (Ron Perlman) to get the Cronos from Jesús by any means. However, de la Guardia constantly abuses and belittles his hapless but brutal nephew who, in turn, thoroughly despises his uncle. Even though Angel puts up with de la Guardia's degrading treatment, he tolerates it in expectation of inheriting his uncle's fortune. This is a contradictory premise because once de la Guardia has the Cronos, he would have everlasting life.

Without going into a detailed plot summary, Jesús and his young granddaughter Aurora (Tamara Shanath) overcome the murderous attempts of de la Guardia and Angel. This unlikely pair, an old man and a little girl, kill their evil antagonists, and Jesús finally destroys the Cronos device. Before earning his well-deserved rest, Jesús undergoes several brutal assaults at the hands of Angel, including being pushed over a cliff in a car. Apparently dead, Jesús is sent to a funeral home which leads to an amusing sequence by Daniel Giménez Cacho as Tito the embalmer. These and other sequences emphasize the metaphorical relation of Jesús Gris with Jesus Christ — his several resurrections after being left for dead.

Another unusual aspect to the film is that the dialogue is almost equally in Spanish and English. "I know how lazy American audiences are to read subtitles," Del Toro remarked at the time. "and this blending makes 'Cronos' an almost un-subtitled movie." There was an all–Spanish version (in which Del Toro himself dubbed the voice of Angel). Ironically, the all–Spanish version, which was made for the Spanish-speaking market in the United States, had a "lackluster" reception in Los Angeles whereas the bilingual, art-house version (which

Guillermo del Toro and Tamara Shanath

Del Toro preferred) "did very well with audiences that go to see cutting-edge, stylized cinema from anywhere in the world," according to Jeff Lipsky of October films, the U.S. distributor.[65]

All in all, 1991 and 1992 were remarkable years for quality Mexican films, a reflection of the proactive policy of IMCINE's director, Ignacio Durán. Among other outstanding films of these two years was Dana Rotberg's (b. 1960) *Angel de fuego* ("Angel of Fire," 1991) which was her second full-length feature (the first was *Intimidad* in 1989).

The setting for *Angel* is "a rundown circus and an evangelical puppet show on the outskirts of Mexico City."[66] With suggestions of Fellini and Buñuel, the film is an unrelenting portrayal of the misery of the circus performers and the spectators on the fringes of a booming Mexico City in the background. Alma (Evangelina Sosa) is a 15-year-old fire-eating trapeze artist who is pregnant with her own father's child. Her father, Renato (Alejandro Parodi), is an old, sick clown and soon dies. The circus

Claudio Brook in Guillermo del Toro's *Cronos* (1992) (Cineteca).

Federico Luppi and Tamara Shanath in *Cronos* (Cineteca).

folk try to convince Alma to abort the fetus or be fired from the circus. She prefers to wander the streets performing her fire-eating act at intersections and begging.

She encounters a group of evangelical puppeteers and is taken in by this new "family" and its strange prophetess Refugio (Lilia Aragón). Refugio has an adult son, Sacramento (played by Roberto Sosa, Evangelina's twin brother), and Noé (Noé Montealegre), an abandoned child taken in by the evangelists. Their puppet shows are based on the Bible, which as Rotberg described in an interview, were her inspiration for this film:

Obviously, my background is Jewish; the first stories that were told to me were these, all of the Old Testament in Hebrew. On the other hand, they were the most gorgeous in the world, because the Bible is marvelous in depicting a fantastic world.... From there emerged the other motive of the film: sacrifice of the innocents.[67]

The puppet play presents the story of Abraham and Isaac, "a story that Alma learns she will have to repeat if she is to be purged of her sin."[68] By film's end, Alma has "become the exterminating angel of Revelations, inflicting God's wrath on an earth that has been found unworthy of [H]is pardon."[69] Elissa Rashkin sums up the denouement:

By the end of the film, Alma has lost her fetus and in revenge has first provoked Sacramento's suicide and then destroyed the circus tent and herself with it. Alma's self-immolation, which is preceded by two gestures of intense

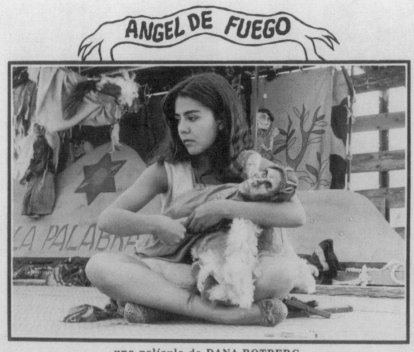

una película de DANA ROTBERG
con: EVANGELINA SOSA · LILIA ARAGON · ROBERTO SOSA
DISTRIBUCION: INTITUTO MEXICANO DE CINEMATOGRAFIA

Evangelina Sosa in Dana Rotberg's *Angel de fuego* (1991) (Cineteca).

tenderness [freeing the caged animals and bidding a silent farewell to her sleeping friends], can be seen as a biblical-scale attempt to cleanse a land that has been over-run by corruption and horror.[70]

Tomás Pérez Turrent saw *Angel de fuego* as a striking exception to the "vacuous optimism" of 1980s Mexico. The film's "aestheticized yet brutal vision" was an appro-priate response to contemporary national reality."[71] By "national reality" he meant the administration of Carlos Salinas de Gortari, then busily engaged in neoliberal economic development — economic uplift by means of open markets and foreign investment — which would qualify Mexico for membership in NAFTA.

Pérez Turrent had no kind words for the tendency of young Mexican filmmak-ers to focus on middle-class settings and stories, in other words, movies about "yup-pies." He chastised another critic who in writing about *Sólo con tu pareja* had congratulated the "current cinema" for abandoning its focus on the "marginalized classes, allowing its "camera to *rise up in society* [emphasis by Pérez Turrent]."[72] Of course, *Sólo con tu pareja* had been a huge box office and critical success, unlike *Angel de fuego* which while garnering much critical praise at Cannes, Havana,[73] Guadalajara, and other film festivals, did not especially attract moviegoers. This seemed to reflect the tastes of the Mexican middle-class audience, which apparently

Evangelina Sosa and Noé Montealegre in *Angel de fuego* (Cineteca).

Roberto Sosa and Lilia Aragón in *Angel de fuego* (Cineteca).

preferred to see itself portrayed on the screen and not the human misery that surrounded them. Perhaps the British critic Nick Roddick summed it up best:

> The audiences who flock to all the festivals are no longer surprised by anything — ultraviolence, ultraminimalism, ultradecadence — everything is absorbed, regurgitated, classified, labeled. Anyone is challenged to do the same with *Angel de fuego*, which won't be so easily digested and defies all labels. I don't know if it is brilliant, pretentious, magical-realist, or just a diamond in the rough.

Pérez Turrent concluded that "in spite of good reviews and the [film festival] audience's enthusiasm ... it will not be easy to sell the film. It will go to many festivals, but selling it will be a little more difficult."[74]

Angel de fuego is reminiscent of two classic masterpieces: Luis Buñuel's *Los olvidados* (1950) and Federico Fellini's *La Strada* (1954). And its gloomy pessimism may be a reflection of Rotberg's work with another director who also possesses a dark vision, Felipe Cazals. She was his assistant in *Los motivos de Luz*, an earlier example of death and despair in the slums.

And if Rotberg's intent was an indirect denunciation of Salinas's policies, it perhaps anticipated such British films as *Brassed Off* (1996) and *The Full Monty* (1997), among others, which contained vehement denunciations of Margaret Thatcher's own neoliberal program. But similar vitriolic exposés of the Salinas administration would not yet be made at this time in Mexico. Nonetheless, Dana Rotberg's film was an impressive example of Mexican film production, and she was just one of a group of women directors to make an impact on the industry in the 1990s.

Gabriel Retes's *El bulto* (1992) was not quite so metaphorical. *Bulto* means a bundle or burden, and the title refers to the film's main character, Lauro Cantillo. He is played by Gabriel Retes, who also wrote and directed the film (and had directed eight previous films). This Rip Van Winkle parable tells of a young radical journalist who is shot on June 10, 1971, in a clash between student protesters and paramilitary forces. He remains in a coma for over twenty years being cared for by his family (who refer to him as *el bulto*). In Patricia Hart's description:

> It is his character's awakening from the coma into a yuppified upper-middle-class Mexico of the nineties that provides Retes with the opportunity to examine the trajectory of Mexican radicalism in that period within a dramatic, familial setting in which each character neatly represents a sector of contemporary society.[75]

A "feel good" movie that was quite the opposite of Rotberg's *Angel de fuego*, was María Novaro's charming and romantic *Danzón* (1991). She is undoubtedly Mexico's best-known woman filmmaker with a vision of her country that is both sentimental and discerning. Novaro, born in Mexico City in 1951, graduated from the CUEC where she made several short films. In 1986 she won an Ariel for best short film with her *Una isla rodeada de agua* ("An Island Surrounded by Water").

Her screenplay "Lola" won her a scholarship to the screenwriting and directing workshops at the Sundance Institute. The screenplay was also awarded first prize in a competition sponsored by Televisión Española which made it possible for her to make the film. *Lola* (1989) won awards at Berlin, New York, and Biarritz, in addition to an Ariel for the best first-time director.[76] The film relates the life of a single mother who tries to eke out a living as a street vendor in Mexico City. She is part of a group of similar marginal people who set up their wares on the sidewalks ever wary of the police. Lola (Leticia Huijara) is married to a rock musician who leaves her and their baby to go on tour to Los Angeles. She finally abandons the congested and dangerous streets of Mexico City to find solace and peace on the beaches of Veracruz.

Novaro's second feature, *Danzón*, starring María Rojo, was a break-out hit. It was the first Mexican film in fourteen years to be invited to the Directors' Section of the Cannes Film Festival. Following Cannes, it played at two commercial theaters in Paris, toured the festival circuit, and soon became an international hit. Sony Classics distributed it in the United States, where it played at art houses in New York and other cities for months. And in Mexico it was the first Mexican film in years to show a profit at the box office.[77]

Rojo plays Julia Solórzano, a middle-aged single mother who works as an operator in the telephone company. She lives a minimally comfortable working-class life, with her teenage daughter and a circle of caring and supportive women friends, especially Silvia (Margarita Isabel). Julia's passion is dancing, specifically the danzón, a

María Rojo and Daniel Regis in María Novaro's *Danzón* (1991) (Cineteca).

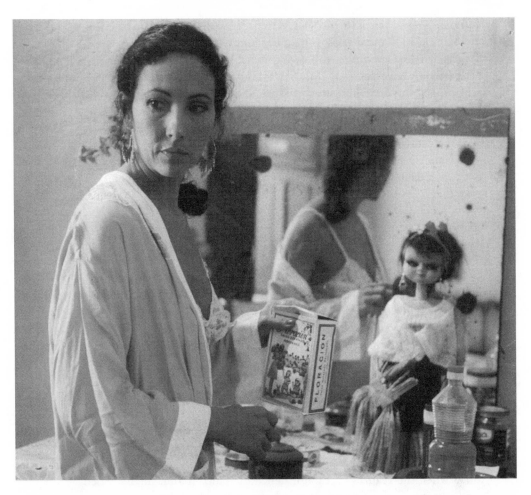

Blanca Guerra in *Danzón* (Agrasáchez).

courtly and intricate dance with specific rules much like the tango. It was originally a Caribbean dance with French/Haitian roots that took root in Cuba from where it was imported to Mexico in the late 19th century through Veracruz.

Julia's dance partner at the dance hall is Carmelo (Daniel Regis), a tall, elegantly dressed, middle-aged man. Julia and Carmelo have no relationship or even contact outside the dance hall, even though they have been steady dance partners, winning many competitions. One evening, he fails to show up and Julia is distressed. She has no interest in dancing with other men and resolves to find Carmelo. She hears that he is from Veracruz and has been falsely accused of theft at the restaurant where he worked as a cook. Julia goes to the restaurant but they have no idea where Carmelo has gone. She resolves to go to Veracruz to find him.

Thus Julia embarks on a journey of self-discovery and personal liberation. She takes a leave of absence from work and travels to Veracruz by train. She takes a room at a cheap hotel run by *doña* Ti (Carmen Salinas), a grumpy but sympathetic woman who has no illusions about men and children. The hotel is not only a residence for legitimate guests but also for prostitutes, especially La Colorada (Blanca Guerra), who befriends Julia and tries to help her find Carmelo.

On her first evening stroll to a popular café, Julia attracts the attentions of a overly friendly Russian sailor (Mikhail Kaminin)[78] who regales her with compliments and propositions in a hilarious mixture of English, Spanish, and Russian. It is a charming and funny scene in which Rojo cannot contain her laughter.

Novaro's style in this scene and throughout the film is observational; she will pause the camera to examine colorful bystanders — a child being bathed with a hose at the train station, a grandmother dancing with her granddaughter in a restaurant, an old man dancing alone. This is especially evident when Julia goes to Zamora Park, where there are outdoor danzón dances. Novaro's camera lingers on the participants — a cross-section of Veracruz's residents of all ages, genders, and colors. Novaro shares Julia's fascination with this warm, exotic, subtropical world with its underlay of Afro-Caribbean culture so different from the harshness and congestion of Mexico City.

In the park she meets Susy (Tito Vasconcelos), a transvestite and cross-dressing performer who had noticed Julia earlier when the Russian sailor was hitting on her. Susy invites Julia to see her act, where he lip-syncs at a cheesy cabaret to an old Cuban song dressed like Carmen Miranda. Julia is fascinated by the grotesque sculptures of large-breasted women on the walls. Susy takes Julia under his wing, teaching her how to dress and use makeup to be more seductive. And he also offers to help her find Carmelo, even asking a group of cooks at a restaurant if anyone like Carmelo had been looking for work.

She looks for a Greek ship at the waterfront having heard that Carmelo might have gotten a job there, but learns from Rubén (Víctor Carpinteiro), a young tugboat captain, that the ship has sailed. This encounter leads Julia to have an affair with the handsome, long-haired, and much younger man. She becomes disillusioned with Rubén when she realizes he cannot dance the danzón and, finally, when he has his long locks cut, making him look much younger.

Julia must return to her job and abruptly departs for Mexico City, leaving a note for Rubén and a gift for Susy. She returns to a happy reunion with her daughter and friends, and when she goes to the dance hall, she is welcomed by the owner and the patrons. As she is dancing with the owner, Carmelo cuts in and they resume dancing wordlessly, with no mention of where he has been or her quest to Veracruz.

Danzón is utterly endearing, not only because of the story and lush photography but also due to María Rojo's sensitive and appealing interpretation of Julia. She is not only Mexico's leading actress, but her unique qualities are highly appreciated. David William Foster wrote:

> Although a woman with very attractive features — audiences most often remember the brilliance of her smile — Rojo goes against the grain of both the standards of young beauty in Western society as a whole and idea of the younger the better for women stars.... Rojo calls attention to the possibility of a beautiful and interesting woman who is older than the dominant form in Mexican society and, therefore, in the erotic imagery found in advertising and the like.[79]

María Rojo in a glamour publicity photograph.

Another writer observed:

> Rojo is perfect for her role; she's old enough to have earned the world-weary lines
> around her eyes, yet still young and sexy enough to turn men's heads. [She brings to
> mind Carmen Maura, the great star of Pedro Almodóvar's early films.*] When she
> returns home, leaving her young lover behind, she seems to have passed a turning point:
> With or without Carmelo, she has decided to live, not merely to exist.[80]

Inevitably, because of its popularity and commercial success, *Danzón* created some
controversy. Tomás Pérez Turrent decried its very optimism and benign portrayal of
Mexican society:

> But the success of *Danzón* is due to, besides its simplicity, the fact that it is a movie
> that does not disturb, does not assault, and in which there are no people who are *dirty,
> ugly, or bad*, a picture that revels in and infects its optimism; that leaves the sensation
> that after all [and with all the misery in spite of the new order] we live in the best of
> all possible worlds.[81]

This was a severe and politicized attack on a successful Mexican film, both at home
and abroad. But it is this very optimism of Novaro's that is appealing. The characters

And such American actresses as Susan Sarandon and Diane Keaton.

in her films are essentially good people who confront life with courage and humor. Not only is there nothing wrong with that, but it is one of the basic elements that appealed to Mexican and foreign audiences. Novaro recalled that when *Danzón* was first screened at Cannes:

> immediately I noticed that the audience laughed a great deal and was very interested.... I imagine that in a festival where they expect much denser movies and suddenly there is one with much happiness and sensuality, the people appreciate it very much. And for me it was a surprise.[82]

Another debate that swirled around *Danzón* was whether it was a "feminist" film. Some critics argued that the centrality of the danzón was anti-feminist since the dance ascribes ritualistic and specific roles to men and women. Yet Julia relies on it to achieve happiness and peace on her own terms. Such controversies can go on and on, usually to excess.[83] Novaro herself was noncommittal on this issue, but described her inspiration for the film:

> The stories I invent are a pretext to create a style and a tone, to explore a world, which in this case is the world of the danzón, of those games of femininity in Mexican music, what we remember of the Mexican cinema of yesterday.... I think that this is a movie that is essential to recuperate ourselves in a moment in which I feel there is a brutal struggle to save the culture of our country. To rescue certain values of Mexicanness is a question practically of life or death.[84]

A film that took on some very basic values of *mexicanidad* was Juan Mora Catlett's *Retorno a Aztlán* ("Return to Aztlan," 1992). The action is set in pre–Hispanic times when a terrible drought is devastating the Aztec Empire in central Mexico. There is a power struggle between the warrior class headed by Moctezuma, and the priests. The priests initiate a journey to find Aztlán, the ancestral homeland of the Méxicas. Once there they will ask the goddess Coatlicue to end the drought. But Ollín, a peasant, begins his own journey, parallel to that of the priests.[85] The film is unique in two aspects: it is one of the very few Mexican films set before the Spanish conquest in 1521,[86] and the dialogue is entirely in Nahuatl, the language of the Aztecs and other pre–Columbian peoples of central Mexico. (The 1943 *María Candelaria* had snatches of Nahuatl). It bears comparison to a later Canadian film, *Atanarjuat: The Fast Runner* (2001), based on an Inuit legend and spoken completely in Inuktitut. Both films are unique, well-done, and difficult for general audiences.

Juan Mora Catlett (b. 1949, Mexico City) studied film, starting in 1968, for six years at the Academy of Fine Arts, Film and Television Faculty in Prague in (then) Czechoslovakia, where this project was born, as he relates it:

> The idea for *Return to Aztlan* came to me while I was studying in Prague. I came from Mexico somewhat overwhelmed by the magnificence of European culture. But in Czechoslovakia, I realized how a nation of barely 14 million people had managed to have a great influence on world culture, with writers like Kafka and Kundera and musicians like Dvorak and Smetana. The reason for this was in the love that the two nations — the Czechs and the Slovaks — had for their culture. This made me think

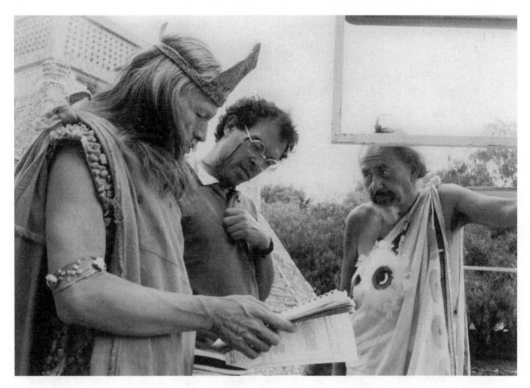

Retorno a Aztlán **director Juan Mora Catlett (middle) discusses a scene with the actors (Juan Mora Catlett).**

about the shame, and sometimes outright contempt, that many Latin Americans have for their own cultural roots, which in many cases are equal to or even richer than the culture they inherited from Europe during colonization, neocolonization, and globalization. My eyes were opened to the great cultural richness of Mexico throughout its entire history and multiculturalism, and I decided to make films based on that premise.[87]

Mora Catlett returned to Mexico in 1975 where he ran "into a bunch of closed doors, great lack of interest, and a kind of phobia and fear."[88] He began working with historians and archaeologists, and after receiving a Guggenheim grant he was able to spend a year working on the script. His first version was "a kind of bad Greek tragedy" due, he felt, to initially studying dramaturgy in Prague. "The gods that inspire Greek tragedy are amplifications of human emotions, and the pre–Hispanic gods are not," he said. "Quetzalcoatl cannot be made into an Olympian entity."[89]

Starting with the idea that Greek tragedy and philosophy arise from questioning Greek myth, Mora Catlett was intent on creating a "Mexican" dramaturgy that questioned the myths of the ancient Mexicans. The result was a labor of research and elaboration, with input from all kinds of experts, which took him ten years and "culminated in a script that was exceedingly strange and which served as a basis for the film."[90] His premise was that since all myths have the same content, or can be considered as diverse versions of the same histories, the potential audience was already

Rodrigo Puebla as Moctezuma and Amado Zumaya is Tlacaelel in *Retorno a Aztlán* (1992) (Juan Mora Catlett).

familiar with the story: the sacrifice of the hero in a moment of chaos to reestablish order. What they did not know was the pre–Columbian narrative styles.

So being faithful to the source material, he created a type of cinematic codex, like the pre–Hispanic codices[91] which were like audiovisual comic books — an oral narration, probably accompanied by music. "It was an interesting experiment," Mora Catlett said, "trying to put aside conventional forms of cinematic narrative and developing one appropriate to this material, trying to find in this way a basis for a filmic aesthetic unique to my culture."[92]

Initially, *Retorno a Aztlán* was going to be in Spanish, which is what the actors spoke. But a serious problem arose: What kind of Spanish did the ancient Mexicans speak? Or how to create a type of Spanish that the audience would accept as traditional Nahuatl translated into Spanish? The first idea was to employ 16th century Span-

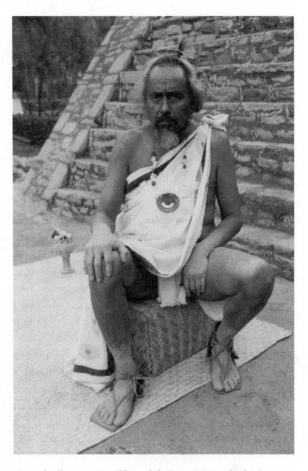

Amado Zumaya as Tlacaelel (Juan Mora Catlett).

ish, but "that gave us a very strange language to read and almost impossible to pronounce."[93] So the decision was made to have the dialogue in Nahuatl, which was the imperial language of the Aztecs, similar to what Latin was for the Roman Empire:

> With the Spanish conquest in 1521, [Nahuatl] was replaced by Spanish, but it survived in isolated communities and evolved into different dialects. For the film we used the language spoken in the 16th century, which is considered a dead language. It was filmed with the actors speaking Spanish and later a historian translated the dialogue into Nahuatl. It was a difficult task, because the translation had to be synchronized with the actors' lip movements, who were speaking a language that had nothing to do with Nahuatl.... Then we faced the problem of the voices because I didn't think there were any actors who spoke the language. Fortunately, I was contacted by a group of actors who had spent a year learning Nahuatl pronunciation for a theatrical project that was never completed. We began dubbing with the historian's help and two indigenous linguists who helped to substitute words or change phrases to fit the lip movements.[94]

Mora Catlett relates an incident connected with the dubbing:

> On the second day of dubbing, the Actors' Union [ANDA — Asociación Nacional de Actores] halted the work, arguing that the film was being dubbed in a language other than Spanish and according to a collective contract it was considered a foreign language for exhibition outside Mexico. And according to the contract, the actors had to be paid a very high salary in dollars. My argument that Nahuatl was the original language of Mexico and in no way could it be considered a foreign language fell on deaf ears. Fortunately, word got out to the media and the next morning when I arrived at the union offices to haggle, the annoyed officials showed me a newspaper with a big headline reading: "ANDA CONSIDERS NAHUATL TO BE A FOREIGN LANGUAGE." They gave me dirty looks and told me "pay the actors what you want!"[95]

Retorno a Aztlán achieves an otherworldly look enhanced by the indigenous music played on authentic pre-conquest instruments and the surrealistic makeup of the actors inspired by drawings in the codices. The pace is slow and the Nahuatl dialogue rather ponderous sounding. It is certainly far from a general audience film, although it did connect with diverse viewers. At a free screening in Mexico City, Mora Catlett saw a four-year-old Indian boy get away from his mother and run into the theater. After a few moments, he saw the boy trying to pull his mother out of the theater, but she did not want to leave. She was fascinated hearing for the first time her native tongue on a movie screen. And after a screening in Austria, the audience maintained a strange silence but didn't leave. When he insisted several times that they say something, a woman answered, "How can you expect us to ask questions after we have participated in a mythic ceremony, in a primeval rite?"[96]

In stark contrast to the highly specialized and unique *Retorno a Aztlán* was the breakout international hit alluded to previously. This was Alfonso Arau's* *Como agua para chocolate* ("Like Water for Chocolate," 1992), based on a best-selling novel of the same name by Laura Esquivel, his wife at the time. It was the highest-grossing foreign film in the United States ($21,665,500) until 1997, when Roberto Benigni's *Life Is Beautiful* surpassed it with $57,598,247 (October 1999) and a slew of Academy Awards.** *Como agua para chocolate* won several Ariel awards, a Golden

*Alfonso Arau is also mentioned in Chapter 5 as writer, director, and star of Calzonzín inspector (1973) and star of Alberto Isaac's Tívoli (1974). His son Sergio Arau, a musician and cartoonist, wrote and directed Un dia sin mexicanos (A Day Without a Mexican) in 2004, starring his wife, Yareli Arizmendi. Conceived as a humorous yet serious "mockumentary" about what would happen if all the Mexicans in California suddenly disappeared, the film made some funny observations about television news and the Border Patrol but was also preachy, uneven, and overly long. It was screened in a few U.S. cities, including Los Angeles, San Francisco, New York, Chicago, and Miami, but was largely panned by the few critics who saw it. Curiously for a Mexican film (produced by Televisa Cine and Altavista Films), the dialogue in Un día sin mexicanos is almost entirely in English; it's somewhat reminiscent of his father's flawed effort, Mojado Power. See David Brooks and Jim Cason, "Un día sin mexicanos busca un diálogo binacional: Sergio Arau," La Jornada, 13 September 2004, Internet Edition and Laura Emerick, "Film spoof raises profile of Mexicans in U.S. society, Chicago Sun-Times, 18 September 2004, Internet Edition. John McMurtrie said the picture "doesn't know what it wants to be: either a goofball satire or a heavy-handed social-message movie." Film Clips, San Francisco Chronicle, 4 June 2004, Internet Edition.

**It in turn was supplanted by Ang Lee's Crouching Tiger, Hidden Dragon (2000), which in the United States grossed $128,067,808 as of October 2001.

Globenomination for best foreign-language film, and various awards and nominations at other film festivals around the world.

In the late 1970s, Arau had gone to Hollywood with the idea of making "Mexican movies for Mexicans living in the United States,"[97] which resulted in *Mojado Power* (1979), a Spanish-language comedy about a Mexican illegal (Arau) in Los Angeles creating a support group of *mojados*, or wetbacks and his rivalry with a Chicano for the affections of a Chicana (curiously, all the Chicano characters spoke perfect Spanish and no English, probably because they were played by Mexican actors). Purportedly a comedy, the movie was silly rather than funny even though it enjoyed some box-office success in Los Angeles. *Mojado Power* was evidently a quickie commercial trifle aimed at a perceived Mexican audience in Southern California and was certainly not an attempt at social commentary.[98]

Arau had been much more successful in getting roles in major Hollywood productions, such as Sam Peckinpah's *The Wild Bunch* (1969) and in *Romancing the Stone* (1984). He did a very funny turn as the Colombian drug kingpin who is a fan of the romance novels written by Kathleen Turner's character.

Pekinpah learned that Arau had just finished his first film, *El aguila descalza*, "so he knew I was a young director," Arau recalled when he was hired to play lieutenant Herrera in *The Wild Bunch*. During the fourteen weeks of shooting, Pekinpah adopted him as a pupil. "I was tremendously lucky to have him as a friend. He was one of my mentors, as both an actor and director," Arau said.[99]

In 1960s Mexico, there was a strong leftist movement and support for the Cuban Revolution accompanied by a rejection of American cinema by leftist directors, and going to Hollywood was seen as a betrayal of the nation. Nevertheless, the enormous success of *The Wild Bunch*, which became a classic, opened doors to Hollywood and Arau was hired by Disney to work in *Scandalous John* (1971) with Brian Keith, his first picture in the United States. (*The Wild Bunch* was filmed in Mexico.) He spent 34 years going commuting between Mexico and Hollywood, studying directing, producing, and financing at UCLA between directing and acting jobs.

Arau began his career in the 1950s when he teamed up with Sergio Corona in a song-and-dance act. In 1960 they went to Cuba where they made a short film, *Alfredo va a la playa* ("Alfredo Goes to the Beach"). Arau then produced and starred in "El Show de Arau" on Cuban television. Then he went to Paris to study pantomime, returning to Mexico in the late 1960s and produced Alejandro Jodorowsky's "Locuras felices" ("Happy Madnesses") for the stage and in 1969 wrote and directed his first feature film, *El Águila descalza* ("The Barefoot Eagle"), a satire on Mexican stereotypes. In 1976 he returned to Cuba to make a documentary, *Caribe, estrella y águila* ("The Caribbean, Star and Eagle") in which through interviews he contrasts the societies of Mexico and Cuba. Arau continued acting until the opportunity to make *Como agua para chocolate* presented itself.[100] Arau's career had been spotty, with long lapses between filmmaking. And some in the Mexican film community regarded with suspicion the years he spent in Castro's Cuba.

Married to Laura Esquivel (they cowrote *Tacos de oro* in 1985, which he directed) during the time she was writing *Como agua para chocolate,* she would give him the chapters to read as they were completed. "As soon as I started reading it, I knew I had to make the film, and I was determined to produce it, to make sure it was seen," Arau said.[101] However, he had doubts about directing it,

> because the theme was so feminine and so emotional, directly related to the melo-dramatic genre, that I always assumed a woman should direct it. And we looked around and interviewed various persons. But I don't know if because she was being support-ive or simply on a hunch, Laura always insisted I direct it, and finally I agreed. But on the condition that she should stay very close to me during shooting.[102]

The Arau-Esquivel collaboration worked very well. Not only was her published novel (1990) a best-seller in Mexico and other countries, but the film was an inter-national box-office hit. In Mexico, hot chocolate is made with water that is brought to a boil before adding the chunks of dark, rich chocolate. "Like water for choco-late" is also said of someone who is in a state of sexual excitement. Like *Babette's Feast*, the 1987 Danish award-winning film that initiated a number of films centered around food, *Como agua para chocolate* used the preparation of exotic cuisine as a metaphor for passion and desire.

On a ranch in northern Mexico near the U.S. border in the late 19th century three daughters live with their tyrannical mother. Tita (Lumi Cavazos), the youngest, by tradition, can never marry so that she can care for her mother Mamá Elena (Regina Torné) until she dies. Tita loves Pedro (Marco Leonardi), but since their love can never be, he agrees to marry the awkward, hard-luck, flatulent older sister Rosaura (Yareli Arizmendi), so as to be near Tita. Tita deals with this impossible situation by pouring all her frustrated passion and desire into the preparation of elaborate meals that "can provoke crying fits, vomiting or raging lust; in which metaphoric, sexual fire leads to literal flames; and in which ghosts of the dead can harass or comfort the living."[103] The middle sister, Gertrudis (Claudette Maillé), liberates herself from the grim household by riding off nude holding onto a rebel soldier and returns years later as a revolutionary general.

Como agua para chocolate was well-made with elements that appealed to an inter-national audience. Artfully photographed by Emmanuel Lubezki in soft-focus warm colors and employing magical realism, it is a melodramatic story of women seeking emotional and sexual fulfillment. The story is carried along by tasty recipes appro-priate to the situation. Arau reflected on his film's unexpected success by saying, "The most rational explanation is that it's a miracle, a divine act."[104] He planned it for a global market, but could not anticipate the scale of its success.

Its success gave the Mexican film industry a big international presence and bought Arau a ticket to Hollywood where he directed *A Walk in the Clouds* (1995). A some-what mystical and sentimental melodrama, the movie brought in a respectable $50,012,507 in box-office receipts in the United States alone. Adapted from a 1942 Italian film, *Quattro passi fra le nuvole*, it starred Keanu Reeves as a young soldier who meets a pregnant girl (Aitana Sánchez-Gijón) on a bus. She asks him to make believe he is the father and brings him to her home, which is a large 400-year-old Napa Valley vineyard owned by her "aristocratic" Mexican-American family. Her father (Giancarlo Giannini) is a tradition-bound patriarchal tyrant, while the grand-father (Anthony Quinn) is sympathetic to the young couple.

XXIV MUESTRA INTERNACIONAL DE CINE

LUMI CAVAZOS
MARCO LEONARDI
REGINA TORNE
MARIO IVAN MARTINEZ

COMO AGUA PARA CHOCOLATE

Dirección
ALFONSO
ARAU

Laura Esquivel and Alfonso Arau on location for *Como agua para chocolate* (1992) (Cineteca).

The film betrays its Italian origin because nothing Mexican in California is 400 years old and Californians of Mexican ancestry don't behave like titled Italians. Yet what was different and refreshing about Arau's film is that he placed Mexicans at the top of the social ladder, unlike the American (i.e., Chicano/Latino) filmmakers who generally focus on poverty, gangs, crime, and social exclusion.[105]

Arau kept working in the United States, mostly directing made-for-television movies, including *The Magnificent Ambersons* (2002). In 2000, he directed *Picking Up the Pieces,* with Woody Allen and Sharon Stone, which most critics panned and it went directly to video. But in 2003 he returned to Mexico to film *Zapata: el sueño del héroe* ("Zapata: The Hero's Dream"), with a $10 million budget put up by private investors (the largest to date of any Mexican film) which had its Mexican premiere on April 30, 2004.[106]

Alejandro Pelayo's *Miroslava* (1992) related the life and death of Miroslava Stern (1925–1955), a popular star of the 1940s and '50s who had worked with a number of the leading Mexican directors, including Luis Buñuel. Born Miroslava Sternova in Prague, Czechoslovakia, she immigrated with her parents to Mexico in 1940. After winning a beauty contest at an exclusive country club dance, she was discovered and appeared in *Bodas trágicas* ("Tragic Wedding"), a 1946 movie directed by Gilberto

XXIV MUESTRA INTERNACIONAL DE CINE

LUMI CAVAZOS
MARCO LEONARDI
REGINA TORNE
MARIO IVAN MARTINEZ

COMO AGUA
PARA CHOCOLATE

Dirección
ALFONSO
ARAU

Lumi Cavazos as Tina in *Como agua para chocolate* (Cineteca).

Martínez Solares. She went on to make twenty-six films, including three in Holly-wood, the most important being Robert Rossen's *The Brave Bulls* (1950). Miroslava even appeared on the cover of *Life* in the edition of July 10, 1950.

She worked with the leading Mexican directors, including Luis Buñuel in *Ensayo de un crimen* in 1955, her last film. On March 10 of that year she committed suicide by overdosing on sleeping pills. She was reportedly found by her friends, the actresses Ninón Sevilla and Carmen Prieto. According to another account it was her house-keeper who discovered her body[107], holding a photograph of Luis Miguel Domin-guín, the famous Spanish matador with whom she was having a torrid love affair when he unexpectedly married an Italian actress. Presumably this was the immediate cause of her suicide, but Miroslava had apparently suffered from deep clinical depression for many years.[108] In fact, many of the circumstances surrounding Marilyn Monroe's death in 1962 reminded Mexicans of Miroslava's life and death.

Alejandro Pelayo's film takes place during the afternoon and evening of Miroslava's death, with frequent flashbacks that provide major biographical details and possible motivations for her self-destructive obsessions. The central narrative is provided by Alex (Claudio Brook), producer of most of her films, who in the form of an interview relates Miroslava's last hours.

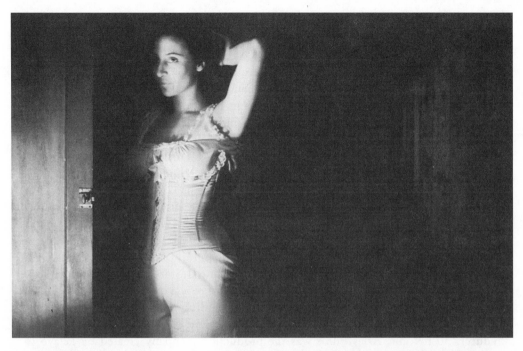

Yareli Arizmendi as Rosaura in for *Como agua para chocolate* (Agrasánchez Film Archive).

On the set of *A Walk in the Clouds* (1995), left to right, Atiana Sánchez-Gijón, Alfonso Arau, Anthony Quinn, and Keanu Reeves (20th Century Fox).

Miroslava was played by United States-born Arielle Dombasle, whose French father took her to Mexico when she was a few months old. She lived in Mexico until the age of 18 when she moved to Paris to pursue a career on the stage and in the movies.[109] After an extensive search throughout Mexico and Europe, Pelayo found this blonde actress whose beauty resembled Miroslava's and who spoke Spanish with a Mexican accent. Pelayo skillfully reconstructed scenes in Prague, using members of the small Czechoslovakian community in Mexico, speaking Czech (with Spanish subtitles).

Miroslava was slow paced and elegant, "an exercise in style," according to Pelayo who said he emphasized production values over straightforward content.[110] It was based on a book by Guadalupe Loeza for which Ignacio Durán, director of IMCINE, purchased the movie rights and approached Pelayo to make the film. The project was quite novel for Pelayo, since he had always produced and written his own politically oriented independent films in the 1980s, such as *Morir en el Golfo* (1989). The tragic story of Miroslava reverberated in Mexico, much like Marilyn Monroe's did in the United States, and the film did quite well, coming in third in the box-office for 1993. It was distributed in Europe but not in the United States, not surprising since Miroslava was practically unknown there.

The film cost $1 million with IMCINE funding 60 percent, the Fondo del Fomento al Cine de Calidad putting up 10 percent, and Tabasco Films, a private producer, 30 percent. Aries Films was the production company created by Pelayo to make *Miroslava*. This was the formula adopted by Durán at IMCINE after 1989.[111]

Another bilingual film that dealt with Mexican multiculturalism was Guita Schyfter's *Novia que te vea* ("May I See You a Bride" or "Bride to Be," 1993), which tells the story of two Jewish Mexican girls, Oshinika (Claudette Maillé, who played Gertrudis in *Como agua para chocolate*) of Turkish Sephardic background and Rifke (Maya Mishalska) of European Ashkenazi descent. Based on a first novel by Rosa Nissán, "part of a cluster of Mexican Jewish writers,"[112] the film is unique in a number of ways not least in that Schyfter is one of a small but significant group of women filmmakers who came to the fore in the 1980s and 1990s. Born in Costa Rica in 1947 of refugee Lithuanian and Ukrainian parents, she moved to Mexico in 1965 where she earned a psychology degree from UNAM in 1969. She went to London to study and then took a production course at the BBC. Returning to Mexico she worked for the Secretariat of Education, producing more than 20 audiovisuals and television documentaries. *Novia que te vea* was her first feature film.[113]

Although most Americans and Europeans do not usually assume an important Jewish presence in Mexico, it has the third largest Jewish population in Latin America, after Argentina and Brazil. There are about 40,000 Mexican Jews, mostly in Mexico City, but smaller groups live in Guadalajara, Monterrey, and Tijuana.[114]

Novia que te vea focuses on two friends. One is Oshinika, who is descended from Turkish Sephardic Jews who arrived in Mexico City in 1927. At the train station, when her ancestors ask a policeman where Jews live, he tells them to go to Lagunilla, a district of many Jewish-owned shops. A Sephardic man overhears them and takes them home with him. Here, and in later scenes of the Sephardic family gatherings, most of the dialogue is in Ladino without subtitles, essentially a 16th century Spanish dialect conserved for centuries after the ouster of Jews from Spain in 1492.

Arielle Dombasle in Alejandro Pelayo's *Miroslava* (1992).

Ari Telch and Maya Mishalska at the Zionist youth camp in Guita Schyfter's *Novia que te vea* (1993) (Cineteca).

Sephardic women socializing in *Novia que te vea*. Angélica Aragón is at left (Cineteca).

The other friend is Rifke, daughter of a well-to-do and progressive Ashkenazi (Eastern European) family who studies anthropology and Nahuatl at UNAM and attends a Zionist youth camp. These activities reflect the conflict between her wish to be Mexican and her family's traditional cultural ties. Her uncle, a death camp survivor, is passionately anti–Zionist and constantly argues (often in Yiddish) with Rifke's father about Israel.

At the university she becomes involved in leftist politics and meets Saavedra (Ernesto Laguardia), a communist student firebrand from a prominent family. When he invites her to lunch at his home, his parents welcome her warmly, but another guest, a journalist, baits Rifke about Jews. He complains that there must be about two million of them in Mexico, because "they are everywhere" and "don't assimilate." Rifke challenges him, as does Saavedra: "Assimilate into what? The great Mexican family?" Attacking the dominant ideology from his leftist viewpoint, he says that few things disgust him more than the idea of la *gran familia mexicana*, "because it assumes that we all want the same thing." To his support of the class struggle, the journalist argues, "In this class society, where are the Jews? Among the exploited?" Rifke argues that "the great Mexican family also has its cultural minorities — the Otomí, the Cora, the Tarahumara, the Huichol, the Nahua ... the Jews." Saavedra adds that "all are Mexican but with different traditions."[115]

Oshinika's struggle, on the other hand, is with her tradition-bound family whose only goal for her is marriage and children. Her desire to study art is sternly opposed by her mother (Angélica Aragón), but her classes are secretly paid for by her sympathetic father. She meets Levy, a Jewish medical student, at a dance which leads her mother to immediately start planning the wedding. Oshinika hates his jokes and mustache and is even more discouraged when he forbids her from ordering more food at a drive-in, because he doesn't want her to get fat. He plans their married life with no input from her, evidence that he will be a controlling, traditional husband — of whom Oshinika's mother approves.

Matters come to a head when Saavedra is arrested during President John Kennedy's visit to Mexico. He with other vocal anti–American radicals are picked up to prevent mischief during the visit. Rifke, upset, goes to Guadalajara to visit her grandmother, and Oshinika accompanies her. Neither girl lets her parents know. When Levy criticizes Oshinika's father for having so little control over his daughter, the father loses his temper and throws Levy out of his house.

Eventually, Rifke marries Saavedra and she becomes a famous author. Oshinika marries the boy she met at the Zionist meetings and becomes a renowned artist. Both have found happiness by assimilating into the broader Mexican cosmopolitan culture while still retaining their Jewish identity. The final scene is at Rifke's son's bar mitzvah where she and Saavedra proudly look on as the boy recites in Hebrew. Saavedra's parents are also present, enjoying the ceremony but still somewhat perplexed at their Jewish grandson.

Novia que te vea is a film rich in details of assimilation, cultural conflict, and accommodation. The dialogue in Ladino, Yiddish, and Hebrew, as well as Spanish, reinforces its message of diversity in Mexican society.[116]

María Novaro's next film, *El jardín del Edén* ("The Garden of Eden," 1994) was also bilingual (and even trilingual with some Zapotec dialogue). Although interesting and well made, it did not enjoy the success of *Danzón*. It was another of Novaro's forays into (for her) an exotic world through the eyes of a bourgeois *chilanga* (resident of Mexico City). The film was set in and around Tijuana and across the border in southern California. This is a region that attracts Mexicans from all over the country, to work in maquiladoras and also to try to cross the border to find work in the United States.

Here five lives intersect: Jane (Renée Coleman), an open-hearted but naïve WASP always thrilled with everything and everyone she encounters in Mexico; her friend Lupita (Denisse Bravo), a Mexican-American single mother organizing a Chicano art exhibit in Tijuana, who is culturally conflicted partly because of her imperfect command of Spanish; Jane's brother Frank (Joseph Culp) who has dropped out of society and spends his days in a beachfront house watching and recording the wailings of dolphins; Felipe (Bruno Bichir), a farmer from the interior who has come to Tijuana to get across the border; and photo shop owner Serena (Gabriela Roel) a widowed mother.

Novaro and her screenwriter sister Beatriz Novaro present a unique picture of the U.S.-Mexico border area, so frequently depicted as a cultural and literal battleground. Individuals from both countries come to Tijuana in search of different things, and in the process try to connect with each other. The portrayals are both sensitive and humorous, and the demographic complexity of both sides of the border is surprising and affecting. Bruno Bichir's performance as Felipe is outstanding, as a scruffy but sensitive and gentle peasant who forms an almost romantic bond with the confused but goodhearted Jane.

Scenes from María Novaro's *El Jardín del Edén* (1994): (top) Renée Coleman attending the bedridden Bruno Bichir; (left) Ana Ofelia Murguía; Gabriela Roel (right) (Cineteca).

The veteran director Jorge Fons made *El Callejón de los Milagros* ("Midaq Alley," 1994) based on a novel by the popular Nobel-winning Egyptian writer Naguib Mahfouz (b. 1911). The novel is about a group of residents of a Cairo neighborhood during World War II. Relocating the setting to Mexico City in the 1990s, Fons tells the interconnected stories of the neighbors who live on a street near the Zócalo, the historic center of Mexico City. It is a dramatic and depressing yet often humorous tale told from the perspectives of the different characters. Although the characters were originally Cairenes, their experiences are convincingly adapted to Mexico City.

The producer Alfredo Ripstein, Sr. (Arturo's father), had purchased the film rights to two of Mahfouz's novels: *Midaq Alley* and *The Beginning and the End*. The latter was filmed by Alfredo Ripstein, Jr., as *Principio y fin* (1993). Leonardo García Tsao observed that "comparisons are inevitable since they are two Mexican adaptations of the same author. But the differences are very clear. While Ripstein creates his own universe, your gaze is considerably more realistic. Ripstein's world is closed, suffocating, while in your film there is much humor, which provides a respite."[117] In response, Fons commented that "I have noticed that the endings of my films are disheartening and rather sad. However, they are nothing like the pure acid that is Arturo's cinema."[118]

El Callejón de los Milagros (literally, "The Alley of Miracles") featured an all-star cast: Ernesto Gómez Cruz, María Rojo, Bruno Bichir, Delia Casanova, Daniel Giménez Cacho, Claudio Obregón, Margarita Sanz, and, in her first Mexican film, Salma Hayek in a highly praised performance.

The film is structured in four acts named for their principal characters: "Rutilio" (Gómez Cruz), the bar owner conflicted by his homosexual urges, unhappy with his

Salma Hayek and Daniel Giménez Cacho in Jorge Fons's *El Callejón de los Milagros* (1995) (Cineteca).

Salma Hayek (right) at the brothel (Cineteca).

wife's (Casanova) sexual demands and his useless son Chava (Juan Manuel Bernal); "Alma" (Hayek), is the daughter of *doña* Cata (Rojo), a card reader and holistic healer who tries to marry Alma off to the well-to-do shopkeeper Don Fidel (Obregón). When he dies from a heart attack before the wedding, Alma is seduced by the pimp José Luis (Giménez Cacho) into prostitution. And in "Susanita" (Sanz), the middle-aged spinster landlady who hungers for love, first flirts with Chava and then marries Rutilio's young but dishonest bartender, Güicho (Luis Felipe Tovar), who steals from her and Rutilio. Chava also takes money from Susanita to go to the United States illegally, after he beats up his father's young lover in a bathhouse. Abel (Bichir) goes along because he needs money to open his own barbershop and marry Alma.[119] In the film's climax, Abel returns and learns that Alma is working in a brothel. He slashes José Luis's face before being stabbed by him. Abel dies in Alma's arms in the street.

"Each life is a Mexican melodrama of the purest essence," commented a reviewer. "*El Callejón de los Milagros* ... is an excellent and revitalized example that melodrama runs through the veins of Mexicans.... It fully belongs to the Mexican movie concept of yesteryear, but with the narrative, descriptive, and moral possibilities offered by today's cinema and liberalism."[120]

The film swept the Arieles in 1995 and received many awards, from best film and acting to set design and cinematography at film festivals in Berlin, Havana, and Valladolid. It was released in the United States but was little noticed, receiving some tepid comments from minor reviewers. Perhaps Americans tended to consider it too melodramatic, too much like a *telenovela*. Mexican (and other Latin American) *telenovelas*

Bruno Bichir gives Ernesto Gómez Cruz a haircut in *El Callejón de los Milagros* (Cineteca).

have an enthusiastic following throughout the world, from Italy and Turkey to Russia and Korea, but Americans know little about them. Another factor may be that Americans have their own soap operas and have scant interest in foreign melodrama. *El Callejón*, while transcending the soap opera structure, is inspired by Mexican melodramas of the 1940s and 1950s, still beloved by many Mexicans.[121]

Arturo Ripstein's next feature, *Profundo carmesí* ("Deep Purple," 1996), while not burning up the box office in Mexico or elsewhere was well-made (as all his movies usually are) and enjoyable (as not all his movies are). Enjoyable might not be the first reaction that comes to mind about a film relating the bloody careers of two serial killers. Described by Roger Ebert as "macabre and perverse"[122] and by Kenneth Turan as "a strange and deeply twisted romance,"[123] the film is part road picture, part melodrama, but principally a deeply disturbing and violent account of two psychotic and dysfunctional people whose ideas of love are derived from soap opera sentimentality.

The film begins in Mexico City in 1949 and unfolds in the open, sunny deserts of northern Mexico, instead of in Ripstein's usual moody, closed-in cluttered interiors (although there are still some cluttered interiors and exteriors in *Profundo carmesí*). And it even has some elements of humor, which is unusual for Ripstein.

The story is based on true-life "Lonely Hearts" murderers Martha Beck and Raymond Fernández. The two preyed on lonely widows and spinsters in the northeastern United States in the late 1940s. In 1969, Leonard Kastle based his cult classic *The Honeymoon Killers* on the pair's murder spree, which was seen as his inversion of *Bonnie and Clyde* (1967). Instead of a physically attractive homicidal couple, he featured a physically repulsive couple. The story interested Ripstein and at first he considered shooting it in the United States in English with American actors.[124] But he opted for changing the setting to Mexico with Garcíadiego writing the script. This was fortuitous for several reasons not least because she insists on writing very detailed directions in her scripts and as a married couple they have developed an intuitive and smooth working relationship.[125]

The essentials of the story are the same in the Mexican setting. Martha Beck is played by the opera-trained Regina Orozco, as Coral, an obese, frustrated nurse and single mother of two who dreams of finding a Prince Charming by placing ads in the personals listings. The Raymond Fernández character is portrayed by Daniel Giménez Cacho as Nicolás, a slick confidence man and gigolo who, until he meets Coral, is limited to hoodwinking vulnerable, lonely women out of their money.

Nicolás answers Coral's enticing ad but is turned off not only by her poundage but by her messy apartment and her two children. Not least of the turnoffs is the pervading odor of formaldehyde emanating from Coral's body (she works in a morgue). But Coral pursues him relentlessly and forces him to have sex with her. She even abandons her two young children at an orphanage to please him. They develop a strange co-dependent relationship in which she becomes his partner in locating vulnerable women. Coral passes herself off as Nicolás's sister and proceeds to murder the women after she and her lover have swindled anything of value out of them.

An amusing aspect of Nicolas's deceptiveness is that, besides being obsessed with not being seen without his toupée, he passes himself off as a Spaniard by affecting a

Regina Orozco in Arturo Ripstein's *Profundo carmesí* (1996) (Cineteca).

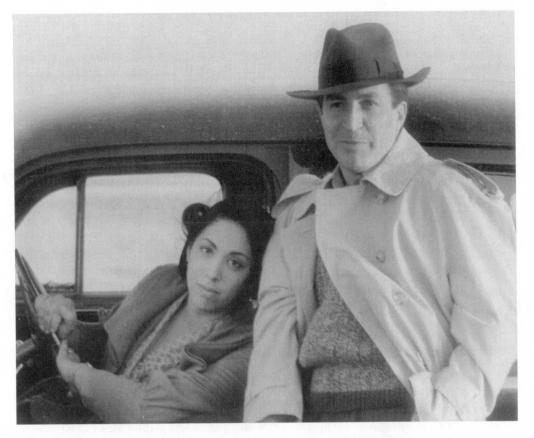

Regina Orozco and Daniel Giménez Cacho in *Profundo carmesí* (Cineteca).

Castilian accent. This makes him appear exotic to his victims, but is especially appealing to an affluent Spanish widow (Marisa Paredes) living in a small northern town. When the authorities finally catch up with Coral and Nicolás, their fate is "Mexicanized." The original American killers, Martha Beck and Raymond Fernández, died in the electric chair at Sing Sing, New York in 1951. In Ripstein's version, Coral and Nicolás are dispatched by means of *la ley fuga*— shot while trying to escape — because in Mexico there is no capital punishment. But to the end, as they lay dying in a muddy puddle, Coral and Nicolás swear eternal love for each other, justifying their unspeakable crimes in the name of true love.

Alejandro Springall's *Santitos* (1998) was a charming comedy that was well received at the Sundance Film Festival but sabotaged in the United States by inept promotion and distribution. It is the story of Esperanza (Dolores Heredia), who sees the image of St. Jude in the dirty window of her oven ("Thank God I ran out of Easy-Off," she tells the priest to whom she also phones in her confessions). An innocent and devout mother, she cannot believe that her daughter has died of a mysterious infectious disease. The authorities seal the coffin, so she believes that her daughter has been kidnapped and is being forced to work in a brothel. This leads Esperanza on a quest, first working as a housekeeper in a local brothel and then going to Tijuana,

The end of the trail for the homicidal lovers of *Profundo carmesí* (Cineteca).

where she thinks her daughter has been taken. Esperanza maintains her innocence in the midst of depravity and eventually meets and falls in love with a Mexican wrestler (who never takes off his mask) in San Diego.

"The charm of 'Santitos' ... is its knowing but joyous life-affirming tone. Both the director ... and the screenwriter, María Amparo Escandón, have done well by Ms. Escandón's novel, on which the film is based," said *The New York Times*.[126] *Santitos* was Springall's directorial effort; he was a producer or production consultant on such films as *Cronos* (1992), *Someone Else's America* (1995), Salma Hayek's *Frida* (2002), and John Sayles's *Casa de los Babys* (2003). *Santitos* did receive some distribution in the United States but it was placed in some theaters without any promotion by an understandably short-lived company. The distributor, Latin Universe, purported to distribute "Spanish-language movies" to the elusive American "Latino" audience. Springall was none too happy with the way his film was handled.[127]

The most successful Mexican film up to that time in Mexico was Antonio Serrano's *Sexo, pudor y lagrimas* ("Sex, Shame, and Tears," 1998), an unsatisfying film that became a phenomenon, staying on movie screens for 27 consecutive weeks. Even though production that year was only eleven films, "the smallest number since the early Thirties," *Sexo* "offered ample evidence that there was a huge middle-class public willing to pay to see Mexican films at the multiplex."[128]

This comedic drama featured two young couples and two world-traveling friends, a man and woman, who reenter the two couples' lives. The story takes place mostly in two apartments across the street from each other in Mexico City. Intellectual Carlos

Dolores Heredia and Demián Bichir in Alejandro Springall's *Santitos* (1998) (Cineteca).

A scene from *Santitos* (Cineteca).

(Víctor Huggo Martín) is not providing as much sex as wife Ana (Susana Zabaleta) needs. Tomás (Demián Bichir), a world-traveling friend of the couple, reappears after many years abroad. Across the street, womanizing executive Miguel (Jorge Salinas) and suffering wife Andrea (Cecilia Suárez) are joined by visiting friend Maria (Mónica Dionne). The presence of guests Tomás and María triggers lust, rejection, infidelities, and other conse-

Demián Bichir in Antonio Serrano's *Sexo, pudor y lágrimas* (1998) (Cineteca).

quences of suppressed love and marital relations among the six friends. This results in Tomás's suicide, which leads to the others' reconciliation.

The movie consists essentially of these yuppies yelling at each other, which soon becomes wearisome, but it was enormously popular in Mexico (and nowhere else) so it is important to try to understand why. According to Susana López Aranda, IMCINE's film festival coordinator, several key factors operated in the success of

Jorge Salinas on top of Susana Zabaleta in one of the scenes that made *Sexo, pudor y lágrimas* so popular (Cineteca).

Sexo, pudor y lágrimas. First among them, "the old movie theaters closed down, and cineplexes began to come in — they provided completely different services than the ones we were accustomed to — good sound, clean facilities, very expensive. It was marvelous, like going to a movie in the United States." Secondly, the film "was directed toward the urban middle class, thirty-somethings, who returned to the movies — a very interesting phenomenon that was not repeated anywhere else. In the United States and Europe there were hundreds of movies of that type [urban romantic comedies]." Incidentally, López Aranda added, this was the second film that Latin Universe attempted to distribute in the United States, and following what she characterized as the "catastrophe" of *Santitos*, it quickly folded.[129]

The improvement of Mexican exhibition facilities is an important reason for the revival of Mexican cinema in the 1990s, which provided world-class facilities for the viewing of Mexican and foreign films. According to López Aranda, "the lower class don't go because there are no cheap movies anymore. They depend on movies made for the video market."[130]

In 2001, there were about 2,000 screens in the country. The largest, Ramírez Cinemas, had about 45 percent of the market. This is the largest and most important chain in Latin America. It had about 55 Cinépolis, 41 Multicinemas, 28 double screen ("Gemelos") and six single-screen cinemas — a total of 835 screens and 198,000 seats. In second place is Cinemex, which operates only in Mexico City. It has 25 percent of the market, with 325 screens and 67,784 seats. In third place is the American firm Cinemark, with 14 percent of the market with 26 complexes, 256 theaters, and 60,000 seats.

These multiplexes offer such amenities as coffee shops, cinecafés, customer services, sushi bars, ticket sales and reservations by telephone and Internet, digital and THX sound systems, large screens for 70 mm formats, free magazines, cybercafés, child care, creperies, 24-hour security, and even low-calorie popcorn in addition to full concession services.[131] In August 2003, Cinemex announced plans to invest 1 billion pesos ($93.3 million) in the construction of eleven multiplexes in the Mexico City area, giving the company 121 new screens, bringing its nationwide total to 501.[132]

A dissenting view was provided by Víctor Ugalde, Technical Director of FIDECINE (Fondo de Inversión y Estímulos al Cine/Fund for Film Investment and Stimulation, a state funding agency created in 2001). Ugalde, who considers himself "first a filmmaker and second a bureaucrat,"[133] said that in the 1980s and early 1990s, Mexican films were produced for the majority of the public, the poor." And, he added, "only a small percentage were made for the middle class — a market which was supplied by independents or state-sponsored producers."

> Suddenly, the profile changed. The government began neglecting the theaters operated by the state-run Compañía Operadora de Teatros, so people would say, "What bad service, they smell, I don't like them." This was state policy to privatize or eliminate state-run exhibition so private firms could come in. Today's [2004] movie ticket of about 47 pesos costs one day's minimum salary, before with one day's salary, six tickets could be bought — enough for the entire family.[134]

Ugalde pointed out another dimension of this shift in production from the poor majority to the affluent minority: "This public [the middle class] did not identify with swarthy heroes because the popular classes are mostly dark-skinned. The new multiplex patrons identify with light-skinned heroes — with *güeros* [blondes]."[135]

Sexo, pudor y lágrimas, besides being full of *güeros*, also benefited from the new clean, modern, and comfortable multiplexes in drawing a young, upscale, middle-class Mexican audience to see a Mexican film that was about *them*. Not that *Solo con tu pareja*, a superior film, did not also reflect the Mexican yuppie culture, but *Sexo* obviously pressed all the right buttons.

A very different set of buttons was pressed by Luis Estrada's *La ley de Herodes* ("Herod's Law," 1999). A black comedy and political satire, it told the story of Juan Vargas (Damián Alcázar), a lowly janitor in the regional PRI headquarters, who is tapped by López (Pedro Armendáriz, Jr.), the local political boss, to become the mayor of San Pedro de los Saguayos, a miserable, dirt-poor village where most of the Indian residents do not speak Spanish and whose three previous mayors have been lynched for corruption.

The only profitable enterprise in the village is the brothel, run by Doña Lupe (Isela Vega), who has traditionally bribed the previous mayors. Vargas, at first enthusiastic and idealistic, soon succumbs to the temptations of his office, accepting not only money but sex. His greed and ambition escalate out of control until he murders López, which only leads to a higher post in the PRI and a career in national politics.

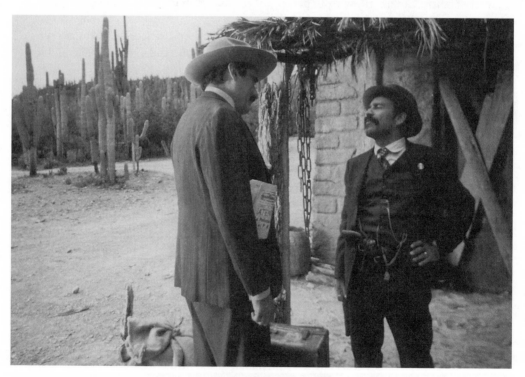

Damián Alcázar (right) and Manuel Ojeda in Luis Estrada's *La ley de Herodes* (1999) (Cineteca).

Damían Alcázar in *La ley de Herodes* (Cineteca).

La ley de Herodes was well made albeit with a sledgehammer approach. That it dealt with official corruption was not especially novel, but that it mentioned the PRI by name led to a major uproar. Even though it was set during the administration of Miguel Alemán (1946–1952), sensitivities were high with the hotly contested presidential election of 2000 looming.

It was scheduled to be screened at the Cineteca Nacional and commercially at the Cinemark 12 multiplex. The Cineteca copy was "out of focus and blurry" while the Cinemark screening was cancelled because of "projector malfunction." Bertha Navarro, member of the Mexican Association of Independent Producers, called the episode "a new form of censorship" as did Isela Vega. María Rojo, a representative in the Chamber of Deputies, called for a congressional inquiry.[136] IMCINE's director, Eduardo Amerena, "a financier and not a movie person,"[137] came under fire for giving in to pressure from government officials to sabotage the film.

The controversy was resolved when IMCINE, under pressure from the film community and the press, gave up its rights to the film and gave Estrada sole ownership, enabling him to "exhibit his film under conditions and at such times that he considers convenient."[138] His film, aided by the notoriety, went on to a successful and profitable run in Mexico. It was shown in the United States and Europe without much of a ripple, although some people greatly overstated its impact by saying it was the film that brought the PRI down. Naturally, foreigners did not respond to it the way Mexicans did.

Roger Ebert's reaction was typical: "The film is bold and passionate, but not subtle, and that is its downfall. Luis Estrada ... uses his characters so clearly as symbols that he neglects to give them the complexity of human beings."[139] One small but obvious disconnect with a non–Mexican audience was the deliberate similarity between the Vargas character and Tin-Tan, the beloved screen comic of the 1940s and 1950s. When López is shown Vargas's picture as a candidate for mayor of San Pedro, he comments, "What, this guy who looks like Tin-Tan?" The joke and the reference would be lost outside of Mexico. Also, the display of a photograph of Miguel Alemán in López's office was quite surprising and even shocking to a Mexican audience, but meaningless to foreign viewers.

Another film worth mentioning is Carlos Bolados's *Bajo California: El límite del tiempo* ("Below California: The Limitations of Time," 1999). It won several Arieles and awards at film festivals in Guadalajara, Buenos Aires, Munich, St. Louis, and Los Angeles. It's the story of a man who sets out to find himself among the deserts of Baja California. He travels from Los Angeles to San Francisco de la Sierra, traverses the landscape and finally arrives at his destination, the primitive paintings of the extinct Indians of Baja California. It resembles Wim Wenders's *Paris, Texas* in that the protagonist (Damián Alcázar) is seeking something elusive, something that he needs in order to feel complete. The film's length lets us share his journey. The landscape is beautiful and desolate, as anyone familiar with Baja California will recognize. As one viewer commented: "An excellent achievement by a Mexican director. Not a movie for everybody, but one that stays with you after you've seen it. The phrase *"el pasado son todos nuestros muertos"* ("the past is all our dead") is very powerful"[140]

In the year 2000, fifteen mostly state-financed feature films were produced in Mexico.[141] But the most successful by far was the privately produced Altavista Films *Amores perros*, written by Guillermo Arriaga and directed by Alejandro González Iñárritu. Badly translated as "Love is a bitch," the film was described perhaps too enthusiastically by one *New York Times Magazine* writer as "the most ambitious and dazzling movie to emerge from Latin America in three decades."[142] González Iñárritu had previously made only television commercials, some 800 for Coca-Cola and Ford, "shot in deep, dirty colors like muddy maroon and feature actors who are not movie-star beautiful — stylistically, mini-prototypes of 'Amores Perros' "[143]

The unifying metaphor for *Amores perros* is dogs: the ones of illegal dogfights, the pampered small white dog in the second episode that is trapped under the floorboard of an apartment, and the pack of mutts that belong to a homeless man. A better translation for the title would be "cruel loves," because the first episode is about Octavio (Gael García Bernal) a working-class youth who participates in illegal dogfights to raise money to get his sister-in-law to run away with him — and he uses his brother's dog Cofi without his knowledge. The second episode is about a well-to-do magazine editor who leaves his wife to move in with a glamorous blonde supermodel. The model's little fluffy dog disappears into a hole in the floor where, she fears, it will be devoured by rats. In the last section, El Chivo (Emilio Echevarría), a revolutionary turned street bum and hit man, is accompanied by a pack of mutts that he has taken in.

Salma Hayek and Fernando Luján in Arturo Ripstein's *El coronel no tiene quien le escriba* (1999). Based on a novel by Gabriel García Márquez, it's the story of a retired colonel who vainly waits for his pension to arrive and grieves for his lost son (Cineteca).

Another scene from *El coronel no tiene quien le escriba* (Cineteca).

The film begins with a wrenching car crash that involves the lives of all the characters. Cofi, a Rottweiler bleeding from a gunshot wound, is in the car driven by Octavio, which smashes into another driven by the model, who consequently is crippled and confined to a wheelchair, thus dampening her sex appeal for her lover. And El Chivo, who happens to be passing by with his cart and dogs, rescues Cofi from the accident and takes him home to nurse him back to health. One day when El Chivo returns, he finds that Cofi has killed his other dogs.

Amores perros depicts Mex-ico City as a violent, brutal place where life is dangerous and precarious. And it is true that many middle-class *chilangos* like González Iñárritu felt insecure in the city, which had experienced a dramatic rise in crime in the 1990s following an economic crisis. This was not unlike New York City before Rudolph Giuliani reduced its high crime rate in the 1990s. (In 2003 he was a consultant for Mexico City on dealing with its crime problems.) And some of the most dramatic and infamous incidents were often reported and played up in the media, both in Mexico and the foreign press — homicides, assaults, bank robberies, taxis whose drivers held up passengers (especially tourists), kidnappings, and other forms of urban mayhem.

Mexico City was acquiring a sordid reputation, which became juicy material for some filmmakers and appealed to middle class audiences in the multiplexes. *Amores perros* then became, to many American and other foreign critics and viewers, something like a documentary of the dangerous environment of Mexico City. Not a few American movie critics assured their readers that Mexico City was a "filthy and savage" place, even though they had never been there.[144] And the brutality of the film's events was intensified by the speeded-up movement and fast cuts which the filmmaker liberally employed, enhancing the time-shifting of three interlocked stories presented in a complex elliptical style by Arriaga's intricate script.[145]

Fittingly, there were the street dogs that have always been a familiar part of the city's mosaic. Mexico City has some of the sweetest and scruffiest street-smart stray dogs of anywhere in the world. Thanks to González Iñárritu, some of these gentle and long-suffering mutts had a chance to be movie stars. He took pains to point out that no dogs were injured in the making of his film — an important factor in

Alejandro González Iñárritu directing *Amores perros* on location in Mexico City.

Emilio Echevarría with his dogs in *Amores perros*.

marketing a film in the United States and Britain. He recounts that at the New York Film Festival a woman walked out during the dogfighting sequences. He assured her that he did not hurt any dogs: "I treated the actors worse than the dogs. I love dogs."[146]

Amores perros benefited from the new multiplexes, setting box office records in Mexico before it was noticed outside the country. Altavista films, which had produced the previous commercial hit, *Sexo, pudor, y lágrimas*, invested $2.5 million (U.S.) in the González Iñárritu/Arriaga film. And its investment paid off handsomely — the film's gross by 2002 in the United States and Europe was well over $6 million. It swept the Arieles and won awards at film festivals around the world, including Cannes, Chicago, Edinburgh, and Tokyo, as well as winning a Golden Globe for best film and being nominated for an Academy Award as best foreign-language film. And it was the first of three Mexican films that did remarkably well around the world in three successive years, the other two being Alfonso Cuarón's *Y tu mamá también* (2001) and Carlos Carrera's *El crimen del Padre Amaro* (2002). Another Mexican filmmaker who found success in Hollywood and Spain was horror/fantasy specialist Guillermo del Toro.[147]

Other films, although not international blockbusters by Mexican and foreign film standards, did well by looking satirically at the country's life and in Leonardo García Tsao's words, by focusing on "figures and situations that any Mexican citizen who watches the news would recognize" and making "friendly allusion to certain neuroses of Mexico City's middle class."[148] For example, another Altavista production, Fernando Sariñana's *Todo el poder* ("All the Power," 1999), did quite well in Mexico with a comic treatment of crime and police corruption. Gabriel (Demián Bichir) is a filmmaker with a preteen daughter, ex-wife, and a girlfriend. At a very upscale country club dinner, the worst nightmare of every Mexico City yuppie occurs: a large gang of masked bandits terrorizes and holds up the partygoers. Gabriel's inquisitive camcorder later happens to record his stolen SUV driven by a cop. From this he uncovers a gang of policemen who operate as thieves and are protected by the police commissioner. The movie is amusing as Gabriel and his friends conduct their own investigation until about the middle, when too many complicated plot turns slow down the action.

Altavista Films also produced *Por la libre* (2000), another middle-class–focused film that was quite appealing. It was a road movie and the title literally means "by the toll-free road." The grandfather of two young cousins dies, and it is his last wish that his ashes be scattered in the bay of Acapulco. However, the family opposes this, everyone is quarreling about the inheritance, and the two cousins, who dislike each other, have been tasked by their grandfather to dispose of his ashes. The cousins have little money, so they cannot take the toll road to Acapulco and have to take the old highway. Once they arrive in Acapulco, they make a most surprising discovery about their grandfather's secret family. *Por la libre* was directed by Juan Carlos de Llaca.

In 2000, Altavista coproduced with Televisión Española, Tornasol Films (Spain), and Tabasco Films (Mexico) María Novaro's entertaining and beautifully photographed film *Sin dejar huella* ("Without a Trace"). A road movie about two women fleeing from villainous men, it was quickly recognizable as Ridley Scott's *Thelma & Louise* (1991) in a Mexican setting. In a question-and-answer session at the San Francisco Film Festival, director Novaro acknowledged her film's resemblance to *Thelma & Louise*, but added that she wanted to make a movie "in which the women don't get punished."[149] But the setting made all the difference.

Ana (Atiana Sánchez-Gijón) is a smuggler of forgeries of pre–Columbian artifacts which she sells to clients in the United States. (She is picked up by Mendizábel [Jesús Ochoa], a sleazy Juárez cop as she crosses the border into Mexico.) Aurelia (Tiaré Scanda) is a young mother in Ciudad Juárez whose boyfriend is involved with drug dealers. Ana manages to elude the police and hops a bus south. Aurelia drops her son off with her sister and also drives south with her baby in a beat-up station wagon. The two women — Ana is Spanish and Aurelia is Mexican — meet in a roadside restaurant where Ana suggests she help with the driving and expenses, preferring that to continuing on the bus. But Ana has no money and is not an experienced driver. She has to reach Yucatan to warn her supplier who makes the bogus figurines that the authorities are looking for him.

So begins the odyssey, a road movie that begins in the border seediness of Ciudad Juárez and finds its denouement in the tropical beauty of Cancún. During the drive, Ana and Aurelia overcome their mutual suspicions and bond while evading their respective pursuers, the menacing Mendizábel and the drug-dealing boyfriend Saúl (Martín Altomaro). Their journey takes them the length of Mexico, from the northern deserts to the lush landscapes of Veracruz, Tabasco, and Yucatan. The songs on the sound track, all subtitled, reflect the music of the regions they pass through. And Novaro unflinchingly shows the poverty of the countryside, including Zapatista graffiti. She conducts the viewer through places and cultures as alien to a middle-class Mexican as they would be to a New Yorker or Londoner. This is emphasized by the Mayan dialogue in the scenes with the artisan and his family.

Perhaps for these reasons the film did not do well in Mexico City, but its lack of distribution in the United States and Europe (it had a short run in Spain) is also puzzling. *Sin dejar huella* would seem to have had enough "folkloric" interest as well as action and comedy to appeal to a wider audience. It just points up once again the vagaries of the movie business. The next Mexican "megahit" had similar elements — a road movie with sex and comedy that also commented on the country's social and economic problems.

Before going on to Alfonso Cuarón's *Y tu mamá también*, it is worth discussing a very specialized film by one of Mexico's veteran filmmakers, Felipe Cazals. In 2000 he made *Su Alteza Serenísima* ("His Most Serene Highness"), an account of the last three days in the life of Antonio López de Santa Anna (1794–1876). He was the infamous 19th century general and eleven-times president who triumphed at the Alamo but lost Texas. He later was recalled from exile to resist the American invasion of 1846–48.[150] To no avail because after the war Mexico had to cede more than half of its territory to the victorious United States.

After making the disappointing *Kino* (1991), about the Jesuit missionary Father Eusebio Kino (1645–1711) who explored and worked in Sonora and southern Arizona, Cazals voluntarily retired from filmmaking. Referring to *Kino*, which he had to film in two parts because he ran out of funding, Cazals said it took nine years for the "wound to somewhat heal" before he decided to film again.[151] It was a time of "reflection on his profession and work, and especially his future."[152]

Su Alteza Serenísima recounts the last three days in the life of Santa Anna (Alejandro Parodi) in his hacienda, Mango de Clavo, in Veracruz. Forgotten and discredited by his countrymen, Santa Anna takes comfort in believing that, in Cazals's words, "he is not a circumstantial man but a providential one. He believes that he is the homeland, the symbol of the country, and for that reason his mistakes should be understood."[153] To keep up his spirits, Santa Anna's wife hires beggars to pay him homage and make him believe that he is still loved and respected by his subjects.

Presented with the Tatu Tumpa award at the Santa Cruz Film Festival in Bolivia, *Su Alteza Serenísima* was not otherwise widely recognized. A slowly paced, enclosed, and, some said, boring art film, it played at a few film festivals and had a moderately successful run in Mexico City.[154] Reflecting on this Cazals said:

> My movies are either successful or esteemed. In this case it was the latter. That means that the 50,000 who watched it in Mexico City are those who attend concerts, art galleries and museums. It's not the hundreds of thousands who watched *El apando* [1975]. *Su Alteza* is not a movie to entertain; it's very demanding to the public.[155]

Cazals, disregarding the middle-class-oriented commercial thrust of Mexican cinema, followed up in 2003 with *Digna ... hasta el último aliento* ("Digna ... Worthy

A scene from Felipe Cazals's *Su Alteza Serenísima* (2000) (Serenísima Films).

Another scene from *Su Alteza Serenísima* (Serenísima Films).

to her Final Breath"), a film about Digna Ochoa, an internationally acclaimed human rights lawyer who was shot dead in her office in Mexico City on October 19, 2001. Amnesty International strongly condemned her murder and demanded that President Vicente Fox immediately undertake a thorough investigation into her death. Ochoa had worked for many years on cases in which public officials, including members of the offices of the attorney general and the armed forces, had been implicated in serious human rights violations.

Cazals, indignant at the official version of Ochoa's death that it was a "simulated suicide," declared that his new film "illustrates the reality of this barbaric Mexico where social justice has not been attained, where nothing changes ... where mass killings take place ... where the assassination of a lawyer like Digna is perfectly feasible.... The official version of a simulated suicide is an insult to the intelligence of all Mexicans." Cazals, ever the tireless crusader for social justice, was still struggling to make his compatriots face up to their consciences and problems. Produced by IMCINE, *Digna ... hasta el último aliento* was screened at the Berlin Film Festival in April 2004 and the Cannes Film Festival in May 2004. Both Cazals and Vanessa Bauche, who portrayed Digna, were invited to the Berlinale.[156]

"A boomlet of celebrated movies in the last three years has prompted predictions of a renaissance in the long-dormant Mexican film industry," wrote Elisabeth Malkin in *The New York Times* in 2003.[157] Clearly, Mexican films were making an impact if they were being discussed in the *Times*. In contrast to most American critics' usually one-dimensional assessments of Mexican films, on the rare occasions they took the trouble, Malkin's article went to some depth on the problems and promise of Mexico's filmmaking. First of all, the "boomlet" referred to *Amores perros* (2000), *Y tu mamá también* (2001), and *El crimen del padre Amaro* (2002). All three featured Gael García Bernal, who won a spot on the 2003 Academy Awards, where he made an anti-war statement on Iraq, and then proceeded in short order to land acting jobs in Hollywood, the United Kingdom, and Spain (with Almodóvar).

Malkin explained the dramatic rise in multiplexes from the middle 1990s which in turn attracted middle-class audiences. Seeking to profit from these developments, Carlos Slim, multibillionaire owner of Teléfonos de México, Prodigy, and other enterprises, partnered with a live-entertainment company to found Altavista Films. Other production companies started up at this time were Argos, Producciones Anhelo, and Titán that "put their money on commercial cinema capable of attracting middle-class audiences without insulting their intelligence."[158]

Alfonso Cuarón's highly successful *Y tu mamá también* in 2001 was produced privately by Jorge Vergara Madrigal's Producciones Anhelo. Vergara is also the founder of Grupo Omnilife, a company that sells nutritional supplements. The film's gross receipts as of July 2002 were $13,622,333 in the United States. In the United Kingdom, by May of the same year, it had taken in £980,438 (UK), and in Spain 1,190,241 Euros. And these figures do not include DVD sales. It still fell short of Alfonso Arau's gross of $21,665,500 in the United States and 3,271,196 Euros in Spain for *Como agua para chocolate*, but still extremely good for a Mexican film.

Like María Novaro's practically ignored *Sin dejar huella*, *Y tu mamá también* was a road movie with attractive Mexican landscapes and social commentary, but a lot

Setting out on their fateful road trip in Alfonso Cuarón's *Y tu mamá también* (2001) are Maribel Verdú, Diego Luna, and Gael García Bernal.

more sex. After his successful *Sólo con tu pareja* in 1991, Cuarón went to Hollywood where he directed the well received *A Little Princess* in 1995 and the less successful big-budget *Great Expectations* in 1998. Even though it starred Gwyneth Paltrow and Ethan Hawke, it got "poor reviews, made no money, and was generally a very tough experience." But if it had not been for that "baroque, claustrophobic" experience of *Great Expectations*, Cuarón said "he wouldn't have realized that he'd lost sight of his ambitions as a director."

It was about that time he was invited to be an adviser to the Sundance Lab in Utah, a program founded by Robert Redford's Sundance Institute, where experienced directors help aspiring filmmakers develop their scripts. Revitalized by the enthusiasm of the novice directors, Cuarón at first was ashamed of himself:

> Why don't you learn from this? Instead of being bitter, why not reconnect to your first enthusiasm? I wanted to do something close to my creative roots, that embodies my culture, my language, my upbringing.[159]

Cuarón returned home to New York, called his brother Carlos, and they resumed work on a script they had started ten years earlier. That script became *Y tu mamá también*, a road movie, a coming of age story, a reflection on life, love, and mortality, and an uncompromising look at the extremes between Mexico's wealth and poverty. All these elements came together artistically in a film that appealed across borders, languages, and cultures.

Tenoch (Diego Luna) and Julio (Gael García Bernal) are two teenagers whose lives revolve around partying and sex. The title refers to Julio — perhaps — jokingly telling Tenoch that he had bedded his mother, after they confess to having slept with each other's girlfriends, who have gone to Europe for the summer. Tenoch's family is wealthy and politically influential, while Julio's clings to middle class status. One day at an upscale garden party to which Tenoch has taken Julio, they meet Luisa (Maribel Verdú), an attractive, late twenty-something from Madrid. She is the wife of Tenoch's cousin, whom Luisa knows is unfaithful. The boys flirt with her and suggest going to an idyllic beach they claim to have discovered. Much to their surprise, Luisa accepts their offer. Julio borrows his sister's beat-up station wagon, and they set off from Mexico City to the coast.

The journey takes them past scenes of rural poverty and ominous groups of soldiers, to which Tenoch and Julio are oblivious in their juvenile, sex-obsessed fantasies. A third-person voice-over narration explains the political and economic background of some of the events and people they come across. Luisa flirts and toys with the boys, but it is obvious she has other thoughts and concerns. The flirting evolves into intense, graphic (but simulated) sex which Luisa controls, and during one three-way encounter she so arouses Tenoch and Julio that the two boys quite naturally kiss each other. Subsequently, they are doubtful of their sexuality and their friendship cools.

Luisa decides to stay at the beach, and the boys return alone to the city. In the last scene, Tenoch and Julio meet in a Mexico City coffee shop some time later and chat uncomfortably. At first discussing college plans, Julio asks Tenoch if he heard that Luisa had died of cancer, that she had known she was terminally ill when she went on the road trip. They part, having started on the road to maturity with Luisa's guidance, but their fragile juvenile friendship is over.

Even though *Y tu mamá también* was one of the first unrated (because of its sex scenes) movies to be nominated for an Academy Award, it came as quite a surprise to Cuarón when Warner Bros. approached him to direct *Harry Potter and the Prisoner of Azkaban* (2004), the third in the enormously popular and profitable franchise.

> I was shocked. I had just made this sexy, scandalous movie, and I don't understand why they were sending me the script. I was unfamiliar with the Harry Potter universe, but I read the books, and I saw the potential. Thematically, it's actually very close to "Y tu Mamá También [*sic*]" Harry Potter is about finding your own identity, and so is "Y Tu Mamá." Harry Potter deals with class, with race, with power. I see this book as a metaphor for our times.[160]

While filming *The Children of Men*, a science-fiction movie, in Hollywood, Cuarón was also working on *México '68*, described as a drama about the student demonstrations in Mexico City during the 1968 Olympics.

And 2002 was the year of *El crimen del padre Amaro*, a controversial and highly profitable film coproduced by Alameda Films, IMCINE, FOPROCINE, and the

State of Veracruz, among others. The director was Carlos Carrera, whose two previous full-length feature films had been the highly praised *La mujer de Benjamín* (1991) and *La vida conyugal* (1993), besides several short films.

El crimen is about Father Amaro, played by Gael García Bernal in a role that further enhanced his visibility around the world. The character is that of a newly ordained priest, young, handsome, and ambitious, who arrives in a village as the assistant to the parish priest, Father Benito (Sancho Gracia). His bishop (Ernesto Gómez Cruz) taps him as a candidate for high church office by recommending him for an assignment in Rome. But Amaro cannot resist the charms of Amelia (Ana Claudia Talancón), an attractive young parishioner, with whom he has a passionate and illicit affair.

Amaro learns that Father Benito is having an affair with his housekeeper and is also laundering money for the local drug dealer to build a modern regional hospital. A left-wing priest, Father Natalio Pérez (Damián Alcázar), works diligently on behalf of the poor (and is perhaps also helping the local guerrillas) and provokes the ire of the church hierarchy. Amaro admires Pérez for choosing his ministry over a church career, even though he won't make the same sacrifice. But Amelia becomes pregnant, and Amaro arranges an abortion. The is botched and Amelia dies. In spite of this tragedy, Father Amaro conceals his "crime," his willingness to sacrifice Amelia and the baby to his church career.

El crimen del padre Amaro not surprisingly was at the center of a public row, led by the Catholic Church and religious lay groups which demanded that the new government of Vicente Fox ban the movie. He refused, which "seemed to usher in a new era of democracy and freedom of expression and the release of 'Padre Amaro' bolstered those hopes."[161]

Ernesto Gómez Cruz as the bishop and Gael García Bernal as Father Amaro in Carlos Carrera's *El crimen del padre Amaro* (2002).

Gael García Bernal and Ana Claudia Talancón in *El crimen del padre Amaro*.

But the assault backfired because the public uproar gave the film invaluable free publicity (as these controversies always do), and millions of Mexicans flocked to theaters, making the film the latest highest grossing domestic movie. The widespread scandals in the United States regarding sexual abuse by priests no doubt helped to sell movie tickets, although Father Amaro committed heterosexual offenses, not pedophilia. Roger Ebert offered this assessment:

> Both sides treat the film as a statement about the church, when in fact it's more of a melodrama, a film that doesn't say priests are bad but observes that priests are human and some humans are bad. What may really offend its critics is that young Father Amaro's crime is not having sex with a local girl and helping her find an abortion. His crime is that he covers up this episode and denies his responsibility because of his professional ambitions within the church. Young Father Amaro thinks he has a rosy future ahead of him.[162]

As indicated at the beginning of this chapter, Alejandro González Iñárritu and Alfonso Cuarón certainly reaped benefits from the enthusiastic reception in the United States and Europe of their Mexican-made films, and Carlos Carrera's film also benefited from the success of *Amores perros* and *Y tu mamá también*. So, too, did Guillermo del Toro, although his *El espinazo del diablo* (2001), a ghost story set during the Spanish Civil War and produced by Pedro Almodóvar in Spain, was not a blockbuster hit, it did do a respectable art house business. He continued making successful fantasy action thrillers in the United States like *Blade II* (2002), and *Hellboy* (2004).

Luis Mandoki is another Mexican filmmaker who is well established in Hollywood. After making four films in Mexico in the 1980s, including *Gaby: A True Story* (1987), he directed the following big studio films in Hollywood: *White Palace* (1990), *Born Yesterday* (1993), *When a Man Loves a Woman* (1994*), Message in a Bottle* (1999),

Amazing Grace (2000), *Angel Eyes* (2001), and *Trapped* (2002). He returned to Mexico in 2004 to make two films: *Casas de cartón* ("Cardboard Houses") and *Amapola* ("Poppy"). Mandoki stated that "to return had been one of my dreams after so many years [in Hollywood]. In Mexico there is a great human richness that does not exist in the United States. Being here has been a rebirth, but I continue to see that the national industry is still having difficulties."[163]

Antonio Serrano's second attempt to penetrate the North American market also failed. The director of the hugely successful *Sexo, pudor y lágrimas* made *La hija del caníbal* in 2003, based on a popular novel set in the 1970s. It was distributed in the United States under the title, *Lucía, Lucía* because, as Roger Ebert observed, "no English-speaking audiences would ... know the title referred to a political, not a dietetic, cannibal."[164]

The film sought to capitalize on the popularity of the other Mexican films, but it had a lackluster reception. Starring the Spanish actress Cecilia Roth as Lucía (the movie was a coproduction with FOPROCINE and Spain), it started out with the Hitchcockian-style disappearance of her husband at the airport where they were to catch a flight to Brazil. Lucía, who writes children's books, then enlists the help of two sympathetic neighbors in her apartment building: one is Félix (Carlos Alvarez-Novoa), an old life-long leftist, veteran of the Spanish Civil War and Castro's revolution, and the other is young, handsome Adrián (Kuno Becker) who is attracted to Lucía. They receive a ransom call from the presumed kidnappers of her husband, which turns out not to be what it seems.

In their investigations they uncover ever-deepening levels of deception indicating Lucía's husband is involved in high-level political corruption. And Lucía also makes things up — she and her apartment go through a series of transformations. The film eventually turns into a road movie where the three amateur sleuths drive up to the U.S. border and encounter a mysterious crime kingpin in a setting reminiscent of a James Bond movie. The movie, while starting off promisingly, eventually goes off in some bizarre directions. As a comedy/light drama/mystery/political/road movie, it tried to deal with too many genres at once.

As already mentioned, in the summer of 2004 Cuarón released the third Harry Potter film. The year before, Alejandro González Iñárritu had made the critically acclaimed *21 Grams* in the U.S.[165] (The title refers to the weight the body supposedly loses at death.) It came about because Sean Penn phoned him in Mexico City to congratulate him on the success of *Amores perros*. At first, he didn't believe it was really Penn — "Sure, and I'm Marlon Brando" he replied.[166]

They became friends, and González Iñárritu later sent Penn a script written by Guillermo Arriaga. "[Sean] called me every 20 minutes while he was reading it. He was reacting like a kid; he kept calling to talk about the scene he'd just read."[167] The end result was *21 Grams,* a film he originally intended to make in Mexico, in Spanish with Mexican actors. But he and Arriaga translated the script and it was shot in the United States with Penn, Naomi Watts, and Benicio del Toro. As in *Amores perros,* "there's an automobile accident, a ghastly car crash that takes three lives and suddenly connects three others."[168]

Epilogue

As I stated, the success of Salma Hayek, Alfonso Cuarón, Alejandro González Iñárritu, and Guillermo del Toro and their decisions to further their careers in the United States pointed up the persistent problems of filmmaking in Mexico. Their experience was emblematic of far-reaching cultural, political, social, and economic changes in Mexico during the late 1980s and 1990s. The film "industry"—if it could be called that—was undergoing many changes in an effort to maintain and, if possible, increase production.

During the administration of Ernesto Zedillo between 1994 and 2000, IMCINE had four directors: Alberto Lozoya, Diego López, Eduardo Amerena, and Alejandro Pelayo. In January 1998, the government created FOPROCINE (Fondo para la Producción Cinematográfica de Calidad/Fund for the Production of Quality Films) which, together with IMCINE, provided seed money for film projects and the revival of film production. With the initial deposit of 135 million pesos and the interest generated, IMCINE and FOPROCINE were able to support the production of 37 films in three and a half years, reactivating film production which increased from 11 films in 1998 to 28 in 2000. Fifteen of these were coproduced with FOPROCINE, which emphasized "art" films, and the thirteen remaining were made by private companies.

In 2001, with the support of the Congress and deputies like María Rojo, another fund was created called FIDECINE, because FOPROCINE had run out of money. FIDECINE backed more commercial films picked by a committee of distributors, exhibitors, and producers, but no filmmakers. An important film produced under this arrangement was *Nicotina* (2003), directed by Argentine-born (but naturalized Mexican) Hugo Rodríguez,[1] described as a "Tarantino-like black comedy."[2] The production team put together for this movie was Cacerola Film, Altavista Films, Videocine, FIDECINE, Cinema Gótika (Argentina), Oberon Cinematográfica (Spain) and a few others.

Alfredo Joskowicz, who succeeded Alejandro Pelayo as IMCINE's director in January 2001, characterized Mexican film production as "uneven" since 28 films were made in 2000, 21 in 2001, 14 in 2002, 29 in 2003, and he was anticipating up to 40 in 2004. In 1998, when FOPROCINE was created, Mexican movies had 3.5 percent of screen time, 8.5 percent in 2001, 9.8 percent in 2002, and 5.6 percent in 2003.

This editorial cartoon by the artist Rocha appeared in *La Jornada* on November 11, 2003. Alluding to the Fox administration's proposal to privatize the principal components of the film industry, the cartoon shows Secretary of Hacienda (Interior) Francisco Gil Díaz (who initiated the proposal) as a Dracula figure about to suck the life blood out of the Mexican cinema, represented by the hapless damsel he is carrying. "Vicente Fox Presents" is rendered in the style of the 20th Century Fox logo. The rest of the text reads "The last roll of the 'The Vampire'—Fiscal reform without a script or reason that pretends to do away with IMCINE, CCC, and Churubusco Studios." At the lower right appear the names of Francisco Gil and two other of Fox's cabinet officials—Elba Esther and Santiago Creel. Incidentally, *El vampiro*, is also the name of a famous 1957 Mexican cult film directed by Fernando Méndez and starring Abel Salazar and Ariadna Welter.

He indicated that Mexico has "more than 3,000 screens around the country, and it has 50 percent of all the Spanish-speaking screens in Latin America, not including Brazil. For American films, the Mexican market is very important: In 1998 Mexico occupied thirteenth place in Hollywood's worldwide receipts, and by 2003 it was in fourth place."[3]

Some of these more positive-sounding statistics might have led the administration of Vicente Fox to propose a controversial measure: to "*desincorporar*," or privatize IMCINE, Churubusco studios, and the film school CCC to help reduce the federal budget deficit. This plan proposed by Santiago Creel, secretary of Gobernación (Interior Department), not surprisingly caused a furor in the film and general arts and intellectual community. The actress María Rojo, also a deputy in the Congress, asked if this consisted of "a macabre joke, or, as my film colleagues say, we are witnessing one more act of schizophrenic cannibalism." Mónica Lozano of Altavista Films said it was "an assault on the nation" and Bertha Navarro of Tequila Gang averred that "the economic proposals ... are of recession, not investment. These gentlemen do not govern for Mexico.... We will not permit this design for domination that seeks to destroy the national identity." Alfredo Joskowicz demanded "an immediate explanation" for including IMCINE in the plan, adding that his agency "has supported 45 percent of the films produced in Mexico, in addition to repositioning Mexican cinema in the most important international forums."[4]

Members of the film community appealed to the Chamber of Deputies to block the administration's proposal. The leftist mayor of Mexico City (his official title is governor of the Federal District), Andrés Manuel López Obrador,* proposed showing "solidarity with the [film] community and preventing the sale of CCC by incorporating it into the University of Mexico City."

Agustín Tapia, director of *Club eutanasia*, which was filming at the time of the controversy, commented:

> At the beginning [of his administration] Fox promised to support the film industry. Our films begin to bear fruit and suddenly they come up with this. We hope this will be no more than just a scare.... It is analogous to *Club eutanasia* and its story, which tells of a home for the elderly that loses its funding. It's like a metaphor. In the nursing home the old people shout: "We want food and more attention, and that, symbolically, is what filmmakers and all the people who make their living from this are asking: work and opportunity. It is nothing if not ironic.[5]

The government, in its defense, insisted that it had proposed eliminating or privatizing seventeen agencies because "it has the obligation of being much more efficient in its use of resources." A Labor Department official, Carlos Abascal Carranza, pointed out that the Churubusco Studios with a staff of 200 employees cost the government 19 million pesos a year ($1,688,962.39 US). Similarly, in the CCC, 80 professors and 40 staff serve 150 students, spending 24 million pesos ($2,133,426.17 US) yearly. Another official said that the government should only maintain "strategic areas to provide the

---

*Andrés Manuel López Obrador is a member of the Partido de la Revolución Democrática (PRD), Party of the Democratic Revolution. In 2005, he was a leading candidate in the 2006 presidential election.

public with a clearer accounting of the resources they give us to administer public affairs: The government should only be involved in strategic sectors, and this should be the criterion with which to decide whether 'Imcine yes or Imcine no.'"[6]

The matter was finally settled when the Mexican Congress rejected these proposals in Fox's 2004 budget plan, thus saving IMCINE, Churubusco, and CCC.[7]

The two-month controversy was noticed beyond Mexico's borders, even inspiring an unusual and strong comment in the editorial pages of *The New York Times*. Observing that "Mexican movies — and moviemakers are hot ... everywhere, that is, but in Mexico," the piece pointed out that the government's proposals would only save $10 million a year as part of "widespread budget cuts." The budget cuts were inspired by a "philosophical shift" in which the conservative Fox administration was trying to implement more free-market policies. Most movie industries around the world have been state-supported, the United States and India being the principal exceptions. But obviously, in most countries it is believed that "government does belong in the movies ... France's film industry lives off more than 50 years of heavy state support. An infusion of state money ... sparked a resurgence of British film."

> Not every poor country should have a national film industry. But Mexico should, and not just because of its history. Like France, Mexico defines itself in large part by what it isn't: it's not the United States. For Mexicans, their films are a defense against being swallowed culturally by America. Despite the best efforts of the Mexican film industry, 80 percent of the movies playing in Mexican theaters come from Hollywood.[8]

It can also be said that the above remarks are perhaps even more germane to the third NAFTA partner, Canada, which supports with public funds the production of both English- and French-language movies. Canadians, a majority of whom are English-speaking but whose French-speaking sector is ever more assertive culturally, are an easily accessible market for American movies and television programming. This blanketing of Canada with American movie and television fare concerns Canadians and presents them with a more difficult task than Mexicans have in defining and maintaining their cultural differences from their powerful mutual neighbor.

In December 2002, Mexico passed a law "allowing it to do what Argentina and France do: tax movie tickets."[9] The law was modest, taxing one peso (10 cents) on every 35-peso ticket with the money going to support Mexican filmmakers. This small amount would have raised about $15 million a year, enabling films to be supported without state funds channeled through IMCINE and FIDECINE. By comparison, France taxes each moviegoer 11 percent.

> But even this tiny sum drew the wrath of the Motion Picture Association [of America], whose head, Jack Valenti, wrote a letter to President Fox. The association, which opposes all box-office taxes, argued that the law inadvertently penalized film distributors. The Valenti letter came after the law had been passed by [Mexico's] Congress, but in Mexico that is rarely the end of the story. Warner Brothers, 20th Century Fox and other American movie distributors have filed lawsuits, which are blocking the collection of more than 80 percent of the funds. It will probably be years before directors see the money.[10]

Many Americans quite naturally bristle at the accusation by leftist critics that the United States uses its economic power in ways that are inimicable to the economies and people of other countries. Valenti's and the MPAA's indignation at Mexico's perfectly legitimate and sovereign attempt to aid its modest film industry certainly does not help dispel the "imperialistic" label that many people throughout the world attach to the United States.[11] And in Mexico it does not create more friends for the United States. After nearly four decades as MPAA president, Valenti announced he would retire in the summer of 2004, "a blessing for us," wryly commented Pelayo.[12]

In addition to the above changes in infrastructure and financing were the broader ideological and cultural changes of the 1990s. Alejandro Pelayo spoke of these in comparing the generations of the 1970s and the young filmmakers of the late 1980s and 1990s:

> The generation of the 1970s — that of Ripstein, of Felipe Cazals — is fundamentally formed by going to Europe, many study in Paris. In the 1960s, there was the concept of auteur cinema, the French New Wave. We in the 1980s were influenced by the filmmakers of the 70s with whom we worked. So we also pick Europe over the United States — we study in Paris, the Socialist countries that in those days gave scholarships. Sergio Olhovich and Sergio Martínez in the USSR, Juan Manuel Torres in Poland, Paul Ledúc, Tomás Pérez Turrent, Felipe Cazals in Paris. I go to London to study. So I didn't even consider the U.S. — for me it was just a place to wait at an airport to change flights from Mexico to Paris or London. It just didn't interest me.
>
> On the other hand, the generation of the 90s, which is formed in the 80s, is influenced by television, video, with a much more rapid language from advertising which had the best technology and resources like fast cameras. At the end of the 80s, Alfonso Cuarón, Luis Estrada, Emmanuel Lubezki, and Carlos Marcovich studied at CUEC, where they had a problem because the director at that time was Marcela Fernández Violante. They wanted to make a short film in English because they intended to distribute it in the U.S. The director said no, they were unhappy, and left CUEC. Well, they have become a brilliant generation and they are all in the U.S., except for Estrada.[13]

The young generation of Mexican filmmakers, that of the 1990s as defined by Pelayo, seemed more comfortable and self-assured about maintaining their national and cultural identity even while immersed in the high-powered and fast-paced filmmaking world in the United States. And even this sense of identity had become more complex, sophisticated, and international. It reflects larger cultural, social, and economic trends in Mexico. Beginning in the 1960s Mexican and other Latin American movie industries were "unified by the principle of radical cinema," explained Donald Ranvaud, a Brazilian producer:

> They were naturally on the left, denouncing social conditions and making films about poverty. This could be very insular. Their attitude was that if the wider world wasn't interested, fine. But that is no longer seen as a justification for making a movie. Directors have realised that they have to think about their audience or perish.[14]

The internationally successful films from Mexico, Brazil, and Argentina "represent a generational sea change ... films made by youngish directors for a still-younger audience (particularly in Mexico where half the audience is under 30) ... the new wave of films is buttressed by gleaming production values and shrewd marketing campaigns. They also come hotwired into an international framework of distribution as never before."[15]

This global distribution network is mostly American — Miramax, 20th Century Fox, and other U.S. giants. Rosa Bosch, founder of Tequila Gang—"Spanish-born, Mexican-affiliated and London-based"— pointed out that the Latin American box office hits like *Amores perros*, *Y tu mamá también*, Argentina's *Nine Queens* (Fabian Bielinsky, 2000), and Brazil's *City of God* (Kátia Lund and Fernando Meirelles, 2002) are "linked by their use of private money.... None of them are financed by state subsidies."[16]

Guillermo del Toro considers state-subsidized films a "fossilized approach." He said that "when you let in private investors, you're suddenly dealing with people who'll make an effort to recoup their capital. So they'll promote your film in a way that would never have happened in the past." Alfonso Cuarón agreed, preferring to secure financing from private investors rather than "corrupt" state agencies. And he was unconcerned that his film was distributed in Mexico by a U.S. multinational: "Of course, I'm not going to defend America's attitude towards Mexico. Historically, it is a very tense relationship. But you have to be pragmatic. Why should I turn down American distribution?"[17]

Alfonso Arau opined: "Some of us have made films that have maintained the idea of a Mexican cinema. We don't make films, we make miracles. NAFTA has given an impulse. Government financing is negative because it's not the most talented who make movies but the ones with most friends, the most political."[18]

Others worry about the effect of globalization on Mexican filmmaking, concerned that American producers will use Mexican directors and actors as a "maquiladora." Víctor Ugalde especially sees these developments as "very worrisome — it's Mexico light, no depth," pointing out a recent Mexican film produced by Disney, *Ladies' Night* (2003), directed by Argentine-born Gabriela Tagliavini. Another romantic comedy about Mexico City yuppies, it had a successful run in Mexico by employing a "North American model of expression."[19] Alejandro Pelayo feels that "commercial and art cinema should coexist. Our politicians think that our film industry should be like that of the U.S., but they don't realize that 90 percent of screen time in Mexico is taken by Hollywood movies, and the remaining 10 percent is fought out by the rest of the world, including Mexican movies. I fear that globalization will doom Mexican cinema."[20]

All of these views reflect the broader complexities of the 21st century world. Globalization — the free flow of capital and business conducted by large multinational corporations — presents problems and opportunities. Understandably, many Mexicans in the arts and cultural fields fear the overwhelming power and influence of American movies and music on their popular culture, just as their counterparts around the world have the same concerns, in Canada, Latin America, Europe, and Asia. But in the world of the 21st century there will be new highly accessible technologies for disseminating popular culture. Digital video camera technology offers a high-quality and inexpensive method of making movies, making it possible for filmmakers all over the world to express themselves and their national cultures.* And widespread satellite and cable telecommunications systems of transmission provide another outlet for disseminating diversified cultural products. This is all made possible by the rapid and unimpeded movement of capital which, in Tom Friedman's words, "can seek out factories and knowledge workers anywhere in the world with greater and greater ease."[21] And this applies to workers in film and the other arts as well. This globalization in turn can lead to further rapid innovations in film, digital, computer, and information technologies that will benefit filmmakers everywhere.

The success of Alfonso Cuarón, Alejandro González Iñárritu, Guillermo del Toro, and Salma Hayek can offer a model for filmmakers working in an international context while still maintaining their national expression. However, Víctor Ugalde worried about American companies trying to interpret "*el imaginario mexicano*," or the Mexican "self image," by setting up production facilities in Mexico to make movies in Spanish with Mexican or other Latin American actors and directors because "their vision is not ours — it's always a superficial one."[22]

These differing points of view are indicative of a healthy debate within the Mexican film community. As the previous chapters of this book have shown, Mexican cinema has undergone a number of crises in its long history and it has always persevered by adapting to changing domestic and international conditions. In the 21st century, no country or culture can maintain itself untouched by cultural and economic influences from outside its borders, especially with the rapidly changing technologies of the mass media. The new generation of Mexican filmmakers, whether they choose to work in their own country or test their talents in the wider world, seemed to be adapting very well to the challenges of the 21st century.

In conclusion, Alfonso Arau's assessment seems to summarize the problems and the possibilities of Mexican cinema:

> We are thinking of a cinema that is global, and not just for Mexico. We are just beginning to reconstruct an industry. We never lacked for talent; we have magnificent writers directors, actors, photographers, technicians — all the elements to make movies that will interest the world. That will happen slowly. Some see globalization as an invasion. But it can also be like a highway with two directions — one from here to there, and another from there to here. One the one hand, it is the great calamity of mankind, on the other we can convert calamity into opportunity. We have no other option.[23]

The road ahead is difficult and uncertain, of that there is no doubt. But if the commitment, creativity, and dedication of Mexico's filmmakers, old and new, are any reflection of the larger society, then both Mexico and its cinema have a promising and probably even exciting future.

The first Mexican director to shoot a film using a digital camera was Arturo Ripstein, hardly a beginner. The movie was Así es la vida (2000), a retelling of the legend of Medea in a seedy and depressing section of Mexico City. Source: Alejandro Pelayo, interview, 15 December 2003.

Appendix 1:
Selected Filmographies

FERNANDO DE FUENTES

Born December 13, 1894, in Veracruz; died July 4, 1958, in Mexico City.

El anónimo (1932)
El prisionero trece (1933)
La Calandria (1933)
El Tigre de Yautepec (1933)
El compadre Mendoza (1933)
Cruz Diablo (1934)
El fantasma del convento (1934)
Vámonos con Pancho Villa (1935)
La familia Dressel (1935)
Las mujeres mandan (1936)
Allá en el Rancho Grande (1936)
Bajo el cielo de México (1937)
La Zandunga (1937)
La casa del ogro (1938)
Papacito lindo (1939)
Allá en el trópico (1940)
El jefe máximo (1940)
Creo en Dios (1940)
La gallina clueca (1941)
Así se quiere en Jalisco (1942)
Doña Bárbara (1943)
La mujer sin alma (1943)
El rey se divierte (1944)
Hasta que perdió Jalisco (1945)
La selva de fuego (1945)
La devoradora (1946)
Allá en el Rancho Grande (1948, remake)
Jalisco canta en Sevilla (1948)
Hipólito el de Santa (1949)
Por la puerta falsa (1950)

Crimen y castigo (1950)
Los hijos de María Morales (1952)
Canción de cuna (1952)
Tres citas con el destino (1953) (Mexican episode, coproduction with Spain and Argentina; other two segments directed by Florián Rey and León Klimovsky)

LUIS BUÑUEL

Born February 22, 1900, in Calanda, Aragón, Spain; died July 29, 1983, in Mexico City. Only Buñuel's Mexican films are listed.

Gran Casino (1946)
El gran calavera (1949)
Los olvidados (1950)
Susana (carne y demonio) (1950)
La hija del engaño (1951)
Una mujer sin amor (1951)
Subida al cielo (1952)
El bruto (1952)
Las aventuras de Robinson Crusoe (1952)
El (1952)
Abismos de pasión (1953)
La ilusión viaja en tranvía (1953)
El río y la muerte (1954)
Ensayo de un crimen (1955)
La muerte en este jardín/La Mort en ça Jardin (1956)
Nazarín (1958)
Los ambiciosos/La Fièvre Monte a El Pao (1960)
La jóven (1961)
Viridiana (1962)

El ángel exterminador (1962)
Simón del desierto (1964)

EMILIO FERNÁNDEZ

Born March 27, 1904, El Hondo, Coahuila;
died in Mexico City on August 6, 1986.

La isla de la pasión (Clipperton) (1941)
Soy puro mexicano (1942)
Flor silvestre (1943)
María Candelaria (1943)
Las abandonadas (1944)
Bugambilia (1944)
Pepita Jiménez (1945)
La perla (1945)
Enamorada (1946)
Río Escondido (1947)
Maclovia (1948)
Salón México (1948)
Pueblerina (1948)
La malquerida (1949)
Duelo en las montañas (1949)
Del odio nació el amor (*The Torch*, English-lan-
   guage version of *Enamorada*) (1949)
Un día de vida (1950)
Víctimas del pecado (1950)
Islas Marías (1950)
Siempre tuya (1950)
La bienamada (1951)
Acapulco (1951)
El mar y tu (1951)
Cuando levanta la niebla (1952)
La red (1953)
Reportaje (1953)
El rapto (1953)
La rosa blanca (coproduction with Cuba, 1953)
La rebelión de los colgados, codirector Alfredo
   Crevenna (1954)
Nosotros dos (coproduction with Spain, 1954)
La tierra de fuego se apaga (coproduction with
   Argentina, 1955)
Una cita de amor (1956)
El impostor (1956)
Pueblito (1961)
Paloma herida (coproduction with Guatemala,
   1962)
Un dorado de Pancho Villa (1966)
El crepúsculo de un dios (1968)
La Choca (1973)
Zona roja (1975)
México norte (1975)
Erótica (1978)

ALEJANDRO GALINDO

Born January 14, 1906, in Monterrey; died
in Mexico City on February 1, 1999.

Almas rebeldes (1937)
Refugiados en Madrid (1938)
Mientras México duerme (1938)
El muerto murió (1939)
Corazón de niño (1939)
El monje loco (1940)
Ni sangre ni arena (1941)
El rápido de las 9:15 (1941)
Vírgen de medianoche (1941)
Konga roja (1943)
Divorciadas (1943)
Tribunal de justicia (1943)
La sombra de Chucho el Roto (1944)
Tu eres la luz (1945)
Campeón sin corona (1945)
Los que volvieron (1946)
Hermoso ideal (1947)
El muchacho alegre (1947)
¡Esquina bajan! (1948)
Una familia de tantas (1948)
Hay lugar para dos (1948)
Confidencias de un ruletero (1949)
Cuatro contra el mundo (1949)
Capitán de rurales (1950)
Doña Perfecta (1950)
Dicen que soy comunista (1951)
El último round (1952)
Los dineros del diablo (1952)
Por el mismo camino (1952)
Sucedió en Acapulco (1952)
Las infieles (1953)
Espaldas mojadas (1953; released 1955)
Los Fernández de Peralvillo (1953)
La duda (1953)
¡…Y mañana serán mujeres! (1954)
Historia de un marido infiel (1954)
Tres melodías de amor (1955)
Hora y media de balazos (1956)
Policías y ladrones (1956)
Tu hijo debe nacer (1956)
Esposa te doy (1956)
Piernas de oro (1957)
Te vi en TV (1957)
Manos arriba (1957)
Echenme al gato (1957)
Raffles (1958)
La edad de la tentación (1958)
El supermacho (1958)
México nunca duerme (1958)

La vida de Agustín Lara (1958)
¡Ni hablar del peluquín! (1959)
Ellas también son rebeldes (1959)
Mañana serán hombres (1960)
La muerte y el crimen (1961)
Corona de lágrimas (1967)
Remolino de pasiones (1968)
Cristo 70 (1969)
Verano ardiente (1970)
Simplemente vivir (1970)
Tacos al carbón (1971)
Pepito y la lámpara maravillosa (1971)
Triángulo (1971)
San Simón de los magüeyes (1972)
El juicio de Martín Cortés (Los hijos de La Malinche) (1973)
Ante el cadáver de un líder (1973)
Y la mujer hizo al hombre (1974)
Las del talón (1977)
Que te vaya bonito (1977)
Mojados (Wetbacks) (1977)
El milagro en el circo (1978)
Dimas el león (1979)
Cruz de olvido (1980)
El sexo de los pobres (1981)
El color de nuestra piel (1982)
Lázaro Cárdenas (1985)
¡México grita! (1986)

LUIS ALCORIZA

Born September 5, 1921, in Badajoz, Spain. Died December 3, 1992, in Cuernavaca, Mexico.

Los jóvenes (1960)
Tlayucan (1961)
Tiburoneros (1962)
Amor y sexo (1963)
Tarahumara (Cada vez más lejos) (1964)
El gángster (1964)
Juego peligroso (1967) (directed segment *Divertimento*; other part directed by Alberto Isaac)
La puerta y la mujer del carnicero (1968)
El oficio mas antiguo del mundo (1970)
Paraíso (1970)
El muro del silencio (1971)
Mecánica nacional (1971)
Esperanza (one part of *Fe, esperanza y caridad*; directors of other two parts: Alberto Bojórquez and Jorge Fons)
Presagio (1974)

Las fuerzas vivas (1975)
A paso de cojo (1978)
Semana santa en Acapulco (Viacrucis nacional) (1980)
Han violado a una mujer (1981)
El amor es un juego extraño (1983)
Terror y encajes negros (1984)
Lo que importa es vivir (1987)
Día de muertos (1988)
La sombra del ciprés es alargada (1990)

ALBERTO ISAAC

Born March 18, 1925, in Colima, Mexico; died January 9, 1998, in Mexico City.

En este pueblo no hay ladrones (1965)
Las visitaciones del diablo (1968)
Olimpiada en México (1969)
Fútbol México 70 (1970)
The World at Their Feet (1970)
Los días del amor (1971)
El rincón de las vírgenes (1972)
Cita en Guadalajara (1973)
Tívoli (1974)
Cuartelazo (1976)
Tiempo de lobos (1981)
Las noches de Paloma (1978)
¡Maten a Chinto! (1990)
Mujerers insumisas (1995)

FELIPE CAZALS

Born July 28, 1937, in Guethary, France. Family emigrated to Mexico four months later. Raised in Mexico City.

Mariana Alcoforado (1965)
La manzana de la discordia (1968)
Familiaridades (1969)
Emiliano Zapata (1970)
El jardín de tía Isabel (1971)
Aquellos años (1973)
Los que viven donde el viento sopla suave (1973)
Canoa (1975)
Testimonios y documentos: Paro agrario (1975)
Investigación científica (1975)
El apando (1976)
Las Poquiánchis (1976)
La güera Rodríguez (1978)
El año de la peste (1978)
Rigo es amor (1980)

El gran triunfo (1980)
Las siete Cucas (1981)
Bajo la metralla (1983)
Los motivos de Luz (1985)
El tres de copas (1986)
Testimonios de la revolución (1986)
Las inocentes (1986)
Burbujas de amor (1991)
Desvestidas y alborotadas (1991)
Kino (1993)
Su Alteza Serenísima (2000)
Digna ... hasta el último aliento (2003)

ARTURO RIPSTEIN

Born December 13, 1943, in Mexico City.

Tiempo de morir (1966)
Juego peligroso (1967) (segment "HO")
Los recuerdos del porvenir (1968)
La hora de los niños (1969)
El náufrago de la Calle Providencia (1970)
Exorcismos (1970)
Crimen (1970)
La belleza (1970)
Autobiografía (1970)
El castillo de la pureza (1973)
El Santo Oficio (1974)
Los otros niños (1974)
Tres preguntas a Chávez (1975)
Tiempo de correr (1975)
Foxtrot (1975)
Matématicas (1975)
Español (1975)
Ciencias sociales (1975)
Ciencias naturales (1975)
Lecumberri (1976)
El borracho (1976)
La viuda negra (1977)
El lugar sin límites (1978)
Cadena perpétua (1979)
La ilegal (1979)
La tía Alejandra (1979)
La seducción (1980)
Rastro de muerte (1981)
Quítele el usted y tratamos (1984)
El otro (1984)
De todo como en botica (1984)
Contra hechos no hay palabras (1984)
El imperio de la fortuna (1986)
Mentiras piadosas (1987)
La mujer del puerto (1991)
Principio y fin (1993)

La reina de la noche (1994)
Profundo carmesí (1996)
El evangelio de las maravillas (1998)
El coronel no tiene quien le escriba (1999)
Así es la vida (2000)
La perdición de los hombres (2000)
La vírgen de la lujuria (2002)

JAIME HUMBERTO HERMOSILLO

Born January 22, 1942, in Aguascalientes, Mexico.

S.S. Glencairn (1967)
Los nuestros (1969)
La verdadera vocación de Magdalena (1971)
El señor de Osanto (1972)
El cumpleaños del perro (1975)
La pasión según Berenice (1976)
Matinée (1977)
Naufragio (1977)
Idilio (1977)
Amor libre (1978)
María de mi corazón (1979)
Confidencias (1982)
Las apariencias engañan (1983)
El corazón de la noche (1983)
Doña Herlinda y su hijo (1985)
Clandestino destino (1987)
El verano de la señora Forbes (1988)
Un momento de ira (1989)
Intimidades de un cuarto de baño (1989)
El aprendiz de pornógrafo (1989)
La tarea (1990)
La tarea prohibida (1992)
Encuentro inesperado (1993)
Danske piger viser alt/ Danish Girls Show Everything (1996) (segment "Why Don't We?")
¿Por qué nosotros no? (1996)
De noche vienes, Esmeralda (1997)
Escrito en el cuerpo de la noche (2002)
eXXXorcismos (2002)
Ausencia (2003)
El Edén (2004)
Dos auroras (2004)
El misterio de los almendros (2004)
Rencor (2005)

MARÍA NOVARO

Born September 11, 1951, in Mexico City.

7 A.M. (1982)

Querida Carmen (1983)
Pervertida (1985)
Una isla rodeada de agua (1985)
Historias de ciudad (1988)
Azul celeste (1988)
Lola (1990)

Danzón (1991)
Otoñal (1993)
El Jardín del Edén (1994)
Enredando sombras (1998) (episode "Cuando comenzamos a hablar")
Sin dejar huella (2000)

Appendix 2:
Useful Addresses

Instituto Mexicano de Cinematografía (IMCINE)
(Mexican Film Institute)
Director: Alfredo Joskowicz
Managing Director, International Promotion and Sales: Susana López Aranda, suslopez @hotmail.com
Insurgentes Sur 674
Col. Del Valle
03100 México, D.F.
Telephone: (5255) 5448 5344/5448 5339
        Fax: (5255) 5448 5380
Promint@imcine.gob.mx
www.imcine.gob.mx

Academia Mexicana de Artes y Ciencias Cinematográficas (AMACC)
(Mexican Academy of Motion Picture Arts and Sciences)
Technical Secretary: Silvia Gil
Av. División del Norte 2462 (3er piso)
Col. Portales, Del. Benito Juárez
03300 México, D.F.
Telephone and fax: (5255) 5688 7079
Ariel@gapsnet.com
www.academia-ariel.org.mx

Asociación Mexicana de Productores Independientes (AMPI)
(Mexican Association of Independent Producers)
President: Federico González Compeán
Atletas 2, Camerino B-201, Edif. Luis Buñuel

Col. Country Club, Del. Coyoacán
04220 México, D.F.
Telephone: (5255) 5689 5344
        Conm. (5255) 5549 3060 Ext. 121
Ampiac@yahoo.com

Asociación Nacional de Actores (ANDA)
(National Actors' Association)
Secretary General: Juan Imperio
Ignacio Altamirano 128 4o piso
Col. San Rafael
06470 México, D.F.
Telephone: Conm. (5255) 5705 0624
                    (5255) 5535 4019
                    (5255) 5592 2162
            Fax: (5255) 5566 6065
General@anda.org.mx

Asociación de Productores y Distribuidores de Películas Mexicanas
(Association of Producers and Distributors of Mexican Films)
Director: Gonzalo Elvira Ávarez
Av. División del Norte 2462, 8o piso
Col. Portales, Del. Benito Juárez
03300 México, D.F.
Telephone: (5255) 5688 7251
                    (5255) 5688 8301
            Fax: (5255) 5688 8810
                    (5255) 5604 3202

Cámara Nacional de la Industria Cinematográfica (CANACINE)
(National Chamber of the Film Industry)

President: Miguel Ángel Dávila
Gral. Anaya 198
Col. San Diego Churubusco, Del. Coyoacán
04120 México, D.F.
Telephone: (5255) 5688 0442
    Fax: (5255) 56888810/5604 3202
Canacine@mx.inter.net
Canacine@terra.com.mx
www.canacine.org.mx/

Centro de Capacitación Cinematográfica (CCC)
(Center for Film Training)

Director: Ángeles Castro Gurría
Calzada de Tlalpan No. 1670
Col. Country Club
04220 México, D.F.
Telephone: (5255) 1253 9490
Sandalia@cc.cnart.mx
http://ccc.cnart.mx/

Centro Universitario de Estudios Cine-matográficos (CUEC)
(University Center for Film Studies)

Director: Mitl Valdez Salazar
Adolfo Prieto 721
Col. Del Valle, Del. Benito Juárez
03100 México, D.F.
Telephone: (5255) 5699 1489/5682 5196
    Fax: (5255) 5536 1799
Mitlvs@correo.unam.mx

Cineteca Nacional
(National Film Archive)

Director: Magdalena Acosta Urquidi
Ave. México Coyoacán No. 189
Colo. Xoco, Del. Benito Juárez
03330 México, D.F.
Telephone: (5255) 5422 1100
    Fax: (5255) 5422 1180
cbloch@cinetecanacional.net
macosta@cinetecanacional.net
masanchez@cinetecanacional.net
www.cinetecanacional.net

Comisión Nacional de Filmaciones (CONAFILM)
(National Film Commission)

National Commissioner: Sergio Molina
Av. División del Norte 2462, 5o piso
Col. Portales, Del. Benito Juárez
03300 México, D.F.

Telephone: (5255) 5688 7813/5688 0970
    Fax: (5255) 5688 7027
Conafilm@prodigy.net.mx
www.conafilm.org.mx

Consejo Nacional para la Cultura y las Artes (CONACULTA)
(National Council for Culture and the Arts)

President: Sari Bermúdez
Arenal No. 40
Col. Chimalistac
01050 México, D.F.
Telephone: (5255) 5662 8199
    Fax: (5255) 5662 6080
www.conaculta.gob.mx/

Estudios Churubusco (ECHASA)

Director: Mario Aguiñaga
Atletas 2
Col. Country Club, Del. Coyoacán
04220 México, D.F.
Telephone: (5255) 5549 3060
    Fax: (5255) 5549 1418
www.estudioschurubusco.com
robespierre@estudioschurubusco.com
magiñaga@estudios-churubusco.com

Dirección General de Actividades Cine-matográficas de la UNAM Filmoteca
(General Office of Film Activities of the UNAM Film Archive)

Director: Iván Trujillo Bolio
Circuito Dr. Mario de la Cueva s/n
Del. Tlalpan
04510 México, D.F.
(located in front of the Faculty of Political
    and Social Sciences)
Telephone: (5255) 5702 2594/5622 9595/
        5622 9583
    Fax: (5255) 5622 9585
Trujillo@servidor.unam.mx
www.unam.mx/filmoteca

Fondo de Inversión y Estímulos al Cine (FIDECINE)
(Fund for Investment and Stimuli)

Executive Secretary: Víctor Ugalde
Insurgentes Sur 674
Col. Del Valle, Del. Benito Juárez
03100 México, D.F.

Telephone: (5255) 5682 8776
   Fax: (5255) 5448 5381
Fidecine@imcine.gob.mx

**Secretaría de Relaciones Exteriores.
   Unidad de Asuntos Culturales
(Department of Foreign Relations. Cul-
   tural Affairs Unit)**
Av. Paseo de la Reforma 175
Col. Cuauhtémoc, Del. Cuauhtémoc
06500 México, D.F.
Telephone: (5255) 5241 3401
   Fax: (5255) 5782 3209
www.sre.gob.mx

**Sindicato de Trabajadores de la Indus-
   tria Cinematográfica (STIC)
(Union of Film Industry Workers)**
General Secretary: Jorge Sánchez Sánchez
Plaza de la República No. 32, 5o y 6o pisos
Col. Tabacalera, Del. Cuauhtémoc
06030 México. D.F.
Telephone: (5255) 5566 6011/5566
      6401/55566 1599
   Fax: (5255) 5535 8797

**Sindicato de Trabajadores de la Produc-
   ción Cinematográfica (STPC)
(Union of Film Production Workers)**
General Secretary: Marcela Fernández
   Violante
Col. San José Insurgentes, Del. Benito Juárez
03900 México, D.F.
Telephone: (5255) 5680 6299
   Fax: (5255) 5593 5990
Ccstpc@terra.com.mx

**Sociedad de Escritores de México
   (SOGEM)
(General Writers Association of Mexico)**
President: Víctor Hugo Razcón Banda
José María Velasco 59
Col. San José Insurgentes, Del. Benito Juárez
03900 México, D.F.
Telephone: (5255) 5593 3147/5593 9976
   Fax: (5255) 5593 6017
Muribe@sogem.org.mx
www.sogem.org.mx/

Notes

Chapter 1

1. Agustin Mahieu, *Breve historia del cine nacional,* 1896–1974 (Buenos Aires: Alzamor Editores, 1976), pp. 7–24.

2. Geraldo Santos Pereira, *Plano Geral do Cinema Brasileiro: História, Cultura, Economia e Legislação* (Benfica, Guanabara: Editor Borsoi, 1973), pp. 61–62.

3. Georges Sadoul, *Histoire du Cinéma Mondial des Origines à nos Jours* (Paris: Flammarion Editeur, 1949), pp. 7–18.

4. He comments: "Malamente puede escribirse la historia de esta etapa [muda] cuando solo se ha logrado ver *una* cinta muda nacional, El automóvil gris; tal es mi caso y el de casi todos los demás estudiosos del cine del país." Emilio García Riera, *Historia documental del cine mexicano,* 9 vols (Mexico City: Ediciones Era, 1969–1978), 1:7; hereinafter referred to as *Historia.*

5. *Salón Rojo (programas y crónicas del cine mudo en México),* vol. 1 *(1895–1920),* Cuadernos de Cine #16 (Mexico City: Dirección General de Difusión Cultural, UNAM, 1968), hereinafter referred to as *Salón Rojo.*

6. *Ibid.,* pp. 7–8.

7. Both the *Enciclopedia de México,* 10 vols. (Mexico City: Instituto de la Enciclopedia de México, 1968), 2: 540 and the *Diccionario Porrúa: Historia, Biografía y Geografía de México,* 2 vols., 3d ed. (Mexico City: Editorial Porrúa, 1970), 1: 435 attribute the establishment of this theater to Salvador Toscano. The confusion seems to stem from the fact that in 1897 Toscano opened his *second* theater, also on Plateros Street (his first locale had been on No. 17 Jesús María Street in early 1897). *Salón Rojo,* p. 17.

8. Quoted in *Salón Rojo,* pp. 9, 11, 14. Unless otherwise noted, all translations are author's.

9. Quoted in *ibid.,* p. 15.

10. *Enciclopedia de México,* 2: 540; *Diccionario Porrúa,* 1: 435.

11. *Salón Rojo,* p. 17.

12. *Ibid.,* p. 18.

13. *Ibid.,* pp. 19–20; Sadoul, *Histoire du Cinéma Mondial,* p. 25.

14. *Salón Rojo,* p. 20.

15. *Ibid.,* pp. 20–21.

16. *Ibid.,* pp. 22–23.

17. *Ibid.,* pp. 25–26.

18. *Ibid.,* pp. 26–27.

19. *Ibid.,* p. 28.

20. Eugenia Meyer, coordinator, *Cuadernos de la Cineteca Nacional: Testimonios para la historia del cine mexicano,* 8 vols. (Mexico City: Dirección de Cinematografía de la Secretaría de Gobernación, 1976), 1: 13.

21. These were as follows: Teatro Riva Palacio, Teatro Apolo, Sala Pathé, Gran Salón Mexicano, Academia Metropolitana, Salón High Life, Salón Art Noveau, Salón de Moda, Salón Verde, Spectatorium, Salón Monte Carlo, El Molino Blanco, Salón Music Hall, Pabellón Morisco, and Salón Cinematográfico (which after November 1906 was renamed Salón Rojo). *Salón Rojo,* p. 35.

22. Quoted in *ibid.,* pp. 35, 37. Eric Rhode observes: "We may find it ironic that a class only recently touched by the hope of literacy should have been the first to give itself over to moving images; but the truth is that the cinema was to be a desperately needed consolation and source of knowledge to the poor, the illiterate and to immigrant communities (as in America) unable to speak the native language." *A History of the Cinema from its Origins to 1970* (New York: Hill and Wang, 1976), p. 21.

23. Moisés González Navarro, *Población y sociedad en México (1900–1970),* 2 vols. (Mexico City: UNAM, 1974), 1:43.

24. *Salón Rojo,* p. 31.

25. Meyer, *Cuadernos,* 1:13. Also see Alejandro Sorondo, "Jorge Stahl Inició de Niño una Carrera Cinematográfica que ha Durado 82 Años," *Excélsior,* 22 September 1976, pp. 9-B, 10-B; and Augustín Gurezpe, "Hoy es el Homenaje a Jorge Stahl Frente al Monumento del 'Ariel,'" *Excélsior,* 8 October 1976, Section Cine, Teatro, Radio y TV, p. 1.

26. *Salón Rojo,* p. 31.

27. *Ibid.* Film runs through the projector at the rate of 10.98 meters a minute.

28. *Ibid.,* pp. 32–33.

29. *Ibid.*, p. 34.

30. The first had been Salvador Toscano's *Don Juan Tenorio* (1898).

31. Emilio García Riera, *El cine mexicano* (Mexico City: Ediciones Era, 1963), p. 14.

32. *Salón Rojo*, pp. 52–53; although Toscano was not responsible for the making of this film, a scene from it can be seen briefly in *Memorias de un mexicano*.

33. Rodolfo Usigli, *Mexico in the Theater*, translated with an introduction by Wilder P. Scott (University, Miss.: Romance Monographs, Inc., 1976), p. 114.

34. *Ibid.*, p. 110.

35. "Una Gran Dama," *Tiempo*, 26 October 1945, p. 30; Daniel Cosío Villegas, gen. ed., *Historia moderna de México*, 8 vols. (Mexico City: Editorial Hermes, 1955–1972), vol. 4, *El Porfiriato — La vida social* by Moisés González Navarro (1957), pp. 801–12.

36. Carlos Monsiváis, "Junto contigo le doy un aplauso al placer y al amor," *Textos* (Guadalajara), año 2, no. 9–10 (1975), p. 39; Ruth S. Lamb, *Mexican Theater of the Twentieth Century; Bibliography and Study* (Claremont, Calif.:Ocelot Press, 1975), p. 7.

37. Raoul Fournier Villada, "He Makes Mexico Laugh," *Américas*, March 1953, pp. 6–8.

38. *Ibid.*, p. 7.

39. *Salón Rojo*, p. 58.

40. *Ibid.*, pp. 58–59.

41. *Ibid.*, pp. 63–65.

42. *Ibid.*, p. 65.

43. Oscar Valdés and Miguel Torres, "En compañía de Max Linder," *Cine cubano* 6, no. 35 (1966): 45–49; *Salón Rojo*, pp. 66–67; D.J. Wenden, *The Birth of the Movies* (London: Macdonald and Co., 1975), p. 28.

44. Pierre Leprohon, *The Italian Cinema*, translated from the French by Roger Greaves and Oliver Stallybrass (New York: Praeger Publishers, 1972), pp. 24–25.

45. "Temporada Dramática," *Tiempo*, 16 March 1945, p. 46.

46. A similar cinema fire in Paris at the Bazar de la Charité in May 1897 took a heavy toll of life, mostly aristocrats. Rhode, *A History of the Cinema*, p. 19.

47. *Salón Rojo*, pp. 59–60, 113–14. The truth of the matter is that the era's nitro cellulose stock was highly flammable and the movie "salons," which were often nothing more than wooden shacks, added to the danger. A fireproof film was not to be available until 1952 with the introduction of acetate-based film stock. Clive Coultass, "Film Preservation: The Archives," in Smith, *The Historian and Film*, p. 35.

48. As is the case with the United States, Mexico does not date its independence from the actual date of administrative separation from Spain. This occurred with the signing of the Treaty of Córdoba on August 24, 1821, by Agustín Iturbide and the last viceroy, Juan Odonojú. A provisional government was set up in Mexico City on September 28. The date that Mexicans observe as independence day is September 16, 1810, which commemorates Father Miguel Hidalgo y Costilla's abortive *jacquerie*.

49. E. Bradford Burns, *Latin American Cinema: Film and History* (Los Angeles: UCLA Latin American Center, 1975), p. 18. Even though Burns erroneously dates the film in 1918, his comments acquire greater significance when it is realized that such a film was produced under an officially anti-indigenous regime, and that it might have reflected an already strong pre-revolutionary current of interest in Mexico's Indian past — and present.

50. Howard F. Cline, *The United States and Mexico* (New York: Atheneum, 1963), p. 122.

51. *Ibid.*, p. 121.

52. *Salón Rojo*, p. 77.

53. *Ibid.*

54. *Ibid.*, p. 79.

55. *Ibid.* The tone of this advertisement is not surprising in view of the campaign of vilification at this time against Madero's provisional government and against him personally. Porfirian elements nostalgic for the "good old days" were still plentiful, and presumably these were the people who responded with their "enthusiastic applause" to the sight of Porfirio Díaz on the screen. For a representative sample of films exhibited in 1912, including comedy shorts by Max Linder and Rabinet, and American westerns, see *ibid.*, pp. 79–80.

56. Quoted from the Salón Rojo's advertisement for *La revolución en Chihuahua, ibid.*, p. 82. Rare films of the campaign against Pascual Orozco can be seen in *Memorias de un mexicano*, including shots of General Victoriano Huerta in the field directing the federal forces. These are among the earliest films taken of combat.

57. Cosío Villegas, *Historia moderna de México*, p. 791.

58. *Ibid.*

59. *Ibid.*, p. 790.

60. *Salón Rojo*, pp. 54–56.

61. *Ibid.*, pp. 95–96.

62. Leprohon, *The Italian Cinema*, p. 28.

63. *Salón Rojo*, pp. 100–101.

64. *Ibid.*, p. 104.

65. *Ibid.*, pp. 112–13.

66. *Ibid.*, p. 125.

67. *Ibid.*, pp. 125–26.

68. *Ibid.*, p. 139.

69. Actually "whistled" — in Mexico an audience generally displays its displeasure not by hissing but by whistling.

70. From *El águila y la serpiente*, quoted in Monsiváis, "Junto contigo le doy un aplauso al placer y al amor," p. 43.

71. Federico Heuer, *La industria cinematográfica mexicana* (Mexico City: n.p., 1964), p. 6; Francisco A. Gómezjara and Delia Selene de Dios, *Sociología del cine* (Mexico City: Sep/Setentas, 1973), p. 48.

72. From E. Bradford Burns's introduction to Beatriz Reyes Nevares, *The Mexican Cinema: Interviews with Thirteen Directors*, trans. Carl J. Mora and Elizabeth Gard (Albuquerque: University of New Mexico Press, 1976), p. xii.

73. John Womack, Jr., *Zapata and the Mexican Revolution* (New York: Vintage Books, 1970), pp. 319, 322–23, 324, 327, 329, 339. Pablo González was a partner in the film company, Azteca Films; the other two were the actress Mimí Derba and the director and producer, Enrique Rosas. García Riera, *El cine mexicano*, p. 16.

74. *Salón Rojo*, p. 144.

75. *Ibid.*, pp. 153, 155.

76. *Ibid.*, pp. 157–58. A list of the players provides what is probably a fairly complete picture of Mexico's film actors at this time.

77. *Ibid.*, pp. 158, 186–87.

78. *Ibid.*, pp. 170–75; *Diccionario Porrúa*, 1: 1146; García Riera, *El cine mexicano*, pp. 14–15.

79. Leprohon, *The Italian Cinema*, p. 45.

80. *Salón Rojo*, pp. 179–80.

81. Leprohon, *The Italian Cinema*, p. 50; García Riera, *El cine mexicano*, p. 12.

82. *Salón Rojo*, p. 185. See also on pages 106–8 the discussion on national traits in films.

83. *Diccionario Porrúa*, 1: 435.

84. For instance in Argentina, along with Brazil, the other major Latin American film-producing country, production consistently lagged behind Mexico's, and the initiatives seemed to be largely in the hands of immigrants. For example, Eugenio Py, a French photographer, was the "Salvador Toscano" of Argentina, installing the first Lumière projector and filming the first footage of public events and street scenes. His first effort was a 17-meter film, *La bandera argentina* (1900), followed by *Visita del Dr. Campos Salles a Buenos Aires* (1900) and *Visita del General Mitre al Museo Nacional*. Eugenio Cardini (1880–1962), a native Argentinian, made *Escenas callejeras* (1902) after constructing, in 1896, the first movie camera ever made in Argentina and "almost undoubtedly in South America." An Italian immigrant, Mario Gallo, who arrived in Argentina in 1905, made *Fusilamiento de Dorrego* in 1908, the first Argentine film made from a script. The Uruguayan Julio R. Alsina (1883–1944) produced a film on Argentina's centennial, *La revista del centenario* (1910). Another Italian, Federico Valle, who had studied with Méliès, arrived in 1911, and until 1930 produced a newsreel, *Film Revista*. In 1915 Humberto Cairo wrote and directed *Nobleza gaucha*, the greatest success of the Argentine film industry to that time. In 1916 Alcides Greca, a Santa Fean, produced *El último malón*. Other notable films of the period were José Agustín Ferreyra's *El tango de la muerte* (1917) and Roberto Guidi's *El mentir de los demás* (1919). Mahieu, *Breve historia*, pp. 11–21. Brazilian production was practically nonexistent prior to 1920, although screenings of foreign films followed the pattern established in the rest of the hemisphere. The period 1913–1922 is referred to as the "*Fase Artesanal*, que inclui as primeiras tentativas de produção organizada, devida mais ao esforço pessoal de pioneiros de que a una estrutura industrial mais consistente." Santos Pereira, *Plano Geral do Cinema Brasileiro*, p. 36.

85. For instance, beginning in 1918 the Guanajuatan Indalecio de Noriega Colombres made the following films: *Carros alegóricos de Chapultepec, Madero en Guanajuato, Corrida de toros, Fuerzas zapatistas, Llegada de don Francisco I. Madero a México, El terrible Pérez, Juegos de beisbol en Guanajuato, La oración de la noche, El molinito, Revista histórica nacional, Caballos de la calle, Pieza teatral, Por ahí viene ya, Madame Butterfly, El año pasado por agua, El bateo, Modelo parisiense, Discurso de Vale Coyote*, and others. His

daughter, María Teresa Noriega, sold them in 1972 to the Centro Universitario de Estudios Cinematográficos for 20,000 pesos. In 1976 she accused its director, Manuel González Casanova, of losing 39 rolls of the "first sound films." González Casanova gave assurances that the films were in the UNAM Filmoteca but that Ms. Noriega had not included the records when delivering the films. See Ricardo Perete, "Desaparecen 39 Rollos con las Primeras Películas Sonoras," *Excélsior*, 11 June 1976, p. C-1 and 15 June 1976, p. B-13.

86. Maria Rita Eliezer Galvão, *Crônica do Cinema Paulistano* (São Paulo: Editora Ática, 1975).

87. García Riera, *El cine mexicano*, p. 13.

88. Meyer, *Cuadernos*, 1: 14.

89. Cline, *The United States and Mexico*, p. 191.

90. *Ibid.*, pp. 192–93.

91. Jesús Abitia was also a friend of General Obregón; in fact, he filmed many of the latter's military campaigns. Reyes Nevares, *The Mexican Cinema*, p. 23.

92. García Riera, *El cine mexicano*, p. 19.

93. *Ibid.*, p. 13.

94. Yet many voices were raised against the film's blatant racism, including those of the NAACP and the president of Harvard University. Wenden, *The Birth of the Movies*, p. 54.

95. Blaine P. Lamb, "The Convenient Villain: The Early Cinema Views the Mexican-American," *Journal of the West* 14 (October 1975): 75.

96. W.A. Swanberg, *Citizen Hearst* (New York: Charles Scribner's Sons, 1961), pp. 296–97. Judging from some typical comments in U.S. newspapers on the eve of our entrance into the war, the nation was on the verge of hysteria over the situation in Mexico. *The Buffalo Express* visualized "hordes of Mexicans under German officers, sweeping into Texas, New Mexico and Arizona." *The New York American* (a Hearst paper) stated: "Mexico ... would retake the Southwest and restore it to barbarism; Japan would take the Far West and 'orientalize' it; Germany and Russia would enslave generations of Americans in the payment of vast war indemnities." Barbara W. Tuchman, *The Zimmerman Telegram* (New York: Dell Publishing Co., 1958), p. 187. The "Plan of San Diego"—a vast Texas-based plot to wrench the former Mexican territories of California, New Mexico, Nevada, Colorado, Arizona, and Oklahoma back from the United States and establish an independent republic affiliated with Mexico—surfaced at this time. Of doubtful authenticity—or perhaps concocted by disgruntled Mexican-Americans working with Mexican and German *provocateurs*—it fed American paranoia. Tuchman speculates that a report of this "conspiracy" reached the German foreign minister, Arthur Zimmerman, and might have inspired his offer to Mexico of an alliance and return of the territories lost in 1848 if it declared war on the United States. *Ibid.*, p. 97. The "Plan" was ostensibly suggested by one F. de P. González, editor of the newspaper *La libertad* in San Diego, Texas. Juan Gómez-Quiñones, "Piedras contra la Luna, México en Aztlán y Aztlán en México: Chicano-Mexican Relations and the Mexican Consulates, 1900–1920," in James W. Wilkie, Michael C. Meyer, Edna Monzón de Wilkie, eds., *Contemporary Mexico: Papers of the IV International Congress of*

Mexican History (Berkeley, Los Angeles, London: University of California Press; and Mexico City: El Colegio de México, 1976), p. 518. Another writer states: "Most authorities, later, suspected the Plan of San Diego was devised either by a German agent to stir up trouble at the United States' back door or by one of the many wealthy American landowners who were being dispossessed in Mexico at this time." T.R. Fehrenbach, *Lone Star: A History of Texas and the Texans* (New York: Macmillan Publishing Co., 1968), p. 691. The Plan of San Diego is available as Senate Document 285, 66th Congress, U.S. Govt. Printing Office and is reprinted in, The Editors of Winston Press, *Viewpoints: Red & Yellow, Black & Brown* (Minneapolis, Minn.: Winston Press, 1972), pp. 257–58.

97. Lamb, "The Convenient Villain," p. 76.

98. *Salón Rojo*, pp. 227–28.

99. *Ibid.*, p. 205.

100. George A. Huaco, *The Sociology of Film Art* (New York: Basic Books, 1965), pp. 25–151.

101. Itzhak Bar-Lewaw, *Introducción crítico-biográfica a José Vasconcelos (1882–1959)* (Madrid: Ediciones Latinoamericanas, 1965), pp. 107–24; José Vasconcelos, *Indología, una interpretación de la cultura iberoamericana* (Barcelona: Agencia Mundial de Librería, 1926), pp. 139–91.

102. Cline, *The United States and Mexico*, p. 203.

103. In 1919 the Ministry of War produced three films, *El Block-house de alta luz, Honor militar,* and *El precio de la gloria*—all directed by Fernando Orozco Berra. These apparently were semi-documentary movies extolling the virtues of the revolutionary soldier. In 1925 Jorge Stahl produced *La linterna de Diógenes*, described by García Riera as propaganda for President Plutarco Elías Calles. These films seem to be the extent to which the Mexican cinema was utilized for political purposes prior to 1930.

104. *Salón Rojo*, pp. 225–26.

105. De Witt Bodeen, "Ramón Novarro," *Films in Review* 18 (November 1967): 528–47.

106. Since Al Jolson's *The Jazz Singer* was released just before *Evangeline*, United Artists had Dolores del Río sing three songs in French, a language in which she was quite proficient, and hurriedly incorporated these scenes into the movie before releasing it.

107. José Gómez Sicre, "Dolores del Río," *Américas*, 19 December 1967, pp. 8–17; De Witt Bodeen, "Dolores del Rio," *Films in Review* 18 (May 1967): 266–83.

108. Mahieu, *Breve historia del cine nacional*, p. 23.

109. García Riera, *El cine mexicano*, p. 20.

Chapter 2

1. *Salón Rojo*, p. 14.

2. Luis Reyes de la Maza, *El cine sonoro en México* (Mexico City: UNAM, Instituto de Investigaciones Estéticas, 1973), p. 11, hereafter *Cine sonoro*. Gaumont personally tested his *cronophone* at the 1920 Paris Universal Exposition. See also Perete, "Desaparecen 39 Rollos," for an account of Indalecio de Noriega Colombres's efforts with a similar sound system in 1918.

3. Rhode, *A History of the Cinema*, p. 269.

4. *Ibid.*, pp. 79–85.

5. Siegfried Kracauer, *From Caligari to Hitler: A Psychological History of the German Film.* 2d ed. (New York: The Noonday Press, 1960) p. 67.

6. Rhode, *A History of the Cinema*, p. 119.

7. *Ibid.*, p. 124.

8. *Ibid.*, p. 154.

9. *Ibid.*

10. Germán Arciniegas, *Latin America: A Cultural History*, trans. Joan MacLean (New York: Alfred A. Knopf, 1967), p. 495.

11. *Cine sonoro*, p. 13.

12. *Ibid.*, and pp. 107–10.

13. Wenden, *The Birth of the Movies*, pp. 178, 179.

14. Alfonso Pintó, "Hollywood's Spanish-Language Films," *Films in Review* 24 (October 1973): 474–83, 487.

15. Joaquín de la Horia, "Fotofónicas en español," *Cinelandia* (December 1929) outlined in *Historia*, 1: 9. Manuel Michel makes the same point about subtitles in "Mexican Cinema: A Panoramic View," *Film Quarterly* 18 (Summer 1965): 48.

16. De la Horia, "Fotofónicas en español," p. 9.

17. One hundred thirteen of these Spanish-language films made by fourteen companies between 1930 and 1935 are listed in Pintó, "Hollywood's Spanish-Language Films," pp. 476–83, 487. The companies were Sono Art-World Wide, Chris Phillips Prods., Hollywood Spanish Pictures Co., Ci-Ti-Go, MGM, First National, Warner Brothers, Universal, Columbia, Paramount (U.S. and Joinville, France), Exito Corp., Ionc./Paramount, Fox, 20th Century–Fox, RNS Ltd., and Metropolitan Pictures Corp. Among other films made after 1935 and which in 1977 were available in the UCLA Film Archive are *La vida bohemia* (1937), Columbia-Cantabria Films starring Gilbert Roland and Rosita Díaz and directed by Joseph Berne; and *Verbena trágica* (1938), Columbia-Cantabria Films, starring Fernando Soler and directed by Charles Lamont.

18. Pintó, "Hollywood's Spanish-Language Films," p. 475; see also idem, "Cuando Hollywood Habló en Español," *Américas*, October 1980, pp. 3–8.

19. The Spanish word here would be *castizo*, "pure," or "correct" as in the Castilian spoken in Castile. In Spanish-American usage, the terms "*castellano*" and "*español*" are employed interchangeably; in Spain, however, a regional nationalist would take exception to "Castilian" being characterized as *the* Spanish language since technically Castilian, Galician, Catalan, Basque, and Valencian are all "Spanish" languages. Fortunately, the latter Iberian distinctions have no bearing on the matter of the Spanish variant employed in Latin-American films.

The 1944 Mexican film *La barraca* was dubbed in the Valencian dialect. Jorge Ayala Blanco, *La aventura del cine mexicano* (Mexico City: Ediciones Era, 1968), p. 244 fn. After the death of Francisco Franco in 1975, more movies in Catalan were made, an important example being Antonio Ribas's *La ciutat cremada* (1977). Roger Mortimore, "Spain," in Peter Cowie, ed., *Inter-*

national Film Guide 1977 (London: Tantivy Press, 1978), p. 253. The Xornadas do Cine Ourense, a Galician film festival, was held in 1977 for the fifth straight year. *Ibid.* See also Stanley Meisler, "In Spain It's Great to Be a Polyglot," *Los Angeles Times,* 27 April 1977, pp. 1–10.

20. *Cine sonoro,* p. 23: see also *Historia,* 1: 20.

21. *Cine sonoro,* p. 22.

22. *Historia,* 1: 20.

23. The influence of the Hollywood movie has been consistently denounced by Marxist film historians, especially with regard to the Latin American film industries. Yet it is interesting to note that up to 1972, Chiang Ch'ing, Mao Tse-tung's widow, lovingly viewed again and again Greta Garbo's *Queen Christina* (1933). "The Rise and Fall of Mao's Empress," *Time,* 21 March 1977, p. 59.

24. Viewed at UCLA Film Archive, December 1976. Columbia-Cantabria Films (1938). Directed by Charles Lamont, produced by Jaime del Amo. With Fernando Soler, Luana de Alcañiz, Juan Torena, Pilar Arcos, Cecilia Callejo, Jorge Mari, Carlos Villarías, Romualdo Tirado, Sergio de Karlo, and Leonor Turich.

25. In 1937, 38 full-length features were produced in Mexico. Garcia Riera, *El cine mexicano,* p. 25.

26. By 1950 it was estimated that 300 theaters in the United States ran exclusively Spanish-language programs and another 100 theaters ran Spanish-language showings once or twice a week. William D. Allen, "Spanish-Language Films in the U.S.," *Films in Review* 1 (July-August 1950): 1, 42–45.

27. Meyer, *Cuadernos,* 1: 66.

28. *Cine sonoro,* pp. 78–79.

29. Ayala Blanco, *La aventura,* pp. 291-92. Cube Bonifant had been a silent film actress; two of her films were Carlos Noriega Hope's *Los chicos de la prensa* (1921) and *La gran noticia* (same year). García Riera, *El cine mexicano,* p. 25.

30. *Cine sonoro,* pp. 132–33; see also Xavier Villaurrutia, *Crítica cinematográfica,* Cuadernos de Cine #18 (Mexico City: UNAM, Dirección General de Difusión Cultural, 1970).

31. "Lupita Tovar was noticed by a Hollywood talent scout at the exclusive girls' she attended in Mexico City. She appeared first in silent Fox films before making the move to Universal and co-starring in the Spanish-language version of 1930s "The Cat Creeps" ("La Voluntad del Muerto"). For the same producer, Czech-born Paul Kohner, she appeared as Eva (the counterpart of Helen Chandler's Mina in the Bela Lugosi original) in Universal's Spanish version of *Dracula.* After making 30 films in both the United States and Mexico, Tovar retired from acting in 1945. Paul Kohner died in 1988. Adapted from *IMDb.com* biography.

32. The first Mexican sound film was actually Raphael J. Sevilla's *Más fuerte que el deber* (Films Tenoch, 1930). It apparently was fairly well received by the Mexican public and demonstrated the feasibility of a national industry based on sound movies. However, the film has been relegated to limbo by most Mexican film scholars who prefer to date the beginning of the sound era with the more commercially successful *Santa* (*Historia,* 1: 17).

Joselito Rodríguez mentions another film, *Sangre mexicana,* for which he had invented a portable, inexpensive sound system. In 1930 he was in Los Angeles exhibiting this movie when representatives of the *Santa* production company arrived seeking to purchase an American sound recording system. Rodríguez says he approached his countrymen to offer his sound system, but when they learned it was invented by a Mexican they ignored him. Finally, the high cost of the U.S.-made systems and Rodríguez's persistence persuaded the *Santa* producers to purchase his system. Martha Aurora Espinosa, "El cine sonoro fue un auténtico invento mío: Joselito Rodríguez," *Uno Más Uno,* 27 January 1981, p. 22.

33. *Ibid.,* p. 27.

34. Salvador Elizondo, "Moral sexual y moraleja en el cine mexicano," *Nuevo Cine,* no. 1 (April 1961), quoted in *Historia,* 1: 27. See also *ibid.,* pp. 25–27; Ayala Blanco, *La aventura,* pp. 128–30; and *Cine sonoro,* pp. 28–29, 259, 264–69.

35. For leftist attacks on Sinclair and *Thunder Over Mexico* see "Thunder Over Mexico" [poster and text], p. 69; "To Upton Sinclair" [poster and text], p. 70; and P. Lorentz, "Thunder Over Mexico" [review], *Film Culture,* nos. 48–49 (Winter-Spring 1970). For other sources on Eisenstein and his stay in Mexico see Marie Seton, *Eisenstein* (Paris: Editions du Seuil, 1967); Gabriel Ramírez, ed., *¡Que viva México!* (Mexico City: Ediciones Era, 1964); Harry M. Geduld and Ronald Gottesman, eds., *Sergei Eisenstein and Upton Sinclair: The Making and Unmaking of ¡Que viva México!* (Bloomington and London: Indiana University Press, 1970); Jean Mitry, *S.M. Eisenstein* (Paris: Editions Universitaires, 1962); Jay Leyda, *Kino, A History of the Russian and Soviet Film* (London: Allen and Unwin, 1960); Sadoul, *Histoire du Cinéma,* pp. 425–30; Rhode, *A History of the Cinema,* pp. 108, 289; Marie Seton, "Vignettes of Eisenstein," *Films in Review* 2 (April 1951): 29–31; synopsis of *¡Que viva México!* in *Experimental Cinema,* no. 5 (1934). This summary of Eisenstein's activities in Mexico is largely based on Alfonso Reyes's account as quoted in *Historia,* 1: 18–19. See also *Cine sonoro,* pp. 236–43 for Adolfo Fernández Bustamante's remarks in *El Ilustrado,* 11, 18, and 25 June and 16 July 1931.

36. For discussions of different national styles in filmmaking see Leprohon, *The Italian Cinema,* p. 20, and for the silent French and German cinemas of the 1920s see Paul Monaco, *Cinema and Society: France and Germany During the Twenties* (New York: Elsevier, 1976), passim but especially chapter 3, "The Film as National Folklore," pp. 68–79. Regarding Eisenstein's influence on Mexican cinema see Glauber Rocha's denunciation in *Cahiers du Cinéma,* no. 195 (November 1967) as quoted in *Historia,* 1: 19–20.

37. *Ibid.,* p. 19.

38. García Riera, *El cine mexicano,* pp. 31–34.

39. *Ibid.,* pp. 37–39.

40. Meyer, *Cuadernos,* 1: 21–29.

41. *Historia,* 1: 38.

42. All these quotes are found in *ibid.,* p. 54. See also Ayala Blanco's analysis in *La aventura,* pp. 131–33.

43. *Historia,* 1:53.

44. *Ibid.*, pp. 57–58.

45. *Ibid.*, p. 59; see also Philippe Pilard's remarks in *ibid.* For García Riera's commentary see *ibid.*, p. 58 and also idem, *El cine mexicano*, pp. 31–32; Ayala Blanco, *La aventura*, pp. 16–22. A retrospective of De Fuentes's work was held in 1976 in Venice. Agustín Gurezpe, "Homenaje a Fernando de Fuentes en la 'Mostra' de Venecia 1976," *Excélsior*, 7 May 1976, p. C-1.

46. *Historia*, 1: 70. The account of the making of *Redes* is taken from *ibid.*, pp. 69–72.

47. Ayala Blanco, *La aventura*, p. 194.

48. *Ibid.*

49. *Historia*, 1: 84–86. A similar theme was used *in La vida bohemia* (1937). In this Columbia-Cantabria production — one of the last of Hollywood's efforts at Hispanic moviemaking — Gilbert Roland portrayed a Parisian writer in love with Rosita Díaz, who eventually dies of tuberculosis. Viewed at UCLA Film Archive, December 1976.

50. Catherine Macotela, "El sindicalismo en el cine (primera parte)," *Otrocine* no. 2 (April-June 1975), pp. 60–61. What later would become the STIC (Sindicato de Trabajadores de la Industria Cinematográfica) was founded in 1919 under the name of Unión de Empleados Confederados del Cinematógrafo (UECC) during a period of intense anarcho-syndicalist activity in Mexico. The Carranza government at this time was also taking steps to regulate the infant film industry; this caused alarm among exhibitors and distributors and led to the organization in 1920 of the Unión de Alquiladores Mexicanos. The first strike called by UECC was in 1925 against the Tampico theater owners who were forced to yield to the strikers' demands and sign collective contracts. Another important strike occurred in 1927 when the advent of sound caused the dismissal of many musicians. *Ibid.*, pp. 60–61.

51. For details on this aspect of the film industries of the Soviet Union and Japan, see Rhode, *A History of the Cinema*, pp. 79–116 and Joseph L. Anderson and Donald Richie, *The Japanese Film: Art and Industry*, foreword by Akira Kurosawa (New York: Grove Press, 1960), pp. 128–30.

52. *Historia*, 1: 90–91, 111.

53. Although there is no evidence that De Fuentes intended these three films as a trilogy, for purposes of analysis they are being considered as such here.

54. *Historia*, 1: 92.

55. José Bohr corroborates this: "Y jamás el gobierno de Cárdenas influyó en la tónica de las producciones; nunca manejó censura de contracensura. Lo único que este hombre buscó fue dar sindicatos para que los trabajadores, artistas, etcétera estuvieran protegidos. Ni una vez rechazaron alguna cinta mía por contener una cosa en pro o en contra." (And never did the Cárdenas government influence the tone of the productions; it never exercised censorship or countercensorship. The only thing this man sought was to provide unions so that the workers, artists, etc. would be protected. Not once did they refuse a film of mine for containing something pro or con." Meyer, *Cuadernos*, 1: 40.

56. For production details, plot outline, and addi-

tional comments by Salvador Elizondo, José de la Colina, and Carlos Monsiváis see *Historia*, 1: 91–97. See also García Riera, *El cine mexicano*, pp. 32–34; Ayala Blanco, *La aventura*, pp. 23–31.

57. *Historia*, 1: 112.

58. *Ibid.*

59. Fehrenbach, Lone Star, p. 75.

60. The surface aspects of the plot are not of major importance since they principally involve the rivalry of two friends for the love of the same girl and the way in which the resulting tensions and misunderstandings are cleared up. For details see *Historia*, 1: 128; for Luz Alba's comments see *ibid.*, pp. 131–32; for Carlos Monsiváis's and Tomás Pérez Turrent's comments see *ibid.*, p. 132. Ayala Blanco has an interesting discussion of the literary origins of *Allá en el Rancho Grande*: it is a free adaptation of a turn-of-the-century Spanish play by Joaquín Dicenta. The *comedia ranchera*'s inspiration from the Spanish *sainete* (one-act comedy) and *zarzuela* (operetta) is also apparent. From the former, it takes the humorous situation and comedy of errors; from the latter, the interludes of lively music. A native source is the Mexico City burlesque or music hall of the 1920s, an observation also made by Luz Alba above. Ayala Blanco, *La aventura*, pp. 64–66. See also García Riera, *El cine mexicano*, p. 34; Reyes Nevares, *The Mexican Cinema*, pp. 1–2; and Alejandro Galindo, *Una radiografía histórica del cine mexicano* (Mexico City: Fondo de Cultura Popular, 1968), p. 133.

61. "Federico Arturo Guízar Tolentino was born on April 8, 1908, in Guadalajara, Mexico. Over the objections of his father he trained early as a singer and, as such, was sent to New York in 1929 to record the songs of Agustin Lara. While there he had a radio show, 'Tito Guízar y su Guitar,' and studied opera. In 1932 he married another Mexican singer, Carmen Noriega. He performed both operatic and Mexican cowboy songs at Carnegie Hall. His 1936 movie "Allá en el Rancho Grande" launched the singing cowboy film in Mexico and succeeded as well in the United States. From there he went to Hollywood, playing with such stars as Roy Rogers, Dorothy Lamour, and Mae West. He continued playing series parts in Mexican television well into the '90s. Tito Guízar died aged 91, survived by a son, two daughters and five grandchildren." From *IMDb.com* minibiography.

62. Tito Guízar was mentioned in a Spanish exercise book used by this author in a New York high school circa 1953 as the best-known "Latin-American troubador." By that time, however, Guízar was somewhat passé south of the border and had long since been supplanted in popularity by both Jorge Negrete and Pedro Infante.

63. Claes af Geijerstam, *Popular Music in Mexico* (Albuquerque: University of New Mexico Press, 1976), pp. 41–45.

64. See Monsiváis, "Junto contigo le doy un aplauso al placer y al amor," pp. 39–56, and idem, "The Culture of the Frontier: The Mexican Side," in Stanley R. Ross, ed., *Views Across the Border: The United States and Mexico* (Albuquerque: University of New Mexico Press, 1978), pp. 50–67.

65. *Historia*, 1: 140.

66. Mahieu, *Breve historia*, p. 31.

67. *Historia*, 1: 117–18.

68. *Ibid.*, p. 146.

69. *Ibid.*, p. 147.

70. *Ibid.*, p. 151.

71. *Ibid.*, p. 135.

72. *Ibid.*, pp. 167–68. See also Bambi, "Lupe Vélez Tuvo Mucha Suerte en su Carrera, Pero no en sus Amores: Edelmira Zúñiga," *Excélsior*, 14 December 1976, pp. 1-B, 2-B, 10B.

73. *Historia*, 1:172. See also Gómez Sicre, "Dolores del Río," pp. 15–16 and Reyes Nevares, *The Mexican Cinema*, p. 18.

74. Since 1931, when Santa was released, a little over 15 million pesos had been invested in the movie industry. The majority of the profits from this capital were obviously not reinvested in the industry, since by 1939 the economic base of the cinema was as unstable as it had been in 1931. *Historia*, 1: 230.

75. See for instance, Emilio Fernández's account of how he and David Silva obtained financial backing for their first film, *La isla de la pasión*, from General Juan F. Azcárate. Reyes Nevares, *The Mexican Cinema*, p. 15.

76. Monaco, *Cinema and Society*, p. 33.

77. *Historia*, 1: 230-31.

78. Román Gubern, *Cine español en el exilio, 1936–1939* (Barcelona: Editorial Lumen, 1976), pp. 13–17.

79. "Muerte del Actor Angel Garasa," *Mañana*, 4 September 1976, p. 62.

80. John Aldape, "In 'mean, sexy' roles Emilia Guiu was a superstar," *The Arizona Republic*, 18 February 1973, p. L-2.

81. Reyes Nevares, *The Mexican Cinema*, p. 66.

82. *Ibid.*, p. 31.

83. *Historia*, 1: 179–80.

84. *Ibid.*, pp. 192–93.

85. *Ibid.*, pp. 202–204. See also Reyes Nevares, *The Mexican Cinema*, pp. 21–42; Meyer, *Cuadernos*, 1: 93–108; García Riera, *El cine mexicano*, p. 63.

86. *Historia*, 1: 254–57; Ayala Blanco, *La aventura*, pp. 40–47.

87. *Historia*, 1: 260.

88. *Ibid.*

89. *Ibid.*

90. *Ibid.*, pp. 260–61; Allen L. Woll, "Hollywood's Good Neighbor Policy: The Latin Image in American Film, 1939–1946," *Journal of Popular Film* 3 (Fall 1974): 278–91; Paul J. Vanderwood, "Images of Mexican Heroes in American Films" (presented at the annual meeting of the American Historical Association, Washington, D.C., 28–30 December 1976), pp. 4–11.

Chapter 3

1. Cline, *The United States and Mexico*, p. 263.

2. *Historia*, 1: 264.

3. Miguel Ângelo, "Brasil: 75 anos de cinema," *O Cruziero*, 15 September 1971, pp. 158–62.

4. *Historia*, 2: 48.

5. *Ibid.*, p. 10.

6. E. Bradford Burns, "National Identity in Argentine Films," *Américas*, November-December 1975, p. 10. See also Raymond del Castillo, "The Cinema in Argentina," *The Penguin Film Review*, no. 4 (1947), p. 101; Mahieu, *Breve historia*, pp. 46–47.

7. *Historia*, 2: 21.

8. *Ibid.*, 1: 274.

9. For an approximation of *cantinflismo*, se *Enciclopedia de México*, 2: 139–40. See also Marie Rose Oliver, "Cantinflas," *Hollywood Quarterly* 2 (1946–1947): 252–56.

10. *Historia,* 2: 12.

11. *Ibid.*

12. García Riera, *El cine mexicano*, pp. 77–78. See also Dr. Raúl Fournier's analysis of Cantinflas's humor in "Necesidad de reir," *Hispanoamericano*, 2 June 1950, p. 28; and E. R. E., "El gran éxito de papá Cantinflas," *Contenido* (Mexico City), July 1979, pp. 33–36.

13. *Historia*, 2: 15–16.

14. Ayala Blanco, *La aventura*, p. 52.

15. Francisco Pineda Alcalá, *La verídica historia del cine mexicano*, prologue by Fernando Morales Ortiz (Mexico City: n.p., 1965), pp. 49–51.

16. Galindo, *Una radiografía histórica*, photograph caption between pages 64 and 65.

17. Reyes Nevares, *The Mexican Cinema*, p. 15.

18. For instance, one million pesos was spent on *Simón Bolívar*. It was filmed at the CLASA studios with 10 days on location in the state of Veracruz. *Historia*, 2: 24.

19. A 1953 Cuban-Mexican coproduction, *La rosa blanca*, with the Mexican actor Roberto Cañedo, was disappointing in its portrayal of José Martí. José Antonio González, "Apuntes para la historia de un cine sin historia," *Cine cubano*, no. 86/87/88 (1973 or 1974), p. 42.

20. Regarding a recent Cantinflas film, *El ministro y yo*, one critic said: "His decadence is complete: the same jokes, exact gestures, identical situations. Naturally, their effectiveness is lessened: the people laugh less, we might even say very little." Miguel Donoso Parejo, "CINE: El ministro y yo," *Mañana*, 24 July 1976, p. 10.

21. Enrique Colina and Daniel Díaz Torres, "Ideología del melodrama en el viejo cine latinoamericano," *Cine cubano*, no. 73/74/75 (1972), p. 19. This is an interesting Marxist analysis of the ideological bases of the commercial Mexican and Argentine cinemas. Predictably, the authors consider the principal themes and values expressed in many films to be "reactionary" and part of a bourgeois "plot" to suppress progressive cultural currents among the people. Many Mexican films have undoubtedly reflected and espoused middle-class values, but it could hardly be otherwise since filmmaking in Mexico (and all other countries) from the beginning was a bourgeois activity for a bourgeois audience. That many of these films might have inculcated middle-class values in the lower-class audiences that flocked to see them is also quite likely, but this was simply a natural process and hardly the result of sinister machinations. Mexico and Argentina to date have not had totalitarian governments that could completely mobilize cultural activities to reflect

"official" values, even if the middle sectors in these countries could ever have agreed on what their "official" values should be. Colina and Díaz Torres, naturally enough since they are Marxists, fail to see that the Cuban cinema is the only one in Latin America that truly and consciously espouses an official viewpoint. This is not meant to deride Cuban films either in their content or technical quality. A Marxist viewpoint is as valid as any other but it does stem, in Cuba, from an absolute centralization of decision making. In Mexico in the 1970s, even though the industry had in effect been nationalized through the centralization of credit facilities in the Banco Nacional Cinematográfico, and content of both scripts and completed films was scrutinized by the Dirección de Cinematografía, a wider range of ideas, from conservative to socialist, have been expressed in Mexican films than in those of revolutionary Cuba.

The theoretical basis for Colina and Díaz Torres is the "hypodermic model and mass society thesis" (Andrew Tudor, *Image and Influence: Studies in the Sociology of Film* [London: George Allen and Unwin, 1974]) which Tudor calls "deeply misleading" (p. 30). He says that this model suggests "people are the passive recipients of whatever the communicators care to 'inject' ... Some versions of the general thesis even go so far as implying conspiracy; media men as manipulators of society" (p. 31). Tudor goes on to say that "We see what we wish to see, and we twist messages around"—a process called "selective perception" (p. 35). He cites the "Mr. Biggott" studies—a series of antiprejudice cartoons shown to a test audience; about two-thirds of the sample "clearly misunderstood" the cartoons' intentions. Observers in this country have noticed a similar reaction to the character of Archie Bunker in the "All in the Family" television series: viewers of similar opinions have tended to identify with Bunker rather than "learn" that bigotry is negative and antisocial.

22. This film, as will be explained in chapter 4, was hardly a standard melodrama. On the contrary, it was an insightful social statement.

23. Meyer, *Cuadernos*, 2: 18; see also pp. 11–23 for Sara García's account of her career. For additional comments on the self-sacrificing yet tyrannical mother image, as visualized in Mexican popular culture, see Aurelio de los Reyes et al., *80 años de cine en México*, Serie Imágenes 2 (Mexico City: UNAM, Difusión Cultural, 1977), pp. 110–11. The image is not that uniquely Mexican, of course; in the United States it is readily recognizable as the "Jewish mother" syndrome, especially in Philip Roth's novel, *Portnoy's Complaint*.

24. However, in *María Candelaria* (1943), Fernández, immediately after the opening credits, juxtaposes a girl's head with pre–Columbian sculptures to emphasize the racial links—a technique directly borrowed from Eisenstein. For additional comments on the Fernández-Figueroa style, see Ayala Blanco, *La aventura*, pp. 35–39, 92.

25. By way of clarification, both these films were produced in English and Spanish-language versions. In Spanish, *The Pearl* (based on a story by John Steinbeck) was, of course, *La perla* (*Historia*, 3: 15*); The Torch* (1949), costarring Paulette Goddard, was *Enam-*orada in its Spanish-language version, with María Félix in the title role. *Ibid.*, pp. 129–34. The dates in the text for both films correspond to the Spanish-language versions. See also Reyes Nevares, *The Mexican Cinema*, pp. 11–19.

26. Carlos Perea in *México Cinema*, 1 July 1942, as quoted in *Historia*, 2: 53.

27. "Balance Cinematográfico," *Tiempo*, 22 January 1943, p. 36.

28. According to its first director, Lic. Carlos Carriedo Galván, in an interview published in *Cinema Reporter*, 1 July 1942, and reprinted in *Historia*, 2: 53–54.

29. For a complete list of board members, see *Historia*, 2: 54, n. 3.

30. "Balance Cinematográfico," p. 36.

31. *Historia*, 2: 54.

32. As García Riera refers to it. *Ibid.*, p. 111.

33. Both García Riera (*Ibid.*) and Mahieu (*Breve historia*, pp. 44–45) attribute this to formula films which appealed to the least demanding and most unsophisticated segments of the Latin American publics.

34. *Historia*, 2: 111. However, toward the end of the war Argentina reversed its policy and declared war on Germany. Raw film stock from the U.S. again became available for Argentine filmmakers; this caused a small panic in Mexican film circles since they realized that this would make Argentine films competitive once again. "Peligro para México," *Hispanoamericano*, 19 April 1946, p. 39. This does not mean that Hollywood movies were completely edged out of the Latin American market druing World War II. For instance, in November 1942, box-office receipts in the Federal District were broken down as follows: Mexican films, 636, 839 (pesos); U.S., 1,253, 110; and Argentine, 63,042. "Balance Cinematográfico," p. 37.

35. "Tres Veces 'Santa'," *Tiempo*, 26 March 1943, p. 39.

36. *Historia*, 2: 111–12.

37. *Ibid.*, pp. 113–14.

38. *Ibid.*, and Reyes Nevares, *The Mexican Cinema*, p. 18. See also "Sin Prejuicios," *Tiempo*, 25 April 1943, p. 59.

39. See Raymond Borde's comments in *Historia*, 2: 169; see also Ayala Blanco, *La aventura*, pp. 195–96.

40. Reyes Nevares, *The Mexican Cinema*, pp. 18–19.

41. *Ibid.*, p. 19.

42. Label applied to a genre of postwar gangster movies set in shabby urban environments and featuring cynical, alienated "antiheroes." Also called "underground movies" by Manny Farber. Howard Hawks's *The Big Sleep* (1946) is considered one of the most important examples of the *film noir* style. Penelope Houston, *The Contemporary Cinema* (Baltimore: Penguin Books, 1966), pp. 65–67. See also John S. Whitney, "A Filmography of Film Noir," *The Journal of Popular Film* 5 (1976): 321–57.

43. *Historia*, 2: 156.

44. "Moral sexual y moraleja en el cine mexicano," *Nuevo Cine*, no. 1 (April 1961) as quoted in *Historia*, 2: 156–57. For a discussion of Fernández and Bracho see Natalia Askenazy, "The Two Kinds of Mexican Movies," *Films in Review* 2 (May 1951): 35–39.

45. CLASA had 10 sound stages and Azteca 18.

H.H. Wollenberg, "Round the World's Studios," *The Penguin Film Review*, no. 1 (1946), p. 53.

46. "Nuevos Estudios," *Tiempo*, 12 March 1943, p. 45.

47. RKO did eventually buy into the Churubusco studios. H.H. Wollenberg, "Round the World's Studios," *The Penguin Film Review*, no. 3 (1947), pp. 39–40. According to Catherine Macotela, RKO and Universal tried to buy the CLASA studios. "El sindicalismo en el cine (primera parte)," *Otrocine*, no. 2 (April–June 1975), p. 65.

48. "Ofensiva Frustrada," *Tiempo*, 17 September 1943, pp. 48, 50.

49. *Historia*, 1: 206 and 2: 90; Macotela, "El sindicalismo en el cine," p. 66. A total of five articles by Macotela traces the complicated unionization process. The first article appears in *Otrocine*, no. 2 (April–June 1975), pp. 60–67. The subsequent articles appear as follows: "(segunda parte)," *Ibid.*, no. 3 (July–September 1975), pp. 57–63; "(tercera parte)," *Ibid.*, no. 4 (October–December 1975), pp. 65–69; "(cuarta parte)," *Ibid.*, no. 5 (January–March 1976), pp. 59–65; and "(quinta parte)," *Ibid.*, no. 6 (April–June 1976), pp. 46–48. Henceforth, references to any of the above articles will be "'(tercera parte),' p. 66," etc.

50. "(segunda parte)," p. 60. In 1934 it was renamed "Unión de Trabajadores de los Estudios Cinematográficos de México" (UTECM). On occasion this name was still being used for STIC until 1944. "Sección 7 vs. Solís," *Tiempo*, 14 April 1944, p. 50. See also "Aniversario Sindical," *Ibid.*, 30 April 1943, p. 42.

51. *Historia*, 2: 207.

52. *Ibid.*

53. "(primera parte)," p. 65.

54. *Ibid.*, p. 64.

55. "(segunda parte)," p. 57.

56. *Ibid.*, p. 61. The STPC had at its inception 2,192 members.

57. *Historia*, 3:14. For a complete account of this complex affair see the series of articles by Catherine Macotela in *Otrocine*, cited above. See also "Ultimo Episodio," *Tiempo*, 14 September 1945, p. 5; and "Alma de España," *Tiempo*, 22 February 1946, p. 35, on the STIC/STPC dispute which was preventing Miguel de Molina, a Spanish dancer, from performing. For additional details on the organization of both STPC and STIC, see Heuer, *La industria cinematográfica mexicana*, p. 121.

58. *Historia*, 2: 286.

59. For elaborations on this, see *Ibid.* and Ayala Blanco, *La aventura*, pp. 241–46. For an interesting view of the Mexican cinema from the other side, that is, from a pro–Franco Spaniard, see Ernesto Giménez Caballero, *Amor a Méjico (A través de su cine)*, Cuadernos de Monografías no. 5 (Madrid: Seminario de Problemas Hispanoamericanos, April 1948). The author attempts to establish that Mexico through its cinema preserves the best of traditional Spanish values. First, the Catholic religion, through such films as *San Francisco de Asís* and *María Candelaria*; second, the Spanish knightly tradition in the films of Jorge Negrete and *Enamorada*; and finally, the picaresque genre in Cantinflas's movies. The work is an attempt to emphasize

that Spain and Mexico remain closely tied by cultural and religious bonds in spite of the Mexican government's hostility to Franco and its support of the Spanish Republic's government-in-exile headquartered in Mexico City.

60. Ayala Blanco, *La aventura*, p. 244. A footnote on this page states that copies of the film were dubbed in the Valencian dialect. There were also plans to have Orson Welles narrate the film for English-speaking audiences. "'La Barraca' en Norteamérica," *Tiempo*, 2 November 1945, p. 41.

61. Galindo, *Una radiografía histórica*, pp. 143–44.

62. "Caja de Sorpresas," *Tiempo*, 30 March 1945, p. 39.

63. Christopher Finch, *The Art of Walt Disney: From Mickey Mouse to the Magic Kingdom* (New York: Harry N. Abrams, Publisher, 1975), pp. 113–14.

64. This in spite of the fact that the project had some powerful backing. William Jenkins's daughter, Elisabeth, was ready to support it at the urging of producer Alfonso Sánchez Tello and journalist Isaac Díaz. In addition, Nelson Rockefeller delayed Robert Trasker's induction into the army until 1943 so he could go to Mexico and work on the script. "'Potrero del Llano,'" *Tiempo*, 20 November 1942, p. 47. Another film, *Espionaje en el golfo*, was made in which the sinking of the *Potrero del Llano* is an incident. "'Charro' Patriótico," *Tiempo*, 6 November 1942, p. 37.

65. *Ibid.*

66. Mexico was the only Spanish-speaking Latin American country to contribute a combat unit to the Allied war effort (Brazil also sent a substantial force to the European theater of war). This was Expeditionary Squadron 201 made up of 300 volunteers from the Mexican air force. It was formed in July 1944 and saw action in the Philippines and Formosa (Taiwan). Cline, *The United States and Mexico*, p. 278.

Chapter 4

1. For a detailed account of these years see Francisco Aranda, *Luis Buñuel: A Critical Biography*, trans. David Robinson (London: Seeker and Warburg, 1975), pp. 116–30.

2. Libertad Lamarque's only recorded comment concerning *Gran Casino* and Buñuel: "En fin, lamento que nunca más, despues de tantos años, volví a filmar con él/Finally, I lament that never again, after so many years, did I ever make another film with him." Meyer, *Cuadernos*, 6: 71.

3. *Historia*, 3: 163.

4. José Luis Ceceña, *Siempre*, 6 August 1969, as quoted in *Historia*, 3: 95–96 fn.

5. *Ibid.*, p. 95.

6. Miguel Contreras Torres, *El libro negro del cine mexicano* (Mexico City: Editora Hispano-Continental Films, 1960), p. 53. See also Joel Edelstein's comments in "Official Statement by the University of the Americas Concerning the Conflict of 1976 and Its Consequences," Santa Catarina Mártir, Puebla, 1 July 1977, Appendix A, p. 23.

7. Contreras Torres, *El libro negro*, p. 55.

8. *Ibid.*, p. 51; Geijerstam, *Popular Music in Mexico*, p. 109. O'Farrill was the owner of XHTV, the first television station in the country; Azcárraga owned XEWTV. Contreras Torres might have meant that Jenkins money was also invested in XEW instead of Azcárraga being associated with XHTV. An interesting note is that Ing. Guillermo González Camarena in 1939 patented a color television system in Mexico and in 1940 registered it in the United States. His system was later adopted by CBS and RCA Victor. "La Televisión en México," *Hispanoamericano*, 17 August 1951, pp. 3–6.

9. *Historia*, 3: 173–74.

10. "Contra un Monopolio," *Hispanoamericano*, 13 February 1953, p. 45. See also "Contra un Monopolio (2)," *Ibid.*, 27 February 1953, p. 42.

11. Felipe Mier Miranda, "La industria nacional cinematográfica mexicana, " (Licenciate thesis, UNAM, 1963), p. 32.

12. A curious bit of dialogue occurs toward the end of the film during the wedding scene between Beatriz and Mr. Roberts before she rushes out to the street to follow Reyes. The judge comments that this marriage of Beatriz to a "foreigner" proves that "Mexicans have no racial prejudice." This might have been a slap by Fernández at Americans because of discrimination and segregation of Mexicans and Mexican-Americans during this time in Texas, California, and other Southwestern states.

13. Perhaps Armendáriz's most bizarre role was in *The Conqueror* (1956) in which he played the brother of Genghis Khan (John Wayne). It was made on location in Nevada near the site of the nuclear bomb tests; many in the cast later developed cancer, including Wayne and Armendáriz. Armendáriz, terminally ill, committed suicide in a Los Angeles hospital. His son, Pedro Armendáriz, Jr., is a leading actor in Mexico and the United States.

14. This pivotal sequence has been inexplicably deleted from the Mexcinema Video Corp. videotape.

15. See *Historia*, 3: 203–207 and Ayala Blanco, *La aventura*, pp. 81–97.

16. Ayala Blanco, *La aventura*, p. 92.

17. *Historia*, 3: 176.

18. Reyes Nevares, *The Mexican Cinema*, pp. 50–51.

19. For the extensive summary on this film see *Historia*, 3: 217–22; Ayala Blanco, *La aventura*, pp. 113–19.

20. Perla Ciuk, *Diccionario de directores del cine mexicano* (CONACULTA/Cineteca Nacional, 2000), pp. 257–58.

21. *Historia*, 3: 272, 275.

22. For an extensive commentary on this film see *Ibid.*, pp. 309–14. Ayala Blanco dedicates a long analysis to *Una familia de tantas* in *La aventura*, pp. 54–63. See also "Sainete Mexicano," *Hispanoamericano*, 29 July 1949, p. 29.

23. Galindo did not get any more specific than this. Personal interview, Mexico City, 7 July 1977.

24. *Ibid.* Galindo had been thinking of making *El juicio de Martín Cortés* for some time. See Galindo, *Una radiografía histórica*, pp. 55–83. See also Reyes Nevares, *The Mexican Cinema*, pp. 29–30; Meyer,

Cuadernos, 1: 93–108; Alejandro Galindo, *¿Qué es el cine?* (Mexico City: Editorial Nuestro Tiempo, 1975); idem, *El cine, genocidio espiritual: De 1900 al "crash" de 29* (Mexico City: Editorial Nuestro/Tiempo, 1971).

25. Personal interview, Mexico City, 7 July 1977.

26. This writer remembers seeing Tin-Tan in just such a costume on the stage of the Alameda Theater in the early 1940s. For biographical details see, *Historia*, 3: 48.

27. "El fabuloso 'Tin-Tan'," *Mañana*, 29 May 1976, p. 56. For Mexican attitudes toward pachucos see Octavio Paz, *The Labryinth of Solitude*, trans. Lysander Kemp (New York: Grove Press, 1961), pp. 12–18. For a discussion of Tin-Tan's pachuco character and its metamorphosis see Monsiváis, "The Culture of the Frontier," pp. 63–64. See also "Authentic Pachuco," *Time*, 10 July 1944, p. 72. Tin-Tan appeared briefly in at least one American film, *Song of Mexico* (1945), a Republic picture. See advertisement in *Hispanoamericano*, 30 November 1945, p. 15. Also see the issue of *Somos* dedicated to Tin-Tan, no. 1941, 29 June 1990.

28. For an assessment of the social significance of popular dances, see Carlos Monsiváis, "Es el baile del pingüino un baile elegante y fino," *Diálogos* (Colegio de México) 13 (September-October 1977): 11–14.

29. *Historia*, 4: 133. See also *Ibid.*, pp. 132–34 for comments from *Cahiers du Cinéma* on Ninón Sevilla, and Ayala Blanco, *La aventura*, pp. 145–52. For comments on *Sensualidad* (1950) see *Ibid.*, pp. 152–54.

30. For an interesting discussion of the genre in relation to culture see Tudor, *Image and Influence*, pp. 223–31.

31. *Historia*, 4: 286, 289.

32. Interview, Mexico City, 7 July 1977.

33. *Historia*, 4: 68–73.

34. *Ibid.*, p. 143; for commentary on *Los olvidados* see pp. 156–76.

35. "El Drama del Pueblo," *Hispanoamericano*, 22 September 1950, p. 24; "'Los Olvidados' y la Crítica," *Ibid.*, 7 March 1952, p. 52. See also Daniel Díaz Torres, "Los Olvidados," *Cine cubano*, no. 78/79/80 (1972), pp. 134–55.

36. Vincent Canby, "Uncovering Luis Bunuel's [*sic*] Mexican Treasures," *New York Times,* 18 January 1976, p. D-13.

37. *Historia*, 6: 25–39.

38. Buñuel's Mexican films are discussed by Aranda in his *Luis Buñuel*, pp. 128–69. See also Freddy Buache, *The Cinema of Luis Buñuel*, trans. Peter Graham (London: The Tantivy Press, 1973), pp. 42–95, 117–37. For a discussion of Buñuel's adaptations of the Mexican melodrama to his own ends, see Daniel Díaz Torres and Enrique Colina, "El melodrama en la obra de Luis Buñuel," *Cine cubano*, no. 78/79/80 (1972), pp. 156–64. For additional data see: Daniel Aubry and J.M. Lacor, "Luis Buñuel," *Film Quarterly* 12 (Winter 1958): 7–9; Emilio García Riera, "La eterna rebelión de Luis Buñuel," *Tiempo de cine*, no. 13 (March 1963), pp. 8–13, 64; idem, "Viridiana," *Film Culture*, no. 24 (1962), p. 74; idem, "The Eternal Rebellion of Luis Buñuel," *Ibid.*, no. 21 (1960), p. 42; idem, "The Films of Luis Buñuel," *Ibid.*, p. 58; Peter Harcourt, "Luis Buñuel: Spaniard and Surrealist," *Film Quarterly* 20 (Spring

1967): 2–19; Kenji Kanesaka, "A Visit to Luis Buñuel," *Film Culture*, no. 41 (1966), p. 60, reprinted in Andrew Sarris, ed., *Interviews with Film Directors* (New York: Avon Books, 1967), pp. 65–74; "Luis Buñuel hace la anatomía del churro cinematográfico," *Cine cubano*, no. 78/79/80 (1972), pp. 112–13; "Filmografía Luis Buñuel," *Ibid.*, pp. 166–75; Emir Rodríguez Monegal, "El mito Buñuel," *Tiempo de cine*, no. 14/15 (July 1963), pp. 7–10; "Entretien avec Luis Buñuel," *Cahiers du Cinéma*, no. 191 (June 1967), pp. 14–18; Fernando Pérez, "Nazarín," *Cine cubano*, no. 78/79/80 (1972), pp. 136–37; Fernando Césarman, *El ojo de Buñuel: Psicoanálisis desde una butaca*, prologue by Carlos Fuentes (Barcelona: Anagrama, 1976); Carol Miller, "El Precio de la Experiencia," *Hispanoamericano*, 11 April 1977, p. 50; Penelope Gilliatt, "Profiles: Long Live the Living!" *The New Yorker*, 5 December 1977, pp. 53–72; Randall Conrad, "'I Am Not a Producer!'—Working with Buñuel," *Film Quarterly* 23 (Fall 1979): 2–11; Ado Kyrou, *Luis Buñuel* (Paris: Editions Seghers, 1970); and Carol Miller, "Luis Buñuel: El Ojo de la Libertad," *Hispanoamericano*, 12 January 1981, pp. 54–57. A recent study is Ernesto R. Acevedo-Muñoz, *Buñuel and Mexico: The Crisis of National Cinema* (Berkeley, Los Angeles, and London: University of California Press, 2003)

39. *Historia*, 5: 145–52; Ayala Blanco, *La aventura*, p. 197; "Misterio y Claridad," *Hispanoamericano*, 20 September 1954, pp. 41–43.

40. *Historia*, 5: 7.

41. See Santiago Reachi's remarks in "A la Conquista del Interés Mundial," *Hispanoamericano*, 27 December 1954, pp. 46–47. See also "Otra Operación de Cimex," *Ibid.*, 9 August 1954, p. 41 for details on how the firm bought up the distributors in the U.S. (Azteca Films) and Cuba (Manuel Espinosa Iglesias's Distribuidora de Películas Continental). Clasa-Mohme remained the independent U.S. distributor.

42. "Premios a la moral," *Hispanoamericano*, 18 January 1953, p. 39.

43. *Historia*, 5: 235–38; "En México se Filmará a Colores," *Hispanoamericano*, 7 December 1953, p. 50; "Películas en Colores," *Ibid.*, 8 February 1954, p. 46. The average cost of a film went from 750,200 pesos in 1954 to 936,300 in 1955. *Historia*, 6: 8.

44. "Emigran Productores a Cuba," *Hispanoamericano*, 29 March 1954, p. 55. However, Cuban actors and technicians protested the "Mexicanization" of moviemaking on the island. "Martí Ganó la Batalla," *Ibid.*, 9 November 1953, p. 47. See also "Actividad Mexicana en el Extranjero," *Ibid.*, 24 May 1954, p. 60; "Pacto con Cuba," *Ibid.*, 14 June 1954, p. 47. For additional background on Cuban cinema and its relation to Mexico in the prerevolutionary period, see Nestor Almendros, "The Cinema in Cuba," *Film Culture* no. 3 (1956), p. 21 and González, "Apuntes para la historia," pp. 37–45.

45. Another method of ensuring at least some distribution of Mexican films abroad was by requiring reciprocity, that is, if foreign films were to be shown in Mexico, the other country had to accept a like number of Mexican films in exchange. Such arrangements existed with Spain, Britain, Argentina, Italy, and Japan.

"Intercambio con España," *Hispanoamericano*, 2 November 1953, p. 44.

46. "Películas de 2 Semanas," *Ibid.*, 28 June 1954, p. 58.

47. *Historia*, 7: 8.

48. See Manuel González Casanova, *¿Qué es un Cine-Club?* (Mexico City: Dirección General de Difusión Cultural, Sección de Actividades Cinematográficas, UNAM, 1961), pp. 11–16; "El CCM," *Hispanoamericano*, 13 July 1951, pp. 42–43; "9 Programas del Cine Club," *Ibid.*, 28 September 1951, p. 48; "3 Grandes Obras," *Ibid.*, 7 December 1951, p. 44; "El Pasado Vuelve," *Ibid.*, 16 May 1952, p. 60, "Labor Fructuosa," *Ibid.*, 11 November 1952, p. 48; and "Exitos del Pasado," *Ibid.*, 3 April 1953, p. 45. The charter of the Federación Mexicana de Cine Clubs is reprinted in *Historia*, 6: 15–19.

Chapter 5

1. Heuer, *La industria cinematográfica*, p. 179.

2. *Historia*, 6: 132; "Acusaciones del 'Indio'," *Hispanoamericano*, 27 September 1954, p. 47.

3. For a detailed analysis of the Mexican political system and its role in economic development see Roger D. Hansen, *The Politics of Mexican Development* (Baltimore: Johns Hopkins University Press, 1971). See also Pablo González Casanova, *Democracy in Mexico*, trans. Danielle Salti (New York: Oxford University Press, 1972). For a later assessment see "Mexico's Reluctant Oil Boom," *Business Week*, 15 January 1979, pp. 64–74; James Flanigan, "Mexican Oil: The U.S. Is Most definitely *Not* in the Driver's Seat," *Forbes*, 22 January 1979, pp. 29–32; idem, "Why Won't the Mexicans Sell Us More Oil?," *Forbes*, 29 October 1979, pp. 41–52.

4. *Historia*, 8: 195.

5. *Ibid.*, p. 194.

6. *Ibid.*, p. 10. The "Santo" series may have been of bad quality but it was remarkably enduring nonetheless as well as continuously profitable. See Agustín Gurezpe, "'Rencor y Envidia Porque mis Películas Siempre Ganan Dinero,' Dice El Santo," *Excélsior*, 6 April 1977, Section Cine, Teatro, Radio y TV, p. 1; and Jorge Ayala Blanco, *La búsqueda del cine mexicano* (1968–1972), 2 vols., Cuadernos de Cine #22 (Mexico City: UNAM, Dirección General de Difusión Cultural, 1974), 1: 295–304.

7. *Historia*, 7: 389.

8. *Ibid.*, 8: 436.

9. *Ibid.*, 7: 321–22.

10. *Ibid.*, pp. 459–60.

11. *Ibid.*, 8: 11–26.

12. *Ibid.*, pp. 358, 361–62.

13. *Ibid.*, p. 354.

14. Jomí García Ascot, "El cine y el escritor," *Cine cubano*, no. 31/32/33 (1966), p. 104.

15. See *ibid.*, pp. 104–105 and *Historia*, 8: 114–36 for an extensive recapitulation of the commentary on this film.

16. See *Historia*, 8: 139–86 for an extensive commentary. See also García Riera, "Viridiana," p. 74; David Stewart Hull, "Viridiana," *Film Quarterly* 15 (Winter 1961/62): 55–56; Buache, *The Cinema of Luis Buñuel*, pp. 117–27; and Aranda, *Luis Buñuel*, pp. 190–205.

17. *Historia*, 8: 292–96. See also Ayala Blanco, *La aventura*, pp. 284–88.

18. See Reyes Nevares, *The Mexican Cinema*, pp. 63–76 and Alberto Isaac, "Cine latinoamericano: reportaje a Luis Alcoriza," *Tiempo de cine*, año 5, no. 20/21 (Spring-Summer 1965), pp. 38–40, 80.

19. Ayala Blanco, *La aventura*, p. 304.

20. Vivian Lash, "Experimenting with Freedom in Mexico," *Film Quarterly* 19 (Summer 1966): 19. Lash writes that 18 films were completed while Ayala Blanco specifies and lists 12. For a complete listing of the films entered in the competition, see Ayala Blanco, *La aventura*, pp. 3–5 and Appendix above, pp. 223–24.

21. Ayala Blanco, *La aventura*, p. 304.

22. *Ibid.*, pp. 308–10. An interesting footnote to the film is that Luis Buñuel appeared in a cameo role.

23. With the exception of Miguel Barbachano Ponce, already well established in film circles as a producer of "quality" cinema.

24. Ayala Blanco, *La aventura*, p. 305.

25. Tomás Pérez-Turrent and Gillian Turner, "Mexico," in Peter Cowie, ed., *International Film Guide* 1976 (London: Tantivy Press, 1977), p. 207.

26. Ayala Blanco, *La búsqueda*, 1: 13. *En el balcón vacío* was premiered at the French Institute and later shown at UNAM. Apparently it was never shown commercially in Mexico. García Ascot, "El cine y el escritor," p. 104. The film is available at the Cineteca Nacional. Also included in the STPC's 1965 awards was distribution of the prize-winning film through the state channels. Independent filmmaking was not any easier in other countries, including the U.S. See for example Janet Stevenson, "Why So Few Independent Feature Films?" *In These Times*, 6–12 December 1977, p. 22.

27. Pérez-Turrent and Turner, "Mexico," in Cowie, ed., *International Film Guide 1974*, p. 237.

28. Ayala Blanco, *La búsqueda*, 1: 11.

29. See Elena Poniatowska's comments in *Historia*, 8: 200 and the *Visión* article quoted in *ibid.*, pp. 202–203.

30. Alan Riding, "Mexico Elects a Symbol," *The New York Times Magazine*, 13 June 1976, p. 14; see also Sergio Zermeño, *México: Una democracia utópica: El movimiento estudiantil del 68*, prologue by Carlos Monsiváis (Mexico City: Siglo Veintiuno Editores, 1978).

31. Much more extensive coverage was given by the U.S. press to the American black athletes who gave a "black power" salute during the playing of the "Star-Spangled Banner" after being awarded their gold medals.

32. See also Elena Poniatowska, *Massacre in Mexico*, trans. Helen R. Lane (New York: Viking Press, 1975), originally published as *La noche de Tlatelolco*: *Testimonios de historia* (Mexico City: Ediciones Era, 1971).

33. Ayala Blanco, *La búsqueda*, 1: 13.

34. *Ibid.*, 2: 333.

35. *Ibid.* For a discussion of the film, see pp. 332–37.

36. *Ibid.*, pp. 339–40. For a discussion of *El grito*, see pp. 337–48.

37. Diaz Ordaz was quoted as saying, "If what you desire is to bury the cinema industry, I will preside over the funeral. The government is not interested in that industry." Galindo, *¿Qué es el cine?*, p. 129. Luis Echeverría had been appointed to the governing board of the Banco Cinematográfico in 1963. *Historia*, 8: 351.

38. Rodolfo Echeverría's professional name was Rodolfo Landa. He had been politically active as well as having been a performer; in 1952 he was elected a deputy to congress. "La Probable XLII Legislatura," *Hispanoamericano*, 13 June 1952, p. 9. Between 1938 and 1965 he appeared in more than 80 movies. He died on March 14, 2004. David Wilt, "Rodolfo Landa Dies," *The Mexican Film Bulletin*, vol. 10, no. 1 (April 2004), p. 1.

39. Cárdenas is considered by some to have been Marxist; Echeverría was nothing of the kind. Many observers looked upon the latter's wooing of the international left as little more than political opportunism.

40. For an assessment of the Echeverría presidency, see Riding, "Mexico Elects a Symbol," pp. 14–15, 19, 22.

41. *Informe general sobre la actividad cinematográfica en el año 1976 relativo al Banco Nacional Cinematográfico, S.A. y sus filiales* (Mexico City: Banco Nacional Cinematográfico, 26 November 1976), p. 11.

42. *Ibid.*, p. 13.

43. *Ibid.*, pp. 11–12.

44. Manuel Michel, "CCC: Un retrato escrito," *Otrocine*, no. 1 (January-March 1975), pp. 62–68.

45. "Edificio," *Cineteca Nacional 1974* (compiled for in-house reference), pp. 30–31.

46. "Acervo," *ibid.*, pp. 35–38; *Informe general*, p. 408.

47. *Informe general*, p. 16.

48. *Ibid.*, pp. 159–60. For more information on CONACINE see *ibid.*, pp. 159–68; for CONACITE I, see pp. 187–91; and for CONACITE II, see pp. 201–204.

49. *Anuario de la producción cinematográfica mexicana, 1970/Mexican Film Production, 1970/Production cinématographique mexicaine, 1970* (Mexico City: Procinemex, n.d.)

50. *Anuario...*, 1971.

51. *Anuario...*, 1972.

52. Alejandro Galindo characterized Alcoriza's *Mecánica nacional* as falsely portraying the way Mexicans behave, and bitterly attacked the Echeverría brothers for their policies toward the film industry. This writer suspects that Galindo's resentment was occasioned by the favoritism shown to young directors like Cazals. Galindo's own pet projects were realized in 1973: *El juicio de Martín Cortés* and *Ante el cadáver de un líder* (the latter his personal favorite), but they were not given the distribution or promotion he felt they deserved. Personal interview, Mexico City, 5 July 1977.

53. There are discrepancies between the Banco's figures and those from Procinemex's *Anuario*. For in-

stance, the latter shows 72 full-length features and 8 independent films for 1971 for a total of 80 films, while the Banco indicates a total of 75. However, the *Informe general* also lists 7 films made by foreign companies in Mexico for a total of 82, a figure not reflected in the table.

54. Interview with Sigifredo García Sanz, Mexico City, 17 July 1977. García Sanz was associated with the film industry from 1947 to the early 1970s, principally in accounting but often becoming involved in other areas of filmmaking. In July 1977, Margarita López Portillo, in her capacity as General Director of Radio, Television, and Cinema — a post created especially for her — ordered a thoroughgoing reorganization of the film industry's financial structure and García Sanz was designated as a consultant to coordinate the project. At the time, he was hopeful that this meant a retreat from state participation in filmmaking.

55. However, it is true that the lowest yearly number of films made up to that time in the decade — 42 films — was made in 1976. "México y Argentina Dominados por el Sexo en su Cinematografía," *Excélsior*, 19 January 1977, Section Cine, Teatro, Radio y TV, p.5.

56. See Sergio Guzik, "A Mass Changes Me More: An Interview with Alexandro [*sic*] Jodorowski," *The Drama Review* 14 (Winter 1970): 70–76. In the same issue, see also "The Mole: Excerpts from a Film Script," pp. 57–69.

57. For more on Jodorowski, see Miguel Barbachano Ponce, "Crítica de Cine: La Montaña Sagrada," *Excélsior*, 6 October 1976, Section Cine, Teatro, Radio y TV, p. 1. Jodorowski expressed impatience with the Mexican public's reception of his films. Complaining about censorship and the cuts he was obliged to make, Jodorowski said that "here in Mexico they are afraid of me, others are not censored." "La Gente de Mexico no Está Preparada Para ver mis Películas: Jodorowski," *Excélsior*, 1 October 1976, Section Cine, Teatro, Radio y TV, p. 1. For commentary on *Fando y Lis* and *El topo*, see Ayala Blanco, *La búsqueda*, 2: 407–15.

58. "Reitera LE que hay Libertad Para Tratarlo Todo en Cine," *Excélsior*, 28 June 1976, p. A-29. See also 'El Gobierno Mexicano Nacionalizó la Industria del Cine y Ahora se Producen Películas que antes se Consideraban 'Tabúes,'" *Excélsior*, 26 October 1976, Section Cine, Teatro, Radio y TV, p. 1.

59. Reyes Nevares, *The Mexican Cinema*, pp. 67–68.

60. Agustín Gurezpe, "Ninguna Película del Nuevo Cine Mexicano Responde a la Necesidad Crítica de la Realidad Actual de Nuestro País," *Excélsior*, 22 July 1976, Section Cine, Teatro, Radio y TV, p. 1.

61. For this, the reader may consult Ayala Blanco's two invaluable works, already extensively cited here: *La aventura del cine mexicano* and *La búsqueda del cine mexicano*, 2 vols.

62. Its gross receipts up to January 1974 were second only to *The Godfather*—7,558,000 pesos. Sam Askinazy, "Mexico's Own Film $600,000 behind 'Godpop,'" *Variety*, 9 January 1974, p. 10.

63. Manolo Fábregas has produced, directed, and acted in Spanish-language versions of *Life with Father*, *My Fair Lady*, and *Fiddler on the Roof*, as well as many other adaptations of hit American shows. Marvin Alisky, "Fábregas's Broadway-to-Mexico Theater," *The Christian Science Monitor*, 2 October 1970, p. 4.

64. See Ayala Blanco, *La búsqueda*, 1: 164–69; Reyes Nevares, *The Mexican Cinema*, pp. 63,69; Marvin Alisky, "Mexico versus Malthus: National Trends," *Current History* 66 (May 1974): 229–30; "Lo Mejor de los Estrenos en 1972," *Hispanoamericano*, 15 January 1973, p. 56; and Angel A. Pérez Gómez, "Luis Alcoriza: Mecánica nacional," *Reseña* (Madrid), año 14, no. 103 (March 1977), p. 29.

65. Ayala Blanco, *La búsqueda*, 2: 503.

66. *Ibid.*, pp. 503–506. See also Alvaro Uribe, "Entrevista a Alfredo Joskowicz," *Otrocine*, no. 3 (July-September 1975), pp. 64–67; José Luis Peralta, "El cambio," *ibid.*, pp. 68–70.

67. For an account of the town and the actual events, see Elsa R. de Estrada, "Ecos de un linchamiento en el pueblo de las bocinas," *Contenido* (Mexico City), June 1976, pp. 72–82. For a description of how the screenplay was written see Tomás Pérez-Turrent, "Una experiencia alrededor de Canoa," *Otrocine*, no. 2 (April-June 1975), pp. 8–12. See also Fernando Gaxiola, "Canoa, memoria de un hecho vergonzante," *Otrocine*, no. 1 (January-March 1975), p. 10; "Reportaje y Denuncia," *Hispanoamericano*, 16 February 1976, p. 59; Antonia Landa G., "Canoa," *Otrocine*, no. 4 (October-December 1975), pp. 14–15; and Martha L. Sepúlveda, "Sobre Canoa," *ibid.*, pp. 16–18.

68. Poli Délano, "El apando," *Otrocine*, no. 6 (April-June 1976), p. 33; Douglas Sánchez, "El apando," *ibid.*, pp. 34–35; Jaime A. Shelley, "Conversación con Felipe Cazals," *ibid.*, no. 3 (July-September 1975), pp. 34–43.

69. Agustín Gurezpe, "'Nunca más Traeré Pistola al Cinto,' Prometió el 'Indio' Fernández ayer en los Churubusco," *Excélsior*, 14 December 1976, Section Cine, Teatro, Radio y TV, pp. 1, 5; Juan de Ayala, "A Ultima Hora el 'Indio' Fernández Tuvo que Pagar $150,000 de Fianza," *ibid.*, 11 December 1976, p. 1; Ayala Blanco, *La búsqueda*, 1: 19–39.

70. See Luis Reyes de la Maza, "De cómo el papá de Martín Cortés se fue mucho pual de Tívoli," *Otrocine*, no. 1 (January-March 1975), pp. 33–39.

71. Reyes Nevares, *The Mexican Cinema*, p. 29.

72. Letter from Christon I. Archer, 1 December 1977. See also Stanley Meisler, "Is This Democracy?" *Los Angeles Times*, 7 March 1976, p. IX-4.

73. Francisco Sánchez, "Tívoli," *Otrocine*, no. 1 (January-March 1975), pp. 19–22; Jaime A. Shelley, "Entrevista con Alberto Isaac," *ibid.*, pp. 23–32.

74. Jesús Salvador Treviño, "The New Mexican Cinema," *Film Quarterly* 34 (Spring 1980): 30–31.

75. There was scant attention paid to Mexican films of the 1970s by American critics. *Canoa*, which won a "Silver Bear" at the 1976 Berlin Film Festival (Ricardo Perete, "¡Corte!" *Excélsior*, 1 October 1976, Section Cine, Teatro Radio y TV, p. 1) was released to general audiences in the United States. However, the Museum of Modern Art in 1977 did acquire for its permanent holdings eight Mexican films including *Actas de Marusia* (*The New Yorker*, 17 January 1977, p. 18). The series was sent on tour around the country and reviewed

by Dennis West ("Mexican Cinema in 1977: A Commentary on the Mexican Film Festival Presently Touring the U.S.," *The American Hispanist* 2 [May 1977]: 6–7, 13–14). For reviews of Paul Ledúc's *Reed: México insurgente* see Lewis H. Diuguid, "AFI's Latin American Film Festival," *The Washington Post*, 17 March 1974, p. E4; Kevin Thomas, "'Reed' Treats Mexico Revolt," *Los Angeles Times*, 9 March 1976, p. IV-8; and Michael Goodwin, "Reed: Insurgent Mexico," *Take One* 4 (December 1974): 31. Rafael Corkidi's *Pafnucio Santo* (1976) was shown at the 15th New York Film Festival—the first Mexican film ever included—and reviewed by Lawrence van Gelder, "Film Festival: Pafnucio Santo," *New York Times*, 27 September 1977. See also Carl Mora, "Mexico's Commercial Films: Sources for the Study of Social History," *PCCLAS Proceedings* 6 (1977–1979): 205–15.

76. Pedro Chaskel, another exiled Chilean filmmaker, praised Mexico for the support it had given Littín: "it represents not only a courtesy, but also backing for the Chilean resistance which struggles for the liberation of our country." He also said that the cameraman Jorge Muller and the actress Carmen Bueno had last been reported in "a concentration camp where they had been tortured." Agustín Gurezpe, "Habla Pedro Chaskel, Chileno en el Exilio—Tarea de Cineastas Latinoamericanos: Luchar por Descolonización Cultural," *Excélsior*, 29 May 1976, p. 30-A.

77. He singled out Tennessee Williams, one of the jurors, as being responsible for the negative vote. Williams had attacked violence in films, presumably with *Actas de Marusia* in mind. Agustín Gurezpe, "Littín Afirma que Perdío en Cannes por un Voto," *Excélsior*, 18 June 1976, p. C-1.

78. It opened at 14 theaters in the Federal District and took in 668,767 pesos in one day's receipts. Miguel Pareja Donoso, "Actas de Marusia," *Mañana*, 24 April 1976, p.10.

79. Betty Jeffries Demby, "The 30th Cannes Film Festival," *Filmmakers Newsletter*, October, 1980, pp. 28–33. The special treatment accorded Littín in Mexico did not fail to elicit criticism; he denied that he "ever pretended to leadership or to take the attitude that he was a hero or saviour of the Mexican cinema … he received the normal salary of a Mexican film director." "Respuesta de Miguel Littín a Avila Camacho," *Excélsior*, 27 October 1976, Section Cine, Teatro, Radio y TV, p. 1. See also Fernando Gaxiola, "'Actas de Marusia'—la posibilidad de un cine popular," *Otrocine*, no. 1 (January-March 1975), p. 9; "Actas de Marusia," *La Revue du Cinéma—Image et Son*, no. 306 (May 1976), pp. 66–67; "Film in Chile: An Interview with Miguel Littín," *Cineaste* 4: 4–9; "Nuevo cine, nuevos realizadores, nuevos filmes: Entrevista a Miguel Littín," *Cine cubano*, no. 63–65 (1970), pp. 1–6; "Premios para 'Actas de Marusia' y 'Universidad Comprometida,' en Huelva," *Excélsior*, 14 December 1976, Section Cine, Teatro, Radio y TV, p. 1; "It's Been a Great Year for International Films," *The Hollywood Reporter*, 26 October 1976, p. 18; "Chilean Exile Makes Hit with 'Letters from Marusia,'" *ibid.*, 26 October 1976, p. 61; David Wilson, "Letters from Marusia," *Sight and Sound* (Winter 1976–1977), pp. 60–61.

80. "El Arte Como Función Social," *Hispanoamericano*, 11 April 1977, pp. 41–42. See pages 39–43 for an interview with Arau. See also Agustín Gurezpe, "En 'Suspenso' la Película que Arau Filmó en la Habana," *Excélsior*, 9 October 1976, section Cine, Teatro, Radio y TV, p. 1.

81. Ricardo Perete, "¡Corte!" *Excélsior*, 29 July 1976, Section Cine, Teatro, Radio y TV, p. 1.

82. From this writer's personal observation, most young Chicanos have little or no fluency in Spanish—a disadvantage that would effectively preclude them from being a major audience for Mexican films, "Chicano" or otherwise. For instance, *Chicano* (1975) was purportedly based on the exploits of the New Mexico land grant activist Reies López Tijerina, yet the film was not shown commercially in New Mexico. At any rate, following the brief spate of publicity on Tijerina as a result of his and his followers' seizure in 1967 of the courthouse at Tierra Amarilla, New Mexico, he retreated into general anonymity with the exception of a visit to President Echeverría that seems to have been reported only in Albuquerque (Tomas Martinez, "Echeverria Meets Group," *Albuquerque Journal*, 13 June 1967, p. 1). The fact that Jaime Casillas, director of *Chicano*, thought that Tijerina was still a major figure among Mexican-American militants points to the lack of knowledge in Mexico regarding the situation. See Charles R. Garrett II, "El Tigre Revisited," *Nuestro*, August 1977, pp. 16–18, 20. Katy Jurado, a well-known Mexican actress with long experience in Hollywood, voiced criticism of Chicanos saying that she "did not understand" the Chicano movement because they are "North Americans" fighting their own country, an attitude which she found "absurd." "Katy Dijo en París que no Entiende a los Chicanos," *El Sol de México*, 22 July 1977, p. E4.

83. David R. Maciel, ed., *La otra cara de México: el pueblo chicano*, prologue by Carlos Monsiváis (Mexico City: Ediciones "El Caballito," 1977), p. 16. The "Chicano public," it seems, prefers the "traditional" package films. The new Mexican cinema with its slow-paced intellectualizing in the European style did not prove popular among Mexican-American audiences according to Gonzalo Checa, president of the California Association of Spanish Film Exhibitors. Carl Hillos, "Gonzalo Checa Espera el Envío de 'Tradicionales,'" *Novedades*, 7 January 1975, Section Novedades en los Espectáculos, pp. 1, 4. See Ayala Blanco's discussion of Mexican Americans in Mexican films and Chicano filmmaking in the United States in *La búsqueda*, 2: 353–58; Carlos Morton, "Why No Chicano Film Makers? Plática con Luis Sedano y Antonio Orgaz," *La Luz*, June 1977, pp. 25–28; Rafael C. Castillo, "Films: Cine Festival," *Nuestro*, December 1979, pp. 51–52; Victor Valle, "Let the Chicano Films Roll," *ibid.*, pp. 51–52; and Jesús Salvador Treviño, "Chicano Cinema" (unpublished paper).

84. Letter from Alfonso Arau, 7 November 1977. In 1979 Arau completed *Mojado Power*, a musical comedy filmed in Tijuana and California. It was produced by AMX Productions. "Alfonso Arau's Latest, 'Mojado Power,'" *The Hollywood Reporter*, March 1979, p. S-18.

85. "En Defensa de una Actriz," *Hispanoamericano*,

13 March 1953, p. 47. See also Larry Ceplair and Steven Englund, *The Inquisition in Hollywood: Politics in the Film Community, 1930–1960* (Garden City, N.Y.: Anchor Press/Doubleday, 1980), pp. 417–18.

86. *Historia,* 7: 367–71. Cantinflas's debut was in the supporting role of Passepartout in *Around the World in 80 Days.*

87. Wini Scheffler, "Foreign Filming Leaves Below-the-Line Income," *Mex-Am Review* 43 (August 1975): 4–5, 7, 9.

88. Luis Torres, "Raices de sangre: First Feature Film Directed by a Chicano," *Somos,* June/July 1978, pp. 17–19; Jesús Salvador Treviño, "Chicano Cinema," pp. 15–16; Armando Mora, "Qué Actores Irán con los Chicanos" and idem, "Actores de la Metrópoli Alternarán con Chicanos," *El Sol de México,* 30 August 1976; Agustín Gurezpe, "El Cine Estadounidense Está Cerrado Para los Actores y Realizadores 'Chicanos'," *Excélsior,* 26 August 1976, Section Cine, Teatro, Radio y TV; and Eduardo de la Vega Alfaro, "Butaca: 'Raíces de Sangre'," *Uno Más Uno,* Mexico City, n.d.

89. For instance, CONACINE II lodged a protest in behalf of STIC when the filming of Mariano Azuela's novel, *Los de abajo,* was assigned to Churubusco. "En Octubre se Rodará 'Los de Abajo,' de Mariano Azuela," *Excélsior,* 13 September 1976, Section Cine, Teatro, Radio y TV, p. 1. See also Agustín Gurezpe, "Técnicos y Manuales Contra los Largometrajes en los 'América'," *ibid.,* 21 July 1976, p. 1; idem, "Es Necesario que se Reanude la Comunicación Entre STIC y STPC," *ibid.,* 10 September 1976, p. 1; idem, "Maximino Molina Pide que se Establezca la Competencia Entre Churubusco y América," *ibid.,* 12 October 1976, p. 1; and Beatriz Reyes Nevares, "Entre cretinos y voraces naufraga el cine mexicano," *Siempre,* 3 January 1973, pp. 40–41, 70.

90. "El Gobierno Mexicano Nacionalizó," p. 1; Gregg Kilday, "Mexico's Revolution in Filmmaking," *Los Angeles Times,* 24 March 1976, p. IV-14.

91. Sam Askinazy, "Echeverria Exit: His Film Reforms Open Up Mexico," *Variety,* 5 January 1977, pp. 16, 56; Agustín Gurezpe, "RE Acabo con el Cine Vacío de 30 Años: que Continúe de Director del Banco," *Excélsior,* 22 May 1976, p. 24-A; Wilson McKinney, "Mexican Film Industry Improving Its Quality," *San Antonio Express-News,* 5 October 1975, p. 8-A; Louis Margorelles, "Le Renoveau Mexicain," *La Revue du Cinéma — Image et Son,* no. 280 (January 1974), pp. 72–90; "Cinéma Mexicain," *ibid.,* no. 295 (April 1975), pp. 20–28; Beatriz Reyes Nevares, "El cine mexicano es hoy de mejor calidad," *Siempre,* 27 December 1972, pp. 42–43; Martha Naranjo, "Echeverria — Giant of Mexican Filmmaking," *The Hollywood Reporter,* 26 October 1976, pp. 1, 64; "Mexico Carves Out Share of World Film Market," *ibid.,* p. 9.

For additional readings on the Echeverría *sexenio* and its impact on films see Alberto Ruy Sánchez, "Cine mexicano: producción social de una estética," *Historia y Sociedad,* no. 18 (Summer 1978), pp. 71–83; Javier Solórzano, "El nuevo cine en México: Entrevista a Emilio García Riera," *Comunicación y cultura* 5 (March 1978), pp. 7–18; David Ramón, "Un sexenio de cine en México," *Comunicación* 21 (March 1977), pp. 24–

33; Emilio García Riera, "Seis años de cine mexicano (1)," *Proceso,* 6 November 1976, pp. 68–69; idem, "Del cine mercantil al cine de autor," *ibid.,* 13 November 1976, pp. 72–73; idem, "El choque con la censura hipócrita," *ibid.,* 20 November 1976, pp. 72–73; Cristina Pacheco, "El Cine, Su Vicio" [interview with Emilio García Riera], *Siempre,* 1 November 1978, pp. 32–34, 70.

92. Agustín Gurezpe, "Reyes Heroles dió Posesión a García Borja en el Banco Cinematográfico," *Excélsior,* 9 December 1976, Section Cine, Teatro, Radio y TV, p. 1.

93. Rubén Torres, "Crean la Productora Nacional de Radio y Televisión, Dependiente de la Sría de Gobernación," *El Heraldo de México,* 5 July 1977, p. 1D.

94. In a letter received by this writer dated 23 July 1980 from Humberto Enríque Hernández, an official of the Secretaría de Gobernación, the CCC is mentioned as being headed by Alfredo Joskowicz. In the same letter it is stated that Benito Alazraki is director of CONACINE and Carlos Ortiz Tejeda is head of CONACITE II. A subsequent description of CUEC as "the only advanced school of cinema in the country" indicated that the CCC was no more. Germán Ramos Navas, "de todos modos CUEC te llama," *Excélsior: Diorama de la Cultura,* 7 September 1980, p. 3. However, as of early January 1981, the film school was still in operation, with Joskowicz in charge. Martha Aurora Espinosa, "Actualización técnica, temática, de exhibición, y distribución, necesidades del cine nacional," *Uno Más Uno,* 13 January 1981, p. 22. See also Pérez Turrent and Turner, "Mexico," *International Film Guide 1981,* pp. 218–21.

95. "Cabos sueltos: Víctimas del pecado: el fin del Centro de Capacitación Cinematográfica," *Nexos* 24 (December 1979), pp. 4–5, 9, 11.

96. According to Ying Ying Wu, "Trying Times in Mexico," *Nuestro,* May 1980, p. 27.

97. *Ibid.*

98. Luis Suárez, "Habla Margarita López Portillo," *Siempre,* 11 July 1979, p. 29.

99. *Ibid.*

100. "Pido buena fe y sentido de responsabilidad para afrontar la crisis del cine mexicano, dice Margarita López Portillo," *Siempre,* 13 June 1979, p. 58.

101. *Ibid.*

102. Wu, "Trying Times in Mexico," p. 27; "Margarita López Portillo Hails Impact of Revitalization of Film Production," *The Hollywood Reporter,* March 1979, p. S-3 (this issue contained a special section on Mexican cinema).

103. "Informe de labores del periodo lectivo del Sr. Manuel Ampudia Girón," *Organo Informativo de la Cámara Nacional de la Industria Cinematográfica,* 10 March 1980, pp. 12–19.

104. *Guyana* was a Mexican-Spanish coproduction with Izaro Films; CONACINE financed 20 percent of the total production costs which were almost $2,600,000. *Variety,* 19 March 1980, p. 39. This was a special issue devoted to Latin American filmmaking. The Mexican section begins on p. 65. See also Alejandro Sigler M.'s interview with René Cardona, Jr., in *Organo Informativo,* January 1980, p. 11.

105. Stephen Klein, "Televicine Rolls Yank Hispanic Link," *Variety*, 28 May 1980, p. 3; "'Televisa' Moves Ahead," *The Hollywood Reporter*, March 1979, pp. 4–5.

106. "Mexican Conglom in U.S. Toehold," *Variety*, 26 March 1980, pp. 1, 99.

107. Televisa's operation prompted a charge by the Spanish Broadcasters of America that the Mexican corporation was monopolizing Spanish-language television broadcasting in the United States. Specific allegations were that Televisa-controlled SIN illegally owned five of its affiliated stations and that it also owned a sales firm which sold advertising to its own network affiliates. In 1980, SIN claimed to have 57 affiliates; in 1988 the number had risen to over 400. Paul R. Wieck, "FCC Investigates Spanish TV Network," *Albuquerque Journal*, 13 September 1980, p. B-8. See also Anne Bagamery, "SIN, the original," *Forbes*, 22 November 1982, pp. 96–99. A controversy arose in 1986 when Jacobo Zabludovsky, the anchor for Televisa's evening news program, "24 Horas," announced he would take over "Noticiero Nacional SIN" originating in Miami. (A specially edited version of "24 Horas" anchored by Zabludovsky was carried by SIN [later Univisión] stations until about 1987.) SIN's news executives, accusing him of being a propagandist for the Mexican government, strongly opposed the move — obliging Zabludovsky to change his plans and remain in Mexico. Carlos Marín, "A Zabludovsky no se le cree por considerarlo vocero del gobierno," *Proceso*, 27 October 1986, pp. 20–25. See also idem, "Alemán reconoce que en información Televisa se autocensura," *ibid.*, 15 September 1986, pp. 6–8. In 1988, the now Univisión network was bought by Hallmark Cards Incorporated after a court ruling that Televisa's ownership of the Spanish-language network constituted an illegal monopoly as well as a violation of U.S. law which prohibits foreign ownership of communications media. In 1987 Telemundo, a competing Spanish-language network, was formed by Henry Silverman of New York; the CEO was Carlos Barra, a Cuban-American. Ignacio González Janzen, "Empresarios estadunidenses desbancan a Televisa en el control de la televisión en español en EU," *Uno Más Uno*, 26 July 1988, p. 24. See also Adolfo Aguilar Zinser, "Mexico's Acrimonious TV Network loses Its Sting," *Wall Street Journal*, 19 August 1988, p. 17 and Marshall Ingwerson, "Spanish-Language TV Now Taps Growing U.S. Hispanic Market," *Albuquerque Journal Entertainer*, 31 March 1989, p. F33 (reprinted from *Christian Science Monitor*).

108. Larry Rohter, "From Reviled Ex-Leader, a Double-Barreled Blast," *New York Times*, 11 November 1988, p. A-4; Matt Moffett, "Mexico's Most-Vilified Former President Writes Best-Seller to Defend His Actions," *Wall Street Journal*, 29 November 1988, p. A14.

109. Ignacio Rodríguez C., "El cine comercial no puede ser elitista," *Organo Informativo*, 10 March 1980, p. 31.

110. Jorge Carrasco, "Luto Nacional," *Hispanoamericano*, 5 April 1982, p. 61.

111. Idem, "Campanas Rojas," *Hispanoamericano*, 29 March 1982, p. 58.

112. John Mosier, "Ambitious Epics: *Cecilia* and *The Red Bells*," *Americas*, Jan-Feb 1983, p. 59.

113. Jorge Carrasco, "Una Buena Película," *Hispanoamericano*, 15 March 1982; see also Julio J. Etienne, "El Buen Cine Mexicano," *ibid.*, 25 August 1987, p. 59.

114. Jorge Carrasco, "Desprecio Malinchista," *ibid.*, 27 Dec. 1982, p. 59.

115. For an interview with Hermosillo and a partial filmography, see Emilio García Riera, "Conversación con Jaime Humberto Hermosillo," *Primer Plano (Revista de la Cineteca Nacional)*, no. 1 (November-December 1981): 3–30.

116. Tomás Pérez-Turrent, "María de mi corazón," in Peter Cowie, ed., *International Film Guide 1982*, p. 205; see also Jorge Carrasco, "Una Buena Muestra de Cine Independiente," *Hispanoamericano*, 18 June 1985, n.p.

117. Jorge Carrasco, "Superhéroe a la Medida," *ibid.*, 20 September 1982, p. 56.

118. For a Santo filmography, see José Xavier Navar, "Imágenes: Las estrellas del colchón," *Su otro yo*, vol. 9, no. 4 (April 1982): 40–41; see also Nelson Carro, *El cine de luchadores* (Mexico City: Filmoteca de la UNAM, 1984.).

119. Jorge Carrasco, "Nuevo Cine Mexicano," *Hispanoamericano*, 11 October 1982, p. 55. A classic example of life imitating art is the phenomenon of "Super Barrio," a masked champion of the poor who appeared after the 1985 Mexico City earthquake. "Dressed in red tights, gold cape, face mask and a shirt emblazoned with the letters SB, Mexico's homegrown superhero leads the fight for fair housing, electricity and sewers here. All it takes is a call to his telephone hotline, and Super Barrio will arrive at the scene of injustice in his Barriomobile, accompanied by lawyers, militants of the Assembly of Barrios and often the press." This real-life superhero kept his identity a secret and gained admittance to meetings and public hearings at the Ministries of the Interior (*Gobernación*) and Urban Development and even Los Pinos, the presidential residence. An ex-professional wrestler, he received film and comic book offers, and even offers to return to the ring, all of which Super Barrio refused: "My struggle is a social struggle, not a commercial one," he said. "We are not confronting Martians, but landlords. Our enemies are not imaginary, but real." Larry Rohter, "The Poor Man's Superman, Scourge of Landlords," *New York Times*, 15 August 1988, n.p. Super Barrio also extended his activities to Mexican communities in the United States. Arturo Gonzalez, Jr., "Not To be Confused with Bird or Plane, Mexico's Caped Crusader Packs a Political Paunch," *People Weekly*, 10 April 1989, pp. 114–115.

120. Carlos Loret de Mola, "Desacato a Gabriel Figueroa: El Cine Desperdiciado," *Siempre*, 24 November 1982, p. 41.

121. Tomás Pérez-Turrent and Gillian Turner, "Mexico," in Peter Cowie, ed., *International Film Guide 1982*, p. 201; for background on Bardem's comment see Carl J. Mora, "The Odyssey of Spanish Cinema," *New Orleans Review* 14, no. 1 (Spring 1987): 13.

122. It seemed that the Mexican cinema had been in a permanent crisis since the 1950s, and even prior

to that. "Like a festering wound eating away at the cinematic structure is the famous crisis. Never had a word been uttered so often, manipulated, and exploited as that permanent crisis of our cinema. Nonetheless, never had a patient survived so robustly such a long illness." Manuel Michel, "Cine mexicano: utopía y realidad," *Plural*, vol. 11-7, no. 127 (April 1982): 67.

123. Carlos Crespo Aragón and Erika Domínguez Cervantes, "José Estrada: Crísis del cine mexicano," *Plural*, vol. 11-9, no. 129 (June 1982): 73.

124. *Ibid.*, p. 74.

125. Erika Domínguez, "Emilio García Riera: Un sexenio de cine mexicano," *Plural*, vol. 12-3, no. 135 (Dec. 1982)

126. "Una Cinematografía Planificada," *Hispanoamericano*, 8 March 1982, p. 57.

Chapter 6

1. Héctor Rivera, "Isaac cree posible levantar un cine en ruinas en un país arruinado," *Proceso*, no. 336, 11 April 1983, p. 50.

2. Tomás Pérez-Turrent and Gillian Turner, "Mexico," in Peter Cowie, ed., *International Film Guide 1982* (London: Tantivy Press, 1983), p. 202.

3. The first was in 1964 (see pp. 107–109), and the second in 1971. The latter was called National Contest of Independent Cinema in Super 8, and resulted in an ideological controversy between proponents of a political cinema led by Paco Ignacio Taibo II and others whose spokesman was Gabriel Retes who favored a more traditional "aesthetic" cinema. Moisés Viñas, *Historia del cine mexicano* (Mexico City: UNAM-UNESCO, 1987), p. 266.

4. *Ibid.*, p. 277.

5. Erika Domínguez, "Dirección del cine mexicano," *Plural*, vol. 12-7, no. 139, April 1983, p. 54.

6. *Ibid.*

7. *Ibid.*, p. 55.

8. *Ibid.*, pp. 55–56.

9. Jorge Carrasco, "Luto en el Cine Mexicano," *Hispanoamericano*, 25 April 1983, pp. 44–47. See also Archibaldo Burns, "Dolores del Río: de sus cenizas, la leyenda," *Proceso*, no. 337, 18 April 1983, pp. 50–53.

10. Michael Wood, "The Discreet Charm of Luis Buñuel," *American Film*, September 1982, p. 38. See also, idem, "Buñuel was always ready for death ... from the moment he was born," *The Listener*, 9 February 1984, pp. 10–12 and Jorge Carrasco, "Un Artista Integro," *Hispanoamericano*, 8 August 1983, pp. 58–59.

11. Luis Buñuel, *Mi último suspiro* (Mexico City: Plaza & Janes, 1982), p. 206.

12. Jorge Carrasco, "Perspectivas Sobre la Cinematografía Nacional," *Hispanoamericano*, 25 July 1983, p. 59.

13. *Ibid.*

14. Tomás Pérez-Turrent and Gillian Turner, "Mexico," in Peter Cowie, ed., *International Film Guide 1985* (London: Tantivy Press, 1986), p. 213.

15. Tomás Pérez-Turrent, "Nocaut (Knockout)," *International Film Guide 1984*, p. 215.

16. Jorge Carrasco, "Vidas Errantes," *Hispanoamericano*, 24 September 1985, p. 46.

17. "Qué es la Cineteca Nacional" [brochure] (Mexico City: Cineteca Nacional, January 1986).

18. "Se Dinamiza la Cineteca Nacional," *Hispanoamericano*, 28 July 1987, p. 65.

19. Jorge Carrasco, "Plan de Recuperación Cinematográfica," *Ibid.*, 19 August 1986, p. 68; see also "Piden Acciones Concretas Para Salvar al Cine," *Ibid.*, 26 August 1986, p. 64.

20. Joan M. West and Dennis West, "Frida," *Cineaste* 16, no. 4 (1988): 54. In 1971 Marcela Fernández Violante made a much-praised short feature entitled *Frida Kahlo*. Moisés Viñas, *Historia del cine mexicano*, p. 268; see also "'We Are Losing Our Identity': An Interview with Mexican Director Marcela Fernández Violante," *Film/Literature Quarterly* 15, no. 1 (1987): 3.

21. Jorge Carrasco, "Una Biografía Poco Convencional," *Hispanoamericano*, 1 April 1986, p. 19.

22. Hortensia Caymares and Luciano Castillo, "Barbachano o la pasión de crear," *Cine cubano* #118 (1987): 60. Not all critics were as enthusiastic about the film — Jorge Ayala Blanco fumed: "Such pathetic boring intellectuals. Any vacuity enthuses them, any childish vision of Frida Kahlo interpreted by an awful actress, with no script, without character development, with no film." *La condición del cine mexicano* (1973–1985) (Mexico City: Editorial Posada, 1986), p. 254. In 1989, Ledúc made *Barroco*, a Mexican-Spanish-Cuban coproduction. Based on *Concierto barroco*, a novella published in 1974 by the Cuban writer Alejo Carpentier (1940–1980), the film attempted to explain Mexican and Latin American history through a series of musical images and no dialogue. His subsequent films, *Latino Bar* (1991) and *Dollar Mambo* (1993) also had no dialogue, but were propagandistic and inferior.

23. Hayden Herrera, *Frida: A Biography of Frida Kahlo* (New York: Harper & Row, 1983).

24. Elliott Stein, "Don Hermosillo and the Sun," *Film Comment*, June 1986, p. 54.

25. Greg Goldin and Marc Cooper, "Mexico's Movies: Now Playing at a Theater Near You," *Southwest Airlines Spirit*, July 1986, p. 54.

26. Interview, Mario Aguiñada, Cineteca Nacional, Mexico City, 30 January 1989.

27. Interview, Marco Bracamonte, marketing manager, VideoVisa, Inc., Los Angeles, CA, 25 October 1988. The United States videocassette market for Spanish-language films, 80 percent Mexican but also including some Argentine, Venezuelan, and Spanish features, has expanded dramatically in the last few years. VideoVisa is among the largest firms with about 300 titles (as of October 1988 and with four or five new titles every month). Others are: Million Dollar Video, Mexcinema, Filmex, and Mexvideo. Some smaller companies are American General Film, Isela Vega Video, Escomex, Pantera Video, and Madera Video. California represents 50 percent of the American market for Mexican films, both for theatrical showings and videocassette rentals with Texas the second largest followed by

Arizona, New Mexico, and Colorado. New York and south Florida are ""difficult"" because of their over-whelmingly non–Mexican Hispanic populations which are generally not receptive to most Mexican film genres. However, musicals featuring *música tropical* do well in Miami. The videos do not have English subtitles. The majority are commercial, low-budget films although VideoVisa has a "Linea Connoisseur" featuring art films; other companies have similar lines. The immigration law of 1986 apparently has also been a factor in the expansion of the Mexican video market in the U.S. Southwest, because Spanish-language movie theaters have been targets for sweeps by INS agents. The resulting drop in attendance has forced many of these theaters to close because their former patrons (the undocumented ones) have resorted to the much safer renting of movies for home viewing.

In Mexico, 30 percent of the country's approximately 16 million households have VCRs which works out to about 4,850,000 sets, the majority in Beta format although VHS has been gaining ground since 1980. Bracamonte explained the reason for the predominance of Beta in Mexico: "The smaller videocassettes were easier to smuggle — a truck could be loaded with one hundred Beta cassettes instead of fifty VHS. But with the opening up of the Mexican economy this will change." Video rentals have proliferated throughout Mexico (and into Central and South America), outlets include specialized shops and video rental sections in department stores, supermarkets, and other businesses. As elsewhere, renting a video is more economical than going to a theater — luxury theaters in Mexico charge 15,000 pesos ($6.60) admission for foreign films and important premieres. By contrast, admission at the Cineteca theaters is 1600 pesos (80 cents), about the same as commercial theaters that show Mexican films. See also Jorge Isaac, "El video ¿complemento o rivalidad con el cine?," *Cámara*, año VII, no. 54 (June-July 1988), pp. 45–48.

28. Larry Tohter, "Film Version of Everyman Wins Mexico," *New York Times*, 6 November 1988, p. 6.

29. Interview, Mario Bracamonte, Los Angeles, 25 October 1988.

30. Ayala Blanco, *La condición del cine mexicano*, pp. 89–94.

31. Interview, Alfredo Crevenna, Mexico City, 7 February 1989. In Japan, it is common to employ Western Caucasian (and occasionally non–Caucasians such as Sammy Davis, Jr.) to promote products in television and print commercials, perhaps a more curious phenomenon; Mexico at least was the colony of a European power which imparted to it a legacy of cultural values that emphasize the European ideal — and of course, unlike the Japanese, many Mexicans are entirely or partly of European descent. Some explanations for the use of foreign models in Japanese advertising were advanced by George Fields in *From Bonsai to Levi's, When West Meets East: An Insider's Surprising Account of How the Japanese Live* (New York and Scarborough, Ontario: Mentor Books, New American Library), 1985. "Loveable and 'tame' foreigners who are kept by Japanese brands help greatly to alleviate the national inferiority complex and create gratitude toward

the brands that were able to hire them." (p. 118) "The use of [Western] stars coincides with the ascension of Japan as an economic colossus." (p. 118) "All these companies were *nonverbally* communicating the fact that they were of international status." (p. 119) And perhaps as a corollary to Mexico: "Foreign stars flood the Japanese screen, but now only newly arrived foreigners are surprised and ask why," (p. 120).

32. Many foreign filmmakers complain about the "dumping" of American films in their countries, which has an inhibiting effect on local production; in effect, expensive Hollywood productions make their profit in the United States and are then made available in Latin America and Europe for extremely low quantities — $25,000 to $30,000 for films that cost up to forty million to produce. Interview, Juan López Moctezuma, Azteca Films, Los Angeles, 26 October 1988; see also Rose Doyle, "U.S. Films Capture European Market," *Europe*, May/June 1984, pp. 44–45; Michael Chanan, *Twenty-Five Years of the New Latin American Cinema*, (London: Channel 4; BFI Books, 1983), p. 3.

33. Interview, Cristián González, Cineteca Nacional, 10 February 1989.

34. Interview, Luciana Cabarga, Mexico City, 8 February 1989. Ms. Cabarga is director of the Morelos State Commission of Film, Theater, and Television, whose purpose is to attract filmmakers to Morelos. (See Appendix 2 for address).

35. Interview, Los Angeles, 26 October 1988. López Moctezuma had extensive experience in making films for non–Mexican audiences. He is best-known for his horror films like *La mansión de la locura* (1971), *Alucarda, Daughter of Darkness* (1975), and *To Kill a Stranger* (1983) with Dean Stockwell, Donald Pleasance, and Aldo Ray. López Moctezuma, together with Alejandro Jodorowsky, Rafael Corkidi, and José Antonio Alcaraz formed the Mexican surrealist film movement of the 1970s. See Phil Hardy, *Encyclopedia of Horror Movies* (New York: Harper & Row, 1987).

36. "Malo, el cine comercial mexicano: Sergio Olhovich," *Uno Más Uno*, 9 April 1988, p. 28; "Exhibirán en los Festivales de Rio de Janeiro y La Habana, la Película Mexicana-Soviética Esperanza," *Excélsior*, 4 September 1988, p. 4-B.

37. José Felipe Coria, "La furia de lo irracional," *Uno Más Uno*, 20 July 1988, p. 28.

38. Goldin and Cooper, "Mexico's Movies...," p. 95.

39. Julio J. Etienne, "El Imperio de la Fortuna," *Hispanoamericano*, 19 May 1987, p. 65; see also Frédéric Sabourad, "Féstivals: 9º Féstival des trois continents à Nantes: La carte de l'identité," *Cahiers du Cinéma*, no. 404 (February 1988): *Le Journaldes*, no. 80, p. VIII and Nelson Carro, "El imperio de la fortuna," *Dicine*, no. 20 (July-August 1987), p. 24.

40. Ayala Blanco, *La condición del cine mexicano*, pp. 375–87; Viñas, *Historia del cine mexicano*, pp. 277–78. For a psycho-politico-social interpretation of *Cadena perpétua*, see Charles Ramírez Berg, "Cracks in the *Macho* Monolith: *Machismo*, Man, and Mexico in Recent Mexican Cinema," *New Orleans Review* 16, no. 1 (Spring 1989): 67–74.

41. Verónica Espinosa, "En México no existe la car-

rera cinematográfica," *Uno Más Uno*, 23 June 1988, p. 23.

42. Interview, Felipe Cazals, Churubusco studios, Mexico City, 9 February 1989.

43. "Un Brillante Cierre de la Muestra," *Hispanoamericano*, 17 December 1985, p. 46.

44. Mauricio Peña, *El Heraldo*, 20 October 1988, quoted in *Cineteca Nacional*, año 6, no. 62, February 1989, p. 19.

45. Jorge Carrasco, "Adiós a Uno de los Grandes del Cine," *Hispanoamericano*, 19 August 1986, p. 66; see also Héctor Rivera, "El Indio, tan intenso en la furia como en la ternura," *Proceso*, 11 August 1986, pp. 42–49: the article also contains pieces by Armando Ponce, "En los últimos años el 'Indio' se dejó arrastrar por la leyenda en la soledad de su casona descuidada," pp. 44–47 and Carlos Monsiváis, "Notas sobre un personaje y una obra," pp. 48–49; the article summarizes his daughter's memoirs of growing up with him, Adela Fernández, *El Indio Fernández, vida y mito* (Mexico City: Panorama Editorial, 1986; a major critical study published just before Fernández's death is Paco Ignacio Taibo I, *El Indio Fernández: El cine por mis pistolas*, Serie Genio y Figura" (Mexico City: Joaquín Mortiz/Planeta, 1986). See also Emilio García Riera, "Emilio Fernández," *Dicine*, no. 22 (November-December 1987), pp. 2–3 and Alejandro Rozado, "Lo trágico en el cine de Emilio Fernández," *Ibid.*, pp. 4–6; part two appears in *Ibid.*, no. 23 (January-February 1988), pp. 10–12. A belated tribute in the United States was given Fernández at the Telluride Festival with a screening of *The Pearl* and clips from other of his films. See M.S. Mason, "Old Mining Town Screens Some Shining Film Nuggets, *The Christian Science Monitor*, 15 October 1985, p. 33.

46. It is beyond the scope of this study to attempt analyses, much less predictions, of the Mexican political situation. Following the election of Carlos Salinas de Gortari on July 1, 1988, the opposition charged fraud and challenged the results in the courts and by means of demonstrations. For instance, opposition delegates jeered Miguel de la Madrid's last State of the Union speech and walked out waving ballots — unheard-of behavior in the Mexican Congress; similar demonstrations broke out at Salinas's inauguration. Accusations of electoral fraud have been common in Mexico; the difference this time was that some in the PRI, starting with Salinas himself, tacitly acknowledged the truth of the accusations. At this writing, Salinas seems to have asserted himself by moving against corrupt officials of the oil workers union and stock manipulators, inspiring an incipient acceptance among the largely skeptical Mexican public which initially saw him as a weak technocrat. Following are some comprehensive early accounts, but for generally reliable reporting on the developing political and economic situation in Mexico, the *Wall Street Journal*, the *New York Times*, and *The Economist* are among the best sources. Matt Moffett, "New Mexican President Is in Political Jeopardy Before Taking Office," *Wall Street Journal*, 31 August 1988, pp. 1, 17; Larry Rohter, "Mexico City Journal: Now, the Urban Sprawl Wonder Diet," *New York Times*, 24 December 1988, p. 4; idem,

"Can He Save Mexico?" *New York Times Magazine*, 20 November 1988, pp. 34–37, 84, 92–93; idem, "Mexicans Hoping for 'Salinastroika'," *New York Times*, 5 January 1989, p. A10; Matt Moffett, "Mexico City's Subsidies Present Stiff Challenges to President Salinas," *Wall Street Journal*, 10 January 1989, pp. A1, A14; Brian O'Reilly, "Doing Business on Mexico's Volcano," *Fortune*, 29 August 1986, pp. 72–74.

47. Interview, Juan López Moctezuma, Los Angeles, 26 October 1988.

48. It is a common sight to see Tarahumara families on the streets of Chihuahua, and others come into contact with the modern world in communities like Divisadero and Creel. Eduardo Benítez, professor of electrical engineering at the Instituto Tecnológico de Chihuahua, told this writer in 1984 that there was just one Tarahumara enrolled in the school in spite of outreach programs to encourage young Indians to assimilate into the mainstream culture.

49. Interviews, Cineteca Nacional, Mexico City, 7 and 10 February 1989. See also, Perla Ciuk, *Diccionario de directores del cine mexicano* (Mexico City: CONACULTA/Cineteca Nacional, 2000), pp. 301–2

50. Interview, Mexico City, 8 February 1989. See also Antonio Berruti, "Pelayo habla de Días Difíciles," *Dicine*, no. 25 (May-June 1988), pp. 12–13.

51. Interview, Mexico City, 10 February 1989.

52. Interview, Mexico City, 2 February 1989.

53. P. 625.

54. "Cine mexicano: utopía y realidad," *Plural*, no. 127 (April 1982): 67. A more recent assessment concludes: "In effect, there has always been talk of a crisis of our cinema, but this referred to content, subject matter, and other artistic matters, but almost never to economic aspects, which in large part influence the others: due to the way in which cinematic policies and the industry are developing, the Mexican cinema has been relegated to being, first, a commercial product, leaving aside its artistic and social aspects, which explains why it fails to reflect Mexican reality." Colectivo Alejandro Galindo, "El cine mexicano y sus crisis," *Dicine*, no. 19 (May-June 1987), pp. 12–13. See also *Ibid.*, part two in no. 20 (July-August 1987), pp. 12–15 and part 3 in no. 21 (September-October 1987), pp. 16–18.

55. J.L. Espinosa, "Al finalizar este sexenio terminan para el cine mexicano 12 años de 'inversión térmica,'" *Uno Más Uno*, 9 August 1988, p. 24.

56. Doyle, "U.S. Films Capture European Market," pp. 44–45.

57. Interview, Mexico City, 10 February 1989.

58. Verónica Espinosa, "Mucho deberán trabajar los nuevos cineastas para mostrar al mundo otra imágen de nuestro cine," *Uno Más Uno*, 28 April 1988, p. 24. For a broad assessment of the difficulties and challenges facing Latin American filmmakers in the face of decreasing audiences, new technologies, increasing costs, and other factors see Paul Leduc, "Nuevo cine latinoamericano," *Dicine*, no. 24 (March-April 1988), pp. 2–5. Leduc also mentions the proposal of Columbia Pictures' David Picker to have the "major studios," in view of the success of *La Bamba*, make films in Spanish, or at least in dual versions, to reach the "enormous

Spanish-speaking public in the United States and throughout the world." Leduc's reaction: "Thus while our audacious producers start to make *churritos* in English, the majors study the possibility of making films in Spanish. *No comments* [*sic*]" (pp. 3–4).

Chapter 7

1. In 2002, his *El espinazo del diablo/The Devil's Backbone*, filmed in Spain and produced by Pedro Almodóvar, received much critical praise and had a successful run in the United States and Europe.

2. Claudia Puig, "Mexico still beckons to these expat directors," *USA Today*, 11 April 2002, p. 4D.

3. See Carl J. Mora, "Poor Mexican Cinema, So Far From *Cahiers du Cinema* and so Close to Latino, U.S.A.: A Cantankerous Essay," *Film-Historia Online*, vol. XIII, no. 3 (2003). The main topic of this piece is the disconcerting tendency of the U.S. media to lump films from Mexico and Latin America (and sometimes even Spain) under the "Latino" label, which at the very least only creates confusion.

4. By August 2003, the total box office receipts was a respectable $25,776,062. "Top Films by Boxoffice," *The Hollywood Reporter*, August 2003, p. F-47.

5. A.O. Scott., "A Celebrated Artist's Biography, on the Verge of Being a Musical," *The New York Times*, 30 October 2002, Internet edition.

6. For instance, characters speak accented English and occasionally punctuate their dialogue with Spanish words for exotic effect. In one scene, Frida (Salma Hayek) calls Diego Rivera (Alfred Molina) "*panzón*" (fatso) and Tina Modotti (Ashley Judd) shouts "*basta*" (enough!) in the party scene. While Paul Leduc's 1985 *Frida: naturaleza viva* authentically employed Spanish, French, and Russian dialogue, Hayek and Taymor have Frida, Rivera, and Trotsky communicating in appropriately (at times inappropriately) accented English. Incidentally, Hayek's *Frida* seems to pay homage to Leduc's film by casting Margarita Sanz, who played a character inspired by Tina Modotti in Leduc's film, as Trotsky's wife.

7. Katy Jurado was nominated for an Oscar as best supporting actress for her role opposite Spencer Tracy in the 1954 western *Broken Lance*. See "Katy Jurado, Mexican Star Who Appeared in 'High Noon.' Dies at 78," *The New York Times*, 6 July 2002, Internet edition. A Mexican newspaper article claimed she received two Oscar nominations but did not indicate for what films. Jorge Caballero, "Katy Jurado, sin homenaje porque falleció en viernes, justifica el enviado de la ANDA," *La Jornada*, 8 July 2002, Internet edition.

8. His U.S. directorial debut, *21 Grams*, was included in the New York Film Festival (October 2003) and released nationwide in November to mostly positive reviews. It starred Sean Penn, Benicio del Toro, and Naomi Watts.

9. "Subcommander Marcos," in David W. Dent, *Encyclopedia of Mexico* (Latham, Maryland, and London: The Scarecrow Press, 2002), pp. 268–270.

10. "After 9/11, Fox Still Waits for U.S. Moves on Mexico," *The New York Times*, 13 September 2002, Internet edition, and "Fox Quesada, Vicente," in *Encyclopedia of Mexico*, pp. 128–132.

11. "In the U.S., it has earned a whopping Dollars 13m (unheard of for an unrated, subtitled movie). Last week its box office takings of pounds 1.3m confirmed it as the UK's most successful Spanish-language film ever." Xan Brooks, "First Steps in Latin," *The Guardian*, 19 July 2002, Internet edition.

12. "Despite the fact that Cantinflas died a millionaire several times over, and was one of the biggest stars ever in Spanish language films, he never forgot where he came from. Much of his money was given over to charitable work, including high-quality, low-income housing for Mexico City's poor. When he died, he was hailed as a national hero, and a protracted period of official mourning followed.

There are two stories about how Mario Moreno Reyes adopted his more familiar professional name. One story goes that he did not want to shame his family, who thought of show business as a less than respectable profession, and so changed his name. The other is that, at one of his first nightclub engagements, a heckler taunted him with, "En la cantina, tu inflas!" ("In the bar room, you talk big!"). For some reason, this amused him, and he shortened the taunt into the professional name of Cantinflas." From biography, Imdb. com

13. David Wilt, "Cantinflas: Unknown Idol," *The Big Reel,* March 1994, p. 104.

14. Raquel Peguero, "Murió Alejandro Galindo, eminente realizador y artífice del cine urbano nacional," *La Jornada*, 2 February 1999, Internet edition.

15. See "María Félix muere en su 88° cumpleaños," *El País* (Madrid), 9 April 2002, Internet edition; Sam Dillon, "María Félix, Feisty Heroine in Mexican Cinema, Dies at 87," *The New York Times*, 10 April 2002, Internet edition; "María Félix Dies," The *Mexican Film Bulletin*, vol. 8, no. 5 (June 2002): 1–2.

16. See "Gabriel Figueroa, 90, giant of Mexican cinema, dies," *CNN.com*, 29 April 1997; Joaquim Ibarz, "Muere Gabriel Figueroa, director de fotografía mexicano," *La Vanguardia* (Barcelona), 29 April 1997, Internet edition.

17. Raquel Peguero, "Falleció el primer *charro cantor* del cine mexicano, Tito Guízar, " *La Jornada*, 26 December 1999, Internet edition.

18. See "Actress Katy Jurado dies at 78," *CNN.com*, 6 July 2002, Internet edition; "Katy Jurado 1925–2002," *The Mexican Film Bulletin*, vol. 8, no. 6 (August 2002): 1–2.

19. Amado Felix, "Legendary tango singer Libertad Lamarque dies at 92," *Salon.com*, 13 December 2000. See also, Arturo Cruz Bárcenas, "Murió ayer Libertad Lamarque, icono de madre abnegada en AL," *La Jornada*, 13 December 2000, Internet edition; Carlos Ares, "Muere en México a los 94 años la actriz y cantante Libertad Lamarque," *El País*, 13 December 2000, Internet edtion.

20. See chapter 1. Lupita Tovar (b. 1911) and Paul Kohner (1902–1988). Kohner was born in what is now the Czech Republic and produced a film in Germany

before emigrating to the U.S. in 1930. He produced Spanish- and English-language movies in Hollywood and later became a famous actors' agent. He and Lupita had two children: Susan Kohner and Pancho Kohner. Susan Kohner (b. 1936) was an actress in the 1950s and 1960s and was nominated for an Academy Award as best supporting actress for her role in *Imitation of Life* (1959), after which she retired from movies to raise a family. Pancho Kohner became a producer, best known for the "Death Wish" movies with Charles Bronson. Susan's two sons, Paul and Chris Weitz ,produced the highly popular albeit lowbrow comedies *American Pie* (1999), *American Pie 2* (2001), and *American Wedding* (2003). They directed the critically acclaimed *About a Boy* (2002) with Hugh Grant.

21. There are a few other well-known Golden Age era stars in Mexico such as Ninón Sevilla and Lilia Prado, but their numbers are dwindling fast.

22. Beginning in April 2004, a film series titled "Cine México" was organized by the Mexican Embassy and the National Gallery. It consisted of a 26-film retrospective of Mexican movies from the silent era to the 1990s. In July, it was presented at Film Forum in New York where the *Times* film critic A.O.Scott viewed them and commented: "While the series ... will certainly provide a fine education in the history of Mexican movies, to recommend it on pedagogical grounds would be unfair to the movies themselves, which include rambunctious comedies, politically tinged quasi-westerns, costume epics, abstract art films and plenty of sighing, swooning, black-and-white tear jerkers. "A Different Mexican Revolution," *The New York Times*, 27 June 2004, Internet edition.

23. Rafael Medina de la Serna, "Rojo Amanecer," *Dicine*, no. 37 (November 1990): 20–21.

24. Alex Cox, "Roads to the South: In Praise of Mexican Cinema." *Film Comment*, vol. 31, issue 6 (November/December 1995, p. 33. Cox is best known for directing *Repo Man* (1984) and *Sid and Nancy* (1986). He directed and appeared in *El patrullero* (1992) in Mexico with Roberto Sosa. He has also acted in Ripstein's *La reina de la noche* (1994) and *La ley de Herodes* (2000).

25. David R. Maciel, "Cinema and the State in Contemporary Mexico, 1970–1999," in Joanne Herschfield and David R. Maciel, eds., *Mexico's Cinema: A Century of Film and Filmmakers* (Wilmington, Delaware: Scholarly Resources, 1999) p. 218. The article does praise the film's other qualities.

26. Medina de la Serna, "Rojo amanecer," p. 21.

27. The movie critic and sociopolitical commentator Michael Medved is the most prominent American conservative leading the attack on Hollywood. Setting the tone for his book in his usual overstated style, he writes, "America's long-running romance with Hollywood is over. As a nation, we no longer believe that popular culture enriches our lives. Few of us view the show business capital as a magical source of uplifting entertainment, romantic inspiration, or even harmless fun. Instead, tens of millions of Americans now see the entertainment industry as an all-powerful enemy. An alien force that assaults our most cherished values and corrupts our children. The dream factory has become the poison factory." Michael Medved, *Hollywood Vs.*

America: Popular Culture and the War on Traditional Values (New York: HarperCollins, 1992), p. 4.

28. Interview with Alejandro Pelayo, Los Angeles, 15 December 2003. At the time, he was cultural attaché at the Consulate General of Mexico. He was director of the Cineteca Nacional from 1997 to 1999 and director of IMCINE from 2000 to 2001.

29. In 1993, Ripstein, along with "sixty eminent 'creative' intellectuals, including Octavio Paz, Carlos Monsiváis, Carlos Fuentes, Gabriel García Márquez, Elena Poniatowska" received a lifelong stipend. The total cost for all recipients was $8 million; the amounts of individual stipends were not specified. Paulo Antonio Paranaguá, ed. *Mexican Cinema*, translated by Ana M. López (London: British Film Institute; Mexico City: IMCINE, 1995), p. 60. See also, Leonardo García Tsao, "Ripstein," in *ibid.*, pp. 212–216. A briefer version of Paranaguá's book was originally published in French to accompany a retrospective of Mexican cinema at the Centre Pompidou in Paris from October 1992 to February 1993.

30. Jorge Ayala Blanco, *La fugacidad del cine mexicano* (Mexico City: Editorial Océano, 2001). Ayala Blanco is a severe critic of Ripstein; the book is full of scathing comments about his films. Obviously Ayala Blanco and Ripstein are not on friendly terms. In fact, Ripstein actually sued Ayala Blanco over negative comments he made of *Mentiras piadosas* (1987) and a book by Emilio García Riera, *Arturo Ripstein habla de su cine con Emilio García* (Guadalajara: Centro de Investigación y Enseñanza Cinematográficas, Universidad de Guadalajara, 1988). As might be expected, both Ripstein and García Riera were highly annoyed. Ayala Blanco recounts this incident in Gabriela Bautista, "Entrevista con Jorge Ayala Blanco," *Plata: Revista de Cine*, 1992, pp. 15–18.

31. J. Hoberman in *The Village Voice*, quoted in Sergio de la Mora, "A Career in Perspective: An Interview with Arturo Ripstein," *Film Quarterly*, vol. 52, issue 1 (Summer 1999): 4.

32. De la Mora, "A Career in Perspective," p. 6.

33. *Ibid.*, p. 4.

34. Arturo Ripstein made this comment during a visit to the University of New Mexico on May 7, 2003. He was there with his wife/screenwriter, Paz Alicia Garcíadiego, to present their film *Profundo carmesí*.

35. Mark A. Uhling, "New Horizons for Mexican Films, *The New York Times*, 22 January 1991, p. B3.

36. De la Mora, "A Career in Perspective," p. 4.

37. From the website for the 43rd International Thessaloniki Film Festival, Nov. 8–17, 2002.

38. Originally written about Diane Lane in *Under the Tuscan Sun* (2003). Roger Ebert, "'Sun' a villa-fied chick flick," *Albuquerque Journal Venue*, 26 September 2003, p. 4.

39. Nelson Carro, "la tarea prohibida," *Tiempo Libre*, December 10–16, 1992, p. 8.

40. His journal, *La relación o naufragios de Alvar Núñez Cabeza de Vaca*, was first published in Spain in 1542. Another edition was published in 1555 which included his adventures in the Río de la Plata province (Argentina) where he served as captain general and adelantado from 1540 to 1543. Dorantes and Castillo

jointly wrote a report about the journey to the Audiencia of Española (Santo Domingo) which was included in subsequent editions. The first English edition was in 1851; a number of others followed including one by Fanny Bandelier in 1905. There were translations into Italian (1565) and French (1837).

41. Leonardo García Tsao, "La conquista según Nicolás Echevarría," *Dicine*, No. 38 (March 1991): 8.

42. *Ibid.*

43. *Ibid.*, pp. 8–9. The film was shown on PBS and a subtitled version was distributed on video. It can be found in the international section of most video stores in the United States. A critical part from the PBS version was cut from the video, with Echevarría's consent — the scene in the cave where Cabeza de Vaca hallucinates and sees his paternal grandfather Pedro de Vera, who conquered the Canary Islands in 1408. Echevarría was unhappy about making the cut, but it was either that or no video release. Echevarría told me this at the Cineteca Nacional in Mexico City on March 17, 2004. In 2002, he made a romantic comedy titled *Vivir mata* ("Living Kills") with an all-star cast including Daniel Giménez Cacho, Emilio Echevarría, Luis Felipe Tovar, and Diana Bracho. He had just completed a television movie on Maximilian, emperor of Mexico during the French intervention of 1863–67.

44. *Ibid.*, p. 8.

45. The Huichol and Cora Indians are neighboring Middle American peoples living in the mountainous areas of the states of Jalisco and Nayarit in western Mexico.

46. García Tsao, "La conquista…," p. 11.

47. Rita Kempley, "Cabeza de Vaca," *The Washington Post.com*, 20 November 1992.

48. Rafael Aviña, "Cabeza de Vaca," *Dicine*, No. 38 (March 1991): 12.

49. "Cabeza de Vaca," *Variety*, 4 March 1991, p. 54. See also, Thomas E. Billings, "Cabeza de Vaca (1991)," *Reviews*, 3 June 1998, Internet editon.

50. A. Fernández Santos, "La condición trágica del descubrimiento y conquista de América," *El País* (Madrid), 25 February 1991, p. 20.

51. Perla Ciuk, *Diccionario de directores del cine mexicano* (Mexico City: CONACULTA/Cineteca Nacional, 2000), p. 161.

52. Nelson Carro, "sólo con tu pareja," *Tiempo Libre*, 31 December 1993, p. 12.

53. *Ibid.*

54. *Ibid.*

55. *Ibid.*

56. Ciuk, *Diccionario*, p. 162.

57. *Ibid.*

58. João Ernesto Salina, "Sólo con tu pareja," *Macrópolis*, 24 December 1992, p. 51.

59. Elsa Fernández-Santos, "Guillermo del Toro afirma que busca "la humanidad del terror," *El País* (Madrid), 13 October 2000, Internet edition.

60. Richard Harrington, "Cronos," *The Washington Post*, 6 July 2000, Internet edtion. Originally published on 22 May 1994.

61. David Wilt, "Los Vampiros: A look at bloodsuckers south-of-the-border, from *El Vampiro* to *Cronos, Imagi-Movies*, Vol. 2, No. 2 (Winter 1994): 50.

See also idem, "El Baron del Terror: The Horror Films of Abel Salazar," *Filmfax* (January/February 1996), no. 56, pp. 32–36, and "Horror Films from South of the Border: An Overview of Neglected Mexican Fantasy Cinema," *Cinefantastique* 27/10 (June 1995), pp. 40–47. Here he discusses little-known Mexican horror films made in the 1930s and 1940s. See also Steve Biodrowski, "Cronos: Director Guillermo del Toro on his fusion of vampirism and alchemy," *Imagi-Movies*, p. 52.

62. Ciuk, *Diccionario*, p. 197.

63. Interview with Alejandro Pelayo on the latter's television series, *Los que hicieron nuestro cine*, quoted in Ciuk, *Diccionario*, p. 197–98.

64. Harrington, "Cronos."

65. *Ibid.*

66. Elissa J. Rashkin, *Women Filmmakers in Mexico: The Country of Which We Dream* (Austin: University of Texas Press, 2001), p. 192.

67. Susana López Aranda, "Dana Rotberg: Entre la realidad y la imaginación," *Dicine*, no. 46 (July 1992): 8.

68. Rashkin, *Women Filmmakers*, p. 199.

69. *Ibid.*

70. *Ibid.*

71. Quoted in ibid, p. 195.

72. Tomás Pérez Turrent, "Angel de fuego y otros asuntos," *Dicine*, no. 46 (July 1992): 7.

73. Not all critics at the Havana festival were united in their praise; Rolando Pérez Betancourt in *Gramma* said the film, "is full of melodramatic phantoms…. The always fascinating world of the circus is the setting for … events that are not unattractive, but lose their power because of the artistic imbalance in which they are shown, including the occasional influence of European masters." "xiv festival internacional del nuevo cine mexicano: El cine mexicano y la crítica," *Tiempo Libre*, 24–30 December, 1992, p. 8.

74. Quoted in Tomás Pérez Turrent, "Angel de fuego y otros asuntos," p. 6.

75. Patricia Hart, "Visual Strategies in Gabriel Retes' Film, *El Bulto*," *Cine-Lit II: Essays on Hispanic Film and Fiction*. (Portland and Corvallis: Cine-Lit Project, 1994), np.

76. Ciuk, *Diccionario*, p. 448.

77. Rashkin, *Women Filmmakers*, p. 167.

78. This scene, which seems improvised, was written into the script. Novaro was dissatisfied with the "Russians" provided by casting, so she went to the Russian Embassy and asked if any of their staff would be interested in appearing in her film. She was told to "take her pick" and she chose Mikhail Kaminin, the cultural attaché. Telecon with María Novaro, 18 March 2004, Mexico City.

79. *Mexico City in Contemporary Mexican Cinema* (Austin: University of Texas Press, 2002), p. 101.

80. Hal Hinson, "Danzon," *Washington Post*. 6 November 1992, Internet edition, p. 2.

81. Tomás Pérez Turrent, "Angel de fuego y otros asuntos," p. 6.

82. Víctor Bustos, "María Novaro: de Lola a Danzón," *Dicine*, no. 40 (July 1991): 11.

83. A thorough review of this question as well as

an analysis of the film can be found in Rashkin, *Women Filmmakers*, pp. 167–99. Another extensive analysis is in David William Foster, *Mexico City in Contemporary Mexican Cinema*, pp. 100–11.

84. Patricia Vega, "Entrevista con María Novaro," *Domingo 25*, August 1991, p. 29. See also Ignacio Escarcega, "Danzón," *Dicine*, no. 41 (September 1991): 21.

85. Hugo Lara, "Retorno a Aztlán," *Dicine*, no. 40 (July 1991): 20.

86. David Wilt informed me that "half of 'Las rosas del milagro' (1959) is set prior to the Conquest (the other half is the Juan Diego-Tepeyac story). Of course, if we want to get into half-movies, 'Chilam Balam' (1955) also has pre–Conquest scenes.... And since the film was never shown, I guess we can't count 'Nezahualcoyotl (El rey poeta)' (1935)." E-mail, 23 April 2004. A Hollywood film, *Kings of the Sun* (1963), had a group of Mayas fleeing from their enemies across the gulf to Florida. Their leader (George Chakiris) encounters a local chief (Yul Brynner); at first adversaries, they join forces to repel the hostile Mayas' seaborne invasion. The actors all spoke Hollywood epic-movie English, however.

87. "Datos personales," e-mail, 19 April 2002.

88. Víctor Bustos and Nelson Carro, "Retorno a Aztlán: El viaje de Juan Mora," *Dicine*, no. 41 (September 1991): 14.

89. *Ibid.*

90. "Datos personales."

91. "A manuscript book, especially of scripture, early literature, or ancient mythological or historical annals. These books contained pictographs and ideograms rather than written script. They dealt with the ritual calendar, divination, ceremonies, and speculations on the gods and the universe. Among these codices are the Vienna Codex, the Codex Colombino, and the Codex Fejérváry-Mayer, all believed to have been produced before the Spanish conquest of the region." *Britannica 2002 Deluxe Edition*.

92. "Datos personales"

93. Bustos and Carro, "Retorno a Aztlán," p. 15.

94. "Datos personales."

95. *Ibid.*

96. *Ibid.* See also, Ciuk, *Diccionario*, pp. 423–24.

97. Arau made this statement to me during a visit to Los Angeles, sometime in the mid–1970s. He had invited me to a screening of *Calzonzín inspector* at the Azteca Films office.

98. For instance, one scene where Arau's character and his Chicano rival are arrested, stripped naked, and deloused by the police is obviously copied — in its detailed display of frontal nudity — from the Swedish film *I Am Curious (Yellow)* (1967). And the final courtroom scene echoes the classic (and much funnier) trial in Cantinflas's *Ahí está el detalle* (1943), but this time with statements about California having been Mexican territory. Which was obvious pandering to some Chicano notions.

99. Interview, 16 March 2004.

100. Ciuk, *Diccionario*, pp. 50–51.

101. Víctor Bustos, "Alfonso Arau: De lo racional a lo sentimental," *Dicine*, no. 47 (1992): 20.

102. *Ibid.*

103. Michael Phillips, "Actors add perfect ingredients to make story's magical, mystical tone work," *Night&Day* supplement, *San Diego Union-Tribune*, 18–24 March 1993, p. 14. See also, idem, "'Chocolate' keeps it all in the family — writer, director and star," *ibid.*

104. Interview, 16 March 2004.

105. Mora, "Poor Mexican Cinema," p. 3.

106. John Hecht, "Filmmaker has revolutionary idea," *The Hollywood Reporter*, 14–20 October 2003, p. 10. Initial reviews were not positive. *La Jornada* said: "Dull like a history book from the Education Secretariat, solemn like a Gogol novel, opportunistic like a video by Ahumada, predictable like a Tom and Jerry adventure, and above all nauseous, the hero's dream will inevitably put viewers to sleep." Jaime Aviles, "La película de Alfonso Arau se estrena hoy en México, con 430 copias." *La Jornada*, 30 April 2004, Internet edition. John Hecht, the Mexico City correspondent for *The Hollywood Reporter*, quoted local media as saying *Zapata* "was poor in acting, cliche-ridden and too Hollywood." E-mail, 4 May 2004. See also Mariana Negrete, "¡Que Viva Zapata! y Zapata cobró vida," *Premiere* (Mexico), April 2004, pp. 63–72.

107. "Miroslava: la muerte enamorada," *Revista de revistas*, (1992), p. 43.

108. For instance, when her parents fled Czechoslovakia they had to leave Miroslava's grandmother behind, which haunted her all her life. Then she learned that Dr. Sternova was not her real father. She had been born from a prior relationship of her mother's. Her mother later met and married Dr. Sternova, and accepted Miroslava as his own daughter. Also, Dr. Sternova was Jewish while Miroslava and her mother were not. David William Foster mistakenly assumes that Miroslava was Jewish (*Mexico City in Contemporary Mexican Cinema*, p. 15). She fell in love with and was going to marry an American pilot she met while studying in the United States, but he was killed in the war. Then she married a Mexican who turned out to be homosexual. In addition, there were rumors of her lesbianism. So by the time she was betrayed by Dominguín, Miroslava was in a precarious emotional state. Juan Jiménez Patiño, "El mito Miroslava: Revisión a su suicidio," *Revista de revistas* (no month, 1992), p. 44. See also, M.I.P., "Miroslava, trágica mujer del siglo XX, *ibid.*, pp. 40–41.

109. "¿Quién es Arielle Dombasle?" *ibid.*, p. 43.

110. Interview, Los Angeles, 15 December 2003.

111. *Ibid.*

112. Foster, *Mexico City in Contemporary Mexican Cinema*, p. 15.

113. Ciuk, *Diccionario*, pp. 561–62.

114. For additional data, see Edward Bernard Glick, "Mexico's Jews — A Model for Survival," *Ethnic News*, vol. 201, no. 20 (15 May 1997), p. 6.

115. Rashkin, *Women Filmmakers in Mexico*, p. 151.

116. Elissa Rashkin provides an excellent detailed analysis in *ibid.*, pp. 141–66. A useful discussion can be found in Foster, *Mexico City in Contemporary Mexican Cinema*, pp. 13–25. However, on p. 18, in discussing the lunch scene with Saavedra, his family, and the hostile journalist, he says it is Oshinika who attends in-

stead of Rifke, and on p. 19 he writes that "Oshinica [*sic*] and her family arrive in Mexico City ... during the Second World War, as refugees from the expanding Holocaust." As the movie indicates, they arrived in 1927 from Turkey and they were Oshinika's grandparents (she of course had not been born yet).

117. Leonardo García Tsao, "Jorge Fons: La posibilidad de conmover," *Dicine*, no. 62 (May-June 1995): 19.

118. *Ibid.*, 19–20.

119. In the novel, these characters go to work at a British army base outside Cairo.

120. Javier González Rubio, "El Callejón de los Milagros," *ibid.*, p. 22.

121. *El Callejón de los Milagros* is available in the United States on VHS and DVD with subtitles.

122. Roger Ebert, "Deep Crimson," *Chicago Sun-Times*, 1 January 1998, Internet edition.

123. Kenneth Turan, "Deep Crimson," *Los Angeles Times*, 11 November 1997, Internet edition.

124. Related to me by Arturo Ripstein on May 7, 2003, in Albuquerque, N.M.

125. Related to me by Paz Alicia Garcíadiego on May 7, 2003, in Albuquerque, N.M.

126. Anita Gates, "'Santitos': Why a Young Widow Went Nobly Into Brothels," *The New York Times,* 28 January 2000, Internet edition.

127. As he told me when he was invited to screen and discuss *Santitos* at the University of New Mexico on July 10, 2000.

128. Leonardo García Tsao, "After the breakthrough of Amores Perros, what's next for Mexican Cinema?" *Film Comment*, July/August 2001, p. 11.

129. Interview with Susana López Aranda, IMCINE, Mexico City, 17 March 2004. A film critic and scholar, she is also the daughter of the eminent actor Ignacio López Tarso.

130. *Ibid.* This is both corroborated and contradicted by a *New York Times* article that stated, "By the early 90s Mexicans stopped going to the movies." Matthew D. Heyman and his Mexican partners, Miguel Angel Dávila and Adolfo Fastlicht, opened their first Cinemex theaters in 1995, which by 2001 had 317 screens in the Federal District, helping to revive Mexico City as an important international market. In addition to building theaters in wealthy districts (and charging higher ticket prices), Heyman "realized that the company needed to tap Mexico City's largest market: the working poor ... by [building] expensive theaters in working class neighborhoods ... [charging] about half as much for tickets." Graham Gori, "An American Directs Mexico City's Cinema Revival," *The New York Times*, 15 July 2001, Internet edition.

131. Jorge Caballero, "Más de 4 mil 600 mdp captaron las salas de cine en México durante 2001," *La Jornada*, 15 January 2002, Internet Edition.

132. John Hecht, "Cinemex greenlights slew of Mexico City multiplexes," *The Hollywood Reporter*, 19–25 August, 2003, p. 8.

133. Ugalde was nominated for an Ariel in 1987 for best adaptation of a screenplay for *Intriga contra México/¿Nos traicionará el presidente?* which was banned. He has written more than 50 scripts for short films and 25 for full-length features, of which 10 have been filmed. He has also written on the film industry for major newspapers and magazines. Ciuk, *Diccionario*, pp. 604–605.

134. Interview with Víctor Ugalde, Mexico City (IMCINE), 18 March 2004.

135. *Ibid.*

136. Yanireth Israde, "Se moviliza la comunidad cinematográfica en defensa de *La ley de Herodes,* filme de Estrada," *La Jornada*, 7 December 1999, Internet edition.

137. As described by Alejandro Pelayo, interview, 15 December 2003.

138. Yanireth Israde, "Estrada se convierte en propietario exclusivo de *La ley de Herodes,*" *La Jornada*, 8 December 1999, Internet edition. See also, "Mexican theater cancels film depicting ruling party corruption," *CNN.com*, 7 December 1999.

139. "Herod's Law," *Chicago Sun-Times*, 10 August 2003, Internet edition.

140. Javier Hernando, in Imdb.com.

141. *Cinema México, Producciones 1998–2000* (Mexico City: CONACULTA/IMCINE, 2000), pp. 30–44.

142. Lynn Hirschberg, "A New Mexican: Alejandro González Iñárritu, *The New York Times Magazine*, 18 March 2001, p. 1. See also, Elvis Mitchell, "'Amores Perros': From Mexico, an Array of Lives United by a Car Wreck," *New York Times*, 5 October 2000, Internet edition.

143. *Ibid.*

144. Two examples: TV producer Bruno Heller said, "Rome of that period was more like Bombay or Mexico City. It was a dirty, wild, savage place." Frank Bruni, "Rendering Unto Caesar's Subjects," *The New York Times*, 5 April 2004, Internet edition; and "Iñárritu is lucky to live in a city, and a country, that are among the world's filthiest and most terrifying places." Andrew O'Hehir, "Amores Perros," *Salon.com*, 30 March 2001. And Tony Scott's *Man on Fire* (2004), with Denzel Washington, extensively exploited this image.

145. For a detailed analysis of this film, see Paul Julian Smith, *Amores Perros* (London: British Film Institute, 2003).

146. *Ibid.*

147. For interviews with these filmmakers (except Carrera), see Puig, "Mexico still beckons to these expat directors," p. 4D.

148. "The Very Latest in Mexican Cinema," *Voices of Mexico*, no. 59 (April-June 2002), p. 46.

149. Quoted from a user's comment on the IMDb.com website for *Sin dejar huella.*

150. Ironically, Santa Anna, prior to Cazals's film, was never portrayed in Mexican films. However, he has appeared consistently in the numerous U.S. movie (more than 20) and television depictions (at least 12) of the battle of the Alamo, the most recent being the 2004 Disney Touchstone production, *The Alamo*, directed by John Lee Hancock, in which Emilio Echevarría plays Santa Anna.

151. Ciuk, *Diccionario*, p. 133.

152. Patricia Dávalos, "'Mi cine es reflexivo, no para divertir', afirma Felipe Cazals," *Crónica*, 20 October 2001, Internet edition.

153. Flor de María Oliva, "Felipe Cazals: A new

era for Mexican cinema," *Pasatiempo, The New Mexican,* n.d. December 2001, p. 59. Cazals was an honoree at the 2001 Santa Fe International Film Festival; in addition to *Su Alteza Serenísima,* there was a retrospective of four of his films from the 1970s: *Canoa, El apando, Los motivos de Luz,* and *Las Poquianchis.* See also, Leonardo García Tsao, *Felipe Cazals habla de su cine* (Guadalajara: Universidad de Guadalajara; Centro de Investigación y Enseñanza Cinematográfica, 1994).

154. The producers were Serenísima Films (Cazals's own production company formed just for this film), IMCINE, and FOPROCINE.

155. *Ibid.*

156. Blanche Petrich and Juan José Olivares, "La película del director mexicano competirá en la selección oficial de la Berlinale," *La Jornada,* 1 February 2004, Internet edition. See also, "Su factura y propuesta la llevaron a la Berlinale, afirman los productores Silva y Kelly," *ibid.,* 9 February 2004, Internet edition.

157. "Mexican Film: High Art, Low Budget," *The New York Times,* 15 July 2003, p. W1.

158. Leonardo García Tsao, "The Very Latest in Mexican Cinema," p. 45.

159. Sharon Waxman, "Filmmaker's Road Picture Steers Him Back to His Roots," *The Washington Post,* 4 May 2002, p. C4.

160. Lynn Hirschberg, "Altering the Script," *The New York Times,* 23 March 2003, Internet edition.

161. Joseph Contreras and Scott Johnson, "Mexico's New Wave," *Newsweek International,* 24 November 2003, Internet edition.

162. "The Crime of Father Amaro (El Crimen del Padre Amaro)," *Chicago Sun-Times,* 15 November 2002, Internet edition.

163. Juan José Juan Olivares, "Reclaman en foro falta de comprensión del gobierno hacia el cine mexicano," *La Jornada,* 5 May 2004, Internet edition.

164. "Lucía, Lucía," *Chicago Sun-Times,* 25 July 2003, Internet edition.

165. See David Hansen, "Holes in the Heart," *Newsweek,* 24 November, 2003; Elvis Mitchell, "Hearts Incapacitated, Souls Wasting Away," *New York Times,* 18 October 2003; and Amy Reiter, "No matter what, life is bigger than death," *Salon.com,* 20 November 2003.

166. Contreras and Johnson, "Mexico's New Wave."

167. *Ibid.* See also, Devin Gordon, "Guiding Actors Through Hell and Back, *Newsweek,* 24 November 2003.

168. Joe Morgenstern, "A Heavyweight '21 Grams': Tragedy Links Its Survivors in a Nuanced Tale of Fate," *Wall Street Journal,* 21 November 2003, p. W12.

Epilogue

1. He arrived in Mexico in 1981 to study journalism. He got into animation and short films, directing his first full-length feature, *En medio de la nada/In the Middle of Nothing* in 1993. Ciuk, *Diccionario,* p. 522–23.

2. Interview, Alejandro Pelayo, 15 December 2003. He provided most of these details about the movie bureaucratic structure.

3. Interview with Alfredo Joskowicz, IMCINE, Mexico City, 18 March 2003. Joskowicz made *Crates* and *El cambio* (both 1971). See Chapter 5.

4. Juan José Olivares, Gabriela Romero, and Raúl Orellanos, "Convoca comunidad cinematográfica a manifestación frente a San Lázaro, el jueves," *La Jornada,* 12 November 2003, Internet edition. See also, "Mexico wants to sell Imcine, Churubusco: Government plans come as a shock," *The Hollywood Reporter,* 11–17 November 2003, p. 113.

5. Juan José Olivares and Laura Gómez Flores, "Dio el pizarrazo inicial de la cinta Club eutanasia; Si peligra el Centro de Capacitación, pasaría a la UCM: López Obrador," *ibid.,* 15 November 2003.

6. Fabiola Martínez, "Paquete económico," *Ibid.,* 16 November 2003.

7. "Lawmakers save Mexican film agencies," *The Hollywood Reporter,* 6–12 January 2004, p. 116.

8. Tina Rosenberg, "Just as Mexican Movies Become Chic Again, the Government Pulls Its Support," *The New York Times,* 11 December 2003, Internet edition.

9. *Ibid.*

10. *Ibid.*

11. For instance, the United States attacked European film subsidies under GATT. In 1994 the United States "threatened to sue the Canadian Government under the terms of NAFTA, insisting that Canadian support of filmmakers was an unfair trading practice." Cox, "Roads to the South," p. 28.

12. Interview, 15 December 2003. For Valenti's announcement, see Jennifer Barrett, "I Survived," *Newsweek,* 26 March 2004, Internet edition.

13. *Ibid.*

14. Xan Brooks, "First Steps in Latin." See also "The Mexicans are Coming!," *Economist.com,* 4 October 2002.

15. *Ibid.*

16. *Ibid.*

17. *Ibid.*

18. Interview, 16 March 2004.

19. Interview, 18 March 2004. Ugalde summarizes his concerns in "A diez años del TLC: La década perdida del cine mexicano," *etcetera,* January 2004, pp. 31–32.

20. Interview, 15 December 2003.

21. Thomas L. Friedman, "What's That Sound?" *The New York Times,* 1 April 2004, Internet edition.

22. Interview, 18 March 2004. Ugalde, however, did help to organize a seminar sponsored by the Motion Pictures Association (MPA) and the Sociedad General de Escritores de México (SOGEM) to train 30 Mexican producers. Said Ugalde: "The MPA, which plans to produce a large number of movies in Spanish with Mexican stories, is seeking talent — together with us — and to professionalize our producers." The seminar was held on May 18, 2004. It was funded by the U.S. Embassy as part of the Mexico–U.S. Bilateral Committee for the stimulation of the film industry. Juan José Olivares, "Realizarán seminario de especialización, con énfasis en el modelo independiente de EU," *La Jornada,* 29 April 2004, Internet edition.

23. Interview, 16 March 2004.

Bibliography

A Note on Sources

The primary sources for the study of Mexican films are, of course, the films themselves. The explosion of first videotapes and then DVDs has made the availability of Mexican (and all other) films infinitely easier. To find subtitled and unsubtitled Mexican films, the easiest method is to use a search engine like Google. Amazon.com also has a wide variety of Mexican videos and DVDs. Other online sources are the Latin American Video Archive, which has a large selection of quality Mexican and Latin American films both subtitled and unsubtitled. Unsubtitled commercial movies are available from Laguna Films, which has links to Azteca Pictures, Condor Pictures, and Cristal Pictures. And in cities with large immigrant Hispanic populations (which is most of the United States now), video rental stores carry many Mexican films. The important Mexican films with subtitles can be found in the international sections of well-stocked video stores such as Blockbuster and Hollywood Video.

For researchers interested in going to the source, the Cineteca Nacional is the obvious destination. Its attentive staff can assist with specific research topics, arrange for screening of films, and put you in touch with directors, performers, and others in the film community. Lic. María de los Angeles Sánchez Gutiérrez, the director of the archives (e-mail: masanchez@cinetecanacional.net), is most responsive and helpful. The Cineteca's address can be found in Appendix 2.

As to published sources, Emilio García Riera's *Historia documental del cine mexicano* is the indispensable work. From 1969 to 1978, nine volumes were published by Ediciones Era, which covered film production from 1926 to 1966. Between 1992 and 1997, a second, revised, and streamlined edition was published by the University of Guadalajara, IMCINE, the Cultural Affairs Department of the Jalisco State Government, and CONACULTA. It consists of 18 volumes: the first 17 contain production notes, synopses, commentaries, and reviews on almost every Mexican film made between 1929 and 1976. Volume 18 is an index to the preceding 17 volumes. It is a truly unique work, unequaled in any other country.

Emilio García Riera was born in Ibiza, Spain, in 1931. In 1939, his family arrived in Mexico as Civil War refugees. He immersed himself in the cinema of his adopted country and became its foremost chronicler. He taught at the University of Guadalajara and wrote articles, books, and screenplays. He served on many international film juries, including Cannes. His career and accomplishments are too extensive to summarize adequately here, but a good biography can be found at www.supermexicanos.com/tintan/garciariera.htm. García Riera died on October 11, 2002, in Guadalajara.

Together with Jaime Humberto Hermosillo, García Riera established a film studies center (Centro de Investigaciones y Enseñanza Cinematográficas/CIEC) at the University of Guadalajara. In 1986, the center initiated a film festival dedicated to showcasing the best of each year's Mexican films, in addition to retrospectives on genres and directors. The Guadalajara Film Festival, held every year in March, is the country's most prestigious, and the best place to check out the latest Mexican films. The university's publishing program also has a series of film books.

David E. Wilt is a librarian at the University of Maryland who tirelessly maintains *The Mexican Film Resource Page* at www.wam. umd.edu/~dwilt/mfb.html. This website contains a wealth of information on all aspects of Mexican movies and links to many official sites, production companies, and all kinds of biographical pages on Mexican movie stars. He also publishes *The Mexican Film Bulletin* about four times a year which, among extensive reviews and plot outlines of many obscure Mexican movies, keeps up the most current obituaries. Wilt is also the compiler of *The Mexican Filmography, 1916 through 2001* (McFarland, 2004).

At this writing, there were no specialized film journals being published in Mexico. The excellent *Dicine* ceased publication in 1994.

Good sources for movie news are the newspapers *La Jornada, Uno Más Uno, Plural,* and *El Financiero*, which carries the lively and provocative film criticism of Jorge Ayala Blanco. *Variety* publishes reviews of major Mexican films, and *The Hollywood Reporter* has occasional articles on the industry. Between 1995 and 2002, the popular Mexican magazine *Somos* published 48 issues, each of which was devoted to a famous Mexican movie actor (see bibliography for complete listing).

I welcome inquiries regarding anything in this book or Mexican cinema in general. My e-mail is gigicarl@swcp.com, and you are welcome to visit my website at www.swcp. com/~gigicarl/.

The following bibliography contains the principal books and articles in Spanish, English, and French on Mexican cinema as well as a basic selection of works on other Latin American countries. Some works on Spanish film are included because of the continual interaction between Mexican and Spanish filmmakers both in the past and currently.

Archives and Libraries Consulted

American Film Institute, Beverly Hills, California
Cineteca Nacional, Mexico City, Mexico
Cinema-Television Library, University of Southern California, Los Angeles, California
UCLA Film Archive, Los Angeles, California
UCLA Theater Arts Library, Los Angeles, California
Zimmerman Library, University of New Mexico, Albuquerque, New Mexico

Magazines and Journals

Cahiers du Cinéma, Paris
Cámara, Mexico City (1981–1989)
Cartel, Mexico City (1947–1948)
Celuloide, Mexico City (1946)
Cine, Mexico City (1938)
Cine al Día, Caracas
Cine-Arte, Mexico City (1986–)

Cineaste, New York
Cine-Club, Mexico City (1955)
Cine cubano, Havana (1960–1988)
Cinelandia, New York (1929–1930)
Cinema Reporter, Mexico City (1938–1951)
Cine Mexicano, Mexico City (1944–1958)
Cineteca Nacional, Mexico City (1983–1989)
Cuadernos de Cine, Bogotá
Dicine, Mexico City (1984–1995)
Film Culture, New York
Film Quarterly, Berkeley, California (volumes 1–5 [1947–1951] were titled *Hollywood Quarterly*; volumes 6–11 [1952–1957] were titled *Quarterly of Film, Radio and Television*)
Films in Review, Somerville, New Jersey
Hablemos de Cine, Lima
The Hollywood Reporter, Los Angeles
Illustrado, Mexico City (1933–1935)
La Revue du Cinéma—Image et Son, Paris
Mañana, Mexico City
México Cinema, Mexico City (1942–1955)
Nuevo Cine, Mexico City (1961)
Ojo al Cine, Cali, Colombia
Organo Informativo de la Cámara Nacional de

la *Industria Cinematográfica*, Mexico City, (1979–)
Otrocine, Mexico City (1975–1976)
The Penguin Film Review, London
Reseña, Madrid
Siempre, Mexico City
Somos, Mexico City (1995–2002)
Tiempo (distributed in the United States under the title of *Hispanoamericano*)
Tiempo de Cine, Montevideo

Newspapers

Cine Mundial, Mexico City
Diario Fílmico Mexicano, Mexico City (1943–1944)
Excélsior, Mexico City
El Heraldo, Mexico City
The Hollywood Reporter
La Jornada, Mexico City
Novedades, Mexico City; see also supplement *México en la Cultura*
El Sol de México, Mexico City
Uno Más Uno, Mexico City
Variety, New York

Books

Abellán, José Luis, ed. *El exilio español de 1939*. 6 vols. Madrid: Taurus Ediciones, S.A., 1976. Vol. 1, *La emigración republicana*, by Vicente Llorens.

Acevedo-Muñoz, Ernesto. *Buñuel and Mexico: The Crisis of National Cinema*. Berkeley: University of California Press, 2003.

Adelman, Alan, ed. *A Guide to Cuban Cinema*. Latin American Monograph and Document Series 4. Pittsburgh: Center for Latin American Studies, University of Pittsburgh, 1981.

Agramonte, Arturo. *Cronología del cine cubano*. Havana: ICAIC, 1966.

Agrasánchez, Rogelio, Jr. *Miguel Zacarías, creador de estrellas*. Guadalajara: Archivo Fílmico Agrasánchez/University of Guadalajara, 2000.

_____, editor. *Mexican Horror Cinema: Posters from Mexican Horror Films*. Harlingen, Texas: Agrasánchez Film Archive, 1999.

_____, curator. *Carteles de la Epoca de Oro del Cine Mexicano/Poster Art from the Golden Age of Mexican Cinema*. Introduction by Charles Ramírez Berg. San Francisco: Chronicle Books, 2001.

_____. *Bellezas del cine mexicano/Beauties of Mexican Cinema*. Harlingen, Texas: Agrasánchez Film Archive, 2001.

_____. *Tears, Passion and Rage: The Heyday of Mexican Movies in the United States (1920–1960)*. Foreword by Carl J. Mora. Jefferson, NC: McFarland, forthcoming.

Alcalá, Manuel. *Buñuel (Cine e Ideología)*. Madrid: Editorial Cuadernos para el Diálogo, 1973.

Alcérreca, Rafael. *Una mirada a los Estudios Churubusco/Un Regard sur les Studios Churubusco*. Mexico City: Estudios Churubusco Azteca, 2002.

Almendros, Nestor. *A Man with a Camera*. Translated from the Spanish by Rachel Phillips Belash. New York: Farrar, Strauss, Giroux, 1984.

_____. *Conducta impropia (Un filme de Néstor Alméndros)*. Madrid: Playor, 1984.

Almoina, Helena. *Bibliografía del cine mexicano, 1960–1985*. Mexico City: Filmoteca UNAM, 1980.

_____. *Notas para la historia del cine en México*. 2 vols. Mexico City: filmoteca UNAM, 1980.

Amo, Alvaro del. *Comedia cinematográfica española*. Madrid: Editorial Cuadernos para el Diálogo, 1975.

Anderson, Joseph L., and Donald Richie. *The Japanese Film: Art and Industry*. Foreword by Akira Kurosawa. New York: Grove Press, 1960.

Aranda, Francisco. *Luis Buñuel: A Critical Biography*. Translated by David Robinson. London: Secker and Warburg, 1975.

Arciniégas, Germán. *Latin America: A Cultural History*. Translated by Joan MacLean. New York: Alfred A. Knopf, 1967.

Armes, Roy. *Third World Filmmaking and the West*. Berkeley: University of California Press, 1987.

Anuario de la producción cinematográfica mexicana, 1970. Mexico City: Procinemex, n.d. Also see *Anuarios* for 1971–1974.

Ayala Blanco, Jorge. *La aventura del cine mexicano*. Mexico City: Ediciones Era, 1968.

_____. *La búsqueda del cine mexicano (1968–1972)*. 2 vols. Cuadernos de Cine #22. Mexico City: UNAM, Dirección General de Difusión Cultural, 1974.

_____. *La condición del cine mexicano (1973–1985)*. Mexico City: Editorial Posada, 1986.

_____. *La disolvencia del cine mexicano: Entre lo popular y lo exquisito*. Mexico City: Editorial Grijalbo, 1991.

_____. *La fugacidad del cine mexicano*. Mexico City: Océano, 2001.

Bardèche, Maurice, and Robert Brasillach. *Histoire du Cinéma*. 10 vols. Paris: André Martel, 1954. Vol. 2, *Le cinéma parlant*, pp. 430–36.

Bawden, Liz-Anne, ed. *The Oxford Companion to Film*. New York: Oxford University Press, 1976.

Besas, Peter. *Behind the Spanish Lens: Spanish Cinema Under Fascism and Democracy*. Denver: Arden Press, 1985.

Blanco, Carlos. *Don Quijote cabalga de nuevo*. Madrid: Editorial Fragua, 1973.

Buache, Freddy. *The Cinema of Luis Buñuel*. Translated by Peter Graham. London: The Tantivy Press, and New York: A.S. Barnes, 1973.

Bukalski, Peter J. *Film Research: A Critical Bibliography with Annotations and Essays*. Boston: G.K. Hall, n.d.

Buñuel, Luis. *Mi último suspiro (memorias)*. Mexico City: Plaza & Janes, 1982.

_____. *Mon Dernier Soupir*. Paris: Editions Robert Laffont, 1982.

_____. *My Last Sigh*. New York: Alfred A. Knopf, 1983.

Burns, E. Bradford. *Latin American Cinema: Film and History*. Los Angeles: UCLA Latin American Center, 1975.

Burton, Julianne, ed. *Cinema and Social Change in Latin America: Conversations with Filmmakers*. Austin: University of Texas Press, 1986.

_____. *The New Latin American Cinema: An Annotated Bibliography of English-Language Sources, 1960–1976*. Cineaste Pamphlet no. 4. New York: Cineaste, 1976.

Bustillo Oro, Juan. *Vientos de los veintes*. Mexico City: Sep/Setentas, n.d.

Campbell, Leon G., Carlos E. Cortés, and Robert Pinger. *Latin America: A Filmic Approach*. Film Series no. 1. Riverside: University of California, Latin American Studies Program, October 1975.

Caparrós Lera, José María and Rafael de España. *The Spanish Cinema: An Historical Approach*. Translated by Carl J. Mora. Barcelona: Centre for Cinematic Research "Film-Historia," 1987.

Careaga, Gabriel. *Erotismo, violencia y política en el cine*. Mexico City: Cuadernos de Joaquín Mortiz, 1981, pp. 86–99 on Pedro Infante.

Carr, Larry. *More Fabulous Faces: The Evolution and Metamorphosis of Dolores del Rio, Myrna Loy, Carole Lombard, Bette Davis, and Katherine Hepburn*. Garden City, NY: Doubleday, 1979, pp. 1–51.

Carro, Nelson. *El cine de luchadores*. Mexico City: Filmoteca de la UNAM, 1984.

Castro, Antonio. *El cine español en el banquillo*. Valencia, Spain: Fernando Torres Editor, 1974.

Cawkwell, Tim, and John M. Smith. *The World Encyclopedia of the Film*. n.p.: A&W Visual Library, November Books, 1972.

Ceplair, Larry, and Steven Englund. *The Inquisition in Hollywood: Politics in the Film Community, 1930–1960*. Berkeley: University of California Press, 1983.

Césarman, Fernando. *El ojo de Buñuel: Psicoanálisis desde una butaca*. Prologue by Carlos Fuentes. Barcelona: Anagrama, 1976.

Chanan, Michael. *The Cuban Image: Cinema and Cultural Politics in Cuba*. London: BFI Publishing; Bloomington: Indiana University Press, 1985.

_____, ed. *Twenty-Five Years of the New Latin American Cinema*. London: Channel 4 Television; BFI Books, 1983.

Cine y revolución en Cuba. Prologue by Miquel Porter. Barcelona: Editorial Fontamara, 1975.

Cinema México: Producciones 1998–2001. Mexico City: Consejo Nacional para la Cultura y las Artes and Instituto Mexicano de Cinematografía, 2002

Cineteca Nacional, 1974. Mexico City: n.p., n.d.

_____, 1975. Mexico City: n.p., n.d.

Cineteca Nacional, Memoria 1976. Mexico City: Cineteca Nacional, 1976, 102 pp.

Cineteca Nacional, Memoria 1977. Mexico City: Cineteca Nacional, 1977, 155 pp.

Cineteca Nacional, Memoria 1978. Mexico City: Cineteca Nacional, 1978, 132 pp.

Cineteca Nacional, Memoria 1979. Mexico City: Cineteca Nacional, 1979, 51 pp.

Cineteca Nacional, Memoria 1980. Mexico City: Cineteca Nacional, 1980, 69 pp.

Cineteca Nacional, Memoria 1981. Mexico City: Cineteca Nacional, 1981, 63 pp.

Cineteca Nacional, Memoria 1982. Mexico City: Cineteca Nacional, 1982, 47 pp.

Cineteca Nacional, Memoria 1983. Mexico City: Cineteca Nacional, 1983, 36 pp.

Cineteca Nacional, Memoria 1984. Mexico City: Cineteca Nacional, 1984, 80 pp.

Cineteca Nacional, Memoria 1985. Mexico City: Cineteca Nacional, 1985, 64 pp.

Cineteca Nacional, Memoria 1986. Mexico City: Cineteca Nacional, 1986, 70 pp.

Cineteca Nacional, Memoria 1987. Mexico City: Cineteca Nacional, 1987, 70 pp.

Cineteca Nacional, Memoria 1988. Mexico City: Cineteca Nacional, 1988, 63 pp.

Ciuk, Perla. *Diccionario de directores del cine mexicano.* Mexico City: CONACULTA/Cineteca Nacional, 2000.

Colina, José de la. *Miradas al cine.* Mexico City: Sep/Setentas, 1972.

_____, and Tomás Pérez-Turrent. *Luis Buñuel: Prohibido asomarse al interior.* Colección Genio y Figura. Mexico City: Joaquín Mortiz/Plantea, 1986.

Comisión Nacional de Cinematografía. *El libro de oro del cine mexicano, 1949.* Mexico City, 1949.

Contreras Torres, Miguel. *El libro negro del cine mexicano.* Mexico City: Editora Hispano-Continental Films, 1960.

Contreras y Espinosa, Fernando. *La producción, sector primario de la industria cinematográfica.* Textos de Cine #4. Mexico City: UNAM, 1973.

Cortés, Carlos E., Leon G. Campbell, and Alan Curl. *A Filmic Approach to the Study of Historical Dilemmas.* Film Series no. 2. Riverside: University of California, Latin American Studies Program, October 1976.

Cosío Villegas, Daniel. *Historia moderna de México.* 8 vols. Mexico City: Editorial Hermes, 1955–1972. Vol. 4, *El Porfiriato — La vida social,* by Moisés González Navarro, 1957.

Cotter, Robert Michael "Bobb." *The Mexican Masked Wrestler and Monster Filmography.* Jefferson, NC: McFarland, 2005.

Cowie, Peter, ed. *International Film Guide.* 21 editions to date. London: The Tantivy Press, 1968–1988.

_____, gen. ed. *World Filmography.* London: The Tantivy Press; South Brunswick, NJ: A.S. Barnes, 1977, pp. 439–56.

_____, ed. *Variety International Film Guide.* Five editions, 1999–2004. London: Silman-James Press, 1999–2004.

Cremoux, Raúl. *La televisión y el alumno de secundaria del Distrito Federal.* Mexico City: Centro de Estudios Educativos, A.C., February 1968.

Cronología de la cultura cinematográfica (1949–1986), Serie: Historia del cine en El Ecuador. Quito: Nueva Editorial, 1987.

Dever, Susan. *Celluloid Nationalism and Other Melodramas: From Post-Revolutionary Mexico to Fin De Siglo Mexamerica.* SUNY Series, Cultural Studies in Cinema/Video & SUNY Series in Feminist Criticism and Theory. Albany: State University of New York Press, 2003.

Diccionario Porrúa: Historia, Biografía y Geografía de México. 2 vols. 3d ed. Mexico City: Editorial Porrúa, 1970. Vol. 1, A–LL.

Eisenstein, S.M. *¡Que viva México!* Prologue by José de la Colina. Mexico City: Ediciones Era, 1971.

El automóvil gris. Introduction by Federico Serrano y Fernando del Moral G. Cuadernos de la Cineteca Nacional #10. Serie Guiones Clásicos del Cine Mexicano. Mexico City: Cineteca Nacional, 1972.

El cine: Desde Lumière hasta el Cinerama. 2 vols. Barcelona: Libreria Editorial Argos, 1965.

Eliezer Galvão, Maria Rita. *Crônica do Cinema Paulistano.* São Paulo: Editora Ática, 1975.

El Topo: A Book of the Film by Alejandro Jodorowski. New York: Douglas Links, 1971.

Enciclopedia de México. 10 vols. Mexico City: Instituto de la Enciclopedia de Mexico, 1968. Vol. 2.

Enciclopedia ilustrada del cine. Barcelona: Editorial Labor, 1969.

Equipo "Cartelera Turia." *Cine español, cine de subgéneros.* Valencia, Spain: Fernando Torres, Editor, 1974.

España, Rafael de. *Las sombras del Encuentro — España y América: cuatro siglos de Historia a través del Cine.* Badajoz: Colección Cine, Diputación de Badajoz, Departamento de Publicaciones, 2002.

Feldman, Simón. *El director de cine: mitos y sometimientos.* Buenos Aires: Granica Editor, 1974.

Fernández, Adela. *El Indio Fernández: Vida y mito.* Mexico City: Panorama Editorial, 1986.

Flores García, Alejandro. *Cinecompendio, 1971/1972.* Mexico City: Editorial A. Posta, 1973.

_____. *Cinecompiendo, 1972/1973.* Mexico City: Editorial A. Posta, 1974.

_____. *Cinecompiendo, 1973/1974.* Mexico City: Editorial A. Posta, 1975.

_____. *Cinecompiendo, 1974/1975.* Mexico City: Editorial A. Posta, 1976.

Font, Domènec. *Del azul al verde: el cine español durante el franquismo.* Barcelona: Editorial Avance, 1976.

Ford, Charles. *Historia popular del cine.* Translated from the French by Leoncio Sureda Guyto. Barcelona: Editorial AHR, 1956.

Foster, David William. *Mexico City in Contemporary Mexican Cinema.* Austin: University of Texas Press, 2002.

40 aniversario cine sonoro mexicano. Mexico City: Comisión Organizadora de los Actos Conmemoratorios del 40 Aniversario del Cine Sonoro Mexicano, November 1971.

Furhammer, Leif and Isaksson, Folke. *Politics and Film.* Translated by Kersti French. New York and Washington, DC: Praeger Publishers, 1971.

Galindo, Alejandro. *El cine, genocidio espiritual: De 1900 al "crash" de 29.* Mexico City: Editorial Nuestro Tiempo, 1971.

_____. *¿Que es el cine?* Mexico City: Editorial Nuestro Tiempo, 1975.

_____. *Una radiografía histórica del cine mexicano.* Mexico City: Fondo de Cultura Popular, 1968.

_____. *Verdad y mentira del cine mexicano.* Mexico City: Aconacagua Ediciones y Publicaciones, 1981.

García Márquez, Gabriel. *La aventura de Miguel Littín clandestino en Chile.* Mexico City: Editorial Diana, 1986.

García Riera, Emilio. *Arturo Ripstein habla de su cine.* Colección Testimonios del Cine Mexicano. Guadalajara: Universidad de Guadalajara, Centro de Investigación y Enseñanza Cinematográficas, 1988.

_____. *El cine mexicano.* Mexico City: Ediciones Era, 1963.

_____. *El cine y su público.* Coleccion Testimonios del Fondo #1. Mexico City: Fondo de Cultura Económica, 1974.

_____. *Historia documental del cine mexicano.* 9 vols. Mexico City: Ediciones Era, 1969–1978.

_____. *Historia documental del cine mexicano.* 18 volumes. Guadalajara: University of Guadalajara, IMCINE, the Cultural Affairs Department of the Jalisco State Government, and CONACULTA, 1992–1997.

_____. *Julio Bracho: 1909–1978.* Coleccion Cineastas de México. Guadalajara: Universidad de Guadalajara, Centro de Investigación y Enseñanza Cinematográficas, 1987.

_____. *México visto por el cine extranjero.* 4 vols. Mexico City: Ediciones Era and Guadalajara: Universidad de Guadalajara, 1987–1988.

_____ and Macotela, Fernando. *La guía del cine mexicano: de la pantalla grande a la televisión, 1919–1984.* Mexico City: Editorial Patria, 1984.

García Tsao, Leonardo. *Felipe Cazals habla de su cine.* Testimonios del Cine Mexicano. Guadalajara: Universidad de Guadalajara, Centro de Investigación y Enseñanza Cinematográficas, 1994.

Geduld, Harry M., and Ronald Gottesman, eds. *Sergei Eisenstein and Upton Sinclair: the Making and Unmaking of Que Viva Mexico!* Bloomington: Indiana University Press, 1970.

Geijerstam, Claes af. *Popular Music in Mexico.* Albuquerque: University of New Mexico Press, 1976.

Gertner, Richard. *International Motion Picture Almanac 1976.* New York: Quigley, 1976, pp. 695–96.

Giménez Caballero, Ernesto. *Amor a Méjico (A través de su cine).* Cuadernos de Monografías no. 5. Madrid: Seminario de Problemas Hispanoamericanos, April 5, 1948.

Gomezjara, Francisco A., and Delia Selene de Dios. *Sociología del cine.* Mexico City: Sep/Setentas, 1973.

González Casanova, Manuel. *¿Que es un cine-club?* Mexico City: Dirección de Difusión Cultural, Seccion de Actividades Cinematográficas, UNAM, 1961.

González Navarro, Moisés. *Población y sociedad en México (1900–1970).* 2 vols. Serie Estudios 42. Mexico City: UNAM, Facultad de Ciencias Políticas y Sociales. 1974.

Greene, Doyle. *Mexploitation Cinema: A Critical History of Mexican Vampire, Wrestler, Ape-Man and Similar Films, 1957–1977.* Jefferson, NC: McFarland, 2005.

Gubern, Román. *Cine español en el exilio, 1936–1939.* Barcelona: Editorial Lumen, 1976.

_____. *El cine sonoro en la República 1929–1936. Historia del cine español II.* Barcelona: Editorial Lumen, 1977.

Guerrero Suárez, Jorge. *Dolores del Río.* Mexico City: By the Author, 1979.

_____. *El Cine Sonoro Mexicano: sus inicios, 1930–1937.* Cuadernos de la Cineteca Nacional #8. Serie Ensayos, Investigaciones y Biografías. Mexico City: Cineteca Nacional, 1987.

Gumucio-Dagrón, Alfonso. *Historia del cine boliviano.* Mexico City: Filmoteca UNAM, 1983.

Haddu, Miriam. *Contemporary Mexican Cinema: History, Space and Identity (1989–2001).* Lewiston, NY: Edwin Mellen Press, 2005.

Hennebele, Guy, and Alfonso Gumucio-Dagrón, eds. *Les Cinémas de L'Amérique Latine.* Paris: Lherminier, 1981.

Hershfield, Joanne. *Mexican Cinema/Mexican Woman, 1940–1950.* Latin American Communication and Popular Culture Series. Tempe: University of Arizona Press, 1996.

_____, and David Maciel, eds. *Mexico's Cinema: A Century of Film and Filmmakers.* Latin American Silhouettes. Wilmington: Scholarly Resources, 1999.

Heuer, Federico. *La industria cinematográfica mexicana.* Mexico City: By the Author, 1964.

Higginbotham, Virginia. *Spanish Film Under Franco.* Austin: University of Texas Press, 1988.

Homenaje a los iniciadores del cine en Mexico (1896–1938). Cuadernos de la Cineteca Nacional #9. Mexico City: Cineteca Nacional, 1979.

Hopewell, John. *Out of the Past: Spanish Cinema After Franco.* London: BFI Books, 1986.

Hijar, Alberto, ed. *Hacia un tercer cine.* Cuadernos de Cine #20. Mexico City: UNAM, 1972.

Huaco, George A. *The Sociology of Film Art.* New York: Basic Books, 1965.

Huss, Roy, and Norman Silverstein. *The Film Experience: Elements of Motion Picture Art.* New York: Harper and Row, 1968.

Informe general sobre la actividad cinematográfica en el año 1971 relativo *al Banco Nacional Cinematográfico,* S.A. Mexico City: Banco Nacional Cinematográfico, January 21, 1972.

Informe general...en el año 1972.... Mexico City: January 23, 1973.

Informe general...en el año 1973.... Mexico City: January 22, 1974.

Informe general...en el año 1974.... Mexico City: January 21, 1975.

Informe general...en el año 1976.... Mexico City: November 26, 1976.

Izaguirre, Rodolfo. *El cine en Venezuela.* Temas Culturales Venezolanos, Serie I. Caracas: n.p., n.d.

Jacobs, Lewis. *The Emergence of Film Art: The Evolution and Development of the Motion Picture as an Art, from 1900 to the Present.* New York: Hopkinson and Blake, 1974.

Jarvie, I.C. *Movies and Society.* New York: Basic Books, 1970.

Jeanne, Rene, and Charley Ford. *Historia ilustrada del cine.* 3 vols. Madrid: Alianza Editorial, 1974.

Johnson, Randal, and Robert Stam. *Brazilian Cinema.* Rutherford, NJ: Fairleigh Dickinson University Press; London: Associated University Press, 1982.

King, John. *Magical Reels: A History of Cinema in Latin America.* New York: Verso Books, 2000.

_____, and Ana M. López, eds. *Mediating Two Worlds: Cinematic Encounters in the Americas.* London: British Film Institute, 1993.

Kracauer, Siegfried. *From Caligari to Hitler: A Psychological History of the German Film.* 2d ed. New York: The Noonday Press, 1960.

Kyrou, Ado. *Luis Buñuel.* Paris: Editions Seghers, 1970.

La *fábrica de sueños: Estudios Churubusco*

1945–1985. Mexico City: Instituto Mexicano de Cinematografía, 1985.

La Fuente, María Isabel de. *Indice bibliográfico del cine mexicano (1930–1965)*. Mexico City: n.p., 1967.

_____. *Indice bibliográfico del cine mexicano (1966–1967)*. Vol. 2. Mexico City: Editorial América, 1968.

Lamarque, Libertad. *Autobiografía*. Mexico City: Javier Vergara, Editor, 1986.

Lamb, Ruth S. *Mexican Theater of the Twentieth Century: Bibliography and Study*. Claremont, CA: Ocelot Press, 1975.

León Frías, Isaac. *Los años de la conmoción, 1967–1973: Entrevistas con realizadores sudamericanos*. Mexico City: Dirección General de Difusión Cultural, UNAM, 1979.

Leprohon, Pierre. *The Italian Cinema*. Translated from the French by Roger Greaves and Oliver Stallybrass. New York: Praeger, 1972.

Littín, Miguel. *El chacal de Nahueltoro, La tierra prometida*. Textos de Cine #5, Serie Guiones 1. Mexico City: UNAM, Direccion General de Difusión Cultural, 1977.

Lizalde, Eduardo. *Luis Buñuel*. Cuadernos de Cine #2. Mexico City: UNAM, Dirección General de Difusión Cultural, 1962.

López Aranda, Susana. *El cine de Ignacio López Tarso*. Guadalajara: University of Guadalajara and IMCINE, 1997.

MacBean, James Roy. *Film and Revolution*. Bloomington: Indiana University Press, 1975.

Madrid, Francisco. *Cincuenta años de cine: Crónica del séptimo arte*. Buenos Aires: Ediciones del Tridente, 1964.

Magaña Esquivel, Antonio. *Los teatros en la ciudad de Mexico*. Mexico City: Colección Popular Ciudad de México, Departamento del Distrito Federal, 1974.

Mahieu, Agustín. *Breve historia del cine nacional, 1896–1974*. Buenos Aires: Alzamor Editores, 1976.

Manchel, Frank. *Film Study: A Resource Guide*. Rutherford, NJ: Fairleigh Dickinson University Press, 1973.

Manvell, Roger, and Heinrich Fraenkel. *The German Cinema*. New York: Praeger, 1971.

Martínez Pardo, Hernando. *Historia del cine colombiano*. Bogotá: Editorial America Latina, 1978.

Martin, Michael T., ed. *New Latin American Cinema: Studies of National Cinemas*. Contemporary Film and Television Series. Detroit: Wayne State University Press, 1997.

Martínez Torres, Augusto, and Manuel Pérez Estremera. *Nuevo cine latinoamericano*. Barcelona: Editorial Anagrama, 1973.

Méndez Berman, León, and Santos Mar. *El embrollo cinematográfico*. Mexico City: Editorial Cooperación, 1953.

Méndez Leite, Fernando. *Historia del cine español*. Madrid: Ediciones Rialp, 1965.

Meyer, Eugenia, coordinator. *Cuadernos de la Cineteca Nacional: Testimonios para la historia del cine mexicano*. 8 vols. Mexico City: Dirección de Cinematografía de la Secretaría de Gobernación, 1976.

Michel, Manuel. *Al pie de la imágen: Críticas y ensayos*. Cuadernos de Cine #15. Mexico City: UNAM, Dirección General de Difusión Cultural, 1968.

_____. *El cine y el hombre contemporáneo*. Prologue by Carlos Fuentes. Cuadernos de la Facultad de Filosofía, Letras y Ciencias #14. Xalapa, Ver.: Universidad Veracruzana, 1962.

Millingham, F. *Por qué nació el cine*. Buenos Aires: Editorial Nova, 1954.

Miquel, Ángel. *Mimí Derba*. Mexico City: Archivo Fílmico Agrasánchez/Filmoteca de la UNAM, 2000.

Mitry, Jean. *Histoire du Cinéma: Art et Industrie*. 3 vols. Paris: Editions Universitaires, 1967.

_____. *S.M. Eisenstein*. Paris: Editions Universitaires, 1962.

Monaco, Paul. *Cinema and Society: France and Germany During the Twenties*. New York: Elsevier, 1976.

Morales, María Luz. *El cine: Historia ilustrada del séptimo arte*. 3 vols. Barcelona: n.p., 1950.

Montalbán, Ricardo, with Bob Thomas. *Reflections: A Life in Two Worlds*. New York: Doubleday, 1980.

Myerson, Michael, ed. *Memories of Underdevelopment: The Revolutionary Films of Cuba*. New York: Grossman, 1973.

Nacional Financiera, S.A. *Statistics on the Mexican Economy*. Mexico City: Nacional Financiera, S.A., 1966.

Noriega, Chon A., and Steven Ricci, eds. *The Mexican Cinema Project*. Los Angeles: UCLA Film and Television Archive, 1994.

Nubila, Domingo di. *Historia del cine argentino*. Buenos Aires: Edicion Cruz de Malta, 1959.

O'Connor, John E., and Martin A. Jackson, eds. *American History/American Film: Interpreting the Hollywood Image*. Foreword by Arthur M. Schlesinger, Jr. New York: Frederick Ungar, 1979.

Palacios More, René, and Daniel Pires Mateus. *El cine latinoamericano: O por una estética de la ferocidad, la magia y la violencia*. Madrid: Sedmay Ediciones, 1976.

Paranaguá, Paulo Antonio, ed. *Mexican Cinema*. London: British Film Institute; Mexico City: Instituto Mexicano de Cinematografía, 1995.

Pastor Legnani, Margarita, and Rosario Vico de Peña. *Filmografía uruguaya*. Montevideo: Cinemateca Uruguaya, 1973.

Pereyra, Miguel. *El lenguaje del cine: Su técnica, su estilo, su arte*. Madrid: Aguilar, 1956.

Pérez, Ismael Diego. *"Cantinflas," genio del humor y del absurdo*. Mexico City: Editorial Indo-Hispana, 1954.

Pineda Alcalá, Francisco. *La verídica historia del cine mexicano*. Prologue by Fernando Morales Ortiz. Mexico City: n.p., 1965.

Portas, Rafael E., and Ricardo E. Rangel. *Enciclopedia cinematográfica mexicana, 1897–1955*. Mexico City: Publicaciones Cinematografistas, n.d.

Ramirez Berg, Charles. *Cinema of Solitude: A Critical Study of Mexican Film, 1967–1983*. Austin: University of Texas Press, 1992.

Ramírez, Gabriel. *El cine yucateco*. Mexico City: Filmoteca UNAM, 1980.

Rashkin, Elissa J. *Women Filmmakers in Mexico: The Country of Which We Dream*. Austin: University of Texas Press, 2001.

Reyes de la Maza, Luis. *Cien años de teatro en México (1810–1910)*. Mexico City: Sep/Setentas, 1972.

_____. *El cine sonoro en Mexico*. Mexico City: UNAM, Instituto de Investigaciones Estéticas, 1973.

_____. *El teatro en México durante el porfirismo, tomo III (1900–1910)*. Mexico City: UNAM, 1968.

_____. *Salón rojo (programas y crónicas del cine mudo en México), vol. 1 (1895–1920)*. Mexico City: UNAM, Dirección General de Difusión Cultural, 1968.

Reyes, Alfonso, Martín Luis Guzmán, and Federico de Onís. *Frente a la pantalla*. Cuadernos de cine #6. Mexico City: UNAM, Dirección General de Difusión Cultural, 1963.

Reyes, Aurelio de los. *Cine y sociedad en México 1896–1930. Volume 1: Vivir de sueños (1896–1920)*. Mexico City: UNAM and Cineteca Nacional, 1981.

_____. *Los orígenes del cine en México (1896–1900)*. Mexico City: UNAM, Dirección General de Difusión Cultural, 1973.

_____, David Ramón, María Luisa Amador, and Rodolfo Rivera. *80 años de cine en México*. Serie Imágenes #2. Mexico City: UNAM, Dirección General de Difusión Cultural, 1977.

Reyes Nevares, Beatriz. *Trece directores del cine mexicano*. Mexico City: Sep/Setentas, 1973.

_____. *The Mexican Cinema: Interviews with Thirteen Directors*. Translated by Carl J. Mora and Elizabeth Gard. Albuquerque: University of New Mexico Press, 1976.

Rhode, Eric. *A History of the Cinema from Its Origins to 1970*. New York: Hill and Wang, 1976.

Riding, Alan. *Distant Neighbors: A Portrait of the Mexicans*. New York: Alfred A. Knopf, 1985, pp. 309–311.

Roberts, John Storm. *Salsa! The Latin Dimension in Popular Music*. New York: BMI, The Many Worlds of Music, issue 3, 1976.

_____. *The Latin Tinge: The Impact of Latin American Music on the United States*. New York: Oxford University Press, 1979.

Román, Ernesto and Figueroa Perea, Mari-Carmen. *Premios y distinciones otorgados al cine mexicano [en] festivales internacionales 1938–1984*. Mexico City: Cineteca Nacional, Departamento de Documentación e Investigación, 1986.

Ross, Stanley R., ed. *Views Across the Border: The United States and Mexico*. Albuquerque: University of New Mexico Press, 1978.

Rovirosa, José. *Cine-Club*. Mexico City: Instituto Mexicano del Seguro Social, 1970.

Rulfo, Juan. *El gallo de oro y otros textos para cine*. Prologue and notes by Jorge Ayala Blanco. Madrid: Ediciones Era and Alianza Editorial, 1980.

Sadoul, Georges. *El cine: Su historia y su técnica*. Translated by Juan José Arreola. Mexico City: Fondo de Cultura Económica, 1952.

———. *Histoire du Cinéma Mondial des Origines a nos Jours*. Paris: Flammarion Editeur, 1949.

Salcedo Silva, Hernando. *Crónicas del cine colombiano 1897–1950*. Bogotá: Carlos Valencia Editores, 1981.

Salt of the Earth. Screenplay by Michael Wilson. Commentary by Deborah Silverton Rosenfelt. Old Westbury, NY: The Feminist Press, 1978.

Sanjinés, Jorge y Grupo Ukamau. *Teoría y práctica de un cine junto al pueblo*. Mexico City: Siglo Veintiuno Editores, 1979.

Santillán, Antonio. *El cine*. Barcelona, Buenos Aires, Bogotá: Editorial Bruguera, 1962.

Santos Pereira, Geraldo. *Plano Geral do Cinema Brasileiro: História, Cultura, Economica, e Legislação*. Benfica, Guanabara: Editor Borsoi, 1973.

Saragoza, Alex M. *Mexican Cinema in Cold War America, 1940–1958: An Inquiry into the Interface Between Mexico and Mexicans in the United States*. ChPEC Working Paper Series. Berkeley: University of California, 1983.

Sarris, Andrew, ed. *Interviews with Film Directors*. New York: Avon Books, 1967.

Schnitman, Jorge A. *Film Industries in Latin America: Dependency and Development*. Norwood, NJ: Ablex, 1984.

Schwartz, Ronald. *Latin American Films, 1932–1994: A Critical Filmography*. Jefferson, NC: McFarland, 2005.

Shaw, Lisa and Dennison, Stephanie, editors. *Latin America Cinema: Essays on Modernity, Gender and National Identity*. Jefferson, NC: McFarland, 2005.

Silva, Alberto. *Cinema e humanismo*. Rio de Janeiro: Pallas, 1975.

Smith, Paul, ed. *The Historian and Film*. Cambridge: At the University Press, 1976.

Smith, Paul Julian. *Amores perros*. London: British Film Institute, 2003.

Solanas, Fernando E., and Octavio Getino. *Cine, cultura, y descolonización*. Buenos Aires: Siglo XXI, 1973.

Taibo I, Paco Ignacio. *El indio Fernández: el cine por mis pistolas*. Colección Genio y Figura. Mexico City: Joaquín Mortiz/Planeta, 1986.

———. *María Felix: 47 pasos por el cine*. Colección Genio y Figura. Mexico City: Joaquín Mortiz/Planeta, 1985.

Taylor, John Russell. *Cinema Eye, Cinema Ear*. New York: Hill and Wang, 1974.

Tigler, Parker. *Classics of the Foreign Film: A Pictorial Treasury*. New York: The Citadel Press, 1962.

Torres, Augusto M. *Cine español, años sesenta*. Barcelona: Editorial Anagrama, 1973.

Trelles Plazaola, Luis. *El cine visto en Puerto Rico (1962–1973)*. Colección Uprex. Río Piedras: Editorial Universitaria, Universidad de Puerto Rico, 1975.

Tudor, Andrew. *Image and Influence: Studies in the Sociology of Film*. London: George Allen and Unwin, 1974.

Usigli, Rodolfo. *Mexico in the Theater*. Translated with an introduction by Wilder P. Scott. University, MS.: Romance Monographs, Inc., 1976.

Valverde, Umberto. *Reportaje crítico al cine colombiano*. Bogotá: Editorial Toronuevo Limitada, 1978.

Vasconcelos, José. *Indología, una interpretación de la cultura iberoamericana*. Barcelona: Agencia Mundial de Librería, 1926.

Vega Alfaro, Eduardo de la. *El cine de Juan Orol*. Mexico City: Filmoteca UNAM, 1985.

———. *Juan Orol: 1897–1988*. Colección Cineastas de México. Guadalajara: Universidad de Guadalajara, Centro de Investigación y Enseñanza Cinematográficas, 1987.

———, and Patricia Torres San Martín. *Adela Sequeyro*. Guadalajara: Archivo Fílmico Agrasánchez, University of Guadalajara, 2000.

Villaurrutia, Xavier. *Crítica cinematográfica*. Edited by Miguel Capistrán. Cuadernos de Cine #18. Mexico City: UNAM, Dirección General de Difusión Cultural, 1970.

Viñas, Moisés. *Historia del cine mexicano*. Mexico City: UNAM-UNESCO, 1987.

Wenden, D.J. *The Birth of the Movies*. London: MacDonald, 1975.

Wilkie, James W., Michael C. Meyer, and Edna Monzón de Wilkie, eds. *Contemporary Mexico: Papers of the IV International Congress of Mexican History*. Berkeley: University of California Press; and Mexico City: El Colegio de Mexico, 1976.

Wilt, David. *The Mexican Filmography, 1916–2001*. Jefferson, NC: McFarland, 2004.

Woll, Allen L. *The Latin Image in American Film*. Latin American Studies, vol. 39, Los Angeles: UCLA Latin American Center Publications, 1977.

Womack, John, Jr. *Zapata and the Mexican Revolution*. New York: Vintage Books, 1970.

Articles

"Actas de Marusia" [review] La *Revue du Cinéma—Image et Son*, no. 306 (May 1976), pp. 66–67.

Alba, Gustavo A. de. "A propósito de Buñuel." *Otrocine* (Mexico City), no. 3 (July-September 1975), pp. 25–26.

_____. "La otra virginidad." *Otrocine*, no. 1 (January-March 1975), pp. 12–16.

Alcalá, Manuel. "Entrevista con Humberto Solás." *Reseña* (Madrid) (March 1977): 26–27.

_____. "Huelva 76: II Semana de Cine Iberoamericano," *Reseña* (February 1977): 35–36.

Aldape, John. "In 'mean, sexy' roles Emilia Guiu was superstar." *The Arizona Republic*, 18 February 1973, p. L-2.

Alisky, Marvin. "Mexico's Rural Radio." *Quarterly of Film, Radio & Television* 8 (Winter 1953–1954): 405–17.

_____. "Mexico versus Malthus: National Trends." *Current History* 66 (May 1974): 200–30.

Allen, William D. "Spanish-Language Films in the U.S." *Films in Review* 1 (July-August 1950): 1, 42–45.

Almendros, Nestor. "The Cinema in Cuba." *Film Culture* no. 3 (1956), p. 21.

Amador, Omar G. "Galanes latinos, Lolita y La Bamba." *Américas*, July- August 1988, pp. 2–9.

Ángelo, Miguel. "Brasil: 75 años de cinema." *O Cruziero* (Rio de Janeiro), 15 September 1971, pp. 158–62.

Aragón, Luis. "Libros: el cine mexicano." *Cine cubano*, no. 17 (January 1964), p. 63.

Askenazy, Natalia. "Movieland Stretches Southward: A Newsletter from Mexico City." *Films in Review* 1 (May-June 1950): 14–43.

_____. "The Two Kinds of Mexican Movies." *Films in Review* 2 (May 1951): 35–39.

Aubry, Daniel, and J.M. Lacor. "Luis Buñuel." *Film Quarterly* 12 (Winter 1958): 7–9.

"Authentic Pachuco." [On Germán Valdez "Tin-Tan"] *Time*, 10 July 1944, p. 72.

Ayala Blanco, Jorge. "Fuensanta: Que triste será la tarde en que te vayas al cine a ver a López Velarde." (La Cultura en México: Suplemento de Siempre) *Siempre*, 20 December 1971, p. xv.

_____. "Pancho Villa en el jardín de los senderos que se trifurcan." *Siempre*, 15 September 1982, p. XVI.

_____. "Western con vihuela." *Cine cubano*, nos. 71/72 (1971), pp. 126- 28.

Azurduy, Victoria. "El cine venezolano: ¿vía crucis?" *Otrocine*, no. 6 (April-June 1976), pp. 4–8.

Beguiristain, Mario E. "Nestor Almendros' Days of Heaven Are Finally Here," *Nuestro*, November 1979, pp. 21–22.

Berg, Charles. "Mexico, Mexico, Ra, Ra, Ra." [review] *Film Quarterly* 32 (Spring 1979): 49–50.

_____. "Canoa." [review] *Film Quarterly* 32 (Spring 1979): 50–52.

Biskind, Peter. "In Latin America They Shoot Filmmakers." *Sight and Sound* (Summer 1976), pp. 160–61.

_____. "Ripping Off Zapata: Revolution Hollywood Style." *Cineaste* 7, no. 2, pp. 11–17.

Bodeen, Dewitt. "Dolores del Rio." *Films in Review* 18 (May 1967): 266–83.

_____. "Ramon Novarro." *Films in Review* 18 (November 1967): 528–47.

Buñuel, Juan. "A Letter on *Exterminating Angel*." *Film Culture*, no. 41 (1966), p. 66.

Burns, Archibaldo. "Dolores del Río: de sus cenizas, la leyenda." *Proceso*, no. 337, 18 April 1983, pp. 50–53.

Burns, E. Bradford. "Film." In *Handbook of Latin American Studies* 38. Edited by Dolores Moyano Martin and Donald E.J. Stewart. Gainesville: University of Florida Press, 1976, pp. 59–69.

_____. "Films." [review of *Los gauchos judíos*] *The Nation*, 16 August 1975, p. 126.

_____. "National Identity in Argentine Films." *Américas*, November-December 1975, pp. 4–10.

Burton, Julianne. Book review of *Nuevo cine latinoamericano, Hacia un tercer cine*, and *Cine, cultura y descolonización*. *Hispanic American Historical Review* 55 (May 1975): 382–86.

_____. "Film." In *Handbook of Latin American Studies* 40. Edited by Dolores Moyano Martin. Gainesville: University of Florida Press, 1978, pp. 57–67.

_____. "Pedro and the Captain." *Film Quarterly* 34, no. 1 (Fall 1985): 30–32.

_____. "The Hour of the Embers: On the Current Situation of Latin American Cinema." *Film Quarterly* 30 (Fall 1976): 33–44.

_____. "*The Traitors*." [film review] *Film Quarterly* 30 (Fall 1976): 57–59.

Butler, Ron. "Cantinflas: Príncipe mexicano de la comedia." *Américas*, April 1981, pp. 7–9.

Cabada, Juan de la. "Mis pasos en el cine." *Otrocine*, no. 1 (January-March h1975), pp. 40–45.

_____. "Mis pasos en el cine (segunda parte)." *Otrocine*, no. 2 (April-June 1975), pp. 34–40.

Carlesimo, Cheryl. "Painting with Light." [article on Nestor Almendros] *American Film* 6 (April 1981), pp. 30–34, 69–71.

Carrasco, Jorge. "Luto en el Cine Mexicano." [obituary on Dolores del Río] *Hispanoamericano*, 25 April 1983, pp. 44–47.

_____. "Un Artista Integro." [obituary on Luis Buñuel] *Hispanoamericano*, 8 August 1983, pp. 58–59.

Casal, Lourdes, and Marvin Surkin. "Recent Cuban Cinema." *Cineaste* 6, no. 4, pp. 22, 52.

Castillo, Raymond del. "The Cinema in Argentina." *The Penguin Film Review*, no. 4 (1947), pp. 100–104.

Caymares, Hortensia, and Luciano Castillo. "Barbachano o la pasión de crear." *Cine cubano*, no. 118 (1987), pp. 59–63.

Chávez, Carlos. "Films by American Governments: Mexico." *Films*, no. 3 (Summer 1940), pp. 20–21.

Chiles, Frederic G., and J. Mraz. "The Historical Film Essay: TODO ES MAS SABROSO CON…" *PCCLAS Proceedings* 4 (1975): 183–86.

Chinchilla, Norma, and Terry Dietz-Fee. "Chile with Poems and Guns: A Strong Analytical Tool." *PCCLAS Proceedings* 4 (1975): 191–92.

"Cine cubano entrevista a Pedro Chaskel, nuevo secretario general de la UCAL." *Cine cubano*, nos. 73/74/75 (1972), pp. 117–19.

Cineaste 4, no. 3, pp. 1–14. [special issue: Latin American militant cinema].

"Cinéma Anti-imperialiste en Amérique Latine." *Cahiers du Cinéma*, no. 253 (October-November 1974)

"Cinema as a Gun: An Interview with Fernando Solanas." *Cineaste*, no. 2, pp. 18–26.

"Cinéma Mexicain." *La Revue du Cinéma—Image et Son*, no. 295 (April 1975), pp. 20–28.

"Cinema Novo vs. Cultural Colonialism: An Interview with Glauber Rocha." *Cineaste* 4, no. 1, pp. 2–9, 35.

Clark, Jaqueline. "Report from the Argentine: Buenos Aires Prefers U.S. and Italian Films." *Films in Review* 1 (March 1950): 16, 48.

Colectivo Alejandro Galindo. "El cine mexicano y sus crisis." [part one] *Dicine*, no. 19 (May-June 1987), pp. 12–13; [part two] no. 20 (July-August 1987), pp. 12–15; [part three] no. 21 (September-October 1987), pp. 16–18.

Colina, José de la. "En busca de una niñez perdida." *Cine cubano*, no. 14–15 (October-November 1963.), pp. 85–88.

_____. "Viridiana." *Cine cubano*, no. 10 (1964), pp. 21–25.

Colina, Enrique, and Daniel Díaz Torres. "Ideología del melodrama en el viejo cine latinoamericano." *Cine cubano*, nos. 73/74/75 (1972), pp. 14–26.

Conrad, Randall. "A Magnificent and Dangerous Weapon: The Politics of Luis Buñuel's Later Films." *Cineaste* 7, no. 4 (1977): 10–18, 51.

Cortés, Carlos E. "The Societal Curriculum and the School Curriculum: Allies or Antagonists?" *Educational Leadership: Journal of the Association for Supervision and Curriculum Development* 36, no. 7 (April 1979): 475–79.

Couselo, Jorge Miguel. "Cine argentino: presente vago y furuo incierto." *Plural*, vol. 12–1, no. 133 (October 1982): 49–53.

Cox, Alex. "Roads to the South: In Praise of Mexican Cinema." *Film Comment*, vol.31, issue 6 (November/December 1995): 26–34.

Crespo Aragón, Carlos, and Erika Domínguez Cervantes. "José Estrada: Crisis del cine mexicano." *Plural*, vol. 11–9, no. 129 (June 1982): 71–75.

Darvell, Michael. "Pan-European: Tapping the Minority Audiences." *Film* (British Federation of Film Societies), series 2, no. 5 (August 1973).

Delpar, Helen. "Mexico, the MPPDA, and Derogatory Films, 1922–1926." *The Journal of Popular Film and Television* 12, no. 1 (Spring 1984): 34–41.

Demby, Betty Jeffries. "The 30th Cannes Film Festival." *Filmmakers Newsletter*, October 1980, pp. 28–33.

Díaz Torres, Daniel. "El cine cubano en América Latina." *Cine cubano*, no. 68 (1971), pp. 67–77.

_____, and Colina, Enrique. "El melodrama en la obra de Luis Buñuel." *Cine cubano*, no. 78/79/80 (1972), pp. 156–59, 162, 164.

Domínguez, Erika. "Disección del cine mexicano." *Plural*, vol. 12–7, no. 139, April 1983, pp. 52–57.

_____. "Emilio García Riera: Un sexenio de cine mexicano." *Plural*, vol. 12–3, no. 135 (December 1982): 45–48.

Dreifus, Claudia. "Carlos Fuentes: When Eternity Moves." *Film Comment*, June 1986, pp. 48–52.

Duarte, Patricia. "Welcome to Ricardo's Reality." *Nuestro*, October 1979, pp. 24–26.

Eceiza, Antonio. "Sobre el cine y la literatura." *Cine cubano*, no. 39 (1967), pp. 26–28.

Ehrmann, Hans. "Latin American Cinema: Film and History." [review of E. Bradford Burns's book] *Film Quarterly* 24 (Summer 1976): 26–27.

"El Arte Como Función Social." [interview with Alfonso Arau] *Hispanoamericano*, 11 April 1977, pp. 39–42.

Ellis, Kirk. "Stranger than Fiction: Emilio Fernandez' Mexico." *The Journal of Popular Film and Television* 10, no. 1 (Spring 1982): 27–36.

"En la Cumbre de la Fama." [article on María Félix] *Hispanoamericano*, 21 November 1955, pp. 40–45.

"Entretien avec Luis Buñuel." *Cahiers du Cinéma*, no. 191 (June 1967), pp. 14–18.

Espinosa, Martha Aurora. "El cine nacional se ha convertido, durante sus 50 años de vida, en un círculo vicioso: Galindo." *Uno Más Uno*, 12 January 1981, p. 23.

Experimental Cinema, no. 5 (1934). [Synopsis for *Que Viva Mexico*].

Falcoff, Mark. "The Uruguay That Never Was: A Historian Looks at Costa-Gavras's State of Siege." *Journal of Latin American Lore* 2 (1976): 239–56.

Fenin, George N. "Perspectivas: Introducción del cine argentino en Estados Unidos." *Tiempo de Cine* (Montevideo), año 11, no. 7 (July-September 1961), p. 13.

Fernández, Carlos. "Nuevamente sobre el cine mexicano." *Cine cubano*, no. 17 (January 1964), pp. 12–14.

_____. "Unas palabras sobre el cine mexicano." *Cine cubano*, no. 7 (1961), pp. 56–58.

"Film in Chile: An Interview with Miguel Littín." *Cineaste* 4, no. 4, pp. 4–9.

"Filmografía del cine cubano." *Cine cubano*, nos. 23/24/25 (1964), pp. 129–42.

"Filmografía Luis Buñuel." *Cine cubano*, nos. 78/79/80 (1972), pp. 166–75.

"5 Frames are 5 Frames, Not 6, But 5: An Interview with Santiago Alvarez." *Cineaste* 6, no. 4, pp. 17–21.

Flores Márquez, Fortunato. "Lo Mejor de los Estrenos en 1972." *Hispanoamericano*, 15 January 1973, p. 56.

_____. "Recopilación Contemporánea." *Hispanoamericano*, 20 November 1972, p. 54.

Fournier Villada, Raoul. "He Makes Mexico Laugh." [article on Cantinflas] *Americas*, March 1953, pp. 6–8, 44–46.

"Fruto del Pueblo." [article on Cantinflas] *Tiempo*, 28 June 1971, pp. 19–21.

Fuentes, Carlos. "El cine y el escritor." *Cine cubano*, no. 31/32/33 (1966), pp. 101–102.

García Ascot, Jomí. "El cine y el escritor." *Cine cubano*, no. 31/32/33 (1966), pp. 103–105.

García Ponce, Juan. "El cine y el escritor." *Cine cubano*, no. 31/32/33 (1966), pp. 106–108.

García Riera, Emilio. "Conversación con Jaime Humberto Hermosillo." *Primer Plano* (*Revista de la Cineteca Nacional*), no. 1 (November-December 1981): 3–30.

_____. "La eterna rebelión de Luis Buñuel." *Tiempo de Cine*, no. 13 (March 1963), pp. 8–13, 64.

_____. "La semana en el cine: Los 50 años de cine nacional." *Uno Más Uno*, 2 January 1981, p. 18; and 3 January 1981, p. 18.

_____. "medio siglo de cine mexicano." *Cine cubano*, no. 31/32/33 (1966), pp. 75–97.

_____. "Seis años de cine mexicano." *Proceso.* 6, 13, and 20 November 1976.

_____. The Eternal Rebellion of Luis Buñuel." *Film Culture*, no. 21 (1960), p. 42.

_____. "The Films of Luis Buñuel." *Film Culture*, no. 21 (1960), p. 58.

_____. "Viridiana." *Film Culture*, no. 24 (1962), p. 74.

García Tsao, Leonardo. "After the breakthrough of Amores Perros, what's next for Mexican Cinema?" *Film Comment*, July/August 2001, pp. 11–13.

_____. "The Very Latest in Mexican Cinema." *Voices of Mexico*, no. 59 (April-June 2002), pp. 42–49.

Garner, Van. "Chile with Poems and Guns: A Counterproductive Model." *PCCLAS Proceedings* 4 (1975): 187–89.

Gaxiola, Fernando. "'Actas de Marusia'— la posibilidad de un cine popular." *Otrocine*, no. 1 (January-March 1975), p. 9.

_____. "Canoa, memoria de un hecho vergonzante." *Otrocine*, no. 1 (January-March 1975), p. 10.

Gerald, Yvonne. "The Comedy of Cantinflas." *Films in Review* 9 (January 1958): 6–11.

Gillet, John. "The Cinema of Luis Buñuel by Freddy Buache." [book review] *Film*, series 2, no. 5 (August 1973), p. 20.

Gilliatt, Penelope. "Profiles: Long Live the Living!" [interview with Luis Buñuel] *The New Yorker*, 5 December 1977, pp. 53–72.

Goldin, Greg, and Marc Cooper. "Mexico's Movies: Now Playing at a Theater Near You." *Southwest Airlines Spirit*, July 1986, pp. 53–54, 87–95.

Gómez, Gloria Cecilia. "El cine mejicano en Colombia." *Cromos* (Bogotá), no. 3094 (4 May 1977), pp. 74–77.

Gómez Sicre, José. "Dolores del Río." *Américas*, December 1967, pp. 8–17.

González, José Antonio. "Apuntes para la historia de un cine sin historia." *Cine cubano*, no. 86/87/88 (1973 or 1974), pp. 37–45.

González Casanova, Manuel. "The Participation of Our Schools in the Defense and Diffusion of National Culture." *The Journal of the University Film Association* 29, no. 2 (Spring 1977): 3–7.

Goytisolo, Juan. "Algunas consideraciones respecto al cine español." *Cine cubano*, no. 10 (1963), pp. 12–15.

Grant, Jacques. "Aprés Royan et à propos du cinéma d'Amérique Latine." *Cinema 74*, no. 187 (May 1974), pp. 40–49.

Green, Marc. "How Much Discipline for the Study of Film?" *The Chronicle of Higher Education*, 15 September 1975.

Greenbaum, Richard. "Luis Buñuel, 1900–1983." *Films in Review* 34, no. 8 (October 1983): 484–86.

Guevara, Alfredo. "IV reseña del cine latinoamericano." *Cine cubano*, no. 12 (July 1963), pp. 54–59.

Gumucio-Dagrón, Alfonso. "Cine obrero sandinista." *Plural*, vol. 11–10, no. 130 (July 1982): 35–40.

Haddad García, George. "Dolores de mi Corazón." *Nuestro*, April 1979, pp. 31–33.

Hairston, Florence. "Use with Caution: These Films Are Biased." *PCCLAS Proceedings* 4 (1975): 171–77.

Harcourt, Peter. "Luis Buñuel: Spaniard and Surrealist." *Film Quarterly* 20 (Spring 1967): pp. 2–19.

H.H. "*El Topo*." [review] *Films in Review*, no. 10 (December 1971).

Hinojosa, Gerardo. "Auandar Anapu: odres nuevos, vino viejo." *Otrocine*, no. 1 (January-March 1975), pp. 46–48.

Hull, David Stuart. "Viridiana." [review] *Film Quarterly* 15 (Winter 1961/62): 55–56.

Isaac, Alberto. "Cine latinoamericano: reportaje a Luis Alcoriza." *Tiempo de cine*, año 5, no. 20/21 (Spring-Summer 1965), pp. 38–40, 80.

Johansen, Jason C. "A New Wave Cresting." *Nuestro*, May 1980, pp. 24–25, 63.

Johnson, Randal. "Film." In Dolores Moyano Martin, ed., *Handbook of Latin American Studies: No. 48—Humanities*, pp. 59–77. Austin: University of Texas Press, 1986.

Kanesaka, Kenji. "A Visit to Luis Buñuel." *Film Culture*, no. 41 (1966), p. 60.

Keel, Erich. "From Militant Cinema to Neo-Realism: The Example of *Pueblo Chico*." *Film Quarterly* 24 (Summer 1976): 17–24.

Konder, Rodolfo. "The Carmen Miranda Museum: Brazilian Bombshell Still Box Office in Rio." *Américas*, September-October 1982, pp. 17–20.

Kovacs, Katherine S. "Miguel Littín's *Recurso del Método*: The Aftermath of Allende." *Film Quarterly* 33 (Spring 1980): 22–29.

Kovacs, Steven. "Las Amazonas de Cine." [article on Venezuelan film board] *Sight and Sound*, Spring 1978, pp. 91–93.

Krohn, Bill. "Brésil, Ma «Fatale Attraction»." *Cahiers du Cinéma*, no. 404 (February 1988), pp. 28–32.

"La Aventura Mexicana." *Hispanoamericano*, 22 March 1976, p. 59.

"La cinematografía mexicana, su historia, su realidad, sus potencialidades." *Militancia: temas del socialismo* 1, no. 1 (September 30, 1974): 55–58.

Lamb, Blaine P. "The Convenient Villain: The Early Cinema Views the Mexican-American." *Journal of the West* 14 (October 1975): 75–81.

Lambert, Gavin. "Nazarin." [review] *Film Quarterly* 13 (Spring 1960): 30–31.

Landa G., Antonio. "Canoa." *Otrocine*, no. 4 (October-December 1975), pp. 14–15.

Lash, Vivian. "Experimenting with Freedom in Mexico." *Film Quarterly* 19 (Summer 1966): 19–24.

"Las Películas Mexicanas en los EE UU." *Tiempo*, 27 April 1945, p. 37.

"La Televisión en Mexico." *Hispanoamericano*, 17 August 1951, pp. 3–6.

"Leopoldo Torre-Nilson Interviewed by Fred Wellington." *Film Culture*, no. 46 (1967), n.p.

Lescale, Aurora. "México Indígena." *Cine cubano*, no. 103 (1982), pp. 108–111.

"Les Jours de L'Amour." [review of Alberto Isaac film] *La Revue du Cinéma — Image et Son*, no 301 (December 1975), pp. 115–16.

Lintz de Nava, Arlene. "Entrevista con Gabriel Retes." *Otrocine*, no. 1 (January-March 1975), pp. 55–61.

"Los Independientes." *Otrocine*, no. 1 (January-March 1975), p. 54.

"'Los Olvidados' y la Crítica." *Hispanoamericano*, 7 March 1952, p. 52.

"Los Próximos 'Arieles.'" *Hispanoamericano*, 13 February 1953, p. 44.

"Luis Buñuel hace la anatomía del churro cinematográfico." *Cine cubano*, no. 78/79/80 (1972), pp. 112–13.

Luna, Andrés de, and Susana Charaund. "Los independientes: entrevista a Eduardo Maldonado." *Otrocine*, no. 6 (April-June 1976), pp. 29–32.

MacBean, James Roy. "Fernando Solanas, An Interview." *Film Quarterly* 24 (Fall 1970): 37–43.

_____. "La Hora de los Hornos." *Film Quarterly* 24 (Fall 1970), pp. 31–37.

Macotela, Catherine. "El sindicalismo en el cine (primera parte)." *Otrocine*, no. 2 (April-June 1975), pp. 60–67.

_____. "El sindicalismo en el cine (segunda parte)." *Octrocine*, no 3 (July-September 1975), pp. 57–63.

_____. "El sindicalismo en el cine (tercera parte)." *Otrocine*, no. 4 (October-December 1975), pp. 65–69.

_____. "El sindicalismo en el cine (cuarta parte)." *Otrocine*, no. 5 (January-March 1976), pp. 59–65.

_____. "El sindicalismo en el cine (quinta parte)." *Otrocine*, no. 6 (April-June 1976), pp. 46–48.

Maffer, Sergio. "México en tres niveles." *Cine cubano*, no. 63/65 (1970), pp. 14–16.

Margorelles, Louis. "Le Renouveau Mexicain." *La Revue du Cinéma — Image et Son*, no. 280 (January 1974), pp. 72–90.

Martínez Ortega, Gonzalo. "El encuentro de un hombre solo." *Militancia: temas del socialismo* 1, no. 1 (September 30, 1974): 64–68.

Matas, Julio. "Theater and Cinematography." In *Revolutionary Change in Cuba*, edited by Carmelo Mesa-Lago, pp. 427–45. Pittsburgh: University of Pittsburgh Press, 1971.

Mekas, Adolfas. "A Letter from Mexico." *Film Culture*, no. 20 (1959), p. 72.

Méndez, José Carlos. "Hacia un cine político: la cooperativa de un cine marginal." (La Cultura en México/Suplemento de *Siempre*) *Siempre*, 1972.

Michel, Manuel. "CCC: Un retrato escrito." *Otrocine*, no. 1 (January-March 1975), pp. 62–68.

_____. "Cine mexicano: utopía y realidad." *Plural*, vol. 11–7, no. 127 (April 1982): 67–70.

_____. "Mexican Cinema: A Panoramic View." *Film Quarterly* 18 (Summer 1965): 46–55.

Miller, Carol. "Luis Buñuel: El Ojo de la Libertad." *Hispanoamericano*, January 12, 1981, pp. 54–57.

Miller, Clyde. "Filmmakers of Churubusco." *Américas*, April 1974, pp. 15–20.

Mistron, Deborah. "A Hybrid Subgenre: The Revolutionary Melodrama in the Mexican Cinema." *Studies in Latin American Popular Culture* 3 (1984): 47–56.

_____. "The Role of Pancho Villa in the Mexican and the American Cinema." *Studies in Latin American Popular Culture* 2 (1983): 1–13.

Monsiváis, Carlos. "Es el baile del pingüino un baile elegante y fino." *Diálogos* (El Colegio de México) 13 (September-October 1977): 11–14.

_____. "Junto contigo le doy un aplauso al placer y al amor." *Textos* (Guadalajara), año 2, no. 9–10 (1975), pp. 39–56.

_____. "Los de atras se quedarán (I) (Notas sobre cultura y sociedad de masas en los setentas)." *Nexos* 26 (February 1980): 35–43.

_____. "Notas sobre la cultura mexicana en el siglo XX: XII. El cine nacional." In *Historia general de Mexico*, vol. 4, pp. 434–59. Mexico City: Centro de Estudios Históricos, El Colegio de México, 1976.

_____. "Proyecto de periodización de historia cultural de México." *PCCLAS Proceedings* 4 (1975): 39–49.

_____. "The Culture of the Frontier: The Mexican Side." In Stanley R. Ross, ed. *Views Across the Border: The United States and Mexico*. Albuquerque: University of New Mexico Press, 1978, pp. 50–67.

Mora, Carl J. "Alejandro Galindo: Pioneer Mexican Filmmaker." *Journal of Popular Culture* 18, no. 1 (Summer 1984): 101–12.

_____. "Cinema, Spanish." In Robert Kern, ed. *Historical Dictionary of Modern Spain*. Westport, CT: Greenwood Press, 1990.

_____. "Introduction," "Feminine Images in Mexican Cinema: The Family Melodrama; Sara García, 'The Mother of Mexico'; and the Prostitute." *Studies in Latin American Popular Culture* 4 (1985): 228–235.

_____. "Mexican Cinema in the 1970s." In Leonard Folgarait, ed., *Mexican Art of the 1970s* (Nashville, TN: Vanderbilt University, Center for Latin American and Iberian Studies, 1984), pp. 37–44.

_____. "Mexico's Commercial Films: Sources for the Study of Social History." *PCCLAS Proceedings* 6 (1977–1979): 205–15.

_____. "México y su revolución vistos por Hollywood." *Historia y Vida* (Barcelona). April 1994, pp. 85–89.

_____. "Motion Pictures: 1960–96." In Michael S. Werner, ed. *Encyclopedia of Mexico*, vol. II. Chicago: Fitzroy Dearborn, 1997: 970–72.

_____. "Poor Mexican Cinema, So Far from *Cahiers du Cinema* and So Close to Latino, U.S.A." *FILM-HISTORIA Online*, vol. XI, no. 3 (2001).

_____. "Spain's Cinema of the 'Autonomies.'" *New Orleans Review* 13, no. 2 (Summer 1986): 32–42.

_____. "The Odyssey of Spanish Cinema." *New Orleans Review* 14, no. 1 (Spring 1987): 7–20.

_____. "Y Ahora para algo Completamente Diferente: Observations on Cinematic Humor in Spain, Mexico, and the United States." *CINE-LIT II Essays on Hispanic Film and Fiction*. Corvallis, OR: Portland State University, Oregon State University, and Reed College, 1995.

Mora, Sergio de la . "A Career in Perspective: An Interview with Arturo Ripstein." *Film Quarterly*, vol. 52, issue 1 (Summer 1999): 4.

Mortimore, Roger. "Buñuel, Sáenz de Heredia and Filmófono." *Sight and Sound* (Summer 1975), pp. 180–82.

Mosier, John. "Actresses and Acting." *Américas*, September-October 1983, pp. 58–59.

_____. "Ambitious Epics: *Cecilia* and *The Red Bells*." *Américas*, January-February 1983, p. 59.

_____. "El cine mexicano: Raúl Araiza." *Américas*, July-August 1982, pp. 57–58.

_____. "Currents in Latin American Film." *Américas*, May 1978, pp. 2–8.

_____, and Alexis Gonzáles. "Marcela Fernández Violante: cineasta singular." *Américas*, January-February 1983, pp. 15–19.

Nicholson, Irene. "Mexican Films: Their Past and Future." *Quarterly of Film, Radio & Television* 10 (1955–56): 248–52.

"Nota de redacción." [review of García Riera's book *El cine mexicano*] *Cine cubano*, no 31/32/33 (1966), pp. 98–100.

Noyola, Antonio. "Retrospectiva del cine mexicano no industrial." *Otrocine*, no. 6 (April-June 1976), pp. 49–57.

_____. "Trece directores del cine mexicano." [book review] *Otrocine*, no. 1 (January-March 1975), pp. 69–71.

"Nuevo cine, nuevos realizadores, nuevos filmes: entrevista a Miguel Littín." *Cine cubano*, no. 63–65 (1970), pp. 1–6.

O'Connor, Chris. "Dolores del Rio: Forever Beautiful." *Modern Maturity*, February–March 1981, pp. 69–71.

Olhovich, Sergio. "Dos directores de cine se critican recíprocamente." *Militancia: temas del socialismo* 1, no. 1 (30 September 1974): 59–63.

Oliver, Maria Rosa [Marie Rose]. "Cantinflas." *Hollywood Quarterly* 2 (1946–1947): 252–56.

_____. "The Native Films of Mexico." *The Penguin Film Review*, pp. 73–79. London and New York: Penguin Books, 1948.

Orme, William A., Jr. "Using TV to Send Social Message." *R&D Mexico*, 16 June 1982, pp. 15–18.

Ostria, Vincent. "L'Enfance de l'Homme." [review of Luis Alcoriza's *Tiburoneros* (*Pecheurs de Requins*)] *Cahiers du Cinéma*, no. 402 (December 1987), pp. 44–46.

Pacheco, Cristina. "El Cine, Su Vicio." [interview with Emilio García Riera] *Siempre*, 1 November 1978, pp. 32–34, 70.

Paz, Octavio. "Nazarin." [review] *Film Culture*, no. 21 (1960), p. 60.

P.C. "El Topo." [review] *Film*, series 2, no. 9 (December 1973), pp. 18–19.

Pensamiento crítico (Havana), no. 42 (July 1970). [Special issue on Cuban cinema.]

Peralta, José Luis. "El cambio." *Otrocine*, no. 3 (July–September 1975), pp. 68–70.

Pérez, Fernando. "Nazarín." *Cine cubano*, no. 78/79/80 (1972), pp. 136–37.

Pérez, Gómez, Angel A. "Luis Alcoriza: Mecánica nacional." *Reseña*, año 14, no. 103 (March 1977), pp. 28–29.

Pérez-Turrent, Tomás. "No es lo mismo los tres mosqueteros que cuatro años después." *Otrocine*, no. 4 (October–December 1975), pp. 4–9.

_____. "una experiencia alrededor de Canoa." *Otrocine*, no. 2 (April–June 1975), pp. 8–12.

Pierre, Sylvie. "Brésil (suite) — Glauber Rocha pourquoi?" *Cahiers du Cinéma*, no. 393 (March 1971): *Le Journaldes*, no. 71, p. II.

_____. "Le cinéma brésilien à Beaubourg: Zut aux exoticophiles!" *Cahiers Du Cinéma*, no. 393 (March 1971): *Le Journaldes*, no. 71, pp. I–II.

Pinto, Alfonso. "Cuando Hollywood Habló en Español." *Américas*, October 1980, pp. 3–8.

_____. "Hollywood's Spanish-Language Films." *Films in Review* 24 (October 1973): 474–83, 487.

Portes, Francisco. "Ignacio López Tarso: el actor y el acento." *Mundo Hispánico* (Madrid), March 1977, pp. 57–60.

Quijada, Miguel Angel. "El joven cine español de la época franquista." *Otrocine*, no. 5 (January–March 1976), pp. 12–17.

Ramírez Berg, Charles. "Cracks in the *Macho* Monolith: *Machismo*, Man, and Mexico in Recent Mexican Cinema." *New Orleans Review* 16, no. 1 (Spring 1989): 67–74.

_____. "Mexican Cinema: A Study in Creative Tension." *New Orleans Review* 10, no. 2 (Summer/Fall 1983): 149–52.

Ramón, David. "Semana del cine mexicano no industrial." *Otrocine*, no. 4 (October–December 1975), pp. 20–22.

_____. "Un sexenio de cine en México." *Comunicación* 21 (March 1977): 24–33. Ramos Navas, Germán. "De todos modos CUEC te llamas." *Excélsior: Diorama de Cultura*, 7 September 1980, p. 3.

"Reportaje a Alberto Isaac." *Tiempo de cine*, año 5, no. 21/22 (Spring-Summer 1965), pp. 41–44.

"Responde a Cine cubano: Alberto Isaac." *Cine cubano*, no. 31/32/33 (1966), pp. 115–16.

"Responde a Cine cubano: Emilio García Riera." *Cine cubano*, no. 31/32/33 (1966), pp. 110–11.

"Responde a Cine cubano: Icaro Cisneros." *Cine cubano*, no. 31/32/33 (1966), pp. 113–15.

"Responde a Cine cubano: José Luis Ibáñez." *Cine cubano*, no. 31/32/33 (1966), pp. 111–13.

"Responden a Cine cubano: Oscar Kantor, David José Kohon, Mabel Itzkovich, Rodolfo Kuhn, Leopoldo Torre Nilsson, Saulo Benavente." *Cine cubano*, no. 31/32/33 (1966), pp. 64–74.

Reyes, Aurelio de los. "El cine como indicador entusiasmado." *Diálogos*, no. 77 (September-October 1977), pp. 30–32.

Reyes de la Maza, Luis. "De como el papá de Martín Cortés se fue mucho para el Tívoli." *Otrocine*, no. 1 (January-March 1975), pp. 33–39.

Reyes Nevares, Beatriz. "Cine mexicano: habla Ricardo Garibay." *Siempre*, 13 December 1972, pp. 40–41.

_____. "El cine mexicano es hoy de mejor calidad." *Siempre*, 27 December 1972, pp. 42–43.

_____. "Entre cretinos y voraces naufraga el cine mexicano." *Siempre*, 3 January 1973, pp. 40–41, 70.

_____. "Salomón Laiter: profeta de un nuevo cine." *Siempre*, 24 January 1973, p. 45.

Rico, María Elena. "Anatomía de un éxito loco: Allá en el Rancho Grande." *Contenido*, June 1976, pp. 20–56.

Rivera, Héctor. "El Indio [Fernández], tan intenso en la furia como en la ternura." *Proceso*, 11 August 1986, pp. 42–48.

_____. "[Alberto] Isaac cree posible levantar un cine en ruinas en un país arruinado." *Proceso*, 11 April 1983, pp. 48–51.

Rodríguez, João Carlos. "El indio y el cine brasileño." *Plural*, vol. 11–12, no. 132 (September 1982): 47–53.

Rodríguez Alemán, Mario. "Entrevista con Antonio Eceiza." *Cine cubano*, no. 39 (1967), pp. 15–25.

Rodríguez Monegal, Emir. "El mito Buñuel." *Tiempo de cine*, no. 14/15 (July 1963), pp. 7–10.

Rossi, Eduardo A. "Lo que el tiempo se tragó." *Otrocine*, no. 3 (July-September 1975), pp. 4–9.

_____. "Veinte años del cine argentino." *Otrocine*, no. 4 (October-December 1975), pp. 44–52.

"Round the World's Studios," *The Penguin Film Review*, no. 1 (1941), pp. 53–54.

Rubia Barcia, J. "Luis Buñuel's *Los Olvidados*." *Quarterly of Film, Radio & Television* 7 (1952–53): 392–401.

Sabourad, Frédéric. "Festivals: 9º Féstival des trois continents à Nantes: La carte de l'identité." [review of Arturo Ripstein's *Imperio de la fortuna*] *Cahiers du Cinéma*, no. 404 (February 1988): *Le Journaldes*, no. 80, p. VIII.

Saderman, Alejandro. "Cine argentino, o de crisis en crisis." *Cine cubano*, no. 31/32/33 (1966), pp. 51–62.

Sánchez, Alberto Ruy. "Cine mexicano: producción social de una estética." *Historia y Sociedad*, no. 18 (Summer 1978), pp. 71–83.

Sánchez, Francisco. "Miguel Littín: poesía y militancia política." *Otrocine*, no. 4 (October-December 1975), pp. 28–33.

_____. "Tívoli." *Otrocine*, no. 1 (January-March 1975), pp. 19–22.

Sanjinés, Jorge. "Cine revolucionario: la experiencia boliviana." *Otrocine*, no. 6 (April-June 1976), pp. 61–70.

Scheffler, Wini. "Foreign Filming Leaves Below-the-Line Income." *Mex-Am Review* 43 (August 1975): 4–5, 7, 9.

Schumann, Jochem. "Ten Years of Cuban Films: 1959–1969." *Publik* (Frankfurt), 1 May 1970.

Schumann, Peter B. "El cine de El Salvador." *Plural*, vol. 12–8, no. 140 (May 1983): 46–48.

_____. "El cine de Venezuela." *Plural*, vol. 12–6, no. 138 (March 1983): 59–65.

Sepúlveda, Martha L. "Sobre Canoa." *Otrocine*, no. 4 (October-December 1975), pp. 16–18.

Seton, Marie. "Vignettes of Eisenstein." *Films in Review* 2 (April 1951): 29–31.

Shelley, Jaime A. "Conversación con Felipe Cazals." *Otrocine*, no. 3 (July-September 1975), pp. 34–43.

_____. "Conversación con Miguel Littín." *Otrocine*, no. 4 (October-December 1975), pp. 34–43.

_____. "El cine mexicano, ¿campeón sin corona?" *Otrocine*, no. 1 (January-March 1975), pp. 2–5.

_____. "Entrevista con Alberto Isaac." *Otrocine*, no. 1 (January-March 1975), pp. 23–32.

_____. "La herencia de los productores, esa ancla enmohecida que puede frenarlo todo." *Otrocine*, no. 2 (April-June 1975), pp. 2–3.

"Simón del desierto." *Cine cubano*, no. 78/79/80 (1972), p. 143.

Somos: Dolores del Río, el rostro del cine mexicano (1995).

Somos: Pedro Armendáriz, la mirada que sedujo al mundo (1996).

Somos: Silvia Pinal, esa rubia debilidad (1997).

Somos: Angélica María, la novia de México (1998).

Somos: Mauricio Garcés, el eterno seductor (1998).

Somos: Marga López, una diva de leyenda (1999).

Somos: Arturo de Córdova, la voz del rostro inolvidable (1999).

Somos: Miroslava, una deslumbrante belleza, una misteriosa tragedia (1999).

Somos: Los Soler, historia de una dinastía irrepetible (1999).

Somos: Carmen Montejo, sigo escribiendo mi historia (1999).

Somos: Luis Aguilar, el gallo más giro del cine mexicano (1999).

Somos: Katy Jurado, estrella en Hollywood orgullosamente mexicana (1999).

Somos: El Indio Fernández, genio y figura del cine mexicano (1999).

Somos: Elsa Aguirre, una belleza para siempre (1999).

Somos: David Silva, campeón con corona (1999).

Somos: El Santo, vida, obra y milagros (1999).

Somos: Las rumberas del cine mexicano (1999).

Somos: Libertad Lamarque, la novia de América (1999).

Somos: María Félix, el mito más bello del cine (2000).

Somos: El talento multifacético de Joaquín Pardavé: actor, director y compositor (2000).

Somos: Lilia Prado, imagen del erotismo y la sensualidad (2000).

Somos: Antonio Aguilar, una vida de corrido (2000).

Somos: Roberto Cañedo, la vida detrás de un galán (2000).

Somos: Gloria Marín, un rostro inlvidable (2000).

Somos: La diosa pantera Tongolele, "Yo nací para bailar" (2000).

Somos: Sara García, la abuelita del cine nacional (2000).

Somos: Tito Guízar y Esther Fernández, pareja inmortal de Rancho Grande (2000).

Somos: María Victoria, voz y encanto de sirena (2000).

Somos: Pedro Infante, el ídolo de México (2001).

Somos: María Elena Marqués, "Uno nace con la belleza que Dios le da y muere con la que merece" (2001).

Somos: Germán Valdés "Tin Tan," de Pachuco a Rey del barrio (2001).

Somos: El placer de ser Sara Montiel (2001).

Somos: Javier Solís, el rey del bolero ranchero/ Rita Macedo, estrella que supo ser actriz (2001).

Somos: Rosita Quintana, "A México le debo lo que soy" (2001).

Somos: Familia artística como pocas: Los Rojo (2001).

Somos: Blanca Estela Pavón, la consentida del pueblo (2001).

Somos: 3 tipos de cuidado (2001).

Somos: Dolores del Río, la mexicana divina (2002).

Somos: Las reinas de la risa (2002).

Somos: Silvia Derbez, una estrella, una historia, una actriz (2002).

Somos: Inolvidables rostros del cine mexicano (2002).

Somos: María Felix, "Todo morirá cuando yo muera" (2002).

Somos: Evita Muñoz "Chachita," niña prodigio del cine mexicano (2002).

Somos: Miguel Aceves Mejía, el rey del falsete (2002).

Somos: Ernesto Alonso, el señor telenovela (2002).

Somos: Lucha Villa, la voz sensual de la canción mexicana (2002).

Somos: Emilio Tuero, el barítono de Argel (2002).

Somos: Lorena Velázquez, reina del cine fantástico; Tere Velázquez, ingenua, bella y sensual (2002).

Somos: Adalberto Martínez "Resortes," rey del baile y de la risa (2002).

Stam, Robert. "Slow Fade to Afro: The Black Presence in Brazilian Cinema." *Film Quarterly*, 36, no. 2 (Winter 1982–83): 16–32.

Stamm [sic], Robert, and Ismael Xavier. "Recent Brazilian Cinema: Allegory/Metacinema/Carnival." *Film Quarterly* 41 (Spring 1988): 15–30.

Stein, Elliott. "Don Hermosillo and the Sun." [on the Third Miami Film Festival and Jaime Humberto Hermosillo's *Doña Herlinda y su hijo* and other of his films] *Film Comment*, June 1986, pp. 53–57.

Sterrit, David. "Puerto Rico: New Presence in Film." *The Christian Science Monitor*, 21 August 1987, pp. 19–20.

Suárez, Joseantonio. "El cine en Portugal." *Otrocine*, no. 4 (October-December 1975), pp. 10–13.

Sutherland, Elizabeth. "Cinema of Revolution — 90 Miles from Home." *Film Quarterly* 15 (Winter 1961/62): 42.

"The Latin-American Film." *The Penguin Film Review*, no. 2 (1947), pp. 34–35.

Toubiana, Serge. "Pour en Réalisme de Rêve." [interview with Ruy Guerra, director of

Eréndira] *Cahiers du Cinéma*, no. 354 (December 1983): *Le Journaldes*, no. 38, pp. III–IV.

Tozzi, R.V. "*Torero!*" [review] *Films in Review* 8 (June-July 1957): 224–25.

Treviño, Jesús Salvador. "The New Mexican Cinema." *Film Quarterly* 32 (Spring 1979): 26–37.

Tuchman, Mitch. "*The Man from Maisinicu*." [review] *Film Quarterly* 30 (Fall 1976): 59–60.

Turner, R.H. "*Macario*." [review] *Film Quarterly* 14 (Winter 1960): 50.

Ugalde, Víctor. "Desmemoria." *Etcetera*. February 2003, pp. 27–28.

_____. "Diversidad cultural." *Etcetera*. October 2003, pp. 36–37.

_____. "El planeta de los simios." *Etcetera*. December 2003, pp. 47–49.

_____. "A diez años del TLC." *Etcetera*. January 2004, pp. 31–32.

_____. "Salas vacías." *Etcetera*. March 2004, pp. 34–35.

_____. "El TLC: La otra conquista." In *Industrias Culturales y TLC: 5 años después*. Mexico City: Red de Acción Frente al Libre Comercio y la Sociedad General de Escritores de México, 2000.

"Una Oportunidad Más." *Hispanoamericano*, 9 February 1976, p. 61.

Uribe, Alvaro. "Entrevista a Alfredo Joskowicz." *Otrocine*, no. 3 (July-September 1975), pp. 64–67.

Valdés, Oscar, and Miguel Torres. "En compañía de Max Linder." *Cine cubano*, no. 35 (1966), pp. 45–49.

Vanderwood, Paul. "An American Cold Warrior: Viva Zapata! (1952)." In *American History/American Film: Interpreting the Hollywood Image*, edited by John E. O'Connor and Martin A. Jackson, pp. 183–201. New York: Frederick Ungar, 1979.

_____. "Filming History: Promise and Problems." *PCCLAS Proceedings* 4 (1975): 179–82. "XXV Aniversario de la Muerte de Pedro Infante." *Hispanoamericano*, 26 April 1982, p. 48.

Viany, Alex. "Cine brasileño: lo viejo y lo nuevo." *Cine cubano*, no. 20 (1964), pp. 8–10, 12–29.

_____. "Production in Brazil." *Films in Review* 2 (February 1951): 28–32.

"Víctimas del pecado: el fin del Centro de Capacitación Cinematográfica." *Nexos* 24 (December 1979): 4–5, 9, 11.

Volman, Dennis. "Brazilian Workmen and Artists Help Filmmaker Recreate a Lost World." [on Carlos Diegues and the making of *Quilombo*] *The Christian Science Monitor,* 23 March 1984, p. 21.

_____. "Film's New Barbarians: Brazilian Directors Strive to Blend Mass Appeal, Artistic Merit." *The Christian Science Montior*, 22 March 1984, pp. 16–17.

"'We Are Losing Our Identity': An Interview with Mexican Director Marcela Fernández Violante." *Film Literature Quarterly* 15, no. 1 (1987): 2–7.

Weinberg, Herman G. "Raíces." [review] *Film Culture* 3 (1957): 17–18.

West, Dennis. "Documenting the End of the Chilean Road to Socialism: *La batalla de Chile*." *The American Hispanist* (February 1978), pp. 13–15.

_____. "Highlights of the First International Festival of New Latin American Cinema." *Review* (Center for Inter-American Relations) 28 (January-April 1981): 53–56.

_____. "Mexican Cinema in 1977: A Commentary on the Mexican Film Festival Presently Touring the U.S." *The American Hispanist* 2 (May 1977): 6–7.

_____. "*One Way or Another (De Cierta Manera)*." *Caribbean Review* 8 (Summer 1979): 42–44.

_____. "Reconciling Entertainment and Thought: An Interview with Julio García Espinosa." *Cineaste* 16, nos. 1–2 (1987–88): 20–26.

_____. "Slavery and Cinema in Cuba: The Case of Gutiérrez Alea's *The Last Supper*." *The Western Journal of Black Studies* (Summer 1979): 128–33.

West, Joan M., and Dennis West. "*Frida*." [film review] *Cineaste* 16, no. 4 (1988): 54, 56.

_____. "*Frida*: An Interview with Paul Leduc." *Cineaste* 16, no. 4 (1988): 55.

White, Arnold. "Films in Focus: Nestor Almendros." *Films in Review* 35, no. 10 (December 1984): 607–609.

Wilson, David. "Letters from Marusia." [review] *Sight and Sound* (Winter 1976/77), pp. 60–61.

Wilt, David. "El Barón del Terror: The Horror Films of Abel Salazar." *Filmfax*, January/February (no. 54), 1996.

_____. "Horror Films from South of the Border: An Overview of Neglected Mexican Fantasy Cinema." *Cinefantastique*, 27/10, pp. 40–47.

_____. "Los Vampiros: A look at bloodsuckers south-of-the-border, from El Vampiro to Cronos." *Imagi-Movies*, vol. 2, no. 2 (Winter 1994), pp. 50–53.

_____. "The Western in Mexico." *The Big Reel*, September 1992.

Woll, Allen L. "Hollywood's Good Neighbor Policy: The Latin Image in American Film, 1939–1946." *Journal of Popular Film* 3 (Fall 1974): 278–91.

Wollenberg, H.H. "Round the World's Studios." *The Penguin Film Review*, no. 3 (1947), pp. 39–40.

_____. "Round the World's Studios." *The Penguin Film Review*, no. 6 (1948), p. 43.

Wood, Michael. "Buñuel was always ready for death ... from the moment he was born." *The Listener*, 9 February 1984, pp. 10–12.

_____. "The Discreet Charm of Luis Buñuel." *American Film*, September 1982, pp. 34–39.

Wu, Ying Ying. "Trying Times in Mexico." *Nuestro*, May 1980, pp. 26–27.

Yakir, Dan. "The Mind of Cinema Novo." *Film Comment*, September-October 1980, pp. 40–44.

Young, Colin. "Letter from Mexico." *Film Quarterly* 14 (Fall 1960): 62–63.

Unpublished Sources

Falcoff, Mark, "Original Sin and Argentine Reality: Peronist History and Myth in *The Traitors*." Paper presented at the twenty-second annual meeting of the Pacific Coast Council on Latin American Studies, Arizona State University, Tempe, 21–23 October 1976.

Geffner, Daniel I. "Cultural Dependency and Film Industry Development in Latin America, 1900–1970." Paper presented at the twenty-third annual meeting of the Pacific Coast Council on Latin American Studies, San Jose, California, 20–22 October 1977.

_____. "Film and Revolution in Latin America: Conceptualizing a Structural Frame-work for Cinema Engagé." Paper presented at the twenty-second annual meeting of the Pacific Coast Council on Latin American Studies, Arizona State Universtiy, Temp, 21–23 October 1976.

Mora, Carl. "*Soy puro mexicano*: Reconciling Nationalism and Support for the U.S. in Mexican Films of the 1940s." Paper presented at Southeastern Conference of Latin American Studies, Mobile, Alabama, March 1–3, 2002.

_____. "Jumpcutting Between the Old and New Worlds: Cinematic Forays in Spain and Latin America." Paper presented at University of Oklahoma, April 18, 1997.

_____. "El contexto histórico de la obra cinematográfica de Luis García Berlanga." Paper presented at Mid-America Conference on Hispanic Literatures, University of Colorado, Boulder, October 12–14, 1995.

_____. "El humorismo cinematográfico en su proyección desde España a Hollywood, pasando por Inglaterra y Méjico." Paper presened at the Spanish Resource Center, Division of Continuing Education, University of New Mexico, Albuquerque, NM, February 22, 1995.

_____. "Emilio 'El Indio' Fernández and *Enamorada*." Paper presented at Vanderbilt University, Nashville, TN, November 11, 1991.

_____. "*Doña Bárbara* and *Enamorada*." Paper presented at Vanderbilt University, Nashville, TN, November 10, 1989.

_____. "Emilio 'el Indio' Fernández, An Overview of his Life and Work." Paper presented at UNAM San Antonio Branch, April 30, 1987, and Guadalupe Cultural Arts Center, San Antonio, TX, May 1, 1987.

_____. "The Elusive Text: Research on Latin American Cinema and its Implications for Area Specialists." Paper presented at XII International Congress of the Latin American Studies Association, Albuquerque, NM, April 20, 1985.

_____. "Mexican Cinema: A Humanistic Assessment." Paper presented at the University of California, Santa Barbara, July 9, 1984.

_____. "The Mexican Cinema, 1896–1976: An Overview." Paper presented at the University of Alabama, Tuscaloosa, March 24, 1980.

Vanderwood, Paul J. "Images of Mexican Heroes in American Films." Paper presented at the annual meeting of the American Historical Association, Washington, DC, 28–30 December 1976.

_____. "Response to 'An Overview of Film and Revolution in Latin America.'" Paper presented at the twenty-wecond annual meeting of the Pacific Coast Council on Latin American Studies, Arizona State University, Tempe, 21–23 October 1976.

Whittaker, Marsha D. "Socio-political History of the Treatment of Women in Mexican Films, 1930–1975." Paper presented at the twenty-third annual meeting of the Pacific Coast Council on Latin American Studies, San Jose, CA, 20–22 October 1977.

Wilt, David. "The OCIAA and the Mexican Film Industry." Paper presented at the Literature/Film Association Conference, Towson University, Maryland, June 1991.

Theses and Dissertations

Amado, G., Francisco Alicia, and Alicia Echeverría. "El cine mexicano, estudio psicológico." Licenciate thesis, UNAM, 1960.

Bermeo, César Adolfo. "The Political Cinema of Latin America: The Dialectic of Dependency and Revolution." Ph.D. dissertation, University of California, Los Angeles, 1981.

Bixby, Barbara Evans. "The Weave of the Serape: Sergei Eisenstein's 'Que Viva Mexico!' as a Multitext." Ph.D. dissertation, University of Florida, Gainesville, 1979.

Cisneros, René. "The Comic Verbal and Nonverbal Expression in the Mario Moreno Cantinflas Film: Meaning and Illocutionary Force." Ph.D. dissertation, University of Texas, Austin, 1978.

Fernández, Henry Cecilio. "The Influence of Galdós on the Films of Luis Buñuel." Ph.D. dissertation, Indiana University, Bloomington, 1976.

Macotela, Fernando. "La industria cinematográfica mexicana. Estudio jurídico y económico." Licenciate thesis, UNAM, 1969.

Mier Miranda, Felipe. "La industria cinematográfica mexicana." Licenciate thesis, UNAM, 1963.

Sandro, Paul Denney. "Assault and Disruption in the Cinema: Four Films by Luis Buñuel." Ph.D. dissertation, Cornell University, Ithaca, NY, 1974.

Schnitman, Jorge Alberto. "The Argentine Film Industry: A Contextual Study." Ph.D. dissertation, Stanford University, Palo Alto, CA, 1979.

Index